Where Human Rights Begin

Where Human Rights Begin

HEALTH, SEXUALITY, AND WOMEN IN THE NEW MILLENNIUM

EDITED BY

WENDY CHAVKIN

ELLEN CHESLER

Rutgers University Press
New Brunswick, New Jersey, and London

Library of Congress Cataloging-in-Publication Data

Where human rights begin : health, sexuality, and women in the New Millennium / edited by Wendy Chavkin and Ellen Chesler.

    p. cm.

    Includes bibliographical references and index.

    ISBN-13: 978-0-8135-3656-9 (hardcover : alk. paper)

    ISBN-13: 978-0-8135-3657-6 (pbk. : alk. paper)

 1. Birth control—Moral and ethical aspects. 2. Contraception—Moral and ethical aspects. 3. Reproductive health. 4. Women's rights. 5. Human rights. I. Chavkin, Wendy. II. Chesler, Ellen.

    HQ766.15.W46 2006

    305.42—dc22

                                              2005004408

A British Cataloging-in-Publication record for this book is available from the British Library.

Manufactured in the United States of America

To our children: Sasha Freudenberg-Chavkin, Jonathan Mallow, and Elizabeth Mallow, who inherit the global challenges this volume presents.

CONTENTS

vii

FOREWORD

MARY ROBINSON

A decade after the progress made at the Vienna, Cairo, and Beijing world conferences on human rights, population and development, and women, we find ourselves at a crucial juncture in the struggle to realize fully women's rights as human rights. Although the movement to protect and promote human rights worldwide is vibrant and growing, we currently face some of the greatest threats to human rights in a generation, including terrorism and the "war" against it, the HIV/AIDS pandemic and related stigma and discrimination, and rising religious fundamentalism in many parts of the world.

Those three landmark conferences played a major role in placing human rights, and particularly the rights of women, on the international agenda. They highlighted explicitly the importance of sexual and reproductive rights. As Eleanor Roosevelt realized long ago, some of the most important rights in the lives of women are also some of the most intimate, from the right to be free from violence in one's home to the right to control one's own sexual and reproductive choices. Yet these are linked, inextricably, to a vast web of increasingly more "public" rights, from the social and economic rights that guarantee a decent standard of living to the civil and political rights that guarantee voice and agency in our lives and societies. Only by realizing our rights on a personal level—in the "small places" that Eleanor Roosevelt referred to, places like our bedrooms, backyards, and boardrooms—will we be able to realize the full scope of human rights to which we are each entitled.

Today sexual and reproductive rights seem to be particularly under threat. In conflict and postconflict situations around the world, women's rights are being deliberately and extensively violated through rape and violence, or violated by default when vital health services, including reproductive health services, are not available. For example, some see the reinstitution of Sharia

law in Nigeria, explored in this volume, as a great threat to women's reproductive and sexual rights, while others maintain that they can work within
its constructs to protect those rights. In the United States, a woman's right to
reproductive choice is at its most vulnerable since the landmark *Roe v. Wade*
Supreme Court decision in 1973. The Bush administration has extended its
opposition to reproductive choice beyond U.S. borders, by withholding funding for organizations that provide vital reproductive health services unless
they agree to abide by the so-called "global gag rule" and by emphasizing
the importance of abstinence over proven HIV prevention methods.

This assault against reproductive rights is all the more troubling because of the fundamental importance of these rights. First, they are essential
to fulfilling the right to health for women and girls. As the 1993 Vienna Declaration and Programme of Action states, women's right to health includes
the right to "accessible and adequate health care and the widest range of family planning services, as well as equal access to education at all levels." This
fundamental principle has been affirmed and built on by United Nations bodies including UN committees on the Elimination of All Forms of Discrimination against Women and on Economic, Social, and Cultural Rights.

Sexual and reproductive rights are, of course, more than a matter of
access to health services. As the Cairo International Conference on Population and Development made clear in 1994, reproductive rights "rest on the
recognition of the basic right of all couples and individuals to decide freely
and responsibly the number, spacing and timing of their children. . . . They
also include the right of all to make decisions concerning reproduction free
of discrimination, coercion and violence." The Beijing Conference Platform
for Action went further, stating clearly that "The human rights of women include their right to have control over and decide freely and responsibly on
matters related to their sexuality, including sexual and reproductive health,
free of coercion, discrimination and violence."

Sexual and reproductive rights are, in essence, about women's empowerment. As the Beijing platform outlined nearly a decade ago, "Good health
is essential to leading a productive and fulfilling life, and the right of all
women to control all aspects of their health, in particular their own fertility,
is basic to their empowerment." Empowerment is about reassuring relationships within the family, the community, and the wider society, and about resisting attempts to justify restriction on the basis of culture. This is why I
have worked throughout my career to help advance the rights of women, including sexual and reproductive rights. When I worked as a lawyer before
the Irish and European courts, I was fortunate enough to be involved in cases

that affected the situation of Irish women. These cases, for example, resulted in the removal of discriminatory taxation of married women, the full participation of women in the jury system in Irish courts, the introduction of legal aid, the abolition of the status of illegitimacy, and the achievement of equal pay and equal opportunity in the workplace. I continued this effort as UN high commissioner for human rights, and now as executive director of Realizing Rights: The Ethical Globalization Initiative. Most recently this new project worked with a number of partners, including Graca Machel, to organize a conference in South Africa on gender and HIV/AIDS, focusing on mobilizing African leadership in the fight against AIDS.

The struggle for women's sexual and reproductive rights is at the frontline of the human rights struggle. Activists are calling for greater protection and fulfillment of these fundamental rights. Healthcare workers and community members are quietly providing vital family planning and reproductive services to women in clinics and hospitals around the world. Women themselves are spreading the word about how to take charge of their own bodies and lives, to protect themselves from HIV and to make informed, healthy, and independent choices about sexuality and about when and how to have a family.

In honor of the efforts of these women and men around the world, and in recognition of the importance of their cause, I am pleased to support this timely and significant book. These essays offer practical lessons and experiences for all of us involved in the effort to realize women's rights. The triumphs and challenges they outline can help inform our own struggles, be they personal or public, in places big or small.

The worldwide women's movement has come a long way since the landmark conferences of the early 1990s. The ongoing struggle for women's rights needs to be given the priority and attention the authors seek.

ACKNOWLEDGMENTS

This book, more than most, owes its existence to numerous individuals and institutions in distant corners of the world and right here in New York City.

First, we thank the Soros Reproductive Health and Rights fellows for the work featured here and for their thoughtful, experienced deliberations throughout the fellowship cycle. Mary Robinson's foreword beautifully sets the stage for the diverse issues explored herein. We thank her for taking the time from a busy schedule to contribute to our effort. We are also most grateful to our selection committee, Vanessa Northington Gamble, Rounaq Jahan, Sylvia Law, JoAnn Mort, and Dorothy Thomas, who culled through more than a hundred worthy applications to pick this fine first group of fellows.

As an important dimension of the fellowship and in preparing this volume, we held two meetings in New York—mini think tanks as we construed them—at which we were also lucky to have the strategic participation of: Karima Bennoune, Charlotte Bunch, Rhonda Copelon, Joanne Csete, Anke Ehrhardt, Lynn Freedman, Vanessa Northington Gamble, Adrienne Germain, Tagreid Abu Hassabo, Rounaq Jahan, Joan Kaufman, Terry McGovern, Alice Miller, Ana Oliveira, Richard Parker, Rosalind Petchesky, Sara Seims, and Tony Whitehead. We thank them all for their wise counsel.

Each chapter of the book was also reviewed by at least two outside experts, who took great care and offered important suggestions. Our thanks to: Mahael Adawy, Babatunde Ahonsi, Karima Bennoune, Charlotte Bunch, Rebecca Cook, Sonia Correa, Sara Costa, Cynthia Dailard, Aida Seif el Dawla, Lynn Freedman, Adrienne Germain, Sofia Gruskin, Joan Kaufman, Michael Kaufman, Michael Kimmel, Barbara Klugman, Terry McGovern, Ros Petchesky, Barbara Pillsbury, Zena Stein, and Tyrene White.

An endeavor such as this relies on behind-the-scenes work, infrastructural support, and vision. At the Open Society Institute, we thank Tiana Norgren, who played a key role in getting this project off the ground; Bergin O'Malley and Aida Henriquez-Brown, for their always good-humored assistance; Leigh Hallingby and John Kowal for some crucial fact-checking; and, of course, Gara LaMarche and Aryeh Neier for infusing the institution with such fine values. Our most profound gratitude goes to George Soros and the entire OSI board of directors for making this program possible, and to Kristin Luker for encouraging them to do so.

At Columbia University, we thank Leslie Davidson, former chair of the Heilbrunn Department of Population and Family Health, Mailman School of Public Health, along with a wonderful, hardworking, smart group of student assistants who are also always good company—Kim Bylander, Felicia Chase Goodman, Sabrina Baronberg, and Lisa Levy. As always, our thanks to Dean Allan Rosenfield, who supports this work both concretely and intellectually, and always as a fellow traveler.

At Rutgers University Press, we are indebted to Kristi Long for her patience as we gathered and edited papers from across the globe, and for her insightful editorial feedback and guidance. We are also extremely grateful to Margaret Case for her careful and thoughtful copy editing of the entire manuscript, to Jane Williamson for editing the chapters in their early stages, and to Esther Hyneman for her editing of the introduction. For the author photographs, we thank our talented friend, Harold Levine.

Finally, enormous thanks and gratitude to the two wonderful, talented directors of the fellowship program, who also provided superb editorial assistance on this volume—first, Stacey Rees and more recently, Sunita Mehta.

Where Human Rights Begin

Introduction

ELLEN CHESLER

> Where, after all, do universal human rights begin? In small places, close to home—so close and so small that they cannot be seen on any map of the world. Yet they *are* the world of the individual person: the neighborhood he lives in; the school or college he attends; the factory, farm, or office where he works. Such are the places where every man, woman, and child seeks equal justice, equal opportunity, equal dignity without discrimination. Unless these rights have meaning there, they have little meaning anywhere. Without concerted citizen action to uphold them close to home, we shall look in vain for progress in the larger world.
> —Eleanor Roosevelt, Remarks at the United Nations, March 27, 1958

Preparing to celebrate the tenth anniversary of the United Nations' Universal Declaration of Human Rights, Eleanor Roosevelt made her way to the organization's imposing new headquarters on Manhattan's East side. The occasion was a small, scarcely noticed ceremony to release a guide for community-based action on human rights. There, in the hope of rekindling interest in the landmark document that had been forged a decade earlier under her skillful leadership, Mrs. Roosevelt casually made the observation quoted above, from which we draw both the title and the inspiration for this book. She insisted upon the potential of universal human rights discourse to transform personal relationships, not just political ones. She encouraged citizens of all nations to enforce respect for human rights and freedoms in their homes and their communities, not to wait for their governments to act (Black, 1999; Lash, 1972).

In recent years the world community, under the umbrella of the United Nations, has dramatically expanded Mrs. Roosevelt's vision by extending formal human rights jurisdiction to the familiar places she identified—the homes and workplaces and communities that govern interactions among individuals.

1

Human rights law is now widely understood as an appropriate construct for informing the conduct and protecting the rights of citizens, and for doing so broadly, not just in terms of their freedom from unwarranted imposition of state power through suppression of assembly and expression, arbitrary arrest, imprisonment or torture—the principal grounds on which human rights violations were long contested.

The application of human rights to private and local realms has called attention to the continuing oppression of women in many parts of the world and has intensified the struggle against state-sanctioned practices that license gender-based subordination, discrimination, and violence. Improving the status of women has become a global priority not only as a moral imperative but also as a necessary condition of achieving human security and guaranteeing progress. Through a series of high-profile meetings over the past several decades, the United Nations has agreed upon a program of action to empower women as an essential first step to accelerate economic growth, reduce poverty, improve public health, sustain the earth's natural environment, and consolidate transitions to democracy in countries long controlled by tyrants. This is no small matter. A near-universal consensus is now calling for fundamental changes in practices that have denied women equality and held them back for centuries.

Universal standards for human rights and development, however, offer no sure cure for the violations of women that persist with uncanny fortitude and often unimaginable cruelty in many places around the world. On the contrary, women and girls are especially vulnerable today as conservative elements rise up to protest the advance of these secular ideas. Attempting to negotiate globalization's assault on their cultures, forces of reaction have made women and the family an arena of intense political conflict.

Women in Afghanistan under the Taliban—forcibly shrouded in burkas, confined to the home, denied education, jobs, and health care, including contraception—provided a graphic representation of this phenomenon. But even with the Taliban's demise, disturbing examples of resurgent fundamentalism persist in the Middle East and elsewhere in Asia, Africa, Europe, and the Americas. Efforts to roll back women's rights—especially their reproductive rights—are under way in many countries of the former Soviet Bloc that are experiencing turmoil as a consequence of democratic and economic transition. They are, of course, notably on the rise in the United States as well, where a quarter century of substantial economic and social progress by women has fueled a fierce backlash in defense of traditional values. This backlash threatens to compromise long-established women's rights at home and undermines U.S. support for international obligations to women—ironically, even as the Bush administration justifies its wars against terrorism at least partly in the name of improving women's status (Chesler, 2004).

How are policy makers and activists faring as they work to translate principles of gender equality now established in international law into meaningful realities in the lives of women and girls? How fragile are these global accords today? What are the remaining obstacles to their realization? Can much be accomplished simply through expanded support of policy and programming on the ground, or will success depend on a broader context of events and circumstances largely unanticipated in the past? How do we proceed in the face of growing unrest around the world brought on by an acceleration in failing states, declining economies, the HIV/AIDS epidemic, and reduced resources available for health and human development? How do we counter a dramatic resurgence of fundamentalism that has led in turn to terrorism, brutal retaliations, and tragic postconflict disarray?

These are large questions, but they can be addressed through narrowly applied research, analysis, and discussion. With those goals in mind, the Open Society Institute of the Soros Foundation Network and the Department of Population and Family Health of the Mailman School of Public Health at Columbia University have cosponsored a two-year fellowship program. The program brought together eight international scholars and activists from around the world to share their experiences and perspectives in the hope of refreshing one another's thinking and providing strategic lessons for continued advocacy and activism on behalf of women's health and human rights. Chosen by a distinguished selection committee from a pool of one hundred applicants, each fellow also agreed to produce an essay written for a broad, general audience. Although each essay is grounded in a local story of interest, it also illumines global challenges by addressing the tensions between new rights paradigms and particular historical circumstances affecting women—and men as well—especially in terms of their sexuality and reproductive health. This book is the product of that labor. Each chapter examines a different country in terms of the obstacles that country faces and the progress it is making in adjusting the exigencies of local cultural, social, political, and economic realities to universal human rights obligations.

This introductory essay also poses a threshold question. What is the historical trajectory of women's rights as human rights? How did we get where we are now? Public policy, as is so often observed, is largely path dependent. How we think and act today is determined by a past that may be unknown to us. Women, in particular, have long been denied fair recognition as historical actors and as agents of political and social change. Understanding the practical processes by which human rights principles came to be applied to women's rights—and the theory that informs them—may arm and embolden us to defeat the obstacles we face in implementing those principles. It seems especially relevant today as we try to unravel the complicated politics of U.S. engagement with the United Nations, and as the United Nations moves forward with its ambitious development goals for the new millennium, which prioritize gender equality and women's empowerment but neglect any specific mention of sexual and reproductive health issues in what many see as a concession to conservative politics. This introduction draws on recent scholarship in order to bring a sobering but still hopeful context to the contemporary program evaluation and policy analysis in the chapters that follow.

The Origins of International Human Rights

Modern human rights doctrine began to take shape in the waning days of World War II, when upon Franklin Roosevelt's death, President Harry Truman appointed his widow to the five-member U.S. delegation of the newly chartered United Nations in London. As first lady, Eleanor Roosevelt had been widely recognized, though hardly universally admired, as an advocate of social and economic justice. She was a passionate critic of racial discrimination long before it was fashionable to defend the civil rights of blacks or other minorities, an ardent defender of the poor and downtrodden, and a faithful proponent of women's equality and rights. As early as 1938, with the country still firmly committed to isolationism, she had published a bestselling book, *This Troubled World,* which envisioned a future governed by collective security agreements among nations that would join in a global peacekeeping body to deter violence and conflict (Black, 1999; Lash, 1972; B. Cook, 1999).

Growing recognition of Nazi crimes turned the attention of America and the world to the kind of security arrangements she had endorsed. The Atlantic Charter, conceived by Franklin Roosevelt and Winston Churchill at a secret meeting in 1941, proclaimed that all people deserved the right to "live out their lives in freedom from want and fear." Within a year, four more countries joined in a formal "Declaration of the United Nations," promising to join the fight against fascist aggression and terror. Growing awareness of the tragic victimization of civilian populations during the war and of the Nazi program of extermination brought pressure for a peace that would be secured not only militarily but also morally. Out of these circumstances was born a doctrine of universal human rights that transcended the sovereignty of nation states.

Among the great powers, enthusiasm for collective security arrangements and human rights came first from individual crusaders such as Mrs. Roosevelt and from churches and secular nongovernmental institutions. H. G. Wells's provocative essay, *The Rights of Man or What Are We Fighting For?*—widely translated and distributed in forty-eight countries—sparked extensive debate about non-Western rights traditions as well as those born of the European Enlightenment. The substantial influence of activists and scholars from the developing world in the evolution of human rights doctrine first became evident when the American Law Institute released a statement of essential rights heavily influenced by Latin American jurists. This later became a blueprint for the Universal Declaration of Human Rights. The International Labor Organization, women's groups, other internationalists, and many progressive religious bodies representing diverse constituencies from countries around the world also added their impassioned voices (Lauren, 2003; Kennedy, 1999; Chesler, 1992).

In the practice of diplomacy, this new way of thinking required nothing short of an intellectual revolution. The conduct of international relations has, in Saskia Sassen's phrase, long constituted a "narrative of eviction," which takes the state as its exclusive subject and relegates all other actors to peripheral roles. Even as Allied forces dropped copies of the Wells book behind enemy lines, tensions developed between human rights advocates and professional diplomats. A postwar planning committee, appointed by President Roosevelt to advise on the formation of the United Nations, could not agree on how to balance idealism about rights for individuals with a mechanism for meaningful enforcement that would also respect national sovereignty (Lauren, 2003; Sassen, 1996; cited in Altman, 2001, 130).

Meeting at Dumbarton Oaks in 1944, the Allied powers resisted the pressure to assign any coercive powers of enforcement to a new international peacekeeping body. And when the UN charter was drawn in April of 1945, the will of the major powers prevailed with the formation of a Security Council they would permanently control and whose actions any one member may veto. Equal representation of all nations was guaranteed through the General Assembly, however, and that body was made responsible for establishing the conditions for respect of rights and for the advancement of higher standards of living—but all with little consideration of what real authority or practical outcomes would issue from this portfolio. This bifurcated arrangement has hobbled human rights enforcement ever since (Lash, 1972; Schlesinger, 2003; Lauren, 2003).

In London, Mrs. Roosevelt was assigned as the American representative to the Social, Humanitarian, and Cultural Committee of the General Assembly (Committee III), considered a relatively insignificant and safe berth by her colleagues on the delegation, including Secretary of State James F. Byrnes and other prominent government officials whose attention was drawn to what they saw as the tougher and more immediate issues of atomic power, European reconstruction, investment, and the like. Committee III, in turn, authorized a Commission on Human Rights, which unanimously elected her chair and head of the committee to draft a human rights declaration.

During the following three years, as she presided patiently and effectively through protracted and contentious debate over the writing of the Universal Declaration of Human Rights, Mrs. Roosevelt earned wide respect as a diplomat from her American colleagues, though never any meaningful enthusiasm for the human rights enterprise. Now the mostly widely translated and disseminated document in history, it bears the unmistakable stamp of her genial temperament and willingness to compromise. The Universal Declaration begins with the bold conviction that "recognition of the inherent dignity and of the equal and inalienable rights of all members of the human family is the foundation of freedom, justice and peace in the world." It demands recognition of rights that transcend the jurisdiction of nation-states and cannot be abrogated by them. It encourages all peoples and all nations to adopt its specific provisions as "a common standard of achievement" and obliges citizens to accept ultimate responsibility as individuals for the enforcement of those rights, but it contains no sanctions for state violations. In Mrs. Roosevelt's own words, it constitutes a set of "ideals" that "men" (she always used what she considered to be a sex-neutral construction) must strive to reach. "Men cannot live by bread alone." Those ideals would only later be made tangible through the definition of binding legal standards (Lash, 1972; Roosevelt, 1948).

Most significantly, the declaration moves beyond traditional civil and political claims to an expanded definition of social citizenship that requires investment in education, employment, housing, and health care. Men might not "live by bread alone," as Mrs. Roosevelt wrote, but they could not stake a meaningful claim on freedom without it. Poverty, hunger, illiteracy, and disease are not conditions in which democracy is likely to flourish (Universal Declaration of Human Rights in Lockwood et al., 1998; Lauren, 2003).

A stunning achievement, the declaration gave rise to the central debate over appropriate boundaries for state obligation to individuals and their personal and social welfare that has in the years since shaped political discourse generally, and the development of the human rights movement specifically. It was Mrs. Roosevelt's achievement, but it also reflected the work of the Soviet representative to the Human Rights Commission, who demanded compensation for the declaration's pious guarantees of political and civil rights, which he saw as empty pronouncements by countries that flagrantly denied rights on the basis of class, race, and sex. He was especially contemptuous of America's then still legally protected racism, a view Mrs. Roosevelt certainly sympathized with. American diplomats, on the other hand, saw these economic and social guarantees as a menacing back door to Communism and an affront to classic liberal principles. For Mrs. Roosevelt, however, the Universal Declaration realized a lifelong understanding about the indivisibility of rights and embodied her conviction that totalitarianism had taken root in the century's economic convulsions, social dislocations, and fears. It embodied her husband's vision, expressed in his final State of the Union address, of a second Bill of Rights that would obligate governments to provide social and economic safeguards (Lash, 1972; Kennedy, 1999; Henkin; 1990).

Mrs. Roosevelt differentiated traditional liberties from new entitlement rights by acknowledging a distinction in how they would be achieved. In her view, civil and political rights constitute inherent obligations that require immediate compliance through international law. Social and economic rights are "aspirational"; they can be achieved only progressively through investments in development. The United Nations would enforce violations of civil and political rights through a complaint mechanism located in the Human Rights Commission, backed up by the threat of economic or military sanctions. Social and economic progress would be advanced through the humanitarian, rights, and development work of the International Labor Organization, along with constituent agencies just being organized, including UNICEF, UNESCO, the Food and Agriculture Organization, and the World Health Organization, with loans and grants from donor countries and with contributions from the newly formed World Bank and International Monetary Fund. In the following six years, in fact, while she remained at the UN, the United States made more than $30 billion in loans and guarantees available for foreign assistance, most for reconstruction in Europe and Japan but including a then sizable $5 billion for the developing world. In addition, a tradition of substantial annual grants to UNICEF and the other UN agencies was established (Lauren, 2003; Roosevelt, 1951).

Although the United States arguably met its obligations to these various UN humanitarian and development agencies, its commitment to human rights quickly fell victim to cold war politics. Under Mrs. Roosevelt's inspired leadership, the UN unanimously adopted the Declaration of Human Rights in 1948 (only Russia and its satellites abstained), and work began immediately to prepare a binding covenant. When a draft was ready three years later, however, the Truman administration objected to the inclusion in a single document of civil and political, as well as social and economic rights. Mrs. Roosevelt tried to negotiate a compromise by preparing two separate covenants, but the Soviets scuttled that arrangement, inflaming public opinion in the United States and fueling hostility to the United Nations within both political parties. The situation worsened as public opinion swung further to the right with the rise of McCarthyism. Following his election to the presidency, Dwight David Eisenhower announced to a shocked world that the United States would not be a party to any human rights treaty approved by the UN and that, despite a prior commitment to nonpartisanship there, Mrs. Roosevelt would not be reappointed when her term at the Human Rights Commission ended. She resigned immediately, and in her absence, the United States effectively withdrew from any constructive role in the evolution of international human rights doctrine, ceding leadership on these issues to the many newly independent states that joined in the wake of the rapid collapse of colonial empires. More than a billion people would secure the right of self-determination in the following two decades, and their commitment to a broad definition of human rights would remain firm (Roosevelt, 1953a and 1953b; Lash, 1972; Lauren, 2003).

With little support from any of the major powers, however, work on the completion of covenants to enforce the Universal Declaration reached a stalemate until 1965, when indignation over the apartheid policies of South Africa led to the adoption of the groundbreaking International Convention on the Elimination of All Forms of Racial Discrimination. This agreement set standards and established mechanisms to monitor the compliance of parties to the treaty and also hear individual complaints. In the throes of its own civil rights revolution, the United States signed the treaty, and the logjam was broken. Within a year, agreement was reached on the International Covenant for Civil and Political Rights and International Covenant for Social, Economic, and Cultural Rights, both of which took over ten years to ratify in the face of considerable opposition from both the Americans and the Russians, who each only signed the one covenant they agreed with (ICCPR and ICESR in Lockwood et al., 1998).

An enforceable system of international law has thus been put into place, but with compromised effectiveness. Wherever domestic remedies for human rights violations do not exist or fail to do their job, international or regional bodies can now be called on with jurisdiction to investigate and prosecute abuses. In the optimistic assessment of historian Paul Gordon Lauren, this has transformed "individual men, women and children from objects of international concern into actual subjects of enforceable international law." Others are less charitable. Although they applaud that human rights have become, in the words of former UN Secretary General Boutros-Boutros Ghali, "the common language of humanity," they bemoan the effective veto the major powers of the Security Council hold over their enforcement. In the United States, where official conviction about human rights has historically been constrained by the powerful influence that conservatives in both parties have exercised, the task of monitoring and enforcing global treaties has fallen largely to nongovernmental organizations such as Amnesty International and Human Rights Watch (Lauren, 2003; Henkin, 1990).

Women's Rights as Human Rights

By the end of World War II, substantial numbers of women around the world were educated, working for wages outside the home and experiencing an unprecedented degree of personal freedom. The war itself had accelerated change, with many thousands of women entering the civilian workforce to fill critical jobs, while others staffed volunteer efforts or supported military operations as nurses and office personnel. Large numbers of women joined the underground resistance in Europe and Japan, and elsewhere they assumed leadership positions in liberation movements. When the UN General Assembly first convened in London, the small party of women delegates, though unable to agree initially on what precise structure the participation of women should take, issued a manifesto calling on all governments of the world to encourage women to engage in public affairs and to share in the work of peace and reconstruction as they had shared in the war and resistance (Fraser, 1999; Lauren, 2003).

Eleanor Roosevelt was one of only eighteen women delegates from eleven countries in a sea of males, but their influence was amplified by the voices of many diverse women in nongovernmental organizations who gathered first in San Francisco and later in London to demand official UN recognition of nonparliamentarians. From the start, this larger group reflected the strong commitments of women from India, New Zealand, the Dominican

Republic, and elsewhere in the developing world to human rights provisions that would assure equal protection on the basis of sex, as well as to equal opportunity for employment of women within the UN system itself. Their vigorous participation belies common accusations in recent years that the UN's ambitious women's rights agenda is solely a recent product of European and American feminism (Gaer, 1998; Fraser, 1999; Schlesinger, 2003).

Almost alone among these women, Mrs. Roosevelt initially opposed efforts to create a Commission on the Status of Women (CSW) wholly independent of the Human Rights Commission. She argued that separate was not likely to be equal in resources or influence, and acknowledged her concern that segregating women's issues would only move them farther from the attention of men, a position perhaps best understood by a remark from Secretary of State Dean Acheson, who famously asked Vijaya Lakshmi Pandit of India, the first woman elected to chair the General Assembly: "Why do pretty women want to be like men?" (Lauren, 2003). But Mrs. Roosevelt ultimately deferred to the majority and instructed the U.S. delegation to introduce a resolution to create the new body. The women of the CSW then played a major role in drafting the Universal Declaration, insisting on gender-neutral language that guarantees rights to "all human beings" not just to "men," as she first wrote. As Hansa Mehta of India protested, "If it says 'all men,' when we go home it will *be* all men" (Fraser, 1999; Black, 1999).

Activist and scholar Felice Gaer best explains how a doctrine according human rights to women had developed. First, the principle that individuals of both sexes have rights to assert against the state was firmly established. A breakthrough had occurred in the nineteenth century, when international treaties were forged to abolish slavery. Similar treaties protecting individual rights then followed, such as those providing victims of war with standing to seek redress. In 1902, the Hague Conventions addressed the conflicts in national laws on marriage, divorce, and child custody that often abrogated the rights of women moving from one place to another. Conventions aimed at combating traffic in women for the purposes of prostitution followed soon after (Gaer 1998).

Second, women had to acquire rights of their own, independent of the rights they had by virtue of their relationships with men. The notion that women's rights should be limited to the protections accorded their fathers or husbands was central to the opposition to women's suffrage, the granting of property and inheritance rights to women, and other reforms. In the late 1800s, and throughout the nineteenth century, a body of literature challenging this assumption had received widespread attention. Mary Wollstonecraft's 1792 tract, *A Vindication of the Rights of Women,* applied to women natural rights theories from the French Enlightenment that upheld the sovereignty of the individual. The 1848 Seneca Falls Declaration of Sentiments and Resolutions claimed autonomy and rights for women in a wide range of civil, political, and private matters. John Stuart Mill's 1869 *Essay on the Subjection of Women* asked whether home and family are women's only natural vocation, or whether in a world where formal work had moved outside the home, women must necessarily follow. Twentieth-century claims by birth control advocates like the American pioneer Margaret Sanger steered these notions in a radical direction by arguing for a woman's inherent right to control her own body, thereby separating sexuality and reproduction, long considered woman's primary role (Gaer, 1998; Fraser, 1999; Chesler, 1992).

By the nineteen twenties, women's movements had achieved victories for suffrage and for some access to safe and legal birth control in Europe and the United States. They had also founded an International Women's Suffrage Association and forged alliances to expand their reach to Asia and Latin America. Then many activists began to move toward what Gaer identifies as the third element necessary to establish women's rights as a human rights— a movement away from laws that provided special protections for women to ones demanding gender equality in every aspect of life—including marriage, ownership of property, inheritance, education, and employment.

The Universal Declaration was the first formal document to claim that discrimination against women is an appropriate matter for international concern, not a category privileged and protected by local sovereignty or by traditional cultural or religious practices governing marriage and family relations. It was the first to recognize that if women are oppressed in private places, they will never be able to exercise their civil and public liberties. To advance women's rights, therefore, it is necessary to address—and the state has an obligation to protect—personal as well as public spheres of conduct. It must intervene to eliminate everyday forms of discrimination. The Universal Declaration establishes broad protections for women as citizens and workers, and it specifically accords to women the rights to free consent in marriage and divorce and the necessary provisions to care for their children. It thus paves the way for the later extension of rights to other areas of women's lives, including inheritance and private property, sexuality and reproduction (Universal Declaration in Lockwood et al., 1999; Gaer, 1998).

Even as the mainstream human rights agenda foundered in the UN's early years, the CSW, operating without much attention from the major powers, negotiated the adoption of legally binding treaties governing women's political rights, nationality rights, consent and minimum age of marriage, property rights, educational opportunities, and labor standards, among other topics. By the 1960s, landmark studies on family planning, housing, health, and human services pushed the body toward a new emphasis on development as a means of advancing women's rights. And in 1967, following several years of careful draftsmanship under CSW's Mexican chair, Maria Lavella Urbina, the UN adopted the Declaration on the Elimination of Discrimination against Women, which consolidated earlier gains and served as a blueprint for the Convention to Eliminate All Forms of Discrimination against Women, passed in 1979 as a legally enforceable document that binds together and expands upon these prior agreements. An interesting sidebar to these developments from today's vantage point was the active participation in drafting the 1967 declaration of Afghan women, who contributed the notion that pervasive discrimination against women warrants granting special privileges as amends, a precursor to the idea of affirmative action (Lockwood et al., 1998; Fraser, 1999).

When the United Nations marked the twentieth anniversary of the Universal Declaration in 1968 at a conference on Human Rights in Tehran, women's rights provided a rare arena of agreement between Soviet delegates, interested in calling international attention to the educational and employment opportunities their government had granted women, and Americans, inspired by the emerging second wave of feminism at home. The conference adopted resolutions encouraging support for programs that advance opportunities for women in education and employment through development assistance, and for the first time identified family planning as a human right. These resolutions began a long debate about how to create an appropriate balance between protecting women's rights, on the one hand, and investing in development programs that address women's long-term needs, on the other.

Ester Boserup's landmark 1969 study, *Women and Economic Development,* which emphasizes the significance of women's economic role in agriculturally based economies of developing nations, spurred government donors and private philanthropists to support income-generating programs for women, along with legal rights projects to advance policies that address gender discrimination in their own countries (Fraser, 1999).

Growing recognition of the importance of gender in development resulted in a commitment by the secretary general to an international women's meeting. The UN's First International Conference on Women was held in Mexico City in 1975, under the inspiring and enduring banner of a dove embossed with the sign representing women. Though most of the parliamentarians continued to be men, many of whom displayed a fairly cynical attitude toward the proceedings, a highly motivated and largely female UN staff, along with nongovernmental organizations supported by U.S. foundations, insured success. Drafting committees controlled by women produced documents that embraced a wildly optimistic plan for achieving gains in areas of civic participation, education, employment, and health care. Enthusiasm was sufficient to designate an UN Decade of Women, and negotiations began to convert the Declaration on Discrimination against Women into a binding convention or treaty (Fraser, 1999; Gaer, 1998; Hartman, 1998).

Adopted in 1979, the visionary Convention to Eliminate All Forms of Discrimination against Women, commonly known as CEDAW or the international bill of rights for women, cautiously acknowledges the importance of women's traditional obligations within the family, but also establishes new norms for women's participation in all dimensions of life. It provides binding protection to a broad range of rights in marriage and family relations, including property, inheritance, and access to health care, with an explicit mention of family planning (though not of abortion). It demands equality for women as citizens with full access to suffrage, political representation, and other legal benefits; it declares their right to education, including professional and vocational training and the elimination of gender stereotypes and segregation. Last, it establishes their rights as workers deserving equal remuneration, social security benefits, and protection from sexual harassment and from workplace discrimination on the grounds of marriage or maternity. In these respects, according to human rights theorist Rebecca J. Cook, CEDAW moves beyond earlier UN conventions guaranteeing a sex-neutral norm usually measured by a male standard to a position that demands a legal response to the pervasive and systemic discrimination against women (R. Cook, 1994; Milani, 2001; CEDAW in Lockwood et al., 1998).

Like all international covenants, the treaty respects national sovereignty and does not impose absolute legal obligations. CEDAW is "self-executing" in those countries whose constitutions or other legal mechanisms explicitly provide for it to be so; but, elsewhere, as in the United States, specific laws must be passed to implement its provisions. CEDAW also provides for the granting of "reservations, understandings and declarations" to accommodate local variations from its standards. Indeed, many signatories do not live up to its obligations, a weakness of all human rights statutes. Many ratifying countries, for example, have reserved on Article 16, which calls for equality in the family Still, they are obliged to submit regular reports to the UN CEDAW committee that semiannually reviews each country's progress toward implementation of the treaty and reports to the General Assembly with rec-ommendations for improvement. CEDAW now also has an "optional proto-col" that allows for a communication procedure from individuals or groups alleging violation of their rights under its provisions and an inquiry proce-dure to permit investigation of alleged violations that are "grave" or "sys-tematic" (see www.law-lib.utoronto.ca/Diana for additional information on the CEDAW protocol).

In a number of countries, including South Africa, Brazil, Australia, Zambia, Sri Lanka, Uganda—and most recently, if ironically, Afghanistan and Iraq—treaty provisions have been incorporated directly into constitutions or bills of rights. Elsewhere the treaty has been used as a basis for specific laws governing workplace practices and property rights, improving access to girls' education, extending maternity leave and child care, requiring legal protec-tion for victims of domestic violence, outlawing female genital cutting, ex-panding family-planning access and curbing sexual trafficking (Milani, 2001; Milani et al., 2004).

In the waning days of his presidency, Jimmy Carter, the first American president to stand firmly behind international human rights principles, hur-riedly signed the convention and sent it to the Senate for ratification, where it has languished ever since, held up by intransigent conservatives who op-pose both international obligations and women's rights. Around the world, 179 countries have now signed the treaty, leaving the United States among a handful of "rogue" states, including Iran, Somalia, and Sudan (Milani et al., 2004). For years, the famously cantankerous senator Jesse Helms attacked CEDAW as the work of "radical feminists" with an "antifamily agenda." "I do not intend to be pushed around by discourteous, demanding women," he bragged on the Senate floor in 1999. Helms is no longer around, but George W. Bush now stands in the way—captive to the conservative base of his party.

A number of specious claims hobble U.S. ratification. Conservative op-ponents have sounded the same alarms that defeated the Equal Rights Amend-ment to the Constitution. They argue that CEDAW abridges parental rights; threatens single-sex education; mandates combat military service for women; demands legal abortion; sanctions homosexuality and same-sex marriage; pro-hibits the celebration of Mother's Day, and other such canards.

In addition, the widespread assumption that American women are al-ready protected by a substantial body of U.S. case law has drained energy from the cause even though U.S. Supreme Court justices Stephen Breyer and Ruth Bader Ginsburg have spoken widely of the positive benefits of apply-ing international standards to the pursuit of equality under U.S. law. Their concurring opinion in *Grutter v. Bollinger*, the recent case upholding the use of affirmative action by the University of Michigan, cited the International Convention on the Elimination of All Forms of Racial Discrimination, which the United States has ratified and which obliges governments in judging racist practices to look not only at intent but also at outcome. Other recent decisions by the Court have similarly invoked international or foreign legal precedents as object lessons or simply as good ideas, in addition to arguments rooted more formally in U.S. sources. In *Lawrence v. Texas,* Justice Anthony Kennedy's majority opinion invalidated a state law criminalizing consensual homosexual sodomy, citing an act of English Parliament and a ruling of the European Court of Human Rights as evidence that, contrary to claims of supporters of the Texas law, criminal prohibitions of sodomy are not universally accepted. Two recent court decisions overturned capital punishment of mentally retarded individuals and minors on the grounds that the U.S. Constitution prohibits cruel and unusual punishments, but also took account of European and international repudiation of the practice (Dorf, 2005).

In a recent article defending workplace affirmative action policies for women and promoting paid family leave and child care, Justice Ginsberg specifically encouraged the use of CEDAW (especially its General Recommendation 25 on "Temporary Special Measures," UN jargon for affirmative action) as a justification for change. Finally, others have argued that the convention might be used to encourage equal representation in Washington, where the U.S. Congress and all executive agencies are exempt from affirmative action laws. This is important because despite substantial gains, women currently hold only 14 of 100 seats in the U.S. Senate, a record 68 of 435 in the House of Representatives, and approximately 20 percent of state legislative positions throughout the country, percentages substantially below the minimum goals for legislative participation by women that Afghanistan and Iraq have now included in their constitutions—with U.S. encouragement (Chesler, 2004).

CEDAW was prepared for adoption at the Second International Conference on Women in Copenhagen in 1980, where fifty-seven countries immediately agreed to ratify. The twenty more necessary for implementation lined up within a year. As a result, despite American objections, the principle of the indivisibility of women's rights was established, and UN emphasis turned to moving women to the center of development strategies. The adage that women perform two-thirds of the world's work, receive one-tenth of total income, and own 1 percent of property, grew out of this meeting (Fraser, 1999).

At Copenhagen, violence against women and children, including battering, sexual assault, and other forms of abuse, was raised for the first time in an international forum and identified as a global issue transcending all cultures. The NGO (nongovernmental organization) forum at the Third International Conference on Women in Nairobi in 1985 then focused attention on this long-unrecognized issue. With over 14,000 women from around the world attending (over twice the number at each of the two prior meetings, including significant numbers from the developing world), a relationship was drawn between culturally sanctioned oppression of women in the home and growing conflict and war within and among nations. No formal recommendations were made, however, about how to resolve the problem. As Gaer observes, the NGO forum provided an opportunity for women to share strategies about how to become "legally literate" and how to begin to redress grievances in their own countries. But although national law was embraced as a tool for positive change, no one at the forum suggested that an international human rights body or procedure be utilized to provide asylum for victims or punish perpetrators of violence against women (Gaer, 1998).

The intellectual breakthrough that made this approach possible came with the 1990 publication of a landmark article in *Human Rights Quarterly* by U.S. activist Charlotte Bunch of the Center for Women's Global Leadership at Rutgers University. "Significant numbers of the world's population are routinely subject to torture, starvation, terrorism, humiliation, and even murder simply because they are female," Bunch wrote. "Crimes such as these against any group other than women would be recognized as a civil and political emergency as well as a gross violation of the victim's humanity. Yet, despite a clear record of deaths and demonstrable abuse, women's rights are not commonly classified as human rights."

Bunch enumerated numerous examples of culturally sanctioned sexism that actually kills women: in prenatal sex selection; in childhood, where girls often receive less food and health care; in pregnancy or illegal abortion, when reproduction combines with poverty and poor health to produce high mortality rates; in wife battery, rape, incest, dowry deaths, genital mutilation, and sexual trafficking. Calling the violence "profoundly political" and identifying it as the result of "structural relationships of power and domination and privilege for men, "she argued for recognition of women's rights as fundamental human rights deserving protection under international law, and she called for the expansion of CEDAW to address questions of violence directly. Drawing on a slogan that actually originated with a women's coalition in the Philippines, Bunch first made the claim later popularized in Beijing in 1995 by Hillary Rodham Clinton that "women's rights are human rights" (Bunch, 1990).

In 1992, CEDAW General Recommendation 19 was expanded so that gender-based violence is now formally identified as a form of discrimination violating fundamental human rights and obligating governments to take action. The UN subsequently published a study titled *Violence against Women in the Family,* which underscores the epidemic proportions of the problem worldwide, its protection "by custom and culture," and its existence "beneath a veil of privacy, guilt and shame" (CEDAW General Recommendation 19, Lockwood et al., 1998; Gaer, 1998; Fraser, 1999).

In *Human Rights Quarterly,* Rebecca J. Cook then reported on the findings of a forum of lawyers from Africa, Asia, the Americas, Europe, and Australia on how to move the women's human rights agenda forward. Many members first questioned the utility of an individual rights approach to the problems of women in most societies, which are disadvantaged by structural injustice and in need of improved social welfare (or a readjustment of burdensome international lending policies) as much as by an absence of rights. But the group then agreed on the value of using human rights instruments to redress injustice, so long as definitions of rights are adjusted to reflect the situation of women more clearly. They argued for a recharacterization of rights categories: for example, gender violence would be compared to torture as a state violation of civil and political rights; maternal and reproductive health policies would be understood as a basic obligation of the state's positive social responsibility to protect women's right to life, liberty, and security. Since multilateral institutions such as the World Bank and the International Monetary Fund are also under the jurisdiction of international human rights accords, some participants also saw the value of using the law to obligate them to ensure that women benefit equally in their investments, or to restructure loans to poor countries whose women are heavily burdened.

The participation of Ken Roth, then a staff member and now executive director of Human Rights Watch, signaled a new interest in women's rights by traditional U.S. human rights organizations. Roth explored the relative merits of applying theories of state accountability developed in other areas of international human rights law to violations of women. States are held accountable for violations under three distinct categories—government agency, which demands treatment of private acts of violence as though they are the acts of government agents; government complicity, which holds the state accountable for failure to act to end violence by individuals; and government responsibility for the unequal application of the law, which would require the complicit state to apply the same level of resources to abuses of women as it does to those of men. Identifying violence against women as an issue has provided an important bridge to established modes of work in human rights. Human Rights Watch had in 1990 begun its own celebrated Women's Rights Division (R. Cook, 1993).

From Human Rights to Human Security: Vienna, Cairo, and Beijing

The fall of communism in Eastern and Central Europe in the late 1980s and the imminent collapse of the Soviet Union occasioned new hope for expansion of the mainstream human rights enterprise to women. However, when organizing began in 1990 for a second World Conference on Human Rights, to be held in Vienna on the forty-fifth anniversary of the Universal Declaration, no mention of women or provisions for inclusion of gender as a category in the program were initially made. In response, Charlotte Bunch convened a working group of women from around the world who were living in the New York area and brought the issue to the first Global Leadership Institute she organized in 1991. The institute developed the idea of an annual campaign of "16 Days of Activism against Gender Violence," linking violence against women to Human Rights Day, which has since grown to involve hundreds of thousands of women around the world in demonstrations, lobbying, media, and other forms of public education and activism. The first campaign issued a petition calling on the UN to recognize gender violence as a human rights violation and to address it at Vienna. The petition was translated into twenty-three languages and garnered more than half a million signatures from 124 countries, through the auspices of the Center for Women's Global Leadership (CWGL), in collaboration with the International Women's Tribune Center.

At the same time, significant regional activism developed around four preparatory meetings in Tunis, San Jose, Bangkok, and Geneva. Drawing on the successful precedent established by women at the 1992 UN Conference on Environment and Development in Rio de Janeiro under the leadership of American politician Bella Abzug, regional advocates organized a disciplined NGO caucus that drew up positive amendments to the conference documents. With great determination, the Global Campaign for Women's Human Rights overcame substantial resistance to including women's rights on the grounds that they are an affront to local cultural prerogatives, and at least a portion of the women's action agenda was included in the draft conference document. Activists, still concerned that the draft failed to identify specific forms of gender exploitation, then worked collaboratively with official government delegations to revise the draft document's statement of principle. That statement finally read: "The human rights of women are an inalienable, integral, and indivisible part of universal human rights." In addition, the violations recognized in the final document included rape as a weapon of war (then much in the news because of atrocities in Bosnia), domestic violence, sexual harassment, and sexual exploitation through prostitution and trafficking, though with no specific timetables for remediation or sanctions (Vienna Declaration and Programme of Action in Lockwood et al., 1998).

A major victory in Vienna was increasing public visibility for the human rights of women. The Global Campaign raised funds to support a professional media campaign, and organized an NGO-sponsored Vienna Global Tribunal with thirty-three dramatic testimonies from women covering war crimes, domestic abuse, violations of bodily integrity, social and economic discrimination, and civil and political persecution. Activists gathered petitions signed by millions of women affirming women's rights as human rights. More than a thousand articles in U.S. newspapers along with substantial coverage elsewhere in the world created new legitimacy for the cause (Bunch and Reilly, 1994; Gaer, 1998).

The following year the world's governments gathered under the auspices of the United Nations to address international population policies and programs, which had grown increasingly controversial despite their success in helping to stabilize birthrates in many places. Women's health and rights activists from around the world attended the International Conference on Population and Development (ICPD) in Cairo, bringing many years of grassroots experience in the reproductive health field and an intense motivation for change. While they emphasized the need for policies and funds to support comprehensive sexual and reproductive health services, they also insisted that population policies, long driven by demographic concerns and by investments in contraceptive technology, should be transformed to reflect a fundamental commitment to reproductive and sexual rights as fundamental human rights. This broader strategy, they argued, would be more humane and more effective than policies narrowly focused on control of women's fertility (Sen et al., 1994).

This is a point not to be taken for granted and one that is often misunderstood. Most of the activists who helped frame the ICPD Programme of Action certainly recognized the fundamental relationship between lowered fertility and the ability of individual women to exercise their rights and realize opportunities outside the home. At the same time, they also appreciated the larger relationship between fertility patterns and collective social and economic outcomes. However strong their disagreements with the past practices of often alarmist and heavy-handed population programs—however serious their commitment to programmatic reforms—they did not deny the benefits of effective family planning to the welfare of individuals, families, communities, and eventually entire countries (Hodgson and Cotts, 1997).

The ICPD agenda provides a rights framework that centers on enabling women to make free and informed decisions about their own bodies, and individuals and couples to have the number of children they want. It also speaks of positive state responsibilities to promote economic and social benefits for women and their families by providing an adequate standard of living and publicly assisted services including, but not limited to, quality health care. Rosalind Petchesky, American activist and scholar, calls this a "double lens," which recognizes the personal and social dimensions of reproductive and sexual rights as mutually dependent rather than in conflict. Or as the platform of DAWN (Development Alternatives with Women for a New Era), an alliance of women largely from the southern hemisphere, put it: "women's reproductive health must be placed within a comprehensive human development framework that promotes all people's well-being and women's full citizenship" (Petchesky and Judd, 1998).

Cairo was also significant because it represented another major victory for the international women's movement, which had begun to organize existing regional networks of women's health advocates in September 1992, coincident with the preparations for Vienna. Under the skillful leadership of Joan Dunlop and Adrienne Germain of the International Women's Health Coalition in New York, an organization that had showcased and helped fund model grassroots activities in reproductive and sexual health since the 1980s, the group drafted a "Women's Declaration on Population Policies." This document was reviewed, revised, and ultimately endorsed by more than one hundred women's organizations across the globe and then sent for signature to other professionals in the health, population and diplomatic communities, including many men. It was followed by "The Rio Statement of Reproductive Health and Justice," signed by 215 women from 79 countries. These documents and the processes that informed them established the trust and built the common ground that resulted in widespread consensus for the values and practical programmatic recommendations in Cairo (Sen et al., 1994, Hodgson and Cotts, 1997).

This occurred in large measure because the women's community not only programmed a successful NGO forum for Cairo, but also demonstrated its growing power by getting many of its members appointed to official government delegations. Deployed in a deft and precise political operation, the women then worked from within the official conference proceedings to influence its outcomes. As in Vienna, the United States delegation in Cairo, appointed by President Clinton and led by Undersecretary of State Tim Wirth, took a leadership role in endorsing the health and rights approach proposed by advocates and defending it to other governments (Chesler, 1997).

The Cairo Programme of Action, endorsed by 79 governments (and even, with some significant reservations, by the Holy See, which represents the Catholic Church at the UN) establishes a twenty-year blueprint to promote human rights and human security by addressing women's empowerment as a central dimension of population issues, sustainable development, and poverty alleviation. It affirms the application of established human rights standards to population and development policies and sets ambitious, though not specific, goals for gender equality. To these ends, it references the Universal Declaration, CEDAW, and other prior UN human rights instruments as a framework. Drawn largely from the women's declaration, its detailed action agenda addresses the need for expanded investment in reproductive health through research, education, advocacy, and the promotion of universal access to quality services. Programming is recommended to integrate improved family planning with maternal and child health care aimed at reducing maternal and infant deaths; screening and treatment for sexually transmitted disease; gynecologic services; sexuality and gender education and counseling; and other health referrals. For the first time in such an agreement, the document endorses services that would address the needs of adolescents as well as adults, and also emphasizes the role of men in respecting women's reproductive rights.

Indeed, the most difficult negotiations at Cairo dealt with the subjects of adolescents and with abortion, both matters requiring deft negotiation with the Holy See and several conservative countries. Cairo affirms that although abortion should never be promoted as a method of family planning, abortion services should be compassionate and safe where permitted by law. Where abortion is not legal, postabortion care should be recognized as a public health obligation, so that dire complications from unsafe abortion are recognized as a public health problem and treated everywhere around the world.

Some of the most contentious debate at Cairo involved the preamble to the Programme of Action, whose final draft includes a provision requiring "full respect for various religious and ethical values and cultural backgrounds." This language appears to qualify the principle of universality of human rights that underlies the entire document. However, a second clause then added by U.S. negotiators demands "conformity with universally recognized international human rights," and the apparent contradiction is not resolved (ICPD Declaration and Programme of Action in Lockwood et al., 1998; Germain and Kyte, 1995).

Preparations for a Fourth World Conference on Women in Beijing in September 1995 began immediately, with regional preparatory meetings hammering out strong draft agreements that endorsed human rights principles for women. Among the participants were countries in Eastern Europe and the Middle East that had never been included before. But a final session to reconcile these drafts witnessed the beginnings of a substantial backlash against UN commitments to women's rights.

Conservatives attacked the language taken from Vienna that subordinated local tradition and culture to universal norms, and they condemned almost all reproductive health and rights provisions from Cairo. They also wrung their hands over the meaning of the term "gender," which, after long use in UN documents, they now attacked as hostile to family values and a code for the endorsement of homosexuality. Efforts were also made to limit the participation of nongovernmental organizations in the official deliberations.

In the following months, a coalition of women's groups and mainstream human rights organizations worked collaboratively with representatives from the American diplomatic team and from various UN agencies in what proved to be a successful effort to overcome these objections. Sympathetic officials in the Clinton administration, recognizing the urgency of the situation, named Geraldine Ferraro, then U.S. ambassador to the UN Commission on Human Rights, as vice chair of the American delegation to Beijing. She, in turn, appointed a team of experts in human rights issues to serve with her. Informal sessions were held over the summer, especially with countries from the key developing world bloc within the General Assembly, then known as the Group of Seventy-seven (G77), that counted many prominent women's rights advocates among their own official delegates. With their help, the G77 overcame opposition within its own ranks and emerged as a strong defender of the two issues most at stake: reaffirmation of the universality of human rights over local custom and culture, and recommitment to gender equality without any compromise to accommodate regional or religious variation. Secretary of State Madeline Albright also met with Cardinal Francis J. O'Connor in New York to try to assuage his concerns about these matters, and once again, Undersecretary of State Tim Wirth led the effort to protect the reproductive rights agreements of Cairo (Gaer, 1998; Meillon and Bunch, 2001).

The Beijing Conference opened with an NGO forum in the town of Huairou, nearly an hour away from the official proceedings in the central city. Neither the rain and mud of an unseasonably stormy August, nor the distance and relatively primitive nature of the facilities, however, could dampen the enthusiasm of more than 25,000 women who attended. Many were first-time participants in UN meetings, and some came from countries of the former Soviet Union, Asia, and Africa, where they had never before had the freedom or opportunity to speak their minds or to travel.

In her opening address to the official parliamentarians—this time, a colorful pageant of nearly equal numbers of men and women, many of them in traditional dress—Pakistan's Prime Minister Benazir Bhutto insisted that traditional Islamic teachings forbid injustice, and blamed discrimination against women on modern, patriarchal traditions that could be reformed. First Lady Hillary Rodham Clinton repeatedly brought the crowd to its feet by reciting a litany of common practices that violate women's rights and demanding remedies in both international and national law. Her closing, which drew on Vienna, has since become a global mantra: "Human rights are women's rights, and women's rights are human rights."

Conference negotiations threatened to bog down, nonetheless, when after informal discussions with a Holy See delegation, American negotiators agreed to endorse language modeled on Cairo that protected religious freedom and reaffirmed the value of motherhood for women. Intervention by representatives of the American Bar Association and other American NGO experts, however, fortified the resolve of the U.S. delegation that no prior protections of human rights would be abridged. The strength of the human rights language incorporated in the Beijing Platform of Action in the end surpassed many expectations, as did the content of the various sections dealing with equal protection for women, violence, sexual and reproductive health and rights, and economic and social rights. The Beijing Declaration, which frames the document, unequivocally restates the Universal Declaration's commitment that "human rights are universal and belong to individuals," and that promotion and protection of those rights is the "sovereign responsibility of each State." It then adds for emphasis that respect for religion, culture, and philosophy "should contribute to the full enjoyment by women of their human rights." When a draft along these lines was read at a briefing for NGOs, the U.S. delegation chair, Secretary of Health and Human Services Donna Shalala diffused tensions by acknowledging to wide applause that "Eleanor Roosevelt couldn't have said it better" (Gaer, 1998; Dunlop and Chesler, 1995).

Thanks to the skillful negotiations of U.S. delegates together with Monique Essad of Guinea and Merwat Tallaway of Egypt, a former CEDAW committee chair, the Beijing Platform of Action actually moves beyond Cairo and earlier agreements in one important respect, the addition of Paragraph 96, still the most discussed and controversial aspect of the document.

> The human rights of women include their right to have control over and decide freely and responsibly on matters related to their sexuality, including sexual and reproductive health, free of coercion, discrimination and violence. Equal relationships between women and men in matters of sexual relations and reproduction, including full respect for the integrity of the person, require mutual respect, consent and shared responsibility for sexual behaviour and its consequences.

The deletion of any explicit references to "sexual rights," which the Europeans earlier had requested, actually reflects a compromise. Nevertheless, this language is broader than any achieved before or since in a UN forum, broad enough to provide married women with protection from husbands who may be carrying a sexually transmitted disease, a concern of HIV/AIDS activists, and also to prevent discrimination based on sexual orientation, another contentious issue at the conference. Although the *New York Times* seemed to trivialize the matter, declaring in a front-page headline that a UN document had guaranteed women "the right to say no" to sex, it was undeniably a major accomplishment. Twenty-nine countries filed reservations about the language, including most of the Islamic states, on the grounds that sexual and reproductive rights should apply only within marriage. The Holy See and several Central and Latin American countries worried that the provision could be interpreted as supporting abortion. Indeed, as a premonition of future difficulties, the Holy See objected generally to the human rights provisions in the platform on the grounds that they foster an "excessive individualism" (Beijing Declaration and Programme of Action in Lockwood et al., 1998; Dunlop and Chesler, 1995; Gaer, 1998).

Ten Years Later, Where We Stand Today

With intellectual and political roots dating back more than half a century, the principle of women's rights as fundamental human rights is now established in international law and is slowly but surely taking hold in the constitutions and case law of many countries. Over the past decade, the United Nations has also firmly embedded the rights for women in an ambitious global development and human security agenda. A seasoned constituency of women and men in both diplomatic and nongovernmental advocacy communities around the world are dedicated to translating these global frameworks into everyday realities, however great the obstacles.

And the obstacles are great. Under George W. Bush, the United States has forged an unlikely, and some would say, unholy, alliance with the Holy See and a handful of Islamic fundamentalist countries at the UN on matters affecting women's human rights. Few Americans are aware of this dangerous, hypocritical backsliding, since the president lays claims to a mantle of activism on behalf of narrowly defined civil rights for women. Nor are they aware of the extent to which the UN is being used as a virtual playground for U.S. Christian social conservatives, since the press has paid only modest attention to these developments. At regional UN meetings marking the ten-year review of the Cairo Programme of Action, for example, Bush appointees repeatedly introduced resolutions stressing sexual abstinence until marriage over contraception, although time and again these resolutions have been firmly repudiated. In 2003, the U.S. delegation disingenuously introduced a toothless resolution on "Women and Political Participation" at the General Assembly in New York, promoting the right of women to hold political office and vaguely encouraging their equal access to education, property and inheritance rights, information technology, and economic opportunity—matters already protected in enforceable UN conventions like CEDAW, which the administration refuses to ratify. The U.S. delegation browbeat enough countries to get the resolution passed, but most have simply ignored it as yet another example of unorthodox diplomatic behavior under this president. Perhaps no action has been as disturbing as the Bush administration's initial refusal to reaffirm the Beijing Declaration and Platform of Action because it endorses rights to sexual and reproductive health care that many conservatives interpret as fostering abortion rights. In this brash but ultimately empty gesture, the United States stood entirely alone, without support from any other countries, and so it finally gave up and signed the tenth year reaffirmation (Chesler, 2004; LaFranchi, 2004).

Though the Bush administration has not been able to enforce its will, the threat of U.S. retribution has had a chilling effect on UN deliberations, dampening enthusiasm for official events to commemorate historic commitments to women's rights or publicly assess progress in meeting goals. The

American retreat on global family planning and women's rights is also worrisome at the national level. At Cairo, the Clinton administration committed to double U.S. annual expenditures for international family planning assistance by the year 2000, but in fact the USAID budget in this category has scarcely grown at all in ten years, not even enough to cover inflation. Assistance from other donors has also leveled off. Moreover, the American reimposition of the so-called global gag rule, censoring speech about abortion by any foreign contractor receiving U.S. funds (an infringement on speech that would be patently unconstitutional for U.S. citizens under our own constitution) has seriously compromised the provision of family planning services in a number of countries where providers refused to comply and lost funding. The additional loss of $34 million annually of U.S. funding for the UN Population Fund because of Bush administration allegations about its work in China has also seriously hurt family planning and women's empowerment programs elsewhere. And by saddling more than a third of U.S. funds for HIV/AIDS prevention abroad with abstinence-only provisions for sexuality education that only religious contractors will enforce, the Bush administration has reduced their effectiveness.

Strong hope lies in the fact that many countries have already translated commitments made at Vienna, Cairo, and Beijing into programs that are having a positive impact on a range of health and social indicators. These include maternal mortality and HIV transmission as well as family planning prevalence. Although progress is uneven, and the alarming spread of AIDS has burdened health resources in a manner unanticipated a decade or more ago, positive results have been achieved even in several of the least developed nations of sub-Saharan Africa where women are at highest risk, such as Malawi, Burundi, Niger, Swaziland, and Zambia. At the same time, countries such as India, Pakistan, Bangladesh, and Egypt, once criticized for their top-down, coercive population policies, have at least in part instituted significant reforms, and the new rights-based, client-sensitive approaches are pushing dramatic, positive trends in key indicators of reproductive and sexual health.

Still, there is simply not enough money to go around. The World Health Organization continues to report alarming statistics: unmet need for contraception among 120 million couples in poor countries; 80 million unintended pregnancies a year; 19 million illegal and/or unsafe abortions that kill an estimated 68,000 women; an HIV infection rate among young African women double that of men, and many hundreds of millions more treatable sexually transmitted infections in young people ages 15–24. The continued burden these statistics place on human security and already fragile health and social welfare systems in poor countries demands what WHO, generally shy of controversy, now talks of as a "mobilization of political will" (Omang, 2004; World Health Organization, 2004).

Although sufficient funds have not followed, the consensus does seem to be holding on what the establishment-friendly *Foreign Affairs,* in an important article by Isobel Coleman calling for U.S. ratification of CEDAW, recently called "The Payoff from Women's Rights." The UN Millennium Development Goals of 2000 identify gender equality and women's empowerment as a third priority, after the eradication of poverty and hunger and the achievement of universal primary education. Though sexual and reproductive health is not addressed explicitly (an oversight most see as a bid to win approval from American and Islamic conservatives), improvements in child and maternal health and the combating of HIV/AIDS are next on the list. Task forces staffed largely by women in the nongovernmental community and convened under the leadership of Jeffrey Sachs and others at Columbia University to plan for the implementation of these goals, are nonetheless emphasizing the importance of including indicators that encourage and allow for the assessment of programs in sex education (especially among youth), the eradication of gender violence, family planning, safe abortion, and other goals of Cairo and Beijing.

At the same time, global institutions such as the World Bank and the International Monetary Fund are now finally talking seriously about substantial debt relief for poor countries so that additional funds will become available to maintain primary health care systems and better meet basic needs. These are positive developments, especially if the United States government at long last repudiates isolationism and its deeply rooted hostility to international entanglements and to human rights. One can only imagine a world where the kinds of money the United States now pours into conventional national security arrangements, including military hardware and personnel, went instead to fund the goals of human rights and security that the UN has boldly prioritized. (Birdsall et al., 2004; Crossette, 2004).

Case Studies

This brings us to the essays prepared for this volume. Each one examines a different part of the world and a different dimension of the women's human rights and development agenda that resonates with the historical developments I have highlighted in this introduction. Each provides a yardstick for measuring compliance with the universal human rights obligations I have examined.

We begin in the Middle East, where Jessica Horn describes the agonizingly slow yet steady progress Egypt is making in eliminating the practice of female genital mutilation and cutting (FGM/C), which was specifically identified at Cairo and Beijing as a violation of women's health and rights. Though officially outlawed as well by Egyptian national law, FGM/C nonetheless continues to be practiced, especially among poor and uneducated families who fear losing control over their daughters and compromising their morality and marital prospects. Horn analyzes successful, community-based programs that have raised awareness of opportunities to guarantee women dignity and provide them security in other ways. These programs are offered in conjunction with general improvements in girls' education and expanded employment opportunities for women. Horn encourages further investment in these approaches as a surer way to eliminate the practice than criminal sanctions against physicians or families, which often unleash harsh opposition and backlash. Although she recognizes the need to see FGM as criminal behavior demanding sanction, she counsels in favor of a more comprehensive approach to reform that respects what many still regard as its virtuous intents.

Ayesha Imam recounts the story of Amina Lawal, whose trial for adultery in the conservative Islamic north of Nigeria attracted extensive international attention. Explaining how local activists engaged local Sharia law from within by using its own provisions to exonerate the young widowed mother, Imam exposes the specific acts under which Lowal was charged and threatened with death by stoning as a social construction born of modern Islamic fundamentalism, not as inherently binding obligations of traditional theology. Her essay makes a strong argument for the value of increased investment in local legal capacity to implement human rights frameworks. It also provides a cautionary appraisal of the value of interventions by international actors, who brought global attention to the case but also enflamed local tensions in the process.

Nearby Uganda is widely considered the first African success story in the fight to contain HIV/AIDS. Yet Uganda has experienced negligible progress in expanding women's access to comprehensive reproductive health care. As a result, fertility has not declined significantly there, as it has in many other parts of the developing world, and maternal and infant mortality have actually increased, draining resources and preventing further gains in health and in social and economic development indicators more generally. Lisa

Richey probes how Uganda's history contributes to this bifurcation in social development. Colonial rule and the country's troubled first years of independence left in place local communities with a concern for social cohesion uncharacteristic of other African settings. These communities have proved highly receptive to public discussion of the serious consequences of HIV and more attentive to government efforts to contain the spread of the disease through so-called ABC policies that encourage sexual abstinence before marriage, faithfulness within marriage, and widespread distribution of condoms. But the same social factors may produce opposite results when the goal is reduced fertility or improvements in infant health that threaten traditional family structures and gender roles, and where some old and established family planning providers still bear a reputation for insensitivity. Until now, containing AIDS has required inspired leadership from the Ugandan government under President Museveni but not the support of a public health infrastructure, which is required for further progress. Richey suggests necessary adjustments in health policies and programs supported by international donors to address all of these circumstances.

From India, Radhika Chandiramani examines the vulnerability of all women and particularly adolescent girls to sexual violence and disease in light of the culture's entrenched sexual conservatism and shyness and its dearth of programs in sex education and awareness. These problems are often overlooked because of India's partial success in revising its once coercive population policies in response to the rights agenda set at Cairo. She sounds an alarm about the growing threat of HIV/AIDS because of widespread reluctance, even by well-established and successful family planning providers, to promote responsible practices, encourage condom use, and provide married women legal recourse against unfaithful husbands. She also analyzes the country's traditionally phobic attitudes toward homosexuality and the hazards of denying widespread evidence of same-sex practices among men who also have sex with women. Her essay maps the boundaries between reproductive health and the guarantees of more broadly defined sexual rights for women first advanced in the Beijing Platform of Action, arguing that the two are inherently bound together—that one cannot be fully achieved without the other.

From Latin America, Benno de Keijzer describes several programs that work with men to challenge social norms equating masculinity with dominance or machismo. Through interventions inspired by Cairo's call for efforts to secure greater male involvement in women's reproductive decisions and outcomes, men are slowly assuming greater responsibility not only in matters of fertility and contraceptive practice but also in parenting and other domestic obligations. These behavioral shifts follow profound economic changes that are driving married women into the paid labor force, mirroring trends already established in more developed countries. Latin men, however, have been especially slow to embrace change and reluctant to give up traditional patterns of male privilege. De Keijzer argues that voluntary efforts to model change need to be scaled up and makes a case for state labor regulations that would grant men time off work to participate in the birthing of their babies, the care of newborns, the education of young children, and other domestic obligations, policies that have worked effectively elsewhere in the world.

Adriana Ortiz-Ortega presents an historical overview of Mexico's sexual politics, long characterized by a "gentleman's agreement" between church and state. This tacit understanding created a "double discourse" that kept abortion officially illegal but readily available to those who could afford to pay ostensibly clandestine, yet easily identifiable and rarely prosecuted providers. In the wake of the country's family planning revolution of the 1970s, a patchwork of abortion reforms was also introduced at the state level that permitted poor women to have an abortion in public hospitals in a variety of circumstances, such as rape or fetal anomaly, but not as a matter of right. However, few providers of such care are available. Since Cairo, Mexican feminists have demanded a rationalization of the situation on human rights grounds and the complete repeal of all criminal sanctions on abortion, while conservatives now in control of the government are calling for a total crackdown on all abortion, rejecting even the long-existing double standard. Ortiz-Ortega suggests several strategies for finding a way out of this impasse.

Edwin Winckler analyzes various efforts under way on the other side of the world in China to reform past abuses and improve the quality of care and services in the country's vast state-run family planning apparatus, while still maintaining strict limits on population growth that the government believes necessary to China's future economic prosperity, social stability, and environmental sustainability. Despite positive changes in China's policies in the wake of Cairo and Beijing, there remains a stubborn resistance to licensing a universal, two-child-per-family state policy that would resolve many internal tensions in China itself, as well as external criticisms of the coercive elements of the existing system. Winkler cogently reports on the varied ways the United Nations Population Fund (UNFPA) has constructively engaged with China to provide demographic modeling and programmatic reforms that are helping to provide confidence in—and greater movement toward—this goal and toward a more client-centered system with fewer top-down restrictions. Winckler's essay sounds another alarm about recent United States policy under the Bush administration, which denies U.S. funding for UNFPA on the grounds—disputed by a bipartisan commission—that it countenances forced abortion in China. This seems especially self-defeating in light of the progress being made there in eliminating such abuses. Winckler instead encourages a more patient stance toward China that elevates what he calls "pragmatic moderation" over moral absolutism. One route to this end is to view the fines imposed by the state on unauthorized pregnancies as a kind of tax paid to society for the additional public burden of raising that child—a form of social savings account in a country where personal taxation is not well established. Indeed, Winckler reports China may be formally moving in this direction.

Martha Davis describes the Kensington Welfare Rights Union, an organization of low-income mothers in Philadelphia, as an example of the successful application of human rights principles to domestic social welfare advocacy in the United States. Affirmative social and economic obligations in the Universal Declaration of Human Rights have helped advocates model parallel provisions in the state laws of Pennsylvania, and Davis argues for more activism to integrate global standards at the subnational level in the United States, particularly in light of the federal devolution of responsibility for social welfare to the states. She makes specific suggestions for applying the privacy provisions of the International Covenant for Civil and Political Rights, which the United States has ratified, to the protection of domestic reproductive health and rights, and also suggests a "trickle-up" approach, whereby local and state gains might be expanded to the federal government. The use of international law by local activists offers rich possibilities for organizing and educating progressive constituencies in the United States, who often respond more positively to its intellectual and moral frameworks than to old and contested domestic arguments. Surveying other local and state groups around the country, Davis paints a vivid portrait of how U.S. activists are bringing human rights back home, even as the federal government under the Bush administration eschews the entire human rights enterprise.

Finally, Wendy Chavkin brings us up to date. She looks at global trends and at local developments observed by our fellows to elicit successful strategies for moving forward—in regions still dealing with high fertility and extreme poverty—and in the many countries now experiencing more rapid than expected demographic transition. This poses new challenges for wedding human rights norms to the obligations posed by rapidly aging and dependent populations. Hers is a sober appraisal that does not neglect the enormous instability that continues to engulf so much of the world, nor the dark forces of reaction that such tragic conditions breed. Yet, she offers cautious optimism.

We, in turn, offer this volume in response to the plaintive cry of Melanesian poet Agnes Dewenis:

> Tell me why as a woman
> I have all this burden
> When God, the Constitution and the
> United Nations all tell me
> You and I are equal in all respects? (Altman, 2001, 122)

On the tenth anniversary of the historic Fourth World Conference on Women in Beijing, we also hope the valiant stories it contains will inspire renewed commitment to advocacy for human rights and security for those everywhere whose aspirations for freedom and opportunity have still not been fully realized.

References

Abusharaf, Rogaia Mustafa. 2001. "Virtuous Cuts: Female Genital Circumcision in an African Ontology." *Differences: A Journal of Feminist Cultural Studies* 12.1: 112–140.

Altman, Dennis. 2001. *Global Sex*. Chicago: University of Chicago Press.

Birdsall, Nancy, Allen C. Kelley, and Steven W. Sinding. 2001. *Population Matters: Demographic Change, Economic Growth, and Poverty in the Developing World.* New York: Oxford University Press.

Birdsall, Nancy, Amina Ibrahim, and Geeta Rao Gupta. 2004. "Task Force 3 Interim Report on Gender Equality." February 1. New York: UN Millennium Project.

Black, Allida M. ed. 1999. *Courage in a Dangerous World: The Political Writings of Eleanor Roosevelt.* New York: Columbia University Press.

Bunch, Charlotte. 1990. "Women's Rights as Human Rights: Toward a Re-Vision of Human Rights." *Human Rights Quarterly* 12: 486–498.

Bunch, Charlotte, and Niamh Reilly. 1994. *Demanding Accountability: The Global Campaign and Vienna Tribunal for Women's Human Rights.* New Brunswick: Center for Women's Global Leadership, Rutgers University; and New York: United Nations Development Fund for Women.

Catino, Jennifer. 1999. *Meeting the Cairo Challenge: Progress in Sexual and Reproductive Health.* New York: Family Care International.

Center for Reproductive Rights and University of Toronto International Programme on Reproductive and Sexual Health Law. 2002. *Bringing Rights to Bear: An Analysis of the Work of UN Treaty Monitoring Bodies on Reproductive and Sexual Rights.* New York.

Chesler, Ellen. 1992. *Woman of Valor: Margaret Sanger and the Birth Control Movement in America*. New York: Simon and Schuster.

————. 1997. "First Thoughts about a Global Program in Women's Reproductive Health and Rights," Memorandum to the Open Society Institute, New York.

————. 2004. "A Progressive Agenda for Women's Rights." In Mark Green, ed., *What We Stand For: A Program for Progressive Patriotism*. New York: Newmarket Press.

Cook, Blanche Wiesen. 1992. *Eleanor Roosevelt, Vol. I: 1884–1933*. New York: Viking.

————. 1999. *Eleanor Roosevelt, Vol. II: The Defining Years, 1933–1938*. New York: Viking.

Cook, Rebecca J. 1993. "Women's International Human Rights Law: The Way Forward." *Human Rights Quarterly* 15.2: 231–261.

————, ed. 1994. *Human Rights of Women: National and International Perspectives*. Philadelphia: University of Pennsylvania Press.

Cox, Larry, and Dorothy Q. Thomas, eds. 2004. *Close to Home: Case Studies of Human Rights Work in the United States*. New York: Ford Foundation.

Crossette, Barbara. 2004 "Reproductive Health and the Millenium Development Goals: The Missing Link." Paper commissioned by the Population Program of the William and Flora Hewlett Foundation Menlo Park, California.

Dorf, Michael C. 2005. "The Use of Foreign Law in American Constitutional Interpretation. http://writ.findlaw.com/dorf.

Dunlop, Joan, and Ellen Chesler. 1995. "Consensus on Women's Rights Cleared the Skies in China." *Christian Science Monitor,* September 29.

Fraser, Arvonne S. 1999. "Becoming Human: The Origins and Development of Women's Human Rights." *Human Rights Quarterly* 21.4: 853–906.

Gaer, Felice D. 1998. "And Never the Twain Shall Meet? The Struggle to Establish Women's Rights as International Human Rights." In Carol E. Lockwood, Daniel B. Margraw, Margaret F. Spring, and S. I. Strong, *The International Human Rights of Women: Instruments of Change*. New York: American Bar Association.

Germain, Adrienne, and Rachel Kyte. 1995. *The Cairo Consensus: The Right Agenda at the Right Time*. New York: International Women's Health Coalition.

Hartmann, Susan M. 1998. *The Other Feminists: Activists in the Liberal Establishment*. New Haven: Yale University Press.

Henkin, Louis. 1990. *The Age of Rights*. New York: Columbia University Press.

Hodgson, Dennis, and Susan Cotts. 1997. "Feminists and Neo-Malthusians: Past and Present Alliances." *Population and Development Review* 23.3: 469–523.

Inglehart, Ronald, and Pippa Norris. 2003. *Rising Tide: Gender Equality and Cultural Change around the World*. Cambridge: Cambridge University Press.

Kennedy, David M. 1999. *Freedom from Fear: The American People in Depression and War, 1929–1995*. New York: Oxford University Press.

LaFranchi, Howard. 2004. "On Family Planning, US vs. Much of the World." *Christian Science Monitor,* March 30.

Lash, Joseph P. 1972. *Eleanor: The Years Alone*. New York: W. W. Norton.

Lauren, Paul Gordon. 2003. *The Evolution of International Human Rights: Visions Seen*. Philadelphia: University of Pennsylvania Press.

Lockwood, Carol E., Daniel B. Magraw, Margaret F. Spring, and S. I. Strong. 1998. *The International Human Rights of Women: Instruments of Change*. New York:

American Bar Association. Includes the major documents on which this essay draws.

Meillon, Cynthia, and Charlotte Bunch, eds. 2001. *Holding on to the Promise: Women's Human Rights and the Beijing +5 Review.* New Brunswick: Center for Women's Global Leadership, Rutgers University.

Milani, Leila, ed. 2001. *Human Rights for All, CEDAW: Working for Women around the World and at Home.* Washington, D.C.: Working Group on Ratification of the U.N. Convention on the Elimination of All Forms of Discrimination against Women. For more on the treaty, also see *www.WomensTreaty.org.*

Milani, Leila, Sarah Albert, and Karina Purushotma. 2004. *CEDAW, The Treaty for the Rights of Women: Rights That Benefit the Entire Community.* Washington, D.C.: Working Group on Ratification of the U.N. Convention on the Elimination of All Forms of Discrimination against Women.

Omang, Joanne, ed. 2004. *Countdown 2015: Sexual and Reproductive Health and Rights for All.* New York: Family Care International, International Planned Parenthood Federation, and Population Action International.

Petchesky, Rosalind P. 2003. *Global Prescriptions: Gendering Health and Human Rights.* London: Zed Books.

Petchesky, Rosalind P., and Karen Judd, eds. 1998. *Negotiating Reproductive Rights: Women's Perspectives across Countries and Cultures.* London: Zed Books.

Reilly, Niamh, ed. 1996. *Without Reservation: The Beijing Tribunal on Accountability for Women's Human Rights.* New Brunswick: Center for Women's Global Leadership, Rutgers University.

Roosevelt, Eleanor. 1948. "The Promise of Human Rights." *Foreign Affairs,* April, in Black, ed., *Courage in a Dangerous World.* New York: Columbia University Press, 1999.

———. 1951. "Statement on Draft Covenant on Human Rights." *Department of State Bulletin,* December 31, in Black, ed., *Courage in a Dangerous World.* New York: Columbia University Press, 1999.

———. 1952. "Reply to Attacks on U.S. Attitude toward Human Rights Covenant, July 14," in Black, ed. *Courage in a Dangerous World.* New York: Columbia University Press, 1999.

———. 1953a. "Eisenhower Administration Rejects Treaty." *My Day,* April 8, in Black, ed., *Courage in a Dangerous World.* New York: Columbia University Press, 1999.

———. 1953b. "ER's Response." *My Day,* April 9, in Black, ed., *Courage in a Dangerous World.* New York: Columbia University Press, 1999.

Schlesinger, Stephen C. 2003. *Act of Creation: The Founding of the United Nations.* New York: Westview.

Sen, Gita, Adrienne Germain, Lincoln C. Chen. eds. 1994. *Population Policies Reconsidered: Health, Empowerment, and Rights.* Cambridge: Harvard University Press.

World Health Organization. 2004. "Strategy to Accelerate Progress towards the Attainment of International Development Goals and Targets Related to Reproductive Health." Adopted by the 57th Annual World Health Assembly, May 2004.

Not Culture But Gender

RECONCEPTUALIZING FEMALE
GENITAL MUTILATION/CUTTING

JESSICA HORN

> The struggle against FGM is a struggle for the liberation of women
> and men from the value system that governs them both. Working
> toward change of this value system is in fact working towards
> changing society as a whole.
> —Statement of the Egyptian FGM Task Force, 1997

The International Conference on Population and Development (ICPD) held in Cairo in 1994 marked a historic turning point in global understandings of health, development, and women's rights. At its best, the Cairo Programme of Action forwarded a holistic vision of the connections between sexual and reproductive health and women's economic autonomy, social and political equality, access to education, and freedom from violence. Beneath these analyses also lay an—albeit hesitant—discussion of the rights of women to control their sexuality and the relevance of this right to achieving health and social justice.

In Egypt, the ICPD discussions ignited charged debate on female genital mutilation/cutting (FGM/C), turning what had been a relatively low-profile issue into a volatile touchstone of national debate.[1] The symbolic relevance of FGM/C for nationalist and religious identity was made explicit in the arguments issued by conservative religious leaders and conservative reaction in the popular press, making FGM/C a battle not only about health or tradition but also about the status of women's rights as a political linchpin in Egyptian national politics (Seif el Dawla 1999). Concerned to demonstrate public support for the Cairo agenda in his address to the conference, the Egyptian minister of health stated that FGM/C was a dying practice in Egypt. However, the next day CNN broadcast footage depicting the circumcision of a young girl in an area of Cairo. In an act of political face-saving, the minister was obliged to react by declaring the government's intent to confront the practice (Seif el Dawla 1999). Subsequent international pressure against FGM/C and pro-FGM/C advocacy by conservative forces in Egypt led to the issuing of an ambivalent decree by the minister of health that restricted the practice to public medical facilities. The partial nature of the ban was clear, going so far as to set a standard fee and special days when families could book appointments (RAINBO 1995). The focus on alleviating the reproductive health risks of FGM/C represented some form of government action in line with the Cairo concerns, but issues of reproductive and sexual rights remained intentionally silenced. In fact, the New Woman Research Centre (1994) argued in a protest statement that the decree "legalizes the inferior status of women in our society" and "legalizes violence against women." In this vein, activists in the post-Cairo period demarcated the same battleground as the state, moving the struggle against FGM/C out of a surface debate on "tradition" to engage the underlying questions of women's rights, citizenship, and gendered social and political power across the public and private domains. This activist engagement carried with it an underlying objective to better the lives of Egyptian women and girls and a clear sense of the state's responsibility in this process.

Global thinking on anti-FGM/C policy and programming has been dominated by analyses of culture and tradition and ways to reconcile universal imperatives of human rights with the values of local cultures. In contrast, a sexual and reproductive rights perspective moves us away from seeing FGM/C as a problem of localized traditions and toward understanding it as a form of gender-based violence, linked to the systematic exclusion of women from agency in social, economic, and political spheres and in relation to choices regarding their bodies. These arguments are intended not to ignore the subjective relevance of culture in people's lives but rather to reveal the gender bias in normative definitions of culture and the ways cultural discourse is used to justify discrimination against women. They also make visible the economic and social inequalities that both shape definitions of culture and help to perpetuate the practice. At a programmatic level, this analysis suggests that sustainable interventions to eliminate FGM/C must address the gendered rationale and material justifications for violent cultural practices and not remain simply a legal denunciation of them as constituting outmoded traditions or a medical intervention against health risks. It also suggests that facilitating women's and girls' access to education, services, employment, and political participation must be a part of sustainable, rights-based strategies against FGM/C.

This chapter analyses Egyptian experiences of anti-FGM/C advocacy and programming as the basis for the argument that women's empowerment, as a process of social and material change, lies at the core of effective strategies to end FGM/C. The analysis is set in the context of shifting conceptualizations of FGM/C in the global arena and in Africa, and the response of African feminists to these formulations. The chapter concludes by assessing the significance of a rights-based, empowerment approach against FGM/C, offering recommendations for future policy and practice.

Conceptualizing FGM/C: Culture, Health, and Rights

The past half century has seen considerable change in the conceptualization of violence against women, with persistent women's rights advocacy transforming the landscape of policy and legislation and definitions of what are deemed unacceptable social practices under international human rights law. The debate on FGM/C within this has been particularly thorny, given that the practice is not universal, with activists on all sides treading carefully amid accusations of intellectual and cultural imperialism. Hesitant government positions on culture and rights have been discordant with progressive analyses by African feminists and women's health advocates (Bennett 2000). These discordances have nevertheless raised important questions concerning the identification of cultural "authorities" and the validity of human rights, and gender-based frameworks for addressing culturally sanctioned violations.

International Debates: Harmful Tradition
or Violence against Women?

The United Nations has provided the primary forum for the international discussion of FGM/C. In the past quarter century, discourse and programming by UN agencies and bilateral donors have shifted from a focus on the health risks of FGM/C, deemed a less controversial entry point (World Health Organization/EMRO 1979), to the need to address gender discrimination. Through the intervention of women's rights activism, the outcome documents of the Vienna (1993), Cairo (1994), and Beijing (1995) world conferences represent an evolving progressivism in the approach to FGM/C and "cultural practices," and a clear positioning of FGM/C as a sexual and reproductive rights concern and as a form of violence against women.[2] These documents also acknowledge that realizing rights to health and bodily integrity will require investments in a broader "enabling environment," in which access to economic opportunities and social and political participation are key. In addition, the language on FGM in the Declaration on the Elimination of Violence against Women (DEVAW) (United Nations 1993), lays important groundwork for the framing of FGM/C as a form of violence. DEVAW classifies FGM as violence in the family (Article 2) and draws a line on the legitimacy of cultural claims when they cross the boundary of women's rights (Article 4). Importantly, DEVAW identifies harm as the result rather than intent of violence, thus overriding the limitations of mainstream human rights in defining violence and acknowledging, in the case of FGM/C, that the often well-meaning intent of circumcisers and kin has grave social, physical, and psychological consequences.[3] Echoing these shifts, the conceptualization of FGM in the Convention for the Elimination of Discrimination against Women (CEDAW), a legally binding document, has developed considerably from the 1990 General Recommendation 14 (CEDAW 1990), which used the term "circumcision" and prescribed educational measures, to the 1999 General Recommendation on Women and Health, which calls for "the enactment of effective enforcement of laws that prohibit female genital mutilation" (CEDAW 1999).

Although the term "women" in human rights instruments and UN documents refers to both women and girls, an additional set of protections for girls has been created under the rubric of children's rights (protecting all those under the age of eighteen), in recognition of the position of girls as legal minors and their dependency on parents for protection and decision making. The Children's Rights Convention currently contains the only legally binding prohibition on harmful traditional practices in international human rights law (Rahman and Toubia 2000). However, although the Committee on the Rights of the Child has been attentive to FGM/C and its effects on children's health and well-being, it "has framed the practice in explicit terms of gender discrimination less frequently" (Center for Reproductive Rights et al. 2002: 71–72).

Regional Debates: FGM in Regional Human Rights Frameworks
The advancement of the global women's rights agenda and persistent lobbying by African women's rights advocates has led to several important shifts in the human rights agenda within the African Union. African commitment to women's rights has also been strengthened in the wake of constitutional reforms in such countries as South Africa and Uganda, where violence against women, economic inequality, and political representation for women

have taken center stage. Biased legal systems and discriminatory cultural practices have been questioned in these processes of reviewing regional and national policy and law, with FGM/C often used as the litmus test of progress
in Africa's willingness to accept women's rights over cultural norms (see
Ibhawoh 2000, An-Na'im 1994).

The regional mandate for human rights is upheld by the African Charter for Human and Peoples' Rights (OAU 1982), adopted in 1981 by the Organization of African Unity (now the African Union). Conceived in the
aftermath of decolonization and liberation movements, the charter embraces
economic, social, and cultural rights and the right to development as central
to the exercise of human rights in Africa. In addition, the charter asserts an
"African" conceptualization of human rights based on individual rights as well
as on duties to family, community, and state, in turn affirming the philosophi-
cal origins and cultural legitimacy of human rights in the African region
(Onoria 2002). The charter's emphasis on the indivisibility of human rights
establishes a potentially strong basis on which to claim women's rights, and
sexual and reproductive rights in particular, given that their realization depends on the fulfillment of all rights (to education, economic security, freedom of thought, and so on). This potential is marred, however, by conferment
of rights to women as they fulfill familial duties (OAU, 1982). This framing
of women's rights is problematic because it establishes the family and traditional values as the context in which women's rights are affirmed, without
recognizing the gender inequalities inherent in both of these spheres. Further, these provisions assume the (heterosexual) family as the "natural" unit
of society, with women's rights confirmed as they fulfill their duties to it.
Seen in this light, these provisions represent an affirmation of the gendered
status quo (though with a view to making it "nicer"), rather than a support
of women's rights to autonomy and choice. That is not to argue that the family is not important in many women's lives, as both marriage and motherhood are often a key source of identity, authority, and economic support for
women in Africa and elsewhere (Petchesky and Judd 1998, Coomaraswamy
1994). Rather, the problem lies in limiting women's identities as "righted"
subjects to their reproductive and conjugal identities, eclipsing the possibility of choice to form (heterosexual) families or not, and failing to acknowledge women's participation in other spheres of life, notably in the economy
and in politics. A feminist reading of the charter thus reveals its twin-track
conceptualization of rights in which men are endowed with general rights to
autonomy in all spheres while women's entitlement is conferred as they stir
the pot of "tradition."

In this context, the Protocol to the African Charter on the Rights of Women in Africa (African Union 2003), adopted by the African Union (AU) in July 2003, represents a victory for the advancement of women's rights. The protocol is the result of a decade of lobbying by African women's rights groups (Wanyeki 2002). It reinforces recent amendments to the Constitutive Act of the AU establishing gender parity and gender mainstreaming in AU mechanisms and gender equality as an AU objective (Maboreke 2003).

Strategies to address "harmful practices" (the rubric under which FGM/C is placed) include awareness campaigns and legislative prohibitions and, notably, a call for states to provide health services, legal supports, and counseling as well as protection for women who are at risk of harmful practices (Article 5).[4] The latter provision shifts the role of state interventions from solely punitive to protective and preventative measures. The protocol also includes economic harm as a consequence of violence (Article 1, para. j). This conceptualization is carried through in recommendations that states provide reparations for victims of violence (Article 4, para. f) and vocational training for victims of harmful practices with a view to making them "self-supporting" (Article 5, para. c). Although the health consequences of violence and harmful practices are mentioned, neither are included in provisions for health and reproductive rights (Article 14). In addition, state measures to address sexual and reproductive health are limited to capacity building in health services, with no mention of the enabling conditions required for women to access these services or to support other aspects of reproductive and sexual well-being.

The protocol places repeated emphasis on the need to eliminate harmful practices, discrimination, and stereotyping, and to transform public opinion to support women's rights, with public education identified as the key mechanism. Indeed, both the African Charter and the protocol confirm the right to a "positive cultural context," with implications for challenging gender-based violations perpetuated on the basis of culture. As Beyani (1994) has argued, the use of the term "positive" cultural values indicates that the charter's architects are aware of the dynamic nature of culture and recognize that unjust aspects of culture can be challenged. With that said, the charter does not identify clear mechanisms by which cultural norms will be defined and revised, leaving what constitutes positive values open to interpretation.

Rethinking the Problem: FGM/C
and Sexual and Reproductive Rights

Attempts to reconcile international human rights with African cultural norms have been closely monitored by African feminists and women's rights activists, who take issue with the static definitions of culture being defended and the absence of women's voices in defining what constitutes culture. Many question the codification of selected social practices as customary law in colonial and postcolonial legislation (see Mama 1997, 2000), raising the concern that "this reification of patriarchal culture has now become a potent tool for denying African women their rights" (McFadden 2001). Critics also take issue with cultural relativist arguments that seek to preserve African cultures in the face of women's rights, yet remain silent on the neoliberal economic policies that effectively undermine the self-determination of communities and hence continuation of their "culture," which is contingent on access to material as well as conceptual resources (Seif el Dawla 1999, Oloka-Onyango and Tamale 1995).

In response, African feminists offer a radicalization of the debate on culture and rights, asking not whether human rights and various African cultural patterns are compatible but rather how the concepts of human rights can be used to create more democratic forms of social organization and a more inclusive cultural imagination (McFadden 2001, Toubia 2002). In line with this argument, Butegwa (1995: 38) explains that rethinking culture entails "looking at culture and religion and other tenets of group identity as tools for the dignity of the group and for individuals rather than as a millstone to keep them in servitude and suffering human indignities."

The feminist critique of culture and concurrent move to see FGM/C as gender-based violence has exposed FGM/C as an issue of inequitable gender power relations and not one of culture per se. Moreover, advocates are aware that FGM/C occurs in contexts in which other human rights affect women's well-being, including domestic violence and rape, high rates of maternal mortality, the gendered spread and impact of HIV/AIDS, a general lack of access to affordable health services and education, employment discrimination, and lack of political representation. From this it is clear that the task of eradicating FGM/C requires not only punitive legislation or awareness programs but also a much broader investment in women's rights, including access to education, employment, political participation, property rights, and legal and judicial services.

Sexual and reproductive rights have provided an important conceptual framework for rethinking the relationships between culture, bodily violation, and women's rights and have provided the impetus to rethink approaches to tackling FGM/C. Mainstream analysis and interventions have focused predominantly on the reproductive and sexual health consequences of FGM/C, including severe bleeding, infection, and obstructed labor, although psychological trauma is now also commonly acknowledged. What sexual and re-productive rights offers is an assessment of the injustice inherent in the rationales behind the practice. FGM/C is performed largely on female children who are neither given adequate information regarding the practice and its consequences nor offered the opportunity to reject it. When children agree to FGM/C, they are often heavily influenced by peer and family pressure and the threat of social ostracism if they dissent. Furthermore, both the surgery and surrounding rituals leave a symbolic reminder of the value of premarital chastity and conjugal fidelity and, in the case of infibulation in particular, of the perceived inappropriateness of women's sexual pleasure (Toubia 1995). A less explored aspect is the role of FGM/C in encouraging heteronormativity and the expectation that a girl's sexuality will ultimately be put to the service of a husband, eclipsing choices regarding sexuality and sexual expression (McFadden 2000). Seen in this light, FGM/C is a clear violation of sexual rights, defined in the Beijing Platform as the right of women "to have control over and decide freely and responsibly on matters related to their sexuality, including sexual and reproductive health, free of coercion, discrimination and violence" (United Nations 1995).

To frame FGM/C as a violation of women's rights is not to ignore women's choice in supporting or performing FGM/C. Indeed one differentiating factor between FGM/C and other forms of gender-based violence is the marked involvement of women in its practice and continuation. A feminist analysis, however, begs further assessment of the reasons for women's complicity. An-Na'im observes that FGM/C is maintained through subtle processes of cultural sanction, which "operates through the socialisation, or conditioning of women in order to induce them to 'consent' to such mutilation being inflicted on their young daughters" (An-Na'im 1994: 177). Although this is true, it is important to note that women's complicity with FGM/C is often informed by a social and economic pragmatism. In contexts in which it is practiced, FGM/C ensures a girl's marriageability and social respectability and thus potential social and economic security. This is compounded in many resource-poor communities where government supports are weak or negligible and social respectability enables access to locally managed services and resources (Abdel Hadi 2003). Furthermore, although women's complicity with social norms is an expression of agency, it is also important to ask what the limited scope of this agency tells us about the nature of the power relations in which women's choices are embedded (Abu-Lughod 1990). That women seek to accommodate rather than contest, or to subtly subvert rather than overtly reject violations is in fact an indication of how limited the choices of resistance are. From a rights perspective, the creation of an enabling environment to expand women's choices thus becomes a critical agenda.

FGM/C Discourse and Anti-FGM/C Interventions in Egypt

Egypt is significant in this discussion of FGM/C and sexual and reproductive rights as the location of the historic conference in 1994; of integrated efforts among NGOs, donors, and government ministries to address FGM/C; and of one of the earliest examples of successful resistance against FGM/C using a model of women's empowerment. Furthermore, the upsurge of activity around FGM/C has had a measurable effect on attitudes toward FGM/C nationally and a localized effect in discouraging the actual practice. Combined, these call for a closer investigation of Egyptian approaches to confronting FGM/C.

The Social and Economic Context of FGM/C in Egypt

Although Egypt enjoys better infrastructure and economic stability than other countries in Africa, gender disparities are apparent in all sectors of the economy and society. Structural Adjustment Policies adopted in the 1970s have gradually displaced the female labor force in the public sector (Seif el Dawla et al. 1998) and, as in other African countries, women are now disproportionately represented in the informal economy and in the lower-paid rungs of the formal economy. Overall, women represent a low 15.4 percent of the labor force (UNDP, INP 2003). Literacy rates have dramatically increased over the past half century, but female literacy is still 63.5 percent of male literacy (UNDP, INP 2003), the result of lower school enrollment rates for girls, particularly in rural areas. The financial burden of school fees combined with gender bias encourages many families to educate sons before daughters.

Although organized efforts have been made since the founding of the Egyptian feminist movement in the 1920s, gender inequalities remain pervasive in social relations as well as in the legal and political systems. Such efforts have been undermined in recent years by the rise of conservative Islam alongside and in reaction to economic liberalization and the insecurities it has created (Guenena and Wassef 1999). The Egyptian justice system is marked by gender inequalities, both in the text of the law and in its biased interpretation by a predominantly conservative, male judiciary. This is particularly clear in laws concerning violence; men are given lenient sentences for domestic violence, whereas women may be given life sentences for similar crimes. Marital rape remains unrecognized by the law. According to Guenana and Wassef (1999: 37), "[t]his difference [in sentencing] is justified by the widespread attitude that a man's honour is dependant upon his wife's virtue."[5]

FGM/C is nearly universal in Egypt, with the Egyptian Demographic and Health Survey (EDHS) reporting a 97.3 percent national prevalence rate among ever-married women. Place of residence (urban/rural), level of education, and participation in wage labor are the key determinants of lower prevalence and support for FGM/C, though prevalence among all social classes and religious groups remains high (DHS 1995, 2000).[6] A comparison between the 1995 and 2000 EDHS shows that although prevalence has not decreased, attitudes toward FGM/C have changed significantly, with 75 percent of ever-married women in favor, a decline of 7 percent from 1995. Support among women earning a wage is significantly lower at 57 percent (DHS 2000). This change is associated with the explosion of public debate around FGM/C incited by the Cairo conference and subsequent anti-FGM/C campaigns.

Tradition figures as the primary reason women give for supporting FGM/C, with the reduction of sexual desire and cleanliness as secondary and tertiary arguments (DHS 2000), echoing the social discourse of FGM/C as a boundary marker for what is considered appropriate sexuality and sexual behavior. Although public rituals marking circumcisions are uncommon in Egypt, FGM/C represents the physical and social conferring of a girl's new identity, confirming her moral and physical "cleanliness" and hence her acceptability for marriage. Due to its strong association with marriage prospects, the event of circumcision is made known to the girl's kin and sometimes becomes neighborhood knowledge. The majority of girls are circumcised between the ages of seven and twelve, and girls are considered mature and ready for marriage at age thirteen (Abdel Hadi 2000), although the average age at first marriage is much later, largely for economic reasons.

Both ethnographic and statistical research have shown that, as has been said, tradition, the control of women's sexual desire, and cleanliness are the dominant explanations for the importance of FGM/C to Egyptian women (DHS 2000, Seif el Dawla et al. 1998, Hoodfar 1997). An innovative study on the relationship between masculinities and the practice of FGM/C in Egypt also demonstrated that men's perceptions play a considerable role in maintaining the social value of the practice (Wassef and Mansour 1999). The majority of the men interviewed supported FGM/C and considered it an essential precondition for marriage. These viewpoints were driven both by the normative beliefs about men's and women's sexuality and the lack of knowledge about the physical and emotional aspects of women's experience of FGM/C. The study also revealed how dependant men are on women's sexual fidelity and subservience as an affirmation of their own masculinity. As the researchers concluded, "FGM is the manifestation of men's perceptions of themselves, their masculinities, their insecurities and their attitudes to women" (Wassef and Mansour 1999: 240).

FGM/C and the State in Egypt

Beliefs and practices around FGM/C at the local level are intimately linked to the political discourse on FGM/C in Egypt, itself an ambivalent political milieu oscillating between the optimistic progressivism of certain NGOs, activists, and scholars, and the protective conservatism of the political mainstream influenced by the attitudes of key Islamic institutions. The Cairo conference had a catalytic effect on the politics of FGM/C in Egypt, both in forcing public discussion on a previously "private" issue, and in exposing alliances among the state, the religious mainstream, and the medical profession in opposition to certain women's rights. In the debates before Cairo, mainstream Islamic and Coptic institutions shared a conservative pro-FGM/C stance, issuing joint statements in the popular press. Activists argued that religious justification for the practice has been propelled less by scripture than by the defense of standards of religious morality, linked implicitly to notions of appropriate gender and sexual behavior. This is particularly evident in the pro-FGM/C stance held until recently by the head of the Egyptian Coptic Church, Pope Shenouda III, given that FGM/C is not mentioned in Christian scripture (Abouzeid 2003). For Islamist commentators, the 1994 ban placed on FGM/C by Minister Abdel Fattah represented a surrender to "Western" agendas and morality. In a demonstration of his moral authority against the state and over the population, the Sheikh of Al-Azhar University reissued a *fatwa* sanctioning FGM/C as Islamic practice. Lobbying by Egyptian NGOs leading up to the Beijing conference in 1995, and the reorganization of the Ministry of Health with a new minister, led to extending the ban on the performance of FGM/C outside of public health facilities. Put into force in 1997, the ban stipulates loss of medical licence and criminal charges, including the charge of manslaughter in the case of death resulting from circumcision, for practitioners found guilty of performing FGM/C.[7] Despite this firmer stance, the ban contains a legal loophole permitting FGM/C when medically necessary and approved by the head of obstetrics and gynaecology in the hospital (Abdel Hadi and Abdel Salam 1999). This ban represents the current legal position of the Egyptian government on FGM/C. Though acknowledged by activists as a step in the right direction, the ban has not been widely publicized, and legal institutions have not placed pressure for its enforcement, leaving it relatively unimplemented. As a result of the visible public debate, however, the formal opinion of both Muslim and Christian institutions in Egypt has changed, with leaders of both Muslim and Christian institutions affirming that no precept in either religion justifies the practice.[8]

Response to government and religious directives on FGM/C in the years following the Cairo conference was led by members of the Egyptian Task Force on FGM, a coalition of Egyptian NGOs, international organizations, donor agencies, individual activists, and government officials. Human rights activists have used constitutional law to counter government and religious mandates promoting the practice of FGM/C as legitimate tradition. In early 1995, women's and human rights activists took the minister Abdel Fattah to court on the grounds that it is illegal under the Egyptian penal code to subject a person to permanent mutilation (Abdel Salaam 2003). Although the appeal was denied, this was nevertheless a bold articulation of women's rights in a seemingly nonnegotiable situation. A similar but successful challenge was made to Islamic religious hegemony when nine members of the Egyptian Organization for Human Rights took action against the Sheikh of Al-Azhar University for his *fatwa* on FGM/C (RAINBO 2000). In the context of heavy-handed government policies and the power of religious conservative forces, these small victories were indeed significant for civil-society activists, who succeeded in igniting a national debate.

Local Successes: Social Change in an Egyptian Village

The battle of the discourses on rights, religion, and tradition waged in the Egyptian media, courtrooms, and NGO meetings has blown open a still volatile debate on the legitimacy of women's rights in Egypt. In this context, the success of an integrated intervention against FGM/C in a rural village in Upper Egypt has become a source of both methodological insights and inspiration for anti-FGM work in Egypt. The changes occurred in the early 1990s in Deir el Barsha, a village situated in a resource-poor governate of Menia in Upper Egypt, and were supported by the long-term initiatives of the Coptic Evangelical Organization for Social Services (CEOSS), an Egyptian NGO. Using a model of participatory development and women's empowerment, CEOSS sought to cultivate local leadership and capacity by supporting local religious and civic leaders, medical practitioners, and a core group of women organized under a village women's committee. The women's committee members oversee the project's classes for young girls, aimed at increasing literacy and social awareness. Women's committee members implement awareness campaigns on FGM/C and also engage in direct interventions on FGM/C through periodic visits to the homes of young girls, with the aim of persuading parents not to circumcise their daughters.

The confluence of shifts in social and educational opportunities and skills for women and girls, and the introduction of community-led public debate about FGM/C in Deir el Barsha led to the drafting and signing of a declaration against FGM/C by village leaders, women's committee representatives, and traditional circumcisers in December 1991 (Abdel Hadi 1998). The declaration represented a critical marker in the process of changing community opinions on FGM/C, in which the involvement of the women's group as stakeholders in community decision making was important. Official recognition of Deir el Barsha's work on FGM/C by the governor of Menia, Egyptian anti-FGM/C advocates hailing Deir el Barsha as a pioneering example, and recent shifts in national government policy supporting anti-FGM/C initiatives have all increased support for the declaration (Abdel Hadi 2003).

The successful initiatives in Deir el Barsha have invited close appraisal by researchers. A study conducted by Abdel Hadi found a considerable shift in opinion and practice in Deir el Barsha, compared with data from a neighboring village where interventions had not taken place, and with national statistics in the 1995 EDHS (Abdel Hadi 1998). Of families in Deir el Barsha, 50 percent circumcised their daughters following the declaration, compared with 84 percent in the control village. Participation in development projects helped account for this change: 41.5 percent of women and 60 percent of men who participated in development projects had uncircumcised daughters, compared with 28.2 percent of women and 28.3 percent of men who did not participate. Majority opinion (70.6 percent) was that this change would continue with continued involvement of CEOSS and the women's committee. The study also found that families felt confident in following through their pledges once they saw the successful marriage and childbearing of uncircumcised women.[9]

A number of planned and unplanned factors led to the change in Deir el Barsha. A weak village economy and the consequent semipermanent migration of men in search of work led to more female-headed households (particularly among older wives) and to women's entry into paid labor to supplement their husbands' incomes. Women thus became household decision makers by default, and began to exercise greater control over household spending than was socially mandated. The decision-making power transferred to women in their husbands' absence also lent greater authority to mothers' views of FGM/C, with opinion among working mothers weighing against it.

Alongside these changes in gender roles were the affirmative policies of the CEOSS development projects that actively encouraged women's participation in leadership, literacy, and awareness raising. The CEOSS project created clearly defined public roles for women in service of community development and allowed the women a forum to discuss issues of community concern and to strategize among themselves, supporting women's right to civic participation and political organization. Girls were important participants in the campaigns and services, a strategy that built their confidence and assertiveness and affirmed their role as change agents. The development of a core of women leaders in the village enabled the founding of the first women's association, the New Women's Association, in 2001 (CEOSS 2003). Importantly, CEOSS staff also intervened when husbands or parents prevented women and girls from participating in the public activities, ensuring support as they challenged convention in the household. The supportive advocacy role of religious leadership in the village added public legitimacy to the anti-FGM/C activities and targeted the dominant perception of FGM/C as a theologically mandated tradition.

The issuing of the declaration required the consensus of the community and support of its key stakeholders and leaders, and carried within it a legacy of activism and advocacy. The village declaration was endowed with a sense of local legitimacy built through a process of collective conceptualization and acceptance by community members themselves. Statements by the religious establishments and government officials against FGM/C has become an additional supporting factor, reinforcing the moral, scientific, and political legitimacy of Deir el Barsha's position. Crucial to achieving community consensus and a reduction in the practice of FGM/C, however, was the active involvement of women in local policy change, education, and publicly contesting tradition as well as actual shifts in the social roles and material possibilities available to women and girls through the development projects. Combined, these factors created the space to question the validity of FGM/C and the opportunity to formulate other social identities, ideas of respectability, and forms of participation for women in the community.

Enlarging the Dialogue: The Egyptian Task Force against FGM

The Egyptian Task Force against FGM was initiated in the lead-up to Cairo, amid the revival of NGO organizing. The involvement of feminist and human rights groups in the Task Force from the end of 1994 shifted its focus from a health to a human rights perspective and concentrated analysis on the social and political dimensions of FGM/C beneath the discourses of religion and culture and tradition. From 1994 to 2000 the Task Force was under the umbrella of the National NGOs Centre for Population and Development (NCPD), which had been established to oversee the implementation of the Cairo Program of Action.[10] Despite this government umbrella, however, the Task Force was nongovernmental in its authority, which gave members greater room to articulate their position amid polarized governmental, civil society, and religious forces.

Assessing the varied needs and existing activities of its members, the Task Force crafted a multidimensional strategy, organized around an NGO mobilization group; an advocacy group, and a research group. The broad gender and rights perspective of the Task Force, and the involvement of diverse actors and institutions, allowed for an expansion of anti-FGM/C efforts beyond the often highly local emphasis of programmatic interventions. A series of workshops led by the Task Force in 1995 trained NGOs on the legal, social, and health aspects of FGM/C and produced educational materials and advocacy messages. Task forces were formed in five regions of Egypt in 1996.

The Task Force was hesitant to support legislation prohibiting FGM/C as a primary measure. The enforcement of punitive legislation against parents without adequate education and anti-FGM/C interventions at community level was seen as ineffective and potentially discriminatory. The Task Force did, however, emphasize the accountability of medical practitioners to stipulations against mutilation in the Egyptian penal code. Debate continues on the appropriateness of human rights language and, in particular, the naming of circumcision as mutilation or violence against women when working with communities (Abdel Salam 2003). Task Force facilitators used local terminology for circumcision (*khittan* or *khittan al banat* in Arabic) when introducing the discussion of FGM/C, but also explained why medically and legally circumcision is a mutilation. The language of "mutilation" and "violence against women" was used in Task Force publications and statements and is now also being used in government campaigns against FGM/C.

New Methodologies: The Comprehensive Social Approach

The Task Force was committed to the development of integrated approaches against FGM/C, with the ultimate goal of creating "an alternative value system reached through consensus that accommodates the rights of girls and women and grants them a sense of entitlement to their own bodies"

(RAINBO 2000: 6). These methodologies were designed to complement the anti-FGM work groups were already doing on the ground, providing a more critical and transformative approach to behavior-change models. With the objective of facilitating change in social discourse, the task force developed the "Comprehensive Social Approach" to inspire discussion and promote the rejection of FGM/C.[11] In contrast to the "harmful traditional practices" model, in which preprepared messages about the health risks of FGM/C and the need for eradication are delivered to a community (RAINBO 2002), the Comprehensive Social Approach helps communities develop their own arguments for ending circumcision while cultivating critical consciousness and analytical skills. Participants are encouraged to speak about their view of what they want for their daughters, as well as their ideas about sexuality and sexual practices, with facilitators supporting critical reflection on their reasoning. Discussions of anatomy are framed by the same analytical perspective. Former Task Force trainer Dr. Seham Abdel Salaam explains: "I started with the brain. It was a great surprise to people because they never thought that the key sexual organ is the brain, and that desire arises in the brain and that they can control desire" (Abdel Salam 2003).

Similar to the Freirean model of popular education, the participatory methodology of Task Force sessions encouraged participants to develop their own rationale for working against FGM/C, drawing on individual and collective conceptions of health, justice, and gender identity. Significantly, the sessions also opened a new social space in which participants from both genders and a range of classes, professions, and ages could openly address the "private" discourses of FGM/C, parental decision making about girl children, and beliefs and perceptions about sexuality. The Task Force used the Comprehensive Social Approach in training and workshops across Egypt in collaboration with implementing organizations. It served as a complement to efforts to transform the socioeconomic position of women through literacy, education, and income-generation projects and changes in legal and political opinion on the issue.

Government Initiatives: National Council for Childhood and Motherhood and the FGM-Free Village Model

After a decade of activism and heated debate, the Egyptian government has begun to actively support initiatives against FGM/C, with first lady Suzanne Mubarak as a key representative of this position. In January 2003 the Egyptian National Council for Childhood and Motherhood (NCCM) inaugurated the Year of the Girl Child, and with it launched the FGM-Free

Villages campaign.[12] The three-year goal of the project is to reduce FGM/C prevalence by at least 40 percent in sixty villages in Upper Egypt (where FGM/C prevalence is the highest). It is a multi-stakeholder project with bilateral donors, UN agencies, and international NGOs collaborating with government ministries, national NGOs, and local implementing organizations.[13]

The NCCM uses a sociocultural approach, seeking to address the social reasoning rather than religious or medical debate around FGM/C, and to encourage the integration of anti-FGM/C into broader development interventions, including literacy classes and the creation of NGO-managed reproductive health programs (NCCM 2003a).The NCCM model builds on the foundational analysis, documentation, and intervention approaches developed by the Task Force in the mid–1990s, amplifying them with an integrated media approach, better monitoring and evaluation, and the creation of enforcement mechanisms to follow up anti-FGM/C declarations made at the local level. The NCCM's status as a government institution facilitates access to the media and the collection of regional and local data. The affirmation of the rights of the girl child are central to the campaign, with anti-FGM/C messages combined with the promotion of girls' education and the campaign against early marriage. FGM/C activities communicate four messages: that FGM/C is an obsolete social tradition, that it is not required by religion, that it does not control sexuality, and that it does not improve hygiene (NCCM 2003b)

The NCCM campaign presents a clear message rejecting FGM/C, replacing what had been an ambivalent state position on the issue. The use of the rights of the girl child also supports public recognition of children's rights and moves away from a model of protection to highlight the need for positive actions to promote girls' social and economic opportunities. As a government-led initiative, this campaign is in a stronger position than the Egyptian Task Force to push for both resource allocation and policy attention to the status of girls in Egypt overall, alongside the efforts to end FGM/C. However, as a government body, the NCCM is limited in the extent to which it can explicitly ask the charged questions around sexuality and sexual autonomy raised by the earlier activities of the NGO-based programs.

With regards to punitive measures, the ministerial decree on the practice of FGM/C by medical practitioners remains largely unimplemented. Both the NCCM and nongovernmental activists are currently focusing on removing the loophole exception within the decree. Although the formal position of medical, religious, and political institutions has begun to shift against FGM/C, the opinion of many key individuals has yet to change, making direct lobbying difficult.

Empowering Social Change

> FGM does not happen in a vacuum. It happens within a discourse
> of power.
> —Abdel Salam 2003

The social and political dynamics of FGM/C in Egypt demonstrate how closely it is linked to the structure of social relations and to prevailing discourses of power through which culture and tradition are defined. Consequently, the situation in Egypt has shown that the full gamut of actors involved in creating and maintaining the social order must be engaged, not just the local residents of urban or rural communities. The analysis presented here demonstrates the value of holistic and participatory methodologies to contest the social logic behind FGM/C and to help negotiate new concepts of well-being and value for girls and women. The success in the village of Deir el Barsha suggests that strategies that encourage rejecting FGM/C are most likely to succeed if introduced alongside measures to increase both opportunities for and the social acceptance of women's increased social and economic visibility and activity. The primary contribution of the Egyptian Task Force has been to create space for dialogue across professional, gender, and religious lines and between activists and Egyptian government representatives. These two premises have been incorporated, in principle, into the new Egyptian government strategy against FGM/C.

Empowerment as an Antiviolence Strategy

In asserting the superiority of women's rights over cultural sanctions, activists work to deliberately transform understandings of tradition and culture that limit the rights and actions of women and girls. The strategy of empowerment provides one blueprint for this process of critical engagement and social change, though its terms and methodologies remain contested.[14] Decisions regarding FGM/C are never made in isolation, and people always measure possible choices against the potential drawbacks and benefits of these choices. Importantly, then, what the process of empowerment requires is an expansion of the range of possibilities conceived of by women and girls while simultaneously expanding the material resources and social acceptability of alternatives that allow transformative choices to be carried through (Kabeer 1999). Central to empowerment is the creation of new or "safe" spaces in which issues of health, gender relations, and sexuality can be discussed and analyzed; access to information needed for informed discussion and choices and to economic resources and protective legislation is also necessary. The concurrent process of securing enabling conditions also seeks to provide real means through which these alternatives will be followed through in women's daily lives, including the identification of new social resources that will be created to replace the "protections" granted by the acceptance of existing social norms. This is particularly important in the case of FGM/C, which, as a normative practice, facilitates women's access to identities and relationships that ensure their social and economic survival.

If, as has been argued here, the decision to circumcise a girl is made with the interests of her future in mind, the alternative of not circumcising must also assure the possibility of a better future for the girl. Hence, combining anti-FGM/C interventions with programs for girls' education, for example, is one way of tipping the balance of this social logic. Questioning the social value of the girl child is also necessary, as is considering the content and quality of the education being provided. We must ask, for example, whether education is simply a means of ensuring a girl will still be a good bride, or if it is also intended to create greater possibilities for her future autonomy whether she marries or not.

Empowerment should inform the method as much as the content of the intervention, with participatory methodologies as a key component. Trying to impose the idea that FGM/C is wrong or a violation of rights on a community that understands it as appropriate and even beneficial is likely to raise resistance and, ultimately, to have little effect on attitudes and practices. Rather, as the Egyptian Task Force argued, rejection of FGM/C must come out of personal and collective reflection and informed analysis of beliefs about FGM/C and its relationship to sexuality, health, religion, tradition, and so on. In this vein, the process of introducing and implementing legislation to help eliminate FGM/C needs to occur in dialogue with affected communities. Legislation should also contain or support measures to better the life chances of girls, not simply punish those who perform FGM/C. Implicit in a methodology of empowerment is not only developing a sense of entitlement to one's body and decisions concerning it but also actively questioning the ways in which this entitlement is structured within prevailing social norms. This process of individual and collective reflection provides a starting point for the slow process of social change.

Although compelling, the notion of empowerment programming raises a number of questions. First is the role of implementing organizations. To propose that an NGO or project can empower someone is, of course, antithetical to the premise of empowerment as a process of developing individual agency. Nevertheless, organizations implementing empowerment projects can become important support systems in the process of change and in mitigating the effects of a potential backlash against the change being sought. As Kabeer (1999: 457) suggests, "in a context where cultural values constrain women's ability to make strategic life choices, structural inequalities cannot be addressed by individuals alone. . . . Women's organizations and social movements in particular have an important role to play in creating the conditions for change and in reducing the costs for the individual."

Following from this observation, it is clear that implementing empowerment programs requires long-term investment in the communities in question, as well as adequate follow-up and monitoring of interventions. Long-term investment is not currently a characteristic of many international NGOs, and thus if they are to counter FGM/C, they must collaborate with and strengthen national and local organizations working at the community level, and in the broader women's rights agenda.

Second is the role of the state in the empowerment process. A review of anti-FGM/C programming shows fairly limited state involvement, in most contexts, beyond legislative and policy reform. Of course, the empowerment of marginalized groups is rarely a priority for most states, and nongovernmental actors often carry a greater commitment to following through the process of change. Furthermore, as argued in the case of NGOs, a state cannot empower its population. Indeed, "[t]hinking of governments as empowering women can quickly lead to a view of empowerment as another welfare handout" (Sen and Batliwala 2000: 19). States do nevertheless have a codified responsibility to provide health services, education, and access to the law, which are also crucial resources for empowerment and provide a potential positive role for states wishing to tackle FGM/C. Active support of women's rights in public and private spheres through policy and legislation is an important component of this.

Third is the role of men in the process of empowerment. It is indeed cause for concern that in a "world authored by men" (Abusharaf 2000), the onus of responsibility to change cultural practice has been placed so heavily on women. NGOs tackling FGM have has made diverse attempts to include men in the process of change, often by encouraging opinion change among male local leaders and religious authorities (Toubia et al., forthcoming) as well as state policy makers and legislators. There has been far less thinking on where men fit in the process of change, however, beyond putting the weight of their social legitimacy behind the work of NGOs. There is need for more research on the relationship of FGM/C to the construction of masculinities and men's perceptions of circumcised and uncircumcised women. The experience in Egypt has shown that creating forums for men to discuss sexuality and gender norms is an important component of changing social attitudes toward FGM/C. Although attitude change towards gender norms is one step, however, social and legislative change to support a transformation of the ways in which men and women relate in the home, in the economy, and in public life is crucial.

Learning from Integrated Approaches to Eliminate FGM/C

As with all issues affecting sexual and reproductive rights, the elimination of FGM/C requires interventions into some of the most intimate and tightly guarded areas of social practice and personal relations. At the same time, the politicization of FGM/C by conservative governments and religious institutions signals how central it is to the maintenance of a particular, highly public, social order and of a gendered status quo. The Egyptian Task Force succeeded in generating critical debate at all levels of society, and in encouraging change in government positions on FGM/C. This furor of public debate opened the way for attitudinal change at national and community levels, and created a more conducive context for the current government-led strategies against FGM/C to roll out.

With that said, although attitudes toward FGM/C have shifted considerably, changes in actual behavior have been much more limited. Comparative data from the EDHS in 1995 and 2000 show that women's support of FGM/C decreased from 82 percent to 75 percent, while the percentage of women with at least one daughter circumcised or intending to circumcise their daughter fell from 87 to 81 percent. The highest support for, and practice of, FGM/C remains among the poorer rural and less educated respondents, and those outside of cash employment (DHS 2000).

To extend the lessons provided by activism in Egypt thus far, it is clear that the context-specific ways in which gender relations and sexuality play out must always form the basis on which programming, research, and policy change on FGM/C is devised and implemented. Furthermore, if we accept that FGM/C is a part of a system of gender inequality, then interventions to address it must work on this broader system and not merely on the specifics of the practice itself. From this premise, a reflection on Egyptian experiences presented in this chapter suggests that the following are central elements of a comprehensive, integrated approach to eliminating FGM/C:

Create spaces and resources for social dialogue that are informed by the local context

- FGM/C exists as an often silenced and hence unquestioned aspect of social relations. Given this, interventions should facilitate the creation of new spaces in which sexuality, gender roles and expectations, and beliefs around circumcision can be critically discussed and potentially transformed. Women's groups, literacy classes, and planned training and workshops are all venues for this new discussion. Advocacy activities can also bring what is often considered a private, unimportant, or shameful discussion into the media and into government policy and law. "New spaces also mean the creation of new consciousness" (Abouzeid 2003).
- Critical reflection on FGM/C and gender norms are aided by increasing access to a range of new information on reproductive and sexual health, sexuality, and laws and policies affecting women's lives, as well as to the conceptual tools needed to critically analyze existing information, beliefs, and practices. It is important to ensure that young women and men are also exposed to these new conceptual resources and encouraged to participate in the social dialogue.
- Cultivating young women's leadership in community education on FGM/C proved successful in Deir el Barsha and could be replicated elsewhere.
- Men should also have opportunities to confront their arguments and knowledge around FGM/C, women's sexuality and health, and the relationship of these to their own masculinities and understanding of gender relations. Interventions could also explore the positive roles men can play in the process of transforming social beliefs and practices harmful to women. More research is needed into men's roles in both perpetuating and eliminating FGM/C and how this varies by context.
- Programmatic activities should be supported and informed by research and analysis into the social, economic, medical, legal, and political dimensions of FGM/C. This both substantiates advocacy activities and helps to tailor programming to the needs of the particular context. Donors should be encouraged to support the creation and maintenance of resource centers on FGM/C and other issues affecting girls and women.

Base dialogue and education processes within interventions to increase social and economic opportunities and justice for women and girls

- FGM/C is a practice linked to conceptions of female reproductive and sexual roles, often limited to the private sphere. Interventions that seek to change the social meanings and practices attached to FGM/C thus need to target the broader context of women's and girls' social options and economic power. In Deir el Barsha the shift in community opinion about and practice of FGM/C occurred in a context of greater opportunities and new roles for both younger and older women that helped to shift the socioeconomic balance sheet against FGM/C.

- Opinion on the explicit use of human rights language in framing FGM/C and other sexual and reproductive rights issues varies, particularly because other legal or ethical frameworks also define parameters of rights and may hold greater moral or political weight than the state-centric and Western-associated language of human rights (see Imam, this volume). With that said, FGM/C has been defined, through advocacy led by activists in contexts where it is practiced, as a violation of human rights, and should be treated as such. The task is thus to popularize this understanding of FGM/C at the community level, while also working to change the position of legislation and policy on the issue. Justice and equity are concepts that exist in all cultural and religious systems and can be drawn upon and discussed in building local discourses of rights.

Engage community leadership at local and national levels to support individual and community change

- Encouraging individual resistance may not be a sustainable strategy if action is not also taken to change the prevailing attitudes toward FGM/C and, in fact, may simply result in further ostracism of the resistant individual. The work of the Egyptian Task Force and the interventions in Deir el-Barsha demonstrate the value of building a broader consensus among opinion leaders as a means of creating a more supportive context for individual, family, and community change. Intervening organizations should thus ensure that key decision makers in the family, community, and state, as appropriate, are included in the change process and are mobilized to set positive standards regarding FGM/C and the treatment of girls overall.
- Governments that commit to addressing FGM/C should be encouraged to review all laws and policies affecting women's rights and autonomy. Policies that support girls' education, women's access to health and other public services, employment opportunities, and property rights are all important components of an integrated strategy to promote women's rights, including an end to FGM/C.

- International and regional instruments provide political precedents for states to introduce laws on FGM/C and other forms of violence against women. The existence of legislation without means to access legal remedies, however, and without adequate programming to change attitudes and behaviors will be, at best, ineffective, and at worst potentially discriminatory. In light of this, legislation against FGM/C should aim to protect girls against the practice of FGM/C, but also be linked to broader legislation to provide services, promote gender equality, and support children's rights and an end to violence against women. The law is an important means of changing social and political discourse by setting new moral standards, and should thus be considered as part of a positive social change process and not only as an instrument of punishment. In addition, advocates should track implementation of new legislation.

Develop a coordinated response among agencies and actors

- The work of the Egyptian Task Force against FGM demonstrates the efficacy of broad-based coalitions in addressing FGM/C as part of the defense of women's rights and health. Such coalitions have the capacity to work at many levels, from legislative and policy level, academic analysis and research, to creating training and education materials and methodologies, implementation of community-level programming. Broad-based coalitions are better positioned to create and implement comprehensive strategies.
- NGOs, service providers, donors, media, and government institutions working on FGM/C must collaborate to ensure coherence of messages and approaches. Collaborative groups also provide a forum for international donors and NGOs to work with national and local NGOs to effectively tailor their programs to the given context.

Conclusion

This chapter has attempted to unravel the tensions between framing FGM/C as a question of culture or of human rights. The work of feminists and women's rights groups on FGM/C, and sexual and reproductive rights more broadly, has shown that FGM/C can no longer be considered in isolation from other issues affecting women's social, economic, and physical well-being. International and regional policy and legislation on FGM/C now acknowledge the gendered source and impact of FGM/C, and question the validity of culture, tradition, and religion as tenets from which to defend the practice. As a form of gender-based violence, FGM/C is implicated not only in the politics of family relations but also in the wider structure of social relations, including those reinforced by state policy.

Both the political debates and practical methodologies that have arisen in Egypt over the course of the past decade provide compelling evidence of the need for integrated approaches to addressing FGM/C and for the centrality of women's empowerment in these approaches. The Egyptian Task Force model affirms the value of broad-based coalitions in dealing with issues of violence that cut across sectors and social and political domains. Furthermore, reframing FGM/C as a question of women's rights represents a successful attempt to move beyond the discussion of culture to confront the assumptions and values that create societal tolerance of the violation of women's bodies. The experience of Deir el Barsha demonstrates the effectiveness of combining community consensus building against FGM/C with new social and economic opportunities and roles for girls and women. Supportive leadership at all levels is required to reinforce the moral consensus against FGM/C and in support of rights to bodily integrity and gender equity.

It is clear that although the explicit terminology of "rights" may not always be used at the local level, it remains both conceptually and practically effective to use the principles of a rights-based framework in devising anti-FGM/C strategies. This framework requires consideration of the ways in which women's rights to their bodies are structured at all levels, from interpersonal relations to the household economy, to legislation and policy, and taking active measures to address inequalities and inequities. Such an approach reaffirms the central vision of the Cairo Program of Action, that integrated strategies supporting women's empowerment are a prerequisite for ensuring health and sustainable development at micro and macro levels.

Notes

I would like to thank the Soros Reproductive Rights Fellowship for facilitating the writing of this chapter, and all the Soros fellows for their engaging commentary and insights. A warm thank you to Madeleine Kennedy-Macfoy, Amal Abdel Hadi, and Nahid Toubia, for reading and commenting on drafts of this chapter, and Seham Abdel Salaam and Amal Abdel Hadi, for their willingness to share their considerable experience and analysis. All shortcomings in the chapter are, of course, my own.

1. I have used the term "female genital mutilation/cutting" (FGM/C) in this paper. FGM was used through much of the 1990s in UN policy documents and by women's rights advocates in the African context and elsewhere, and the more value neutral FGC is a recent addition by USAID and other governmental agencies.

"Circumcision" is used in the text to describe the act of FGM. FGM/C "comprises all procedures involving partial or total removal of the external female genitalia or other injury to the female genital organs whether for cultural, religious or other non-therapeutic reasons" (World Health Organization 2000). FGM/C is practiced in twenty-eight African countries as well in parts of Asia and the Middle East, and is also practiced by immigrant populations from these countries in Europe, North America, and Australia. The World Health Organization estimates that 100 to 140 million women have undergone FGM/C worldwide.

2. Consultations within the African women's movement consolidated a locus of support for progressive positions on FGM/C and other sexual and reproductive rights issues addressed in the consecutive conferences. Although positions on reproductive rights and the highly contested sexual rights varied among African states, the official African position at Beijing was supportive, in light of need to counter pervasive violence against women and the HIV/AIDS pandemic (Klugman 2000).

3. Although there is some agreement that FGM can be regarded as "cruel, inhuman and degrading treatment" under the Torture Convention, it is not possible to claim FGM/C as a form of torture, given that definitions of torture require the *intentional* infliction of harm (Rahman and Toubia 2000: 25–26).

4. Provisions to address harmful practices are also presented in the African Charter on the Rights and Welfare of the Child (OAU 1990), which entered into force in 1991. Although explicit mention of FGM is not made, Article 21 calls on states to "take all appropriate measures to eliminate harmful social and cultural practices . . . in particular . . . those customs and practices discriminatory to the child on the grounds of sex and other status." Regarding implementation, Article 16 on child abuse and torture proposes "legislative, administrative, social and educational measures" and the establishment of special monitoring units as protective and preventative measures.

5. There is a rich tradition of qualitative literature on gender relations and sexual politics in Egypt, which, due to space limitations, cannot be reviewed extensively here. Recent ethnographies have explored the discourses of virtue and honor in relation to women's sexuality and how these interact with and are affected by market forces, class, age, and discourses of masculinity (see Ali 2002, Hoodfar 1997, Abu-Lughod 1993).

6. As Abdel Hadi and Abdel Salam (1999) documented in the late 1990s, many Egyptian medical professionals have historically approved of FGM, which facilitated the increasing medicalization of FGM documented in the 1995 EDHS.

7. The medical profession in Egypt represents an important contingent to target in anti-FGM/C campaigns and education. A recent study showed considerable support for FGM/C by Egyptian physicians. The lack of adequate discussion of the sexual function of the external genitalia and on FGM/C in medical education means that social rationales hold greater influence over physicians' attitudes rather than does medical reasoning (Abdel Hadi and Abdel Salam 1999). Abdel Salaam (2003) notes that many medical students have not been exposed to intact genitalia and are hence not aware of the functions or form of the external genitalia.

8. The grand sheykh of al-Ahzar and a representative of H. E. Pope Shenouda III made this statement before representatives of twenty-eight African and Arab coun-

tries at the Afro-Arab Expert Consultation on Legal Tools for the prevention of Female Genital Mutilation held in Cairo in June 2003.

9. The association between FGM/C and marriageability is a common reason for continuing the practice in many African contexts. Mackie's (2000) analysis of the anti-FGM work by TOSTAN in Senegal finds a similar relationship between a group's willingness to stop circumcising their daughters and the reassurance that uncircumcised girls will be marriageable. However, although assuring that uncircumcised women can be married makes the rejection of FGM socially feasible for many, it does not challenge the gender norms framing the practice.

10. The closure of the NCPD in 2000 and a change in Task Force leadership led to a reconstitution of the Task Force, with many of the original members leaving.

11. Dr. Seham Abdel Salam, former Task Force member and head of the Task Force resource center, was instrumental in the development of this approach.

12. The NCCM is the highest national authority responsible for policy making, planning, coordination, monitoring, and evaluation of activities relating to child protection, development, and welfare. Its objective is also to "ensure that all women enjoy their rights to safe and healthy motherhood and to support their roles within families and society at large." The NCCM was established in 1988 by presidential decree stipulating NCCM decisions as mandatory and binding on all government ministries. See http://www.nccm.org.eg.

13. The project is facilitated by a donor assistance group made up of bilateral donors, UN agencies (UNDP, UNICEF, UNFPA), and international NGOs (Population Council and CEDPA).

14. See Oxaal and Baden 1997; Sen and Batliwala 2000; and Parpart et al. 2002 for definitions and critical assessments of "empowerment."

References

Abdel Hadi, A. 1998. *We Are Decided: The Struggle in an Egyptian Village to Eradicate Female Circumcision.* Cairo: Cairo Institute of Human Rights Studies.

————. 2000. "Female Genital Mutilation in Egypt." In M. Turshen, ed., *African Women's Health.* Trenton, N.J.: Africa World Press.

————. 2003. Personal communication, August 28. Cairo. Coordinator, New Woman Research Centre.

Abdel Hadi, A., and S. Abdel Salam. 1999. *Physicians: Attitudes towards Female Circumcision.* Cairo: Cairo Institute for Human Rights Studies.

Abdel Salaam, S. 2003. Personal communication, September 19. Cairo. Consultant.

Abouzeid. A. 2003. Personal communication, August 21. London. Programs Manager, RAINBO.

Abu-Lughod, L. 1990. "The Romance of Resistance: Tracing Transformations of Power through Bedouin Women." In P. R. Sanday and R. Goodenough, eds., *Beyond the Second Sex: New Directions in the Anthropology of Gender.* Philadelphia: University of Pennsylvania Press.

————. 1993. *Writing Women's Worlds: Bedouin Stories.* Berkeley: University of California Press.

Abusharaf, R. M. 2000. "Revisiting Feminist Discourses on Infibulation: Responses from Sudanese Feminists." In B. Shell-Duncan and Y. Hernlund, eds., *Female "Circumcision" in Africa: Culture, Controversy and Change*. Boulder: Lynne Rienner.

African Union. 2003. Protocol to the African Charter on Human and People's Rights on the Rights of Women in Africa. Adopted 11 July. http://www.africa-union.org/ Official_documents/Treaties_%20Conventions_%20Protocols/Protocol%20on %20the%20Rights%20the%20Women.pdf.

Ali, K. 2002. *Planning the Family in Egypt: New Bodies, New Selves*. Austin: University of Texas Press.

An-Na'im, A. 1994. "State Responsibility under International Human Rights Law to Change Religious and Customary Law." In R. J. Cook, ed., *Human Rights of Women: National and International Perspectives*. Philadelphia: University of Pennsylvania Press.

Bennett, J. 2000. "Thinking Sexualities." *African Gender Institute Newsletter.* http:// web.uct.ac.za/org/agi/pubs/newsletters/vol7/lead7.htm.

Beyani, C. 1994. "Towards a More Effective Guarantee of Women's Rights in the African Human Rights System." In R. Cook, ed., *Human Rights of Women: National and International Perspectives*. Philadelphia: University of Pennsylvania Press.

Butegwa, F. 1995. "International Human Rights Law and Practice: Implications for Women." In M. Schuler, ed., *From Basic Needs to Basic Rights: Women's Claim to Human Rights*. Washington, D.C.: Women, Law and Development International.

CEDAW (Committee on the Elimination of Discrimination against Women). 1990. *General Recommendation No. 14: Female Circumcision.* http://www.un.org/ womenwatch/daw/cedaw/recomm.htm.

———. 1999. *General Recommendation No. 19: Violence against Women.* http:// www.un.org/womenwatch/daw/cedaw/recomm.htm.

CEOSS (Coptic Evangelical Organization for Social Services). 2003. *Empowerment: From Theory to Practice*. Cairo: Ceopress.

Coomaraswamy, R. 1994. "To Bellow Like a Cow: Women, Ethnicity, and the Discourse of Rights." In R. Cook, ed., *Human Rights of Women: National and International Perspectives*. Philadelphia: University of Pennsylvania Press.

Center for Reproductive Rights and University of Toronto International Program on Reproductive and Sexual Health Law. 2002. *Bringing Rights to Bear: An Analysis of the Work of UN Treaty Monitoring Bodies on Reproductive and Sexual Rights*. New York: Center for Reproductive Rights.

DHS (Demographic and Health Survey). 1995. *Egyptian Demographic and Health Survey.* Cairo: National Population Council and Macro International.

———. 2000. *Egyptian Demographic and Health Survey.* Cairo: National Population Council and Macro International.

Guenena, N., and N. Wassef. 1999. *Unfulfilled Promises: Women's Rights in Egypt.* Cairo: Population Council.

Hoodfar, H. 1997. *Between Marriage and the Market: Intimate Politics and Survival in Cairo.* Berkeley: University of California Press.

Ibhawoh, B. 2000. "Between Culture and Constitution: Evaluating the Cultural Legitimacy of Human Rights in the African State." *Human Rights Quarterly* 22(3): 838–860.

Kabeer, N. 1999. "Resources, Agency, Achievements: Reflections on the Measurement of Women's Empowerment." *Development and Change* 30: 435–464.

Klugman, B. 2000. "Sexual Rights in Southern Africa: A Beijing Discourse or a Strategic Necessity?" *Health and Human Rights: An International Journal* 4(2): 132–159.

Maboreke, M. 2003. "African Union Closing Comments." *AMANITARE Voices* 3: 25.

Mackie, G. 2000. "Female Genital Cutting: The Beginning of the End." In B. Shell-Duncan and Y. Hernlund, eds., *Female "Circumcision" in Africa: Culture, Controversy, and Change.* Boulder: Lynne Rienner.

Mama, A. 1997. "Sheroes and Villains: Conceptualising Colonial and Contemporary Violence against Women." In J. Alexander and C. Mohanty, eds., *Feminist Genealogies, Colonial Legacies, Democratic Futures.* New York: Routledge.

———. 2000. "Transformation Thwarted: Gender-Based Violence in Africa's New Democracies." *African Gender Institute Newsletter.* http://web.uct.ac.za/org/agi/pubs/newsletters/vol6/transf.htm.

McFadden, P. 2000. "Sexual Health and Sexual Rights for African Women." *Southern African Political and Economic Monthly* 13(7): 22–24.

———. 2001. "Cultural Practices as Gendered Exclusion." In *Discussing Women's Empowerment: Theory and Practices.* SIDA Studies No. 3. Stockholm: Swedish International Development Agency.

NCCM (National Council for Childhood and Motherhood). 2003a. *Eliminating Female Genital Mutilation: An Egyptian Roadmap: Breaking the Wall of Silence—A Decade of Lessons and Experience.* Cairo: NCCM.

———. 2003b. *The FGM-free Village Model: A National Partnership.* Cairo: NCCM.

New Woman Research Centre. 1994. *Statement on the Decree Legalising Female Genital Mutilation in Public Hospitals.* Cairo: New Woman Research Centre.

OAU (Organization of African Unity). 1982. *African [Banjul] Charter on Human and Peoples' Rights.* OAU Doc. CAB/LEG/67/3 rev. 5, 21 I.L.M. 58. Adopted June 27, 1981.

———. 1990. *African Charter on the Rights and Welfare of the Child.* OAU Doc. CAB/LEG/24.9/49.

Oloka-Onyango, J., and S. Tamale. 1995. "The Personal Is Political, or Why Women's Rights Are Indeed Human Rights: An African Perspective on International Feminism." *Human Rights Quarterly* 17(4): 691–731.

Onoria, H. 2002. "Introduction to the African System of Protection of Human Rights and the Draft Protocol." In W. Benedek, E. Kisaakye, and G. Obertleiner, eds., *The Human Rights of Women: International Instruments and African Experiences.* London: Zed Books.

Oxaal, Z., and S. Baden. 1997. *Gender and Empowerment: Definitions, Approaches and Implications for Policy.* Bridge Report no. 40. Brighton: Institute of Development Studies.

Parpart, J., S. Rai, and K. Staudt, eds. 2002. *Re-thinking Empowerment: Gender and Development in a Global/Local Word.* London: Taylor and Francis.

Petchesky, R., and K. Judd, eds. 1998. *Negotiating Reproductive Rights: Women's Perspectives across Countries and Cultures.* London: Zed Books.

Rahman, A., and N. Toubia. 2000. *Female Genital Mutilation: A Guide to Laws and Policies Worldwide.* New York: Zed Books.

RAINBO (Research, Action and Information Network for the Bodily Integrity of Women). 1995. *Female Genital Mutilation in Egypt: The Recent History.* New York: RAINBO. Collection of primary documents.

———. 2000. *Breaking the Silence: An Egyptian Experience.* New York: RAINBO.

———. 2002. *A Framework for Design, Monitoring and Evaluating Anti-FGM Programs: A Report of the Female Genital Mutilation Review, Evaluation and Monitoring Project, 2001–2002.* London: RAINBO.

Seif el Dawla, A. 1999. "The Political and Legal Struggle over Female Genital Mutilation in Egypt: Five Years Since the ICPD." *Reproductive Health Matters* 7(13): 128–135.

Seif el Dawla, A., A. Abd el Hadi, and N. Abdel Wahab. 1998. "Women's Wit Over Men's: Trade-Offs and Strategic Accommodations in Egyptian Women's Lives." In R. Petchesky and K. Judd, eds., *Negotiating Reproductive Rights: Women's Perspectives across Countries and Cultures.* London: Zed Books.

Sen, G., and S. Batliwala. 2000. "Empowering Women for Reproductive Rights." In Harriet Presser and Gita Sen, eds., *Women's Empowerment and Demographic Processes: Moving beyond Cairo.* Oxford: Oxford University Press.

Toubia N. 1995. *Female Genital Mutilation: A Call for Global Action.* New York: RAINBO.

———. 2002. "Editorial." *AMANITARE Voices* 1:1. London: RAINBO.

Toubia, N., L. Morrisson, J. Chege, P. Greene, and E. H. Sharief. Forthcoming. "Methods, Models and Indicators to Measure Progress in Stopping Female Genital Mutilation." In *Culture Health and Sexuality* (forthcoming).

United Nations. 1995. *Fourth UN World Conference on Women, Beijing Declaration and Platform for Action.* UN Doc. A/CONF. 177/20.

United Nations. 1993. *Declaration on the Elimination of Violence against Women.* UN Doc. A/48/49.

UNDP, INP (United Nations Development Program, Institute for National Planning). 2003. *Egyptian Human Development Report 2003.* Cairo: UNDP, INP.

Wanyeki, L. M. 2002. "OAU Optional Protocol on Women's Human Rights." *AMANITARE Voices* 2: 5–6. London: RAINBO.

Wassef, N., and A. Mansour. 1999 *Investigating Masculinities and Female Genital Mutilation in Egypt.* Cairo: NGO Centre for Population and Development.

World Health Organization. 2000. *Female Genital Mutilation.* Fact sheet No. 241.

World Health Organization/EMRO. 1979. *Traditional Practices Affecting the Health of Women and Children: Female Circumcision, Child Marriage, Nutritional Taboos. Report on a Seminar, Khartoum.* Geneva: World Health Organization.

Women's Reproductive and Sexual Rights and the Offense of *Zina* in Muslim Laws in Nigeria

AYESHA M. IMAM

Amina Lawal was convicted of adultery in March 2002 and sentenced to stoning to death.[1] In the wake of a new Sharia penal code in Katsina state, religious right vigilantes instigated a case against her for having a child after divorce without remarrying. The alleged father swore that he had not had sexual relations with her and was released. These events occurred during a heated controversy in Nigeria about the nature and desirability of Sharia, rights in Muslim laws, constitutional rights, international human rights, and their relationship(s) to each other. Ms. Lawal's case was immediately adopted by a coalition of Nigerian nongovernmental organizations (NGOs) that provided her with lawyers, safe houses, medical care, and emotional support over the eighteen-month ordeal. She also became the object of world attention, media, and protest campaigns, many of which excoriated "Islamic law" as brutal and called on Nigeria's president to pardon her and repeal the Sharia Acts. In September 2003, Amina Lawal won her appeal in the state Sharia Court of Appeal and was acquitted (*Lawal Kurami v. the State*).

Ms. Lawal's is perhaps the best known of the five cases involving adultery and stoning since the passage of Sharia penal codes in several Nigerian states beginning in 2000. The offense of *zina* or unlawful sexual intercourse includes both adultery, punished by stoning to death, and fornication, punished by whipping. In some states, men may be imprisoned also. Two earlier defendants, Safiya Tungar-Tudu and Hafsatu Abubakar, who were convicted in October and December 2001, respectively, had both appealed successfully, again with the assistance of Nigerian women's and human rights NGOs. The conviction of Fatima Usman and Ahmadu Ibrahim two months after Ms. Lawal's conviction was still on appeal at the time of writing (March 2005), as was the last case, in Jigawa state. So far, no sentences of stoning have been upheld or carried out. However, over a score of fornication cases have led to convictions, with sentences of whipping carried out, and some men have been imprisoned as well as whipped.

These cases have opened up issues that are relevant to ensuring and developing women's reproductive and sexual rights in a way that recognizes and respects both local cultures and contexts and international rights agreements. Rising religious right identity politics in Nigeria and around the world, including the United States, on the one hand, and crude antiterrorism policies that are often blatantly Islamophobic on the other, must both be considered—along with romanticizing practices that oppress women in the name of culture.[2] Local cultures can be microcultures in small communities. They can also embody transnational belief systems (whether religious or secular) that have become rooted in the everyday practices in large or small communities. Most often, local cultures are complicated mixtures of many ideologies and social practices structured by power relations, with the common factor of being part of the daily practices of life in a given community. To respect the beliefs, tenets, and practices of both local cultures and international human rights agreements requires a double "claim and critique" strategy. This consists of claiming ownership of both local cultures and of international human rights discourses (including the right to participate in defining the content of each), while privileging neither local nor international as automatically superior, and thus being able to critique both. Strategies for promoting rights in particular situations are not mechanically given by either local or international tenets, but are necessarily contextual to specific history, politics, and place. They frequently involve interplay between local and international discourses.

There are two premises for claiming and critiquing both local and international discourses. The first is that the point of espousing human rights principles is to ensure that people actually enjoy rights as part of their mundane day-to-day lives. This requires—especially for reproductive and sexual rights—that they be claimed and respected by local cultures of understanding and ways of living and not be merely written texts. Celestine Nyamu-Musembi refers to Mahmoud Mamdani's insight that "wherever there [is] oppression, there must come into being a conception of rights. . . . [Thus] human rights are both universal and particular: universal because the experience of resistance to oppression is shared among subjugated groups the world over, but also particular because resistance is shaped in response to the peculiarities of the relevant social context" (Nyamu-Musembi 2002). If particular formulations of rights are perceived as imposed, whether by foreigners or national elites, they are less likely to have local legitimacy and be respected. Human and women's rights activists must move between local, national, and international levels to develop resonances between local, national, and international understandings of rights.

The second premise is that international human rights understandings are also social and historical products, which are affected by the power politics and the cultural and historical traditions of the dominant groups in their contexts. Although some international human rights agreements may be more advanced than particular local cultures on some issues in some places and times, they may also lag behind on other issues, in other places, at other times.

The dominant understanding of what human rights are at any particular time depends on the power of the various people involved to assert their definitions over those of others. Understanding this makes it possible to recognize Western European influences on the construction of rights today, but to accept, nonetheless, the universality of the notion of rights, even when they differ in particulars.[3] Furthermore, human rights cannot be static but must be continually reconstructed by women and men whose lives are impacted by them. Universalizing human rights means not simply asserting that they are universal but also constructing rights that speak to peoples of different cultural, historical, gender, and class backgrounds.[4] Universalizing international constructions of rights requires recognizing diversity and including ideas and principles that may not hitherto have been part of the dominant language of human rights. Here the struggle for the recognition of women's rights as human rights and the development of international reproductive and sexual rights provide good examples (see Imam 1998).

Human rights approaches need to move beyond the notion of culture (including religion) as a static barrier to human rights and toward a notion of culture as constantly remade historical constructions containing potential resources as well as obstacles—as Amilcar Cabral (1973) elucidated long ago. Human rights "outreach" should not mean simply "bringing the message to the grass roots," as revealed in existing treaties and so on. This denies the influence of Western cultural constructs on dominant rights definitions and locates all obstacles to the realization of rights in an unchangeable and monolithic "other" culture or religion.[5] Thus developing international and universalizing human rights must be seen as a multiway process.

The proposed approach requires strategically drawing from and negotiating both local cultural-religious norms and traditions (which may be simultaneously transnational and are always complex and multiple) and formal national and international rights regimes. Women's groups have often been extremely creative in this process, framing and drawing upon and improving international covenants in ways that make sense in local contexts. Including the rights of rural women in the Convention for the Elimination of All Forms of Discrimination against Women (CEDAW) or the rights of the girl child in the Beijing Platform of Action, for example, were due largely to the efforts of African and other non-Western women. Other examples include using CEDAW as the basis for mock tribunals and test cases, adopting it as local law, and highlighting the similarities between it and progressive constructions of religious, customary, and secular national laws and practices.

Typically women's rights are posed in opposition to family, religious, or ethnic community rights. For instance, Muslim women are often accused of being "Westernized" and traitors to the Muslim community if they demand rights. Such oppositions ignore asymmetrical gender power relations and assume current male-dominant constructions of cultural norms as static and unchangeable. This thereby legitimates the power of beneficiaries of the status quo. However, women are as much part of the family and community as men are. What is challenged is not necessarily the community itself but rather the current definitions of the culture and norms of that community and the powers of cultural gatekeepers to maintain their definitions in the face of demands from other community members. Thus women may be asserting their right to participate in defining the norms of their communities as well as, or sometimes rather than, their rights to leave that community and choose another.

Against this background, this chapter looks at the politics and activities around the *zina* cases under the Sharia penal codes in Nigeria. It assesses the strategies and effectiveness of local women's and human rights activists as well as of external actors, including international human rights organizations, the mass media, and thousands of individuals across the world.

The Development of the Sharia Acts and Sharia Penal Codes in Nigeria

Identity politics, meaning the political use of a group identity based on ethnicity or religion to mobilize resources and exclude others from access to power and resources, is not new in Nigeria. Identity politics was institutionalized in the last period of colonial rule in the British policies of "indirect rule" and the "tripartite federation" (see Ibrahim 1989). Despite some political challenges and counter efforts, this trend has continued in independent Nigeria, with "federal character" and other policies directing attention to subnational identities defined as competing with each other. Nonetheless, for the first time since independence, laws have been enacted specifically because they are religious. The context for this includes religious resurgences and the growth of both ethnic and religious identity politics in the 1980s and 1990s, along with the obvious failures of independence and nationalist promises, which led to cynical disillusionment with politics as corrupt and self-serving. The economic and social problems caused or exacerbated by policies influenced by the World Bank and the International Monetary Fund include both an absolute and a relative increase in poverty. Consequently, not only the rural and urban poor but even high-level professionals such as university professors find access to health care, education, and infrastructural services difficult. Such policies also contributed to a massive deterioration in education and health standards and access. These declines took place without the promised increases in industrial and manufacturing capacity or foreign investment, as deregulation facilitated capital flight and corrupt practices. Furthermore, the substantial devaluation of the national currency, the Naira, from parity to the U.S. dollar to the current rate of about N130:$1 further fuelled inflation and poverty (see, among many others, Olukoshi 1993, Osaghae 1995).

Ironically, despite the growth of religious essentialism and religious right tendencies, the new laws were not directly the result of pressure from a religious group. Faced with a small and recently created state with little infrastructure or capital, few natural resources or people with high formal education, the newly elected governor of Zamfara state needed to court popularity—through "Sharianization."[6] Sanusi (2004: 81) pointed out that "the politicians who started the reforms do not have a record of Islamist activism. They seem to have exploited an issue that has for decades had emotional political appeal. . . . In 1999, with elections gone by, the Muslim north had lost political power, thus compounding the sense of vulnerability due to its weak economy and educational backwardness. Its politicians had become discredited as corrupt, power-hungry incompetents. Northern Muslims felt increasingly alienated and insecure. Religion remains for most of them the last anchor for stability." The international environment, including the apparent Islamophobic policies in Palestine and the wars in Afghanistan and Iraq, also contributed to a siege mentality among Muslims. Hence the "defense of Islam" rhetoric was likely to be effective.

Reactions to Sharianization

Condemnations of Sharianization were rife in Nigeria. Christian and other non-Muslim communities feared the imposition of Muslim religious laws. Human rights and other NGOs were concerned about the religious rights of non-Muslims, the violation of constitutional provisions of secularity in the state, and the "barbaric" nature of some of the punishments enacted. Women's rights activists were concerned that Sharianization would be used as a rationale to discriminate against women and restrict their rights, since the first announcement of Sharianization in November 1999 included a restriction on women's movements in public.

Muslim communities in Nigeria are extremely varied (see Hélie-Lucas 1993), and the reactions to Sharianization were correspondingly varied. Members of Muslim communities may, of course, also be members of human rights and women's rights NGOs and activist communities, and several reacted in the same manner as many non-Muslim human rights activists. Ironically, there was spirited opposition among some who had consistently stood for the "Islamization" of Nigeria, like Ibrahim el-Zakzaky of the Muslim Brothers, on the grounds that passing and implementing harsh punishments without first ensuring just socioeconomic relations is not Islamic. This was also the stand taken by some Muslim progressives whose political activities had hitherto been wholly secular (see Mohammed et al. 1999). A few, like Lawal Batagarawa, a respected Hausa poet and radical political and national independence activist, warned of the political abuse of religion, only to be met with abuse and threats of violence. But many members of Muslim communities who were uneasy about Sharianization felt that they had no solid basis on which to protest. As Muslims, they felt that they could not simply oppose Sharianization, but neither did they feel that they were adequately equipped to criticize, as they did not read Arabic or have years of study of *fiqh,* Islamic jurisprudence. Hence there was an uneasy public silence, despite private misgivings. Others felt that protest was futile, as we shall see.

Nonetheless, extending Sharia as a legal system had widespread support in Muslim communities in both the north and southwest of Nigeria. In each Sharianizing state, thousands of people—most of them men, since women are largely secluded in northern Nigeria (Imam 1994)—made their way from rural villages, from other states in Nigeria, and from neighboring countries to enthusiastically celebrate the official inaugurations. A number of factors contributed to this support. One element was identification with religious or regional communities that offered some hope, following the presidential election of a "born-again" Christian from the southwest (President Obasanjo) and the general loss of credibility of politicians.[7] This was perhaps most evident among the middle-class educated and political elites, with the strongest backing for the new laws coming from the Izala and other proto-Wahhabi movements that support severe penal laws, but that had not previously advocated action to change the state or its policies (Sanusi 2004).[8]

Many associated Sharia with morality, beleiving that strong punishments would curb immoral behavior and widespread public violence, thus increasing public security. Ensuring safety and security is even more important for the poor than for the wealthy, who resort to private security companies. Immorality referred not only to sexuality but more particularly to corrupt state and government practices. It is, after all, the poor who suffer most from corrupt practices, because it is they who most need the infrastructure and social services that are lacking. Furthermore, the introduction of Sharia criminal law was widely expected to end judicial corruption and the slowness of the judicial process, which often means many accused persons are held in pretrial detention for longer than the possible maximum sentences. In addition, because the charity tithe (*zakat*) is one of the "five pillars of Islam," many people expected a serious social welfare program to result from Sharianization.

Mass support for Sharianization was so strong that the governors of eleven other states either decided to follow suit or were pushed into passing similar acts for fear of being seen as anti-Sharia. Playing the "Sharia card" has largely worked. The conservative political elite in northern Nigeria have been able to use the mass support for Sharia to criticize the federal government and to increase their otherwise lower access to centrally controlled national resources, following the shift of power in the 1999 elections to the largely Christian southwest/middle belt alliance.

Sharia was also welcomed by some Christians as a means of justifying a move toward "Christian law" for themselves. Yet others justified it as a rationale for their own support for increased local state autonomy vis-à-vis the federal state, especially in the delta region and the southeast.

The net effect of the Sharia Acts and the politics around them has been to give increased power and authority to conservative religious essentialism and identity politics. Many vigilantes have reacted by assuming that the acts justify their imposition of practices that have no legal basis at all, such as conservative dress codes for women, controls on women's movements and use of public transport, or prohibiting music and dancing at private social ceremonies, including single-sex events. Vigilantes sometimes act individually and sometimes as *hizbah* committees claiming the right to monitor and enforce Sharianization, both as ad hoc groups and with overt state support (especially in Zamfara state). Women's rights activists and those women who refuse to abide by the religious right's notions of how they should dress, or who work outside the home, or who refuse to sit in the back seat in taxis and buses have been threatened and sometimes physically attacked. The staff and volunteers of women's organizations that provide sex education and contraceptive information, as well as drivers who carry women in their taxis, buses, and motorcycles have also been intimidated or beaten up.[9] To criticize Sharianization, even mildly, was regarded as anti-Sharia, anti-northern Nigeria, and anti-Islam, even by some convicted under the new acts, who were therefore unwilling to appeal their convictions.

Some Constitutional and Legal Issues

The new Sharia penal codes created some new offenses in Nigerian law,[10] mostly around sexuality, like the *zina* laws and the prohibition of lesbianism.[11] The codes also recognize stoning, retributive punishments,[12] and blood fines.[13] In theory, these laws apply to Muslims only, thereby evading the charge that the Sharia Acts constitute the imposition of a state religion.[14] It remains an open question whether Muslims have the right to choose to be governed by general Nigerian law without having to renounce their religious identity.[15]

One issue that may arise is through what route the criminal appeals from state Sharia courts will pass. The Nigerian constitution states that all death penalty cases are eligible for review by the Supreme Court.[16] It also provides that appeals from state Sharia courts of appeal are heard by a panel of a minimum of three judges of the Federal Court of Appeal learned in Islamic law, and from there to the Supreme Court. However, the new criminal offenses and the jurisdiction of state Sharia courts over them are creations of state law.[17] The constitution gives the Federal Court of Appeal jurisdiction over appeals from state Sharia courts of appeal in civil proceedings, but does not mention criminal jurisdiction one way or the other.

So far all the appeals have been won at the level of state Sharia courts of appeal. However, the women's and human rights groups declared they would support appeals from the state to the Federal Court of Appeal, if necessary. Opponents of the appeals have likewise declared their intention to challenge the jurisdiction of the Federal Court of Appeal, should this happen. Their opposition is not simply procedural; it is also political. Their claim is that, although they would be Muslim, the judges in the Federal Court of Appeal and the Supreme Court would not be likely to properly adjudicate Muslim laws, because their training has been in secular laws, procedures, and criteria (that is, British-influenced practices, with Christian historical traditions).

A still unresolved and ambiguous area is that of the contradictions and gaps between the new Sharia penal codes and the criminal procedure codes that determine procedures and evidence. What counts as evidence? What are the procedures? How are offenses actually defined? Many Sharianizing states have not revised criminal procedure codes to clarify and spell out these issues. For instance, what should constitute evidence of *zina* is not defined in any of the Sharia penal codes or in the criminal procedure acts. Hence, whether the dominant position in Maliki jurisprudence, that pregnancy outside marriage is in itself sufficient evidence of *zina*, will hold or not, or what constitutes voluntary and repeated confession, among other concerns, are subject to debate. Judges frequently refer to offenses and to texts in Arabic, which are not accessible to most defendants or litigants or to many of the court personnel themselves. The common stance of orthodox medieval Muslim jurisprudence, which stipulates that two women witnesses are the equivalent of one man on most issues, is another concern. Although some of these issues have now been addressed in a recent judgment, others are yet to be raised in the courts.[18]

Whether the Sharia Acts themselves or the nature of the punishments are subject to international human rights law has been debated. Nigeria is a state party to several international human rights covenants, including the Convention against Torture and Other Cruel, Inhuman or Degrading Treatment or Punishment. However, as in many other countries, although such agreements may give rise to obligations under international law, unless they have been specifically incorporated into domestic law, they give no basis for claims in national courts, despite their moral force. The only human rights treaty that has been domesticated in Nigeria is the African Charter for Human and Peoples' Rights. International human rights law may enter Nigerian law through case law, and judges have cited CEDAW, for instance, in a number of cases. This is extremely unlikely to happen in the Sharia courts as currently staffed.

Parallel to the international law argument is that the Sharia Acts are contrary to rights recognized in the Nigerian constitution. Human Rights Law Service, a Nigerian organization, has tried to establish this through the courts, but the Zamfara State High Court (not a Sharia court), held that they could not bring such a case, being neither Muslim nor resident in the state of Zamfara.[19] Nigeria currently has a very narrow position on locus standi so that only a direct victim or his or her guardian can initiate a case.

Since independence, Nigeria has had multiple and parallel legal systems of general (usually referred to as secular), Muslim, and customary laws, with family and personal status issues most often addressed in Muslim or customary laws.[20] All of them are administered through and implemented by state legal and judicial institutions. Thus Nigeria has always had different laws for different communities (by religious faith, by ethnicity, and for those choosing general/secular law instead), and women have always had different rights in different systems. For instance, women's access to divorce is better under Muslim than secular or customary laws, and women's access to inheritance is greater in secular than in Muslim law, but greater in Muslim laws than in most customary laws, with the exception of some variations in Yoruba customary laws. Arguing that legislation based on Muslim law is in itself unconstitutional, regardless of the content or scope, is thus unlikely to hold water. The major issue, then, is whose version of Muslim law will hold sway.

Whose Version(s) of Sharia?

Despite claims to the contrary, Sharia is neither directly God-given (that is, revealed in the Qu'ran) nor uniform throughout the Muslim world or history. Some Sharia provisions such as stoning to death for *zina* are not in the Qu'ran. There are Qu'ranic verses that many developers of Sharia chose not to include, such as that women and men are each other's protectors and friends (9:72).[21] Some things, such as slaves, used to be legal in Sharia but are no longer.[22] In parts of the Muslim world a man having up to four wives simultaneously is legal. In other parts this is not permitted at all. The law in both cases is derived from the same verse in the Qu'ran (4:3).

In principle, Muslim laws are developed first by reliance on the Qu'ran. If there is no explicit provision, a second source is the *sunnah* (the traditions of the Prophet), usually as recounted in the *hadith*.[23] Then there is *ijma*, a consensus about what the law is, attained by *qiyas* (analogy) and through *ijtihad* (interpretative reasoning). However, at each stage there are disagreements that have led to diversities in Sharia. Although the words of the Qu'ran are unquestioned, what they mean, how they should be understood in contemporary times, which verses take priority, and how they should be construed in *fiqh* (Islamic jurisprudence) and thence into Sharia (Muslim laws) is and has always been subject to discussion or even controversy.

Similarly, there are disputes as to what constitutes the *sunnah*, or which of the *hadith* are valid and authentic. Of the thousands of *hadith* that have been collected, some scholars have accepted fewer than thirty as authentic, and have proceeded to undertake jurisprudence largely without relying on *hadith*.[24] Another issue is whether *isnaad* (validity of transmission) or *matn* (consistency of content with the Qu'ran) are more important in relying on *hadith*. Even the criterion of consensus is contested, given the range of opinions within as well as among jurists of different persuasions. Whose consensus is to be accepted? Is it the consensus of the *ulema* (Islamic scholars, often self-selecting and self-referencing groups of men) only or the Muslim community as a whole (including women)?

Currently, there are four main schools of Islamic jurisprudence among Sunni Muslims, who constitute about 80 percent of all Muslims. At one point there were nineteen simultaneously existing schools of thought. Shi'a Muslims also have schools of legal thought.[25] Although there are obviously many similarities, there are also wide divergences, including many on women's rights and autonomy. For instance, in Maliki legal traditions, pregnancy outside of marriage is evidence of *zina*, but no other school agrees.[26] Maliki *fiqh* also recognizes a father's right of *ijbar* (to choose a husband for his young never-married daughter), which is not found in Hanafi. Indeed, the Hanafi school permits men and women to choose their own marriage partners without a marriage guardian, which is not recognized by Maliki, Shafi, or Hanbali schools. On the other hand, only the Maliki school categorically recognizes the right of women to divorce, regardless of the consent of their husbands. There is also a wide range of opinion among jurists of the various schools on the right and capacity of women to be leaders, witnesses, judges, or to be politically active, as well as to use contraception and under what conditions.

The scholars for whom these schools of law were named did not see themselves as setting down a God-given legal code to be obeyed by all Muslims for all time. On the contrary, they were quite categorical that Muslims were not obliged to follow them if they did not believe that their reasoning from the Qu'ran and the *sunnah* were right. They had no intention of making their views final and binding on all Muslims. Imam Malik cautioned: "I am but a human being. I may be wrong and I may be right. So first examine what I say. If it complies with the Book and the Sunnah, then you may accept it. But if it does not comply with them, then you should reject it" (Amin 2000).

Imam Malik twice refused the caliphs of his day to make the *al-Muwatta* (his treatise on *fiqh*) state law on the grounds that it would not be the religious duty of Muslims to obey such laws if they did not believe his formulations to be correct. In the views of the very founders of the schools of Islamic jurisprudence, good Muslims were precisely those who questioned, and *fiqh* was not seen necessarily as state law. Yet, when Abdullahi An-Na'im (1998) argued that Sharia cannot be state law because Muslims have different views as to what is religiously required, he was abused as apostate. Other Muslim jurists have argued for a separation between religious obligations and state law, particularly in multifaith states. It is ironic that the founders' names are invoked by the religious right in precisely the opposite fashion to what they intended.

The stereotype of a single, uniform, divinely revealed "Islamic law" is thus false, whether in terms of historical or empirical accuracy or as jurisprudential principle. However, this myth has been useful to Muslim conservatives and the religious right, as well as to Islamophobes in the West. As Ruud Peters (Peters and Barends 2001) has pointed out, the recent establishment of Sharia legislation in Pakistan, Libya, Iran, and Sudan has been the result of identity politics. Zainah Anwar (2004) makes the same point for Malaysia, and documents how, as a result of playing this "more pious than thou" political game of laying claim to Muslim identity, it is the most conservative and restrictive positions that are both legislated and insisted upon as the sole legitimate stance.

The same trend can be seen in Nigeria regarding reproductive and sexual rights. On the issue of *zina*, for instance, there are at least three discernable possibilities. One is to regard *zina* as a sin that Allah will punish directly, except where there are voluntary and repeated confessions. Another is to see the law as a deterrent and thus to keep or reinstate laws that require high standards of proof and evidence, resulting in few prosecutions and extremely rare convictions.[27] The third is the recent aggressive enforcing of morality through restrictive legislation and enthusiastic prosecutions. The latter describes the recent situations in Iran and Sudan as well as Nigeria.

Similarly, there is a range of juristic opinions on fertility management. The majority of Muslim jurists have agreed that fertility management, including the use of contraception and early abortion, is permissible, that pleasure in sexual intercourse is a right for both women and men, and that Islam does not sanction female genital mutilation. Despite this, the religious right in Nigeria have described fertility management as promoting immorality and *zina* and have attempted to prevent it.

By continuing to pose the issues as a choice between the "strict" versus the "loose/liberal/moderate" application of a uniform Islamic law, Muslim religious extremists and essentialist identity politicians prevent progressive

Muslim scholars and rights activists from establishing the legitimacy of their positions in *fiqh*, in Sharia, or in nonreligious laws. Ironically, many progressives and leftists in the West do the same, dismissing critical voices from within the Muslim world as Westernized and inauthentic. It is important to recognize dissenters as equally authentic members of the community.

Organizing in Nigeria

The first group to be active on Sharianization's potential to violate women's rights was BAOBAB for Women's Human Rights. BAOBAB's work rests on recognizing the historicity and specificity of all discourses of rights and the need for their continual reconstruction. For instance, BAOBAB has been active in a comparative study of women's rights under customary, general (secular), and religious laws in the Muslim world. It has also worked with understandings of the Qur'an that provide knowledge through which women in Muslim communities can criticize oppressive practices and claim rights. BAOBAB produces legal literacy leaflets, including ones on divorce, child custody, and women's protection from violence in all Nigerian systems of law and in international human rights. These leaflets are used to train paralegals who work with community-based organizations and with local NGOs. They are also used widely in legal consciousness workshops that focus not just on knowledge of current law but also on demystifying law and on strategies for changing it when necessary. The paralegal and legal consciousness training has addressed international human rights conventions and policies, as well, subjecting them to the same process of analysis and critique.

BAOBAB has initiated a series of bridge-building workshops in which women's rights activists and others examine women's rights in religious and customary laws and practices in both Muslim and non-Muslim communities in Nigeria.[28] Each group analyzes and critiques its own community's norms and practices before applying the same analysis to other communities. This process builds an informed understanding of women's rights in diverse communities. It also helps to establish trust and working together empathetically in practical solidarity. The groups then come together to build common platforms and strategies for women's rights in all communities, drawing on their previous analyses and on international human rights discourse.

BAOBAB collaborates with other women's and human rights groups in Nigeria, including the Women's Rights Advancement and Protection Alternative (WRAPA), which took the lead in defending Amina Lawal. The approach BAOBAB pioneered has three components: defense of those convicted under the new Sharia penal codes; demystifying the notion of Sharia laws; and working to build common platforms to defend and promote women's rights across diverse communities.

Defense of Those Convicted under the New Sharia Penal Code

The strategy in defending those convicted under the new Sharia penal codes was to deliberately focus on appeals in the Sharia courts, for a number of reasons. First, something needed to be done to protect the individuals concerned, and appeals include a stay of execution of sentences, thereby buying time. Second, there was the generally held view (supported by BAOBAB's research) that the higher courts, including the state Sharia courts of appeal, but especially the Federal Court of Appeal panel of judges "learned in Islamic law," have historically been more fair to women than have lower Sharia, customary, or secular courts. Furthermore, trying to put pressure for pardons on the same state governors who signed the penal codes would have been ineffective in the current political climate. Finally, even if the constitutionality of the Sharia Acts and Sharia penal codes themselves could be challenged successfully in the general courts, doing so would certainly have alienated the majority of the Muslim communities in Nigeria, given their initial support for Sharianization.

Through appealing, the use of arguments in *fiqh* would help to expose the deficiencies in the acts and the bias against women in their implementation. It would also promote alternative juristic views to the conservative positions being insisted upon by the religious right and conservatives as the only authentic, legitimate position in Muslim laws. Although the appeals were argued in the Sharia court system, they also drew on rights in Nigerian constitutional law (see Yawuri 2003, WACOL 2003) on the grounds that the Sharia penal codes and the Sharia courts themselves are governed by the Nigerian constitution.

In addition, an acquittal, unlike a pardon, indicates that no conviction should have been made, and thus is a vindication of the person wrongly convicted. Finally, both conservative Muslims and the religious right intelligentsia promoted the view, backed by the threat of direct action and vigilante-instigated rioting, that any criticism or appeal of convictions is anti-Islam. Thus one reason to pursue appeals in the Sharia system was to demonstrate that people have a right to appeal and to challenge injustices, including those perpetrated in the name of religion. Therefore, in defense of those convicted under the Sharia penal codes, NGOs came together to support victims through the appeals. These began with BAOBAB and its supporting legal strategy team, and include the Coalition for the Protection of Women's Rights in Secular, Customary and Religious Laws (sixty NGOs) and the Sharia Stakeholders Group (eighteen NGOs and individuals).

Demystifying Sharia

To demystify the nature of Sharia as Muslim law, groups and individuals have organized seminars, workshops, training, and public discussions; been interviewed on radio and television talk shows; given public lectures; written articles and papers; and published pamphlets and books. This includes groups like the Constitutional Rights Project (2000), BAOBAB, the Women's Action Collective (WACOL) with Women's Action Research and Documentation (WARDC; Ezeilo and Afolabi 2003), and the Nigerian office of the International Human Rights Law Group, as well as individuals like Sanusi Lamido Sanusi and Iman.[29] Explaining that Sharia is not divine but merely religious, and is neither uniform nor unchanging requires uncovering the historical specificities of Muslim laws, the development and diversity of Muslim jurisprudence, the progressive potentials for women's rights, and the legitimacy of reforming current Sharia laws.

Demystifying Sharianization in Nigeria also involves critiques of the current class and gender bias in content and implementation. The poor have been the most subjected to harsh punishments. There have been fewer convictions of men than of women for adultery or fornication. Moreover, men convicted of violent sexual offenses, such as rape and sexual assault, have received less severe punishments (usually fines, imprisonment, or acceptance of pleas of illness and insanity), despite the stronger punishments available in the Sharia penal codes that are routinely meted out for consensual sex outside marriage. Women have clearly been discriminated against. Judges have ignored or dismissed women's allegations of rape and coercion in *zina* cases. Charges of adultery/fornication brought against women used different and discriminatory standards of evidence than those used for men—that of pregnancy outside marriage.

Bringing this information and criticism to public discussion debunks the claim that any critique of Sharianization is tantamount to being anti-Islam. It also lays the basis for demanding reform of the Sharia acts and Sharia penal codes, instead of accepting conservative and retrograde versions.

Working Together to Defend Women's Rights

It is important in a diverse multiethnic and multireligious state like Nigeria to work across communities, as well as within Muslim communities.

Hence the Coalition for Protection of Women's Rights in Secular, Customary and Religious Laws and the Sharia Stakeholders Group include national NGOs and smaller regionally based NGOs from different parts of the country; women's and human rights NGOs and activists; and Muslims, Christians, and secularists, who work together on the *zina* cases.

It has become clear in these coalitions that most NGOs and individual activists, whether or not they have Muslim backgrounds or any direct involvement with Muslim communities, are not demanding the repeal of all religious laws. They chose this strategy with varying motivations. For many, it is pragmatism. In the context of highly politicized religious debate, in which there is a siege mentality and religious laws have long been in existence, demanding repeal would be ineffective if not counterproductive.[30] For others, it is that the beliefs of legislators always influence laws, regardless of whether or not they are formally designated religious laws. The problems arise not around whether laws have content that is legitimated on religious grounds, but on whether laws promote or violate rights. For example, consequent to the alignment of the Republican Party with the Christian right, the Bush administration has attempted to prohibit abortion both in the United States through such means as banning so-called partial birth abortions and internationally through the gag rule. Both the current versions of Nigerian Sharianisation and the current policies and legislative efforts of the Bush administration restrict women's reproductive and sexual rights. Both are clearly influenced by religious beliefs. Nonetheless one is designated religious, the other is formally secular. Furthermore, the assumption that secular laws are necessarily progressive does not survive a cursory examination of laws, for patriarchy has been around a long time and influences secular as well as religious thought. Hence, it is the content of laws that are critical, rather than their formal designation as religious or secular (see Imam 2000, WLUML 2003a). The Coalition for the Protection of Women's Rights has therefore focused on explaining and mobilizing cross-community support for women whose rights are violated. The coalition also takes up the defense of women under customary and secular laws simultaneously with the defense of the *zina* cases, in order to emphasize the similarities underlying discrimination in different contexts and systems of laws.

Other collective initiatives include: the Transition Monitoring Group, which was set up initially to monitor election processes in Nigeria; BAOBAB's bridge-building workshops; the Network for Police Reform in Nigeria; and the Legislative Coalition against Violence against Women, which has submitted a bill protecting against gender-based violence to the federal legislature. Crucially, these coalitions have drawn upon international human rights law and discourses while simultaneously pointing out that they are not solely the domain of the West. For instance, eleven of the twenty-two countries that initiated what became CEDAW are Muslim, seven of which are Muslim majority states, while the other eleven are Third World or Eastern European countries. Hence CEDAW should be seen as also reflecting their concerns, rather than just those of the West. Indeed, the United States is one of the few countries in the world that has refused to ratify CEDAW. Rights-based NGOs in Nigeria have worked collaboratively with and across different rights discourses—borrowing, combining selectively, and reconstructing different elements of them to mobilize multifarious communities in support of rights development and protections.

Developments since 1999

Since the passing of the Sharia Acts and penal codes in late 1999, several developments indicate the effectiveness of these approaches. As the critics predicted and continue to make clear, the political maneuverings behind the Sharia Acts were not intended to create a just and peaceful Muslim society. There have been few attempts to collect the charity tithe and use it for social development and welfare of the poor. Prosecutions and convictions under the Sharia penal codes have overwhelmingly been of poor and nonliterate women and men. Except in Kano state, the Sharia penal codes have not prescribed severe punishments for crimes like embezzlement, and theft convictions have been primarily for stolen bicycles or cows. Those in positions of power who embezzle millions in public resources have been untouched.

Within Muslim communities, many people have become publicly critical about Sharianization. Muslim women continue to defy the religious right and vigilantes by dressing as they see fit, going outside their homes, and working outside the household. As the appeals succeed, and none has yet been lost, those convicted under the new Sharia penal codes are increasingly and publicly seeking help, and human rights activists no longer have to persuade them that appealing is acceptable. This is in marked contrast to the first case, of Bariya Magazu, when BAOBAB activists spent weeks persuading her parents, other relatives, and village opinion leaders to appeal, and had difficulty finding lawyers willing to take her case. Indeed, communities now openly support and defend victims. For instance, Safiya Tungar-Tudu's fellow villagers hid her from BAOBAB activists offering legal support until they were convinced that she would be helped rather than harmed by these strangers. Similarly, the head of Amina Lawal's village warned local vigilantes against taking direct action and to allow the legal process to stand. Clearly people are feeling more empowered to fight rights violations.

The judgment in Ms. Lawal's case is important, adding to the prior successful appeals. Although it sets a legal precedent only in Katsina state,[31] the definitions of *zina* are exactly the same in the twelve states with new Sharia penal codes, which makes it difficult to ignore. The majority position was sweeping, accepting every single ground of the appeal. The Katsina State Sharia Court of Appeal expressly departed from the dominant view of the Maliki school by holding that pregnancy outside of marriage is not evidence of *zina*, thus confirming the arguments of the activists on the existence and permissibility of diversity in Muslim jurisprudence. The court also upheld standard Muslim jurisprudence that confessions need to be voluntary and repeated, and that they can be withdrawn at any point right up to the commencement of the sentence. In so doing, the court implied that the prosecution needed to provide proof in the form of four witnesses of good character to the act of intercourse for women as well as men, which is a standard position in Muslim jurisprudence and a criterion difficult to achieve.

The judgment undercuts the religious right and vigilantes who routinely report women with children born outside of marriage, and their partners, to the police and insist that the police charge them on this ground alone. It also restores the onus of proof to the prosecution, and thus removes the discrimination against women that was evident in the prosecution of the cases. Although *zina* remains on the books, the overturn of Ms. Lawal's conviction has made new *zina* charges less likely (there have been no new ones in the eighteen months since), and should make it extremely unlikely that prosecutions would be successful.

The challenge to the exclusive claim of authenticity and legitimacy of the religious right's version of Muslim law has also had positive effects, as more people are now aware of the historicity and culture, class, and gender specificity of particular provisions in Muslim laws, the existence of progressive alternatives, and the legitimacy of dissent and diversity in Muslim discourses. More and more Muslims are speaking up critically about Sharianization. For example, Kano state attempted to pass a bill requiring veiling for women that would have used different colors of head coverings to indicate their marital status and, thus, presumed sexual status and availability. It was defeated by a combination of direct protests by Kano women (an extremely rare phenomenon where women are widely secluded) and representations from the traditional conservative *ulema* (religious scholars). The *ulema* had not been involved in passing the acts, but had hitherto refrained from criticizing them publicly. Even the conservative religious Federation of Muslim Women's Associations of Nigeria has recently criticized Sharianization (*ThisDay* 2003), after flatly refusing to do so at its inception in 1999. Leading personalities are also criticizing Sharianization publicly (for instance Uwais 2002). Indeed in August 2003, Muslim progressives engaged for the first time in direct public debate with members of the religious right.[32] Significantly, many Muslim critics of Sharianization are now willing to be publicly identified and to make their views widely known. In this climate, even some members of the religious right have conceded a need for reform not only of faulty implementation but also of content.

There are also hopeful developments in non-Muslim communities, which constitute 50 to 60 percent of Nigeria's population. Initially, they expressed the same sort of wholesale outrage against the notion of Sharia and presented many of the stereotypes about Muslim laws as unchanging and uniformly strict, with "barbaric" and "savage" punishments that are always misogynistic. Over time, coverage in the southern-based national press has remained critical of what has been happening in Sharianization, but with fewer of the stereotypical attitudes that could be used to justify further backlash in the Muslim communities. This is in part because of the increased willingness of the Nigerian press to carry articles of informed opinion and dissent from within the Muslim community about Sharia law. The Nigerian press has also covered criticisms of Sharianization and of the religious right by Nigerian women's and human rights activists, and reported their activities in defending rights using more nuanced language.[33] A majority of Nigerian activists agree that it is important for communities to mount internal critiques of rights violations and construct public debates around the nature of rights.

The International Arena

Gabeba Baderoon noted that "with the rise of 24-hour international news organizations based in the United States and Britain, a powerful, though unarticulated geography is at work in world news. There is a symbolic center from which a gaze is aimed with disembodied equanimity at the rest of the globe" (Baderoon 2002). That would explain why the international media coverage of Sharianization in Nigeria and of Ms. Lawal's case in particular has been so remarkably consistent. News stories and commentaries have focused overwhelmingly on the cruel, inhuman, and barbaric punishments of Islamic law. The media have focused on international human rights organizations' demands for a pardon to save Ms. Lawal's life, Muslim-Christian conflict in Nigeria, and graphic descriptions of stonings to death as defined in Iran and other places, since there have been none in Nigeria.

There have also been thousands of petitions in many languages, aimed at defending Ms. Lawal (more than 31,300 hits in a Google search). The majority of those in English or French followed the same themes as the international media, but went several steps further to assert quite inaccurately that the Supreme Court of Nigeria had upheld Ms. Lawal's conviction and therefore that the carrying out of the sentence was imminent. The most widely circulated petition also included false claims that similar petitions had led to pardons in previous cases in Nigeria, asking viewers to sign on to an Amnesty International petition, which several million people did. Petitions also called for the president of Nigeria to veto or repeal the Sharia Acts and to pardon Ms. Lawal. The Nigerian NGOs supporting Ms. Lawal and others viewed these petitions as unhelpful and issued open letters asking the petitioners to desist (see BAOBAB 2003a and b).

Since Ms. Lawal's acquittal, the majority of international news stories and petition Web sites have credited the successful appeal to international media coverage and protests (and sometimes they are given the sole credit, as in CNN News September 25, 2003). They have also diminished the significance of the judgment acquitting her by describing it as merely technical.

International solidarity is important to local rights struggles, and international campaigns and petitions have the potential to be spectacularly successful, as in the case of Zara Yacoub in Tchad in the mid-1990s.[34] However, how solidarity is demonstrated is critical and must depend on the specific context. In the case of Ms. Lawal and several others, the NGOs supporting the appeals felt that huge (and often stereotypical) media coverage and international petitions would not be appropriate. It seems that very little notice of this was taken, however, given the plethora of protests, petitions, and campaigns, not a few issued by international human rights organizations. Although the concern expressed worldwide has been heartwarming, how it was expressed sometimes hindered the actual protection and defense of women's and human rights in Nigeria.

There is considerable overlap between the orientalist gaze of the international media and the self-presentation of the religious right as the sole possessors of the legitimate position on Islam and Muslim laws. Both present "true" Islam as universally strict and controlling of women, with harsh inflexible punishments. And both hold that only those who hold these views are true believers entitled to talk on behalf of Islam and Muslim communities. People with other views are labeled as moderates or Westernized, with doubts raised about their legitimacy or devoutness. The international media and protests have largely ignored the existence of considerable dissent among Muslims about the nature and content of Muslim laws. They have also tended to ignore or downplay protests and campaigns in Nigeria and the existence of previous successful appeals in the Sharia system. This tendency to treat the Muslim world as monolithic only helps to legitimize the religious right's monopolistic claim to speak for all Muslims and to delegitimize the assertions of progressive scholars and rights activists. The use of terms like "inhumane" and "barbaric" to describe Islamic law, without acknowledging the challenges of Muslims, may have led to soul searching among Muslims and as well as shocked outrage among non-Muslims. But it also led many Muslims, including those concerned about the *zina* victims, to feel defensive about Islam and made it easier for the Muslim religious right to dismiss protests as biased against Islam.

International protests may also be dismissed as hypocritical. The response of many Nigerians has frequently been to ask why people in the West are apparently so concerned about the life of one Muslim woman in Nigeria, when they have been killing large numbers of Muslim men, women, and children and are responsible for the horrors of war and its aftermath in Iraq. They point to the war in Afghanistan and ask why, if one concern was women's status under the Taliban, are women still at risk, and why U.S. funds promised to support girls' education, the women's ministry, and programs to protect and promote women's rights are still not forthcoming. Trying to point out that there is a difference between governments and their people is hard in the face of inaccurate and insensitive petitions issued not by the state but by individuals.

The insensitive language of many of the petitions and international news stories gave rise to real fears that the religious right and vigilantes would use this as an excuse to evade the appeal process and take direct action against Ms. Lawal and her defenders. In the case of Bariya Magazu in 2000, the Zamfara state administration implemented her sentence of 100 lashes, notifying her only the night before, precisely to spite international protests and national demonstrations and forestall the appeal process. The possibility that insensitive language would inadvertently fuel a Muslim religious right backlash manifested in rioting directed at non-Muslims was also a realistic fear, on the basis of previous instances such as the rioting over the Miss World contest in 2002.

Calls for President Obasanjo to prohibit Sharia punishments and pardon Ms. Lawal were misdirected, as a federal president has no authority to veto state legislation or to pardon someone convicted in state courts. These calls also ignored the possible violent repercussions if a "born again" Christian were to attempt to veto Muslim laws, even if he had the authority to do so.[35] Thus, these petitions did not support the work of establishing due process and respect for rights in law that Nigerian women's and human rights groups have been working to achieve.

Finally, there was an insistence on the importance and effectiveness of international campaigns and media coverage. These ignored the prior existence of local activism, protest, and campaigns, the facts of previous successful appeals in the Sharia system, and that no pardons have been granted or needed. The clear implication is that it is the pressure and power of external foreign interests that is important and not the strengthening of local cultures of rights. However, asserting the priority of external pressure for defending rights is not likely to convince the community of the correctness of those asserted rights. On the contrary, they tend to feel that foreign values are being imposed upon them and to resist such perceived imposition. If women's human rights abuses are not to be continued at concrete everyday levels, then it is the local community that must be convinced not to accept injustices, even if those injustices are perpetrated in the name of Islam or other strongly held beliefs.

Much more helpful were relations with such organizations as the international solidarity network Women Living Under Muslim Laws (WLUML) or the International Association of Women Judges (IAWJ). From the first, despite the misgivings of some of its activists, WLUML respected the Nigerian groups' request not to circulate an international alert and used its networks to develop arguments that aided the successful appeals. WLUML also continually stressed and gradually convinced its partners in Nigeria of the need to provide information internationally. WLUML then helped to craft and disseminate such messages by posting them on its Web site. Similarly, when alerted to the inaccuracies and dangers of the petitions, the IAWJ circulated appeals not to support them, asked how they could support the defense efforts, publicized material, and helped raise funds to cover the legal costs of the defenses.

Following BAOBAB's open letter asking for a cessation of the international petitions, both the Amnesty International Secretariat and Amnesty's U.S. country section responded, issuing press releases distancing themselves from the petitions and supporting the local groups. Indeed, following the appeals not to sign onto the petitions, many organizations and individuals contacted the Nigerian defense teams to check out subsequent petitions. Several others also posted the open letters on their Web sites, thus helping to counter the damage done by the inaccurate petitions. A few individuals and organizations sent donations to support the work. Throughout the period, sensitively written letters helped to move discussion forward.[36] Many people responded to the early appeal to help craft arguments and provide material on *zina* and the successes and failures of strategies and tactics in other countries. These examples of international solidarity were not always uncritical; however, they relied on dialogue and negotiation when there were disagreements over analysis and strategy—and some shifts of local and international strategy and policy did take place.

Strategies for Moving Forward

Using local structures and mechanisms (judicial appeals, informal dispute resolution, mock tribunals organized by local NGOs, networks of sympathizers, and campaigns) to resist retrogressive laws or interpretations of laws and the forces behind them is the priority. Doing so strengthens local counterdiscourses and often carries greater legitimacy than outside pressure. Further, using local structures and discourses can really address the local political power struggles that are behind the political use of religions and ethnicities.

Having established strong defenses against the prosecution of *zina* offenses, Nigerian women's and human rights groups recognize the necessity of moving forward on reforming the laws. This requires expanding public education on Muslim laws, juristic opinions and *ijtihad*, and debate on the contents of laws. Reforming laws also requires continuing the painstaking work of building solidarity among a variety of actors to develop shared understandings and common strategies and platforms for women's and human rights.

Local groups need to find ways to influence the mass media, especially the international media, to provide coverage that is both more accurate and nuanced and therefore less likely to provoke religious right backlash, feed Islamophobia, or contribute to the refusals of those erring on the side of being too culturally sensitive to admit that rights violations exist. Similarly, the willingness and ability of local groups to negotiate with and influence the strategies of international organizations must be strengthened.

Informed and respectful international solidarity is needed. Those outside must be both more respectful of the analyses and agency of those activists most closely involved in the issues on the ground, and therefore more knowledgeable about the situation, and of the wishes of the women and men who are directly suffering rights violations. To be informed, activists must answer a number of questions: Would a particular response make things better or worse? For which individuals or groups of people? How? Would another sort of response be more effective? Is what is being requested feasible and legal? What sort of language would be most appropriate? Are the facts presented accurate? Is there enough information that the specifics are not lost in over-generalization?[37]

Informed and respectful solidarity also means finding out about the groups involved at national and local levels (and internationally). This is particularly the case when there may be more than one group advocating different things. Who are the groups? What are their past histories? What constituencies do they work with or represent? What areas of rights do they work in? Why are they asking for a given kind of strategy or support? What are their reputations?[38] Respectful solidarity further requires recognizing that while neither locals nor internationals can automatically be assumed to have a monopoly on the best analysis or the most effective strategy possible, it is locals who have to live with the consequences of any wrong or mistaken decisions.

Women's and human rights activists and organizations must campaign at their own local levels as well as in the international arena. Those who are from or based in the more powerful countries have particular problems. The foreign policies of their governments have consequences for their credibility and therefore effectiveness as human rights critics and advocates in the international arena. Many, and not only in the religious right, dismissed criticism of human rights violations from individuals and organizations in the United States or United Kingdom because of those governments' war on Iraq.

The mass demonstrations against the Iraq war in Canada and the United Kingdom were not well reported in the international media, nor, in the case of the United States, in the national media, which reinforces the importance of working with the mass media. Furthermore, the control of more and more media outlets by fewer and fewer corporations plays a large part in the lack of diversity of coverage and of opinion in the media. It is necessary to be concerned about media control and to support alternative media.

Westerners and others from powerful countries may find it as effective to restrain their own governments from foreign policies that help create and support the conditions for power and credibility of the religious right as to criticize the actions of the religious right directly. The policies of international financial institutions such as the World Bank, the International Monetary Fund or, increasingly, the World Trade Organization far too often result in worsening economic conditions for most people—conditions in which more and more people are willing to hear and be influenced by the religious right. Ironically, the growth of religious identity politics and the religious right is aided by private foundation and/or government support for the "charity work" of religious groups. The charity work of providing schooling, food, orphanages, and so on is needed because of these very economic policies, but gratitude has often translated into leveraging support for the legitimacy of the religious right (WLUML 2003b). It is heartening to know that human rights organizations have begun to focus more on economic rights and to consider cooperating with social movements such as that around the World Social Forum. Campaigning for governments and media to support international policies that sustain economic justice and rights would give hope worldwide so that poverty and uncertainty do not continue to be conditions in which religious right sentiments and actors find support for discourses and laws that violate rights.

Notes

1. I am grateful to the anonymous reviewers of the draft, who helped me clarify this paper.
2. This is done in the name of cultural relativity or cultural sensitivity in the West, or by invoking authenticity and tradition elsewhere.
3. To admit European/Western culture as a dominant influence in historical construction, language, and modes of formulation is not to concede sole influence. As one anonymous reviewer pointed out, "many countries/civilizations/cultures/scholars have made and are making contributions to this tradition. There is a powerful historical argument that can be made, for example, that Islamic law played a huge part in influencing the early development of international humanitarian law."
4. While recognizing that the hitherto privileged may object anyway.
5. For instance, in the assumption that life imprisonment is not inhumane or constitute torture, but whipping is. For peoples with a nomadic history, it may well be the reverse. See Sanusi 2003 for more polarizing examples; see also Merry 2003 in relation to women's rights in Hawaii.
6. The Nigerian term coined to describe the passing of the Sharia Acts, but which is also linked with the notion that Sharia is a religiously required way of life and not limited to any actual legal text.
7. It should be noted that although northern Nigeria is often referred to as Muslim, at least two states in the north are dominantly Christian. Several others are split evenly between Muslims and adherents of other religions. There is also a strong Muslim presence in the southwest of Nigeria, whose population is divided roughly 50:50 between Muslims and others (mostly Christian). Sharia Acts have not been

passed in the southwest states so far, but there have been voluntary adoptions of the same content as the Sharia penal codes.

8. The full name of Izala is the Jamaatu Izalat al-Bid'ah wa Iqamat al-Sunnah (Group for the eradication of innovation and establishment of tradition).

9. As yet, there are no reliable figures on total numbers of convictions of whom or for which offenses, or the numbers of people victimized by vigilantes, but see Imam 2004 for a brief discussion.

10. I deal here only with those which are more or less directly relevant to the defense in *zina* cases.

11. Previously sodomy was prohibited, but not specifically homosexuality. The new Sharia criminal legislation follows this. However, the new Sharia penal codes also explicitly prohibit lesbianism for the first time.

12. Following the principle that "as you have done to others, so shall be done unto you" in assaults and killings, for example.

13. Where the victim or his/her family may choose to accept fines from the offender in lieu of their being punished by the state.

14. Nevertheless, on several occasions vigilantes have imposed their version of Sharia on non-Muslims. In one case in Kano state the vigilantes were prosecuted (*The Guardian*, January 10, 2001). In other states however, state governments have not taken action to rein in vigilante impositions on non-Muslims or claims that Sharia must apply throughout "Muslim territory."

15. This is a risky proposition, given that some Muslim laws make apostasy punishable by death. Although this has not been enacted in Nigeria, vigilantes are unlikely to be halted by that fact.

16. General secular law in Nigeria maintains the death penalty for capital offenses.

17. Criminal offenses are not on either the concurrent or exclusive legislative lists, which divide subjects of legislation between state and federal authority. In Nigeria's federal structure, the state has residual powers of legislation.

18. The Katsina Sharia Court of Appeal held that pregnancy outside marriage does not constitute evidence of *zina*. Nor does a confession made in front of a judge without legal representation (*Lawal Kurami v. the State*).

19. Human Rights Law Service's documents, including the two subsequent appeals, can be found at www.hurilaws.org.

20. The so-called Sharia states are the twelve states where Sharia Acts and penal codes have been passed, although Sharia for personal status is also available in another six states and in the Federal Capital Territory.

21. That is, they protect each other equally—men are not the protectors of dependent, weak women. Likewise, the use of the term "friends" implies an egalitarian relationship, not superiority or inferiority.

22. Like the Bible and the Torah, the Qu'ran counsels slaves to obey their masters wholeheartedly. However, the Qu'ran also explicitly praises freeing slaves as a means of attaining Paradise. In the early centuries of Islam, it was legal to own slaves in the Muslim world. Muslim jurisprudence developed conditions and limits (such as that the child of a slave woman and a free man is free, that slaves are permitted to buy their freedom, that Muslims could not be made slaves, that the free can only be made slaves during a jihad in which they refuse to convert, and

so on). Presently, no Muslim majority state, whether secular or religious, allows slavery.

23. The events in the life and the sayings of the Prophet, often collected in a series of anecdotes referred to as *hadith*. The most well-known collection is Sahih Buhari.

24. Including the founder of one of the four accepted schools of Sunni *fiqh*.

25. The Maliki school is dominant in North and West Africa. The Hanafi school is influential in Lower Egypt, South and West Asia (including Bangladesh and India). Shafi is strong in East Africa and Southeast Asia, including Indonesia (the largest Muslim state). Hanbali law (Wahhabi) is found in Saudi Arabia. Shi'a Islam is found mostly in Iran and Iraq.

26. Nor do a substantial minority of scholars within the Maliki tradition.

27. Such as the doctrine of *shubha*—if there is any doubt, avoid conviction.

28. These workshops have now been extended to West Africa, at the express request of women's rights activists in Mali, Senegal, Gambia, Liberia, Sierra Leone, Ghana, and Benin.

29. The nom de plume of a Muslim woman lawyer who chooses to remain anonymous. She has published a series of articles in the newspaper *ThisDay*.

30. By contrast, in Senegal, where the population is 95 percent Muslim, no strong siege mentality or politicization of Muslim religious identity vis-à-vis other religious communities exists. So an attempt by the Muslim religious right in 2003 to reform the family code in religious conservative terms was defeated by a coalition of Muslim secularists, Muslim progressives, women's and democratic rights groups, and Catholic groups.

31. And there are also (contested) views that Sharia does not recognize case precedents.

32. International Conference on Sharia Penal and Family Law in Nigeria in the Muslim World, Abuja, August 2003.

33. For instance, in 2001 *ThisDay* headlined one story "Nigerian Woman Wins Award for Anti-Sharia Campaign," that is, it used terms most likely to damage a reasoned critique of the Sharia acts from within Muslim discourses. Despite protest, *ThisDay* did not apologize. However, it followed subsequently with articles explaining the nature of the campaign and with more nuanced and less stereotypical coverage.

34. Yacoub was the subject of a death *fatwa* (legal opinion) following her video against female genital mutilation. After consultation and with her permission, an international letter writing campaign to the president of Tchad was launched by WLUML (Women Living Under Muslim Laws), which she credits with having saved her and others' lives (Hoodfar and Pazira 2000).

35. Although there were other steps that the Obasanjo administration might have taken, rather than hoping that the issue would go away by itself (see Imam 2004).

36. Hajiya Aisha Ismail, then minister for women's affairs, remarked how helpful she had found a letter from Shirkat Gah (a Pakistani NGO) in her remonstrances with the governor of Zamfara state over Bariya Magazu (Ismail 2001).

37. Hoodfar and Pazira (2000) give a concise introduction to issues around campaigning and solidarity.

38. This can be daunting, but checking their Web sites (if they have them) and the Web sites of groups such as WLUML (www.wluml.org), Women's Human Rights Net (www.whrnet.org) or Women's Learning Partnership (www.learningpartnership.org) can help—all these are international networks of women's rights organizations and/or individuals.

References

Amin, A.R.A. Noor. 2000. "The Evolution of Legal Thought in Islam." In Muslim Women's Research and Action Forum, eds., *The Need for Ijtihad or Intellectual Reasoning,* 23–78. Colombo: Muslim Women's Research and Action Forum.

An-Na'im, Abdullahi. 1998. "Shari'ah and Positive Legislation: Is an Islamic State Possible or Viable?" Paper presented at Professor Noel Coulson Memorial Lecture, School of Oriental and African Studies, University of London, December 7.

Anwar, Zainah. 2004. "Islamisation and Its Impact on Laws and the Law-making Process in Malaysia," In Ayesha Imam, Jenny Morgan, and Nira Yuval-Davis, eds., *Warning Signs of Fundamentalisms*, 71–78. London: Women Living Under Muslim Laws. An earlier version can be found at: http://www.whrnet.org/fundamentalism/doc/doc-wsfmeeting-2002.html.

Baderoon, Gabeba. 2004. "Revelation and Religion: Representations of Gender and Islam in Media, Recalling 11 September 2001 from a South African View." Presented at the Conference on Warning Signs of Fundamentalisms: International Solidarity Network Women Living Under Muslim Laws (WLUML), London, November, 2002. http://www.whrnet.org/fundamentalism/doc/doc-wsfmeeting-2002.html.

BAOBAB for Women's Human Rights. 2003a. "Please Stop the International Amina Lawal Protest Letter Campaigns." www.wluml.org and www.baobabwomen.org.

———. 2003b. "Not So—Re: Amina Lawal Set to Be Stoned." www.wluml.org and www.baobabwomen.org.

———. Forthcoming. *Paralegal Training Modules.* Lagos: BAOBAB.

Cabral, Amilcar. 1973. *Return to the Source.* New York: Monthly Review Press.

Constitutional Rights Project. 2000. *The Place of Women under Sharia.* Lagos: Constitutional Rights Project.

Ezeilo, J. N., and A. A. Afolabi, eds. 2003. *Sharia and Women's Human Rights in Nigeria: Strategies for Action.* Lagos: WARDC/WACOL.

Guardian, The. January 10, 2001 (Nigeria).

Hélie-Lucas, M. 1993. "Women and Development in 'Islamic' Countries." Paper presented at Conference on Women, Islam and Development, organized by the Netherlands Ministry of Foreign Affairs. The Hague, September 15.

Hoodfar, H., and N. Pazira. 2000. *Building Civil Societies: A Guide for Social and Political Activism.* Grabels, France: WLUML.

Ibrahim, J. 1989. "The State, Accumulation, and Democratic Forces in Nigeria." Paper presented at C.E.A.N., Université de Bordeaux I.

Imam, A. 1994. "'If You Won't Do These Things for Me, I Won't Do Seclusion for You': Local and Regional Constructions of Seclusion Ideologies and Practices in Kano, Northern Nigeria." Doctoral thesis, Social Anthropology, University of Sussex at Brighton.

————. 1998. "Engendering Universal Human Rights." In *A Human Rights Message,* 93–100. Sweden: Ministry of Foreign Affairs. http://www.si.se/eng/elinks.html.

————. 2000. "Women's Rights in Muslim Laws (Sharia)." In *The Place of Women under Sharia,* 16–31. Lagos: Constitutional Rights Project.

————. 2004. "Women, Muslim Laws and Human Rights in Nigeria." Africa Program Occasional Paper 2. Washington, D.C.: Woodrow Wilson International Center.

————. 2004. "Fighting the Political (Ab)Use of Religion in Nigeria: BAOBAB for Women's Human Rights, Allies and Others." In Ayesha Imam, Jenny Morgan, and Nira Yuval-Davis, eds., *Warning Signs of Fundamentalisms,* 125–134. London: Women Living Under Muslim Laws. An earlier version can be found at www. whrnet.org/fundamentalism/doc/doc-wsfmeeting-2002.html.

Ismail, Aisha. 2001. Personal communication, Abuja, March 27.

Lawal Kurami v. the State. 2003. Katsina State Sharia Court of Appeal. September 25.

Merry, S. E. 2003. "Constructing a Global Law? Violence against Women and the Human Rights System." *Law and Social Enquiry* (December).

Mohammed, A. S., S. H. Adamu, and A. Abba. 1999. "Human Living Conditions and Reforms of Legal Systems: The Talakawa and the Issue of the Shari'ah in Contemporary Nigeria." Paper presented to conference on the Shari'ah and the Constitutional Process, Zaria, November 17–18.

Nyamu-Musembi, C. 2002. "Towards an Actor-Oriented Perspective on Human Rights." IDS Working Paper 169. Brighton: Institute of Development Studies. www.ids.ac.uk/ids/bookshop/wp/wp169.pdf.

Olukoshi, A., ed. 1993. *The Politics of Structural Adjustment in Nigeria.* London: James Currey and Heinemann.

Osaghae, E. E. 1995. "Structural Adjustment and Ethnicity in Nigeria." Research Report no. 98. Uppsala: Nordika Afrikainstitutet.

Peters, R., and M. Barends. 2001. "The Reintroduction of Islamic Criminal Law in Northern Nigeria—A Study Conducted on Behalf of the European Commission." Lagos: European Commission.

Sanusi, S. L. 2003. "Democracy, Rights and Islam: Theory, Epistemology and the Quest for Synthesis." Paper presented at international conference on Shari'ah Penal and Family Law in Nigeria and the Muslim World. International Human Rights Law Group, Abuja, August 5–7.

————. 2004. "Fundamentalist Groups and the Nigerian Legal System: Some Reflections." In Ayesha Imam, Jenny Morgan, and Nira Yuval-Davis, eds., *Warning Signs of Fundamentalisms,* 79–82. London: Women Living Under Muslim Laws. An earlier version can be found at www.whrnet.org/fundamentalism/doc/doc-wsfmeeting-2002.html.

ThisDay. 2001. "Nigerian Woman Wins Award for Anti-Sharia Campaign." http://allafrica.com/stories/200205220383.html.

————. 2003. "'Why We Are Not Ripe for Sharia,' Says President of Moslem Women Association." August 17. www.thisdayonline.com.

Uwais, M. 2002. "The Impact of Sharia in Nigeria, Its Development and Strategies Adopted against Its Misapplication." Paper presented at Association of Women in Development conference, Guadalajara, September.

WACOL. 2003. *Safiyyatu's Case.* Enugu: WACOL. Court documents translated from Hausa by Ibrahim Ladan.

WLUML. 2003a. *Knowing Our Rights: Women, Family, Laws and Customs in the Muslim World.* Lahore: Women Living Under Muslim Laws.

————. 2003b. "With Her Feet on the Ground: Women, Religion and Development in Muslim Communities." http://www.wluml.org/english/newsfulltxt.shtml?cmd [157]=x–157–20149%20&cmd[189]=x–189–20149.

Yawuri, A. M. 2003. "Issues in Defending Safiyyatu Husseini and Amina Lawal." Paper presented at international conference on Shari'ah Penal and Family Law in Nigeria and the Muslim World. International Human Rights Law Group, Abuja, August 5–7.

Uganda

HIV/AIDS and Reproductive Health

LISA ANN RICHEY

In one of the large conference rooms at the Kampala Sheraton I sat together with Ugandan Ministry of Health officials, most of the Ugandan Bureau of Statistics, representatives from non-governmental organizations (NGOs), international donor agencies, and service providers. We were gathered to hear findings from the Ugandan Demographic and Health Survey (UDHS) on indicators of population, health, and nutrition. After the usual official welcomes, the mission director from the organization that funded the survey reported findings that she termed "disturbing trends." The most prominent of these was that, although the overall prevalence rate of modern contraception had increased, there had been no decline in fertility, contributing significantly to Uganda's high population growth rate. According to the speaker, the "serious implications of rapid population growth" were linked to poverty, infant and child mortality, and immunization rates. Other disturbing trends in Uganda's health data were briefly mentioned, but the list—malaria, childhood diseases, poor antenatal care and unsafe deliveries, and girls' education—did not include HIV/AIDS. Although Uganda has been known for its AIDS "success," data still show that 5 percent of the population is living with the disease. The multiple linkages between HIV/AIDS and reproductive health were not part of the day's discussion. Findings were presented chapter by chapter, thus HIV/AIDS was discussed only when its time came in chapter 11, the last presentation of the day. Today, reproductive health activists have reoriented debates away from population problems and toward women's health and rights. How then did "overpopulation"—not AIDS prevention or treatment, or women's empowerment, or the lack of health care—command the center of discussion at this meeting on reproductive health?

Uganda has been presented as the first African success story in the fight against HIV/AIDS, and boasts one of the most effective women's movements in Africa. This chapter examines the relationship between global reproductive health and AIDS discourses in Uganda to understand how combating the AIDS epidemic and promoting women's reproductive health and rights intermingle, compete, and/or complement each other in an African setting. Given the outspoken leadership on HIV/AIDS, we might expect that official attention would be expanded to include issues of women's reproductive health and rights, making for a strong national program to implement the Cairo framework. Yet Uganda has experienced no decline in fertility rates, infant mortality rates have risen, and access to reproductive health services is limited. In comparing the policy responses in the two areas, we see strong national leadership on AIDS, but no coherent vision on reproductive health. The analysis is based on available demographic and health data and on interviews with informants from government, donor organizations, and NGOs conducted during four months of fieldwork in 2002 and one month in 2004. The Ugandan success in HIV/AIDS policy has been important for its donors, and international assistance is critical to health care provision in Uganda. However, the implementation of reproductive health has been limited, and its non-AIDS related components have been largely unsuccessful. This chapter argues that the future of successful reproductive health policy and continuing success in AIDS policy will be shaped by the increasing demand for AIDS treatment which, like other components of the reproductive health agenda, will require investments in the health care delivery system.

The current success in Uganda's struggle against AIDS is being read to suggest that policy does make a difference, even in changing intimate behavior, and that leadership is an important factor, or perhaps *the* important factor, in distinguishing Uganda's program from those in other African countries. But if Ugandan leadership on HIV/AIDS, arguably *the* reproductive health issue, is so successful, then why do we not see similar levels of success in other aspects of reproductive health and rights? In short, it is because neither the Ugandan government nor civil society groups, including feminist ones, have made it a top priority, and donors seem to remain more concerned about fertility control than about women's empowerment or providing other types of reproductive health services.

Uganda's Political Background

Uganda was once known as the pearl of Africa, but British colonial rule pitted the southern-based Baganda group against other ethnic groups, especially those in the north. Unequal regional development, ethnic favoritism, and the imposition of a bureaucratic authoritarian colonial system, unsurprisingly, did not give way to a democratic or accountable political system at independence in 1962. Politics revolved around constituencies based on religion, ethnicity, language, or region, and for more than two decades, conflict was the norm. The country experienced five official coups d'état in the twenty years following independence. The violence that drove out or killed off Uganda's politically disfavoured ethnic minorities under the regimes of Obote and Idi Amin was long regarded as the standard by which other African political crises were measured. After the military victory of the National Resistance Army, the very first official act of the government was to suspend party politics on the grounds that party competition exacerbated ethnic conflict in Uganda (Goetz 2003b). Ironically, Uganda's violent political history and its conflict-weary society may have contributed to a broader political mandate for Museveni's social agenda around HIV/AIDS.

The "no-party" government of the National Resistance Movement (NRM) has brought political stability to most of the country (although the ongoing civil war in Uganda's north is a frequently overlooked exception). Yet over time, the NRM has concentrated power in the hands of its leadership to the exclusion of dissenting groups. The NRM leadership claims to have formed a grass-roots movement—generated from above. Still, Ugandans and international donors appear to accept the stability/democracy trade-off of Museveni's "broad-based" governance. The NRM has held several elections since 1986, but no real competition against Museveni has ever been allowed. Most important for its international relationships, the NRM has prioritized economic growth based on neoliberal reforms that led to a significant average economic growth rate of 7.1 percent per year in the late 1990s. The economic turnaround from state control to free market, with measurably high rates of success, has provided credibility for Museveni's leadership. However, the capitalist success story has also come under scrutiny. A recent report stated that although the economy grew and poverty was reduced in the 1990s, inequality actually increased (Okidi and Mugambe 2002). Still, Museveni's charisma and pragmatism and Uganda's important role as an economic success story have led the international community to ignore red flags involving domestic human rights violations and Uganda's interference in the politics of its neighbors. Uganda's success in combating the AIDS epidemic has been an important component of ensuring that the country remains the darling of international donors.

The Ugandan Women's Movement

The Ugandan women's movement has been one of the most powerful civil society forces in national politics since the NRM takeover in 1986 (Tripp 1999, 2000, 2001; Goetz 1998). Until recently the country had a female vice president—the first in Africa—and women were appointed to key positions in government ministries, special commissions, and elsewhere, and to cabinet posts. Women's organizations were active in drafting the 1995 constitution, which includes many provisions enhancing the position of women, such as requiring a minimum of one-third female representation in local government. Also, the national parliament has been one-quarter female since the 2001 elections (Goetz 2003b) and was approximately 18 percent female from 1989 to 2001 (Tripp 2000). Uganda's female parliamentary representatives have tended to focus more than their male colleagues have on health, education, child welfare, sexual assault, and gender equity (Tripp 2000).

The international women's movement has been critical in mobilizing the push for women's rights and status in health debates internationally (Berkovitch 1999). Yet, for all its power, the Ugandan women's movement has been unable or unwilling to focus debate on reproductive and sexual health and rights nationally. One reason may be that the women's movement has not made reproductive health and rights a high-priority issue, just as population issues have been consistently disregarded by Ugandan feminists (Kirumira 1998). Another reason is the institutional constraint placed on women's activism by the NRM government. Movement politics have always been socially conservative, articulating an agenda that remains popular with the country's churches. The "no-party" system discourages any articulation of political interests outside of the movement, and women's access to politics is primarily through a system of special seats reserved for parliamentary representation of districts and an additional 30 percent of seats reserved for women in local government (Goetz 2003a).

Institutional representation for women preceded political mobilization of the women's movement in Uganda and has been used to control women's activism rather than to respond to it (Goetz 2003a). Ugandan women did not demand representation; it was granted them as a favor by Museveni's NRM government. Although the women's movement has been among the most effective political forces in Ugandan civil society, it accomplished this by sticking to a relatively conservative gender agenda, particularly on issues of sexuality. When the women's movement tried to overstep the boundaries acceptable to the NRM, by mobilizing to ensure women's property rights in new legislation on land titling and ownership in 1997, for example, it failed (Kawamara-Mishambi and Ovonji-Odida 2003). Despite its comparative strength in the African context, where civil society is generally weak and conservative on gender issues, the Ugandan women's movement has not, thus far, been an effective force for promoting reproductive health and rights.

Uganda's Policy Responses to AIDS and Reproductive Health

The Ugandan HIV/AIDS policy's success has become ubiquitous. In the early 1990s, Uganda reported the highest infection rates in the world, with an estimated 15 percent of the population living with HIV/AIDS. Yet by 2001, the country had managed to bring the prevalence down to 5 percent (Hogle 2002). The greatest declines in HIV incidence are thought to have taken place in the late 1980s and early 1990s. Figures from Uganda's National AIDS Control Programme suggest that the prevalence and incidence of HIV/AIDS are declining across all age groups and socioeconomic levels (Kirumira 2001).[1] The country hosts one of the biggest AIDS care centers in Africa south of the Sahara, the Joint Clinical Research Center in Kampala, and was among the first recipients of the World Bank's Multi-Country HIV/AIDS Program I funding.[2] Also, Uganda received funding in both rounds of the Global Fund and was the eleventh largest recipient of 130 bodies requesting funding.[3] Uganda's policies on HIV/AIDS and reproductive health follow the same blueprints as those in most other developing countries. Yet thus far, the AIDS policies have achieved far more success than have any facet of the reproductive health policies.

Reasons for Uganda's HIV/AIDS Policy Success

Uganda was one of the first countries to recognize AIDS as a major obstacle to development and to launch a multisectoral approach to combating the disease. A formal AIDS Control Programme was established in the Health Ministry in 1986, the year the NRM came to power.[4] Soon after seizing power, Museveni sent his top military officers to Cuba for military training. Several months later at a conference in Zimbabwe, Cuba's President Fidel Castro approached Museveni with the startling news that eighteen of the sixty officers had tested positive for HIV. According to the popular version of this story, Castro took him aside and said "Brother, you have a problem" (Allen 2002). This encounter provided the impetus for Museveni to place AIDS at the top of his agenda and also characterized his military approach to AIDS as a threat against which the Ugandan people must mobilize and fight.

In 1992 the Uganda AIDS Commission was established under the office of the president to act as the coordinating body for all AIDS activities in the country. Funded by major donor agencies, the Ugandan government has promoted a multipronged strategy to combat AIDS, including public information campaigns, research, voluntary testing and counseling, safe blood transfusions, school health programs, home-based care for people living with AIDS, and a broad campaign to treat STDs. In March 2000, the government published a National Strategic Framework for HIV/AIDS to reinforce the objectives of the earlier policies and to expand their scope for coordination and capacity building, in-depth surveillance and a general baseline survey of the population, and better treatment of HIV-positive Ugandans (Parkhurst 2001; Government of Uganda et al. 2000).

Three broad unwritten policies are the key elements of the country's creative response to AIDS and distinguish it from the limited capacity of other states in dealing with the epidemic: leadership, diversity of approach, and openness (Parkhurst 2001). The role of Uganda's President Museveni in speaking about AIDS as a threat to all Ugandans, calling on all groups to get involved in the fight against the disease, and thus reducing the stigma and discrimination surrounding the disease has been critical to policy successes. However, the timing and context of Museveni's actions were critical. The Ugandan population had suffered more than fifteen years of repressive rule and violence, so the takeover by Museveni and the NRM was greeted with optimism and an intense desire for change. This historical period was ripe for radical policy reform, and the population may have been uniquely ready for new statements; therefore, "few leaders could expect to have the same impact on their populations as Museveni did in 1986" (Parkhurst 2001).

Museveni's leadership on AIDS was linked to democratization and the reconstruction of local government as a means of rebuilding social cohesion in the country (De Waal 2003). When the World Bank convened two "learning events" to discuss Uganda's progress, on the premise that "optimism now exists in the fight against AIDS in sub-Saharan Africa due to the dramatic declines in HIV prevalence observed in Uganda," they placed particular importance on the country's "social cohesion" (World Bank 2001). Social cohesion is defined as "the norms and social relations embedded in the social structures of societies that enable people to coordinate action to achieve desired goals" (World Bank 2001). In the aftermath of such high political instability, social cohesion has been an important goal of the NRM government, and Museveni's leadership in communicating AIDS facts while rebuilding social cohesion was necessary for combating HIV/AIDS, while Museveni's success also enhanced social cohesion.

The second unwritten policy—diversity—refers to the variety of approaches used and the differing scales of their implementers. Messages are often tailored to very specific local clientele, and it is just this diversity that has provided "something for everyone" in the fight against AIDS. Large donor-financed international NGOs, community-based groups, church- and mosque-based projects, women's groups, farmer's groups, physicians, and many others have been responsible for implementing AIDS projects. More than 1,020 agencies were engaged in HIV/AIDS control activities, according to an official count in 1997, and approximately 60 percent of them were nongovernmental (UAC 1997, cited in Parkhurst 2001). Ugandan NGOs, such as The AIDS Support Organization (TASO), are regularly cited as models for community-based service provision.[5] Furthermore, the Ugandan state did not push any single approach too strongly and thus avoided much of the potential backlash from conservatives that might have been associated with such controversial activities as aggressive condom promotion (Parkhurst 2001).

Finally, the unwritten policy of "openness" has been a useful strategy in a variety of contexts. Kirumira (2001) points to the country's open policy toward the pandemic and "perhaps the most vigorous IEC [information, education, and communication] and program support services for HIV/AIDS prevention and control in sub-Saharan Africa." Respondents to Parkhurst's interviews described "openness" in terms of Museveni's willingness to talk about AIDS, the society's ongoing attempts to destigmatize the disease, general freedom of speech and the press, the state's acceptance of outside and international organizations, and, finally, the openness of the Ugandan economy—an issue that is critical to international donors who want to insure that their monies are managed according to neoliberal economic policies (Parkhurst 2001).[6] However, we see a quite different picture of reproductive health.

Population Policy and Consequences of the Lack of Leadership on Reproductive Health

The Ugandan state has been evasive in its population policy discussions, using its history of ethnic and religious cleavages to justify governmental inattention at the national level (Kirumira 1998). International interpretations of the "population problem" (Hartmann 1995) have influenced program efforts in Uganda, and the emphasis placed on population control by international donors has set them against some Ugandan leaders. Uganda's national family planning program dates back to the late 1950s, but Ugandan leadership has failed to see population policy as more than simply the equivalent of family planning. Some government representatives argue that Uganda has lost many people in the twenty-five years of civil unrest and the AIDS epidemic, so the population control policy is unnecessary (Kirumira 1998). The NRM government did not express enthusiastic support for the international population control policies that predated the Cairo conference, and it remains unclear how much it supports contemporary policies to promote reproductive health (Lane 1994; Presser 2000). Also, the politics of funding have led policy and program managers to support or develop programs that can attract quicker and better funding, often focusing narrowly on contraceptives instead of on broader health services (Kirumira 1998).

In 1995, however, Uganda endorsed a national population policy whose goal is "to influence the future demographic trends and patterns in desirable directions in order to improve the quality of life and standards of living of the people" (Government of Uganda 1999). This policy is supposedly being expanded to incorporate the post-Cairo vision of reproductive health. In 1999, the Ministry of Health developed a minimum reproductive health package to reflect national priorities (Ministry of Health 2001). This vision can be understood through the goals of the Reproductive Health Division of the Ministry of Health: to increase the contraceptive prevalence rate from the current 15 percent to 30 percent, to reduce the total fertility rate from 6.9 to 5.4, to increase the percentage of supervised deliveries by trained personnel from 38 percent to 50 percent, to strengthen reproductive health manpower [sic] capacity in all districts, and to improve the Health Management Information System for routine monitoring of reproductive health services in forty-five districts as well as at the national level (Reproductive Health Division 2001). Preventing or treating HIV/AIDS is conspicuously missing from these original reproductive health goals, but its absence was noted in a Reproductive Health Division publication (Ebanyat 2002).

When the 2000–2001 Uganda Demographic and Health Survey was released, it showed that the total fertility rate had remained constant at 6.9 births per woman between 1995 and 2000; this was interpreted in donor and some government circles as a signal that family planning programs were not doing enough. Anecdotally, donors in Uganda described both personal and institutional attempts to push Museveni to provide leadership on the population problem equal to that given to the HIV/AIDS epidemic.

Although fertility decline is still important to its donors, Uganda is an intriguing outlier in recent discoveries of East African fertility transition. In the late 1960s, fertility rates were similar throughout East Africa, ranging from 6.6 to 7.1. Today Kenya's fertility rate is 4.7, Tanzania's is 5.8, and Uganda's remains at nearly 7 (Vavrus and Larsen 2003).[7] Lloyd, Kaufman, and Hewett (1999) argue that Uganda and Tanzania have lower levels of contraceptive use than expected when compared with other African countries with similar levels of educational attainment. Yet, more Ugandan than Tanzanian women are using family planning.[8] Nuwagaba (1997) suggests that "ignorance" about modern contraception, such as the belief that contraceptives lead to sterility, may be responsible for low levels of use in Uganda. Yet Uganda has been as successful as Tanzania in increasing levels of contraceptive awareness.[9] Nuwagaba (1997) states that Uganda is still a pronatalist society with a heavily entrenched value for children as labor sources, although this claim is not empirically based.

The apparent stagnation in Ugandan fertility levels actually masks increasingly unequal birth rates between rich and poor. When fertility rates were analyzed according to socioeconomic status, it was shown that fertility levels increased by nearly one child per woman for the poorest two quintiles over the past five years, and decreased by around one child for the richest 40 percent (Ministry of Finance 2002). Health equity is critical in meeting even the narrowest goals of Cairo, including fertility reduction.

AIDS may also account for the lack of fertility decline in Uganda (see Kirumira 1996). A recent study of the impact of sexual behavior changes on HIV and fertility in Uganda found an increase in the age of sexual debut and a decline in nonregular partners, but that these had little impact on fertility (Bessinger, Akwara, and Halperin 2003). This study also confirmed that childbearing is increasing among the youngest cohort of women (ages 15–19) (Ministry of Finance 2002). As I have argued elsewhere, this fertility pattern may reflect young women's fear of AIDS and their desires to reproduce at all costs, even if it means risking exposure to the disease (Richey 2002).

Uganda's reproductive health policies have failed to reduce fertility levels, and they have been even less successful in improving many of the other aspects of reproductive well-being. A startling 22 percent of all maternal deaths are caused by unsafe, illegal abortions, and only 30 percent of all clinical facilities offered postabortion care (Knudsen 2003). Only 21 percent of health centers at level three and above offer any level of emergency obstetric care (Orinda and Mboye 2003). According to a recent government report, "Infant mortality, child mortality, and maternal mortality have remained high and stagnant over the last 5 years in Uganda, in spite of good economic growth" (Ministry of Finance 2002). Comparing data from the 1995 UDHS with those from 2000, we see a disturbing trend in most variables related to maternal and child health. Infant, neonatal, and child mortality levels have risen, and maternal mortality has dropped slightly (from 527 to 505). Fewer children with diarrhea were taken to any health unit for treatment, and the level of fully immunized children fell from 47 percent to 37 percent. Perhaps the most startling reproductive health indicator from these data is that the number of women delivering with the assistance of skilled health care providers has not improved significantly over the past ten years, remaining at a mere 39 percent in spite of government targets for improved coverage (Ministry of Finance 2002). Furthermore, only 5 percent of women gave birth in facilities equipped to provide emergency obstetric care (Orinda and Mbonye 2003).

In May 2001, the National Policy Guidelines and Service Standards for Reproductive Health Services were adopted to address all the components of reproductive health: safe motherhood, family planning, adolescent health, prevention and management of unsafe abortion, reproductive tract infections (including STDs and HIV/AIDS), infertility, cancers, obstetric fistulae, and gender-based violence. These guidelines have a specific policy objective: "to integrate the management of STI/HIV/AIDS into all reproductive health services and to strengthen existing strategies to reduce mother-to-child transmission of HIV" (Ministry of Health 2001). In practice, however, it is not clear that these policies are being implemented, and the guidelines themselves are not well circulated, even among Ministry of Health workers in Kampala. One informant questioned the possibility of implementing thirteen strategic objectives when the basics of health care are not even in place. Cynicism over the possibility of translating policy into genuine concerns for women's health continues; as one district medical officer put it, "The Ministry of Health does not care about anything other than their Pajeros [fancy cars] and their allowances. They don't care about women" (Tripp 2000).

Implications of Uganda's Dependence on International Donors: The Case of HIV/AIDS

Even though combating AIDS has had domestic support in Uganda, international donors are critical to financing the country's implementation efforts. The increasing level of international interest in Ugandan AIDS policy has had an ambivalent reception in Uganda. More money is flowing into the projects, but the state and, in some cases, its nationals are losing autonomy and decision-making power. Uganda's AIDS success is important to donors, and donors are important to Uganda. Total donor support for all AIDS-related programs from 1989 to 1998 was approximately $180 million—an estimated 70 percent of total expenditures on AIDS in the country (Hogle 2002). Similarly, international donors finance approximately 90 percent of all investments in reproductive health, so donor priorities are critical in shaping policies and programs (Ebanyat 2002).[10]

The Need for Success

The Ugandan success in AIDS reduction has been an extremely important part of its characterization as a "good" government to potential donors. Any challenges to the success of its policies have been met with denial and outrage by the Ugandan state and the international AIDS community. It appears that the national Ugandan AIDS success was claimed initially on the basis of a creative reading of limited data. Yet over time, the country has actually achieved the successes it previously claimed, as declining rates have been documented throughout the country.

In July 2002, *The Lancet* published a controversial piece arguing that the Ugandan "HIV/AIDS success story" was "based on misinterpretation of epidemiological data" (Parkhurst 2002).[11] The article's point was not to dispute Uganda's decreasing incidence rates, but that claims of national decline were made and accepted before there was any valid empirical evidence to support them. Parkhurst suggested many reasons for the pressure to claim success, even prematurely. First, Uganda's donors pressured the government to show results. Second, the international media attention to the horrors of AIDS in Africa raised expectations that something be done. Third, avoiding donor fatigue in Uganda is important to insure a continuing flow of funds to countries that are good performers. And finally, local health care workers received a morale boost from statistics offering the perception that they have been effective in the face of a deadly pandemic (Parkhurst 2002). The work questioning Uganda's success was politically sensitive in Uganda's donor countries as well, resulting in an article in *The Economist* explaining that Parkhurst's work caused "pandemonium in Uganda" and "was denounced as slanderous by officials and AIDS researchers."

Both the *Lancet* article and its reception by the international community raise important questions about the relationship between international donors and the Ugandan state and about the importance of "success" to demonstrate effective governance. Harrison (2001) has identified Uganda as a "post-conditionality" regime reflecting the character of the relationship between states that have significantly embraced neoliberal economic reforms and the donors that continue to finance them. There is a mutual dependence between donors and the state. Donors identify states they consider to be good reformers and then are eager to see further success to justify their past policies and selection of states for interventions. In Uganda, it may be that such success has distracted both the government and its donors, causing them to turn a blind eye to the vast improvements needed in public health care.

Ideology, International Funds, and Approaches

Although there is no question that Uganda has been portrayed as *the* AIDS success story among a field of poor performances, the search continues for answers to how Uganda has managed to lower its infection rates while most other African countries have been unable to. Many different approaches, implemented through various agencies under diverse and sometimes even conflicting strategies, have been at work in Uganda since the early stages of the epidemic. The resulting success has been claimed by proponents of each strategy as proof that their approach is the way forward in the fight against AIDS. Recently, the American popular press and some politicians have embraced one strand of the Ugandan approach—Abstinence, Be faithful, use Condoms (ABC)—and tried to sell it as a more effective, less costly public health strategy compared with condom promotion and safe-sex education (Pitts 2003). One USAID official is quoted as saying that "the historical approach to HIV has been little A, little B, and big C. The public health community at large did not believe in abstinence, but Africans were far ahead of the public health community on this. . . . The core of Uganda's success story is big A, big B, and little C" (Ibid.). However, the claimed success of ABC was based on questionable evidence (Shuey et al. 1999) and this does not reflect the actual approach to HIV/AIDS in Uganda, which has included multiple tactics. It is unlikely that any single component alone could have achieved what the multiple strategies accomplished. "Love Faithfully" would not have been possible without the alternative of "Love Carefully." Two studies, one funded by USAID and the other by the Alan Guttmacher Institute, compared changes in variables representing the A, B, and C approaches from nationally representative UDHS and Global Programme on AIDS (GPA) surveys. Both studies concluded that "changes in all three of the factors investigated—abstinence, monogamy, and condom use—probably contributed to lower risk of HIV infection, at least for some women and men and some age and marital groups" (Singh, Darroch, and Bankole 2003).

A selective reading of Uganda's success has been used to justify measures like the Pitts Amendment, which reserves at least one-third of US HIV/AIDS prevention funds for "abstinence-until-marriage" programs (Pitts 2003). A U.S. Congressman criticized a proposed donor initiative for not doing enough to follow the Uganda model. The President's Emergency Plan for AIDS Relief: US Five-Year Global HIV/AIDS Strategy, released on February 24, 2004, goes even further by allocating 33 percent of all prevention funds to "abstinence-only" programs by 2006 (Center for Health and Gender Equity 2004).

Misrepresenting the Uganda model can have policy implications that are dangerous for Ugandan women, however. For example, the potentially harmful effects of abstinence and fidelity-only messages for women are never noted by conservatives. Critics have pointed out that messages such as "be faithful" or "stick to one partner" can actually increase the vulnerability of women who mistakenly believe that their own fidelity will protect them from contracting HIV within a long-term relationship (Abdool-Karim 1998; Tallis 2002). HIV prevalence rates for sub-Saharan African women peak at around twenty-five years of age, which means that the majority of women are contracting HIV within marriage, and three recent studies have shown that more than 80 percent of women who were infected with HIV were monogamous (Center for Health and Gender Equity 2004). Yet, even if married women realized that they may be at risk of HIV, their options for self-protection within their marital sexual relationships are limited. The societal expectation that women must be sexually available to their husbands on demand and the high rate of violence and sexual coercion within marriage put women at high risk of HIV, and this has not been adequately addressed by the Ugandan state or its donors (see Karanja 2003). Raising the issue of condom use within marriage can increase a woman's risk of violence, and exiting a violent marriage is likely to expose women to other relationships of sexual risk, when they are not "protected" by a regular partner. Although the current U.S. global AIDS strategy claims to draw lessons from Uganda, it misrepresents the country's comprehensive effort against the disease in ways that could undermine, rather than support, Ugandan efforts.

Implications of Uganda's Dependence on International Donors: The Case of Reproductive Health

Unlike its AIDS policy, in which a variety of approaches with a common goal are used to tackle the enemy, the Ugandan state has had no singular vision

for reproductive health policy. In contrast, different state actors present conflicting visions about population control, family planning, and reproduction,
and Museveni has remained conspicuously silent, in contrast with his outspoken leadership on AIDS issues. The leader of one reproductive health organization explained: "Imagine if the level of attention given to HIV/AIDS
were given to a number of other issues related to reproductive health—for
example, changing people's attitudes towards health care. 'All mothers should
go for five antenatal care visits!'—imagine if he [Museveni] were shouting
that and more women went to antenatal care and postnatal services where
family planning is integrated. We need more of a push towards these issues"
(Omomuhangi 2002). The result of the state's inattention is that programs and
projects are implemented mostly through the state or international NGOs, and
are led by donor funding and priorities. The reproductive health agenda is
now being implemented through what were previously donor, ministry, and
local family planning institutions. Although some have argued that family
planning structures are appropriate for HIV and reproductive health interventions (Pillai, Sunil, and Gupta 2003), the vestiges of population control still
permeate many family planning interventions on the ground. For example,
one of Uganda's largest major reproductive health projects seemed mired in
population-control logic, rather than prioritizing health and rights. An expa-
triate employee of the project stated: "[Project name] is trying to get people
to use modern methods of family planning. Here it's been politically incor-
rect to tell people to have small families. Social marketers decided we should
be promoting it [contraception] in terms of health and child spacing, but nothing suggests that they should have fewer. . . . We thought that if you could
get people to use modern family planning, then the TFR [total fertility rate]
would go down, but obviously that was a wrong assumption" (interview,
anonymous 2002). Total fertility rate as the indicator of reproductive health
success or failure reduces the myriad goals of Cairo to the singular focus on
decreasing fertility rates, which is not popular with the Ugandan government
or with many Ugandans.

AIDS policies and population policies have not been brought together
under the larger rubric of reproductive health; instead we find competing bu-
reaucracies at all levels of implementation. In the words of Dr. Florence
Oryem-Ebanyat, the first ministry official in charge of reproductive health,
"Although a lot of policies are in place, dissemination has been rather limited
for stakeholders both at national and lower levels, and have not therefore been
translated into action" (Ebanyat 2002). When AIDS interventions have been
linked to family planning at the local level, well-intentioned AIDS interven-

tions have sometimes been considered suspect because of associations between expatriate-associated health projects and racism, mistrust, and abuse.

Consequences of a Narrow Focus on Contraception

Government officials have said in interviews, informal conversations, and public statements that fertility reduction through increased contraception is still important to Uganda's donors and that issues such as reproductive-related cancers receive hardly any support. Some of these officials believe that donors have placed undue focus on contraception, and others considered it a reasonable response to Ugandan demographic realities. For example, one Ministry of Health representative has expressed concern that family planning was dwarfing other reproductive health concerns, stating: "I'd like to change the concept from 'family planning' to 'planning for the family.'" Another Ministry of Health representative stated in an interview: "As far as we are concerned, safe motherhood should be really one of the most important programs, and I must say the support has been diluted. In fact, I have been in this office for a long time and one of the things which used to—I felt uncomfortable about—was at the time when USAID came into this country they were not willing to put in resources to look at other elements [aside from family planning]" (interview, anonymous 2002). However, a contrasting opinion was expressed by the assistant commissioner for reproductive health in an interview: "Of course, it [fertility reduction] is in the back of everybody's mind . . . but I don't think I could blame them really! If they are putting in money to see some tangible development, I think it would be better if fertility was really matching the development" (interview, Ebanyat, 2002).

The reproductive health agenda is challenged in Uganda by the lack of funding concentration in the area in light of the new sectorwide approach to development funding (SWAP), a lack of leadership focused on reproductive health issues, and a narrow interpretation of the agenda by donors remaining outside of SWAP. Implementing the components of Uganda's reproductive health agenda requires adequate funding, particularly for those programs less likely to be supported by donors. In 1999, the Maternal and Child Health Department was restructured and became the Reproductive Health Division. Although this project was a priority for the first fiscal year (2000–2001), the Ugandan Ministry of Health representative responsible for the division at that time stated her belief that inadequate resources had been allocated to support the many activities meant to encompass reproductive health. According to her assessment, one reason for the lack of funding was SWAP. In theory, SWAP would consolidate donor assistance for use in the areas prioritized by the government.[12] In practice, some officials believe that SWAP has resulted in less funding for reproductive health today than in the past, because donations that were once made specifically for reproductive health are now spread across several programs. Furthermore, other informants have suggested that the lack of a clear priority for reproductive health within the overall health ministry may be responsible for its lesser emphasis within SWAP. Indeed, as Askew and Berer (2003: 55) argue, "sexual and reproductive health is not yet seen as a priority health issue in every country, or by all international stakeholders." The current Ministry of Health representative for reproductive health is trying to consolidate support for emergency obstetric care within the context of SWAP, but mobilizing resources for specific projects in a SWAP context remains a challenge (Orinda and Mbonye 2003).

Some donors also remain outside of SWAP, notably the United States Agency for International Development (USAID) and the UN agencies. These donors maintain their own agendas for funding that emphasize the aspects of reproductive health that are most important to them: HIV/AIDS and family planning. In a move that has created some controversy, the United Nations Population Fund has considered joining SWAP as well. Without coherent and consistent emphasis from the government or the major donors, the non-family–planning aspects of reproductive health lack any clear funding stream, and the HIV/AIDS-related aspects are not integrated into the routine of reproductive health care.

One of the dangerous consequences of a lack of integration, as argued by Baylies (2001), is that AIDS has made reproductive choice an illusion when women are not able to make meaningful decisions to protect their health and reproduction. One way that the vestiges of the fertility control agenda places women at risk of AIDS is when married women are discouraged from using condoms as contraception in favor of more effective hormonal means (Baylies 2001). Furthermore, the successful promotion of condom use for AIDS prevention at times when one is neither abstinent nor faithful strengthens the method's association with illicit sex, thus making it unappealing to most couples in committed relationships (Baylies 2001). Access to family planning services is limited in Uganda, and when women do receive services, it is not in an environment that supports women's decision making. Clinical data from Kiboga District Hospital confirm that long-acting hormonal injections are by far the most popular contraceptive dispensed and one of only three methods available, together with pills and condoms (Knudsen 2003). A recent Ugandan study confirmed that women preferred these products to male

condoms and that even when their use involved negotiation with male partners, women perceived them as empowering and enabling them to control
their reproductive health (Green et al. 2001). Offering female-controlled methods such as foam, gel, or the sponge is a missed opportunity for the health
care system.

Dilapidated State of Public Health Care

In the mid-1960s, Uganda boasted one of the best health care systems
in Africa, consisting of "an excellent national referral and teaching hospital
and a hierarchy of government health units and district hospitals, as well as
many mission-run facilities" (Whyte and Birungi 2000). Between 1976 and
1988, however, the number of patients attending government health units fell
by half. Years of war, economic decline, and structural-adjustment-related cuts
left Ugandan public health in ruins.[13] A recent Human Rights Watch report
argued that the private sector, NGOs, and community-based organizations
have begun restoration of health services together with the government, but
that inadequate medical supplies, lack of trained staff, and limited access for
Ugandans living in rural areas still prevail (Karanja 2003). The 2000–01 annual report from the Reproductive Health Division listed the following constraints: reduced staffing, inadequate funding, lack of supplies such as
contraceptives and "maternal drugs," insufficient fuel and maintenance funds
for division vehicles, and a dearth of communication and computer facilities. Research conducted by the Delivery of Improved Services for Health
(DISH) project noted that inadequate supplies and frequent incidents of running out of stock of STD drugs, condoms, and contraceptives, together with
a lack of basic equipment and clinic expendables, discourages use by clients
who see no reason to travel long distances to attend poorly equipped health
units (DISH 2003).

A large proportion of Ugandans with STDs either treat themselves at
home or seek care from private practitioners instead of using the public health
clinics. Lack of trust was the reason patients gave for avoiding these clinics
in favor of private practitioners (Walker et al. 2001). The private providers
said that their clinics were more conveniently located, had longer open hours,
and provided private confidential consultations, so they were more trusted
in the community. Furthermore, both the providers and patients emphasized
the importance of personal relationship, developing a good rapport, polite-
ness, and trust—all cited as lacking in the public clinics. The issue of cost
was discussed in the study, and although public clinics are theoretically cheaper,

the lack of medicines and constant demand for informal "payments" to every health worker encountered makes receiving treatment at public facilities a similarly costly endeavor (Walker et al 2001).

A similarly disheartening picture evolves from the findings of a Ministry of Health study on risk factors for maternal mortality. This retrospective study of maternal deaths in twenty hospitals from fifty-four randomly selected health centers in twelve randomly selected districts identified inadequate supplies of antibiotics, intravenous drug fluids, and blood for transfusion as among the top risk factors for maternal mortality in Uganda (Mbonye 2001).[14] Jane Mpagi of the Ministry of Gender suggested that in this context the condom policy reflects a "male bias," and that to address the majority of women we also need a "glove policy," since women are most likely to be caregivers for AIDS patients (Mpagi 2003).

Scaling Up: Challenges for HIV/AIDS and Reproductive Health

Ugandan HIV interventions were able to succeed in spite of the constraints in the health care system because of HIV's status as a health emergency and because the behavioral and educational focus did not demand the same level of infrastructure as other reproductive health needs did. Providing health care services is not sufficient to enable women to improve their reproductive health; they must be able to exercise their reproductive rights in practice as well. However, as HIV/AIDS care shifts to include treatment, a health care system that promotes reproductive health and rights will be necessary for success in Uganda. Uganda's historically NGO-oriented approach to AIDS is unlikely to meet the challenges of the new phase of the epidemic.

Constraints, Challenges, and Assets for Scaling Up

Calls to "scale up" treatment for AIDS in the future highlight questions about what kind of system will be necessary and what kinds of effects AIDS treatment will have on other kinds of health care needs, such as those of reproductive health.[15] Ranson et al. (2003) constructed a country typology to analyze the various constraints identified in poor countries.[16] Using publicly available sources, they tested three approaches for constructing a classification that could inform strategic choices for scaling up. The variables examined were: literacy; the number of nurses per 100,000 population; diptheria, pertussis, and tetanus (DPT) coverage; control of corruption; government effectiveness; access to health services; and gross domestic product (GDP) per capita. Like most other sub-Saharan African countries, Uganda ranked in the lowest quartile in number of nurses per 100,000 population and in the second lowest quartile for DPT coverage, control of corruption, access to health services, and GDP per capita. However, Uganda was ranked in the third quartile for government effectiveness, a higher position than would be expected for a government of its status and its performance on the other indicators.[17] Thus, Uganda is one of the countries that could be expected to effectively manage the resources necessary to provide public health care, if those resources were forthcoming.

The Ugandan government signaled a positive shift in its policy by agreeing to increase health sector spending with money it receives from the Global Fund (Wendo 2003). The new funds are to be used for the purchase of antiretroviral drugs and for improving medical infrastructure. Yet the difficulties of wedding decentralized service provision with improving access for poor people are likely to increase with the integration of AIDS treatment as part of Ugandan's health care expectations. Kivumbi and Kintu examined the government's attempts to place "safety nets" in the form of exemptions and waivers of user fees for health care. Qualitative data from the districts of Mukono and Mbarara showed that district local governments had little motivation to extend exemptions to their constituents, as they were more interested in raising revenue to meet recurrent costs of service provision than in providing equitable access to health care (Kivumbi and Kintu 2002). Yet health equity is particularly important for improving reproductive health outcomes, as providing health services even to the majority of the population may still not reach those persons at highest risk of maternal, infant, and childhood death (Erickson 2003).

Uganda has been noteworthy for its decentralized approach to scaling up levels of voluntary testing and counseling for HIV/AIDS (Contact Group on Accelerating Access to HIV/AIDS-Related Care 2001). The Ministry of Health was recently restructured at the behest of international donors to comply with decentralized development policy. Jeppsson et al. (2003) analyzed this restructuring and concluded that although the foundation has been laid for the Ministry of Health to function in its new role as coach more than player, the move toward a functioning relationship between the ministry and service-delivery levels is still incomplete. Effective policy responses to the new realities of AIDS treatment will require a well-funded, capable state with goals of health equity. These are the same requirements as those needed to implement the other aspects of the reproductive health agenda.

In spite of a new recognition that a "capable state" is needed, the foundation for improving state capacity has been overwhelmingly eroded through the neoliberal policies of the past twenty years and their corresponding neglect of the state in favor of NGOs.[18] De Waal argued that AIDS treatment will require much more than ad hoc policies: "The HIV/AIDS pandemic in Africa has unfolded at a time when the dominant approach to social action in Africa has been an NGO model. Unfortunately, while a case can be made for pluralist heterodoxy in grassroots community development programmes, public health programmes demand a certain rigour if they are to succeed: 'empowerment' must go with a robust attention to the medical and epidemiological bottom line" (de Waal 2003).

Consequences of Dilapidated Public Health Facilities on HIV/AIDS

The ongoing impact of HIV/AIDS on the already overtaxed and under-supported state health care system takes many forms. One of the less obvious ones is, ironically, the result of AIDS-prevention campaigns. Birungi (1998) described how the dilapidated state of the Ugandan public health services has led to a loss of trust in the treatments these clinics offer. This skepticism, coupled with anti-AIDS education campaigns that warn people against the dangers of sharing unsterilized needles, has led Ugandans to engage in medical "self-help." Birungi shows how injection technology (syringes, needles, and injectables) has been domesticated and personalized in Uganda, as people want to receive injections under their own control from people whom they trust at home. Although the culture of the injection in Uganda and other parts of Africa has historical roots in colonial medicine (Vaughan 1991), the AIDS epidemic and its prevention campaigns have joined with a dysfunctional health care system to intensify personal injection practices as part of health care in contemporary Uganda. The extent to which unsafe medical procedures are responsible for transmitting HIV in Africa has recently been the subject of intense debate. An American study estimated that nearly one-third of new HIV infections in Africa were likely to have been caused by infected needles, not sexual encounters (Brewer et al. 2003; Gisselquist et al. 2003; Gisselquist and Potterat 2003); however, these figures were immediately disputed by UNAIDS (UNAIDS/WHO 2003). Although the heterosexual transmission of the epidemic in Uganda has not been called into question, the relationship between inadequate health care and transmission is an important issue.

As treatment becomes increasingly central to AIDS in Uganda, leadership and commitment to accessible health care delivery systems will be necessary to integrate AIDS into a reproductive health care approach and to up-grade reproductive health systems to successfully deal with AIDS. Treatment activist organizations in Uganda, as in other parts of the Third World, are creating demand and raising expectations that AIDS is a treatable disease. The UN special envoy on HIV/AIDS in Africa described a visit to Uganda's Joint Clinical Research Center in August 2003: "The country is obsessed with treatment and is pursuing it single-mindedly . . . it is projected that some two hundred thousand would today qualify for treatment. Seventeen thousand are currently being treated through the public sector, civil society sector, and private sector combined—and the target is to have sixty thousand in treatment by the end of next year, which would make it the largest public sector programme of its kind on the continent. They are not cowed by infrastructure. They are not cowed by human resource capacity. They are, quite simply, determined to keep their people alive" (Lewis 2003). Access has become a popular political issue in Uganda, as the government announced in the national newspaper the *New Vision* on August 13, 2002, that it would provide free antiretrovirals to two thousand people across the country. There are also ongoing discussions about launching a manufacturing plant for generic antiretrovirals in Kampala. Mike Mukula from the Ministry of Health told the press: "This is a matter of national priority and urgency to have the drugs locally manufactured." The Ugandan Ministry of Health announced in the press: "a total of 10,000 people or one-third of the 30,000 antiretroviral users in Africa are in Uganda" (IRIN News 2003). The government has announced a planned partnership with AIDS Healthcare Foundation to scale up treatment clinics in Masaka District to reach "as many as 10,000 Ugandans" by the summer of 2004 (AHF Global Immunity 2003), and the Ministry of Health official responsible for antiretrovirals claims to be able to provide drugs to all Ugandans who need them in the near future.

Preferential access to antiretrovirals, in which some senior members of the government and army are provided with free or subsidized AIDS treatment, provides strong incentives for staying in office, leading to deleterious governance implications (de Waal 2003). Local media reports confirm the political significance of treatment access with headlines like the *New Vision*'s "Ugandan government gives ARVs to LRA [the revolutionary force in the northern civil war] commanders to persuade them to denounce rebellion."

We will see increasing pressure on the Ugandan government to expand the scope of AIDS treatment beyond the well-funded pilot projects to include increasing numbers of Ugandans. As argued by Dabis and Ekpini (2002), "Prevention of mother-to-child transmission must become a universal standard of care in Africa." It is equally important, however, to insure that this universal standard is one that upholds women's reproductive rights, not one that pits women against their children in a struggle for the right to survival. The prevention of mother-to-child transmission component of the U.S. Global AIDS Strategy includes no clear indication of how pregnant women will receive follow-up treatment for antiretrovirals, whether these women will receive comprehensive reproductive health care, or whether preventing mother-to-child transmission will eventually move beyond pregnant women to insure that *all* women have equitable access to both AIDS treatment and reproductive health care, irrespective of their pregnancy status (Center for Health and Gender Equity 2004).

Barnett and Whiteside (2002) have suggested that AIDS has many lessons to teach us not only about preventing and treating the disease but also about health, well-being, and development. "It may be the epidemic that enables us to respond to the need for a common global public health." In Uganda, AIDS and reproductive health have existed as artificially separate agendas competing for funding and attention. Because of their different goals and scope, the two agendas could be implemented in different ways: AIDS through decentralized, multiple targeted strategies promoting change in sexual behavior, and reproductive health through improved medical service provision.

Yet Uganda's donor dependence for AIDS and reproductive health program support means that donors will have to take on new priorities if these agendas are to be successful. The well-publicized commitment President Bush made to spend $15 billion fighting the pandemic over the next five years shows signs of not living up to its potential in implementation. The first year saw only $2 billion requested for disbursement, and spending is overseen by the new "Global AIDS coordinator," a former pharmaceutical company head and Republican Party activist and donor (Boonstra 2003). In addition, USAID spending on infectious-disease programs will decrease 32 percent in 2004, and child survival and maternal health efforts will decrease 12 percent from the previous year's request (Boonstra 2003). Although the U.S. Global AIDS Strategy emphasizes integrating HIV prevention with antenatal care, safe labor and delivery practices, breast-feeding, malaria prevention and treatment, and family planning, the cuts in funding for reproductive health and shifts of other funds away from this sector suggest a further undermining of these essential services (Center for Health and Gender Equity 2004).

In Uganda today, "most of all, AIDS is associated with suffering and death. Being a victim is stigmatised, not so much because of how you contracted it, but because of the prognosis" (Whyte 2002). Removing the stigma of AIDS in these circumstances requires transforming the disease from terminal to treatable. As treatment options expand, coordination between treatments and their providers, integration of various types of care for AIDS-related illnesses, and referrals (both vertically and horizontally) will not be possible without a stronger, more focused and effective government role. Although the Ugandan government has taken credit for its laissez-faire approach toward reducing HIV prevalence rates, it faces different challenges as the nature of the epidemic is altered according to the realities of treatment.

Conclusions

Treating AIDS and reproductive health as separate agendas is counterproductive to the promotion of women's reproductive health and rights in countries like Uganda. Both could be usefully integrated into the Cairo vision of reproductive health as a basic human right and the fundamental value of human agency (Freedman 1999). AIDS discourses and implementation strategies shape many aspects of reproductive health. First, AIDS has forced sexuality and gender into discussions that had previously been dominated by biomedical, functional explanations of how contraceptives could bring down population growth. Second, AIDS activists both nationally and internationally can be credited with expanding and promoting discussions of gender, including sexual and domestic violence, marital relations and communication, and links between gender oppression and poverty. Similarly, campaigns for the rights of people living with AIDS and those who are HIV positive could be expanded to include the rights of all people to bodily integrity, including control of their reproduction and sexuality. Finally, AIDS activists' demands for adequate health care could be extended to include the right to health care for all illnesses, not just those that are HIV related.

At the program and project level, AIDS has been linked with reproductive health most often through condom-promotion family planning interventions, and little or nothing is done about HIV prevention, healthy sexuality, sexually transmitted diseases (STDs), or AIDS treatment in the context of reproductive health services. Yet, AIDS projects to diagnose and treat STDs are sometimes thought of as providing the "health" aspect of reproductive health, substituting for further investments in maternal and child health. It would be particularly detrimental if HIV/AIDS is allowed to eclipse all other aspects of reproductive health, in light of the recent funding targeting the disease. However, AIDS only comes into a "normal" family planning visit when it is mentioned in relation to condoms as one contraceptive option. Meaningful integration of AIDS and health into local service provision is necessary for realization of reproductive health and rights in Uganda.

Uganda's multipronged "something for everyone" approach to AIDS prevention could be translated into a successfully integrated reproductive health strategy; however, the challenges of treatment and providing basic health care require extensive strengthening of the Ugandan health care system. Infrastructure, employment, training and supervision of health care workers, accessible supplies including but not limited to pharmaceuticals, and integrated policies for achieving health equity are necessary for improving sexual and reproductive health and for continuing to meet the HIV/AIDS pandemic with success. Although domestic policy and management factors are necessary, in resource-poor countries like Uganda, they are not sufficient means for providing health services. Financial commitments must be forthcoming from international donors, particularly to countries in which needs are great and public health leadership has been proven. However, national leadership to promote Ugandan policy objectives and provide a sense of investment worthiness for international development will continue to be important for domestic health care. Political reform, including meaningful strategies toward openness and democratization, would expand the possibilities for Uganda's women's organizations to support more politically challenging issues such as those of reproductive rights. Priority setting, direction, and coordination will be necessary to a greater extent than in the past, even though promoting a diversity of approaches could be helpful in implementing an agenda as wide ranging as Cairo. Again, this requires comprehensive planning at the government level. Expanding health care access for all Ugandans will be critical for achieving further success in reproductive health.

Human rights should provide the foundation for a new generation of integrated policies that promote healthy sexuality, informed and consensual reproductive choices, and the development of the individual and her or his society. However, AIDS policies and reproductive health policies come with their own histories, stakeholders, and agendas, and the points of conflict and cohesion between them must be understood so that policy rhetoric and material interventions move toward an integrated vision of promoting Ugandans' basic human rights. In many ways, if there is an example of success in these realms, we have good reasons to look for it in Uganda. To the extent that the dual implementation of the reproductive health and AIDS agendas poses particular challenges in Uganda, however, we can anticipate similar challenges in other developing countries and begin working to overcome them.

Situating a new generation of integrated approaches to reproductive health within family planning and HIV/AIDS structures that have been historically separate, vertical, and donor driven is proving challenging in Uganda. Reproductive health is still under the heavy cloak of population-control initiatives, at least as family planning has been politicized in Uganda. It will take a real shift in the implementation of reproductive health policies at the clinic level to begin to reshape relationships, build trust, and change perceptions. This is unlikely to happen as long as Uganda's donors and lenders are still focusing on the country's fertility rate as the indicator of success in this realm. Integrating HIV/AIDS prevention and treatment into the structures of maternal and child health is critical but remains difficult, especially because of the stigma that still surrounds the disease, even in an African country renowned for its openness.

Rethinking Ugandan policy dilemmas may help to expand the frameworks of Cairo and Beijing to more fully incorporate the challenges presented by the African AIDS epidemic. The successes in some aspects of reproductive health promotion, notably decreasing HIV prevalence rates, as well as the failures in others—for example, rates of assisted deliveries—result from multiple priorities competing for limited resources. The reproductive health agenda is vast and expensive, but it arises out of the struggles of women for adequate access to quality health care that respects their human rights. However, as AIDS treatment activists have continued to stress, "expensive" is a question of political priorities, and integrating HIV services within programs providing other sexual and reproductive health interventions should offer cost savings (Askew and Berer 2003).

Given that the predominant mode of HIV transmission is through heterosexual intercourse and that childbearing is almost universal in Uganda, a meaningful reproductive health agenda must serve men and women and address gender inequality while incorporating HIV/AIDS. Together, AIDS prevention and treatment, reproductive health services, and family planning based on choice not imposition form the minimal interventions necessary for promoting a reproductive health and rights agenda in Uganda. Educating women to demand their rights of bodily self-determination and creating institutional contexts in which these rights are respected are necessary for both women's fertility choice and sexual decision making. Grounding health interventions in a framework of human rights brings attention to both the gender disparities and geopolitical inequalities at play (Stein 2000). This assumes that AIDS should neither be left out of reproductive health nor allowed to subsume all of its resources.

Whether AIDS becomes an overwhelming disease burden sapping the

Ugandan health care system or whether it holds the potential to introduce unprecedented levels of interest and funding will depend on three factors. First, success depends on whether the government expands its unwritten AIDS policies of leadership, diversity of approaches, and openness to apply to larger issues of reproductive health care and public health service provision. Ugandan women's groups have an important role to play in articulating these issues. Second, success is contingent upon whether the state can act more effectively as a coordinator of various types and levels of public health intervention. And finally, it will depend on whether the crisis of reproductive health and promoting reproductive rights receives adequate and ideologically unbiased consideration and funding from international donors whose attention has previously gone to HIV/AIDS prevention and family planning.

Notes

I would like to thank the Soros Reproductive Health and Rights Fellowship at the Heibrunn Department of Population and Family Health at the Joseph L. Mailman School of Public Health, Columbia University and the Open Society Institute for support while writing this paper; the Danish Institute for International Studies where I was based during most of the writing period; the Government of Uganda and Makerere Institute for Social Research for hosting my fieldwork; Lara Knudsen for research assistance with interviews; and all the Ugandan respondents for their insights. Any shortcomings in the work remain the responsibility of its author.

1. Kirumira points out that HIV/AIDS prevalence and mortality figures are inherently subject to error, and he gives a fair assessment of the data limitations. Still, his conclusion is that the decline is "real," although the measurements may be imprecise (Kirumira 2001).
2. The $500 million Multi-Country HIV/AIDS Program (MAP) for Africa is one of the largest potential funding sources for access to HIV/AIDS treatment. This fund provides loans for HIV/AIDS prevention and treatment with an emphasis on vulnerable groups, communities, and civil society organizations in Africa.
3. The Global Fund to fight AIDS, Tuberculosis and Malaria is one of the largest sources of funding for HIV/AIDS commitments in poor countries. Uganda was approved a total of $96,719,638 in the two rounds, as documented by the Global Fund Observer; www.aidspan.org/globalfund/grants.
4. Uganda's AIDS Control Programme was one of the first programs of this kind in Africa (Parkhurst 2001).
5. TASO was one of the case studies on "scaling up" strategies in a recent publication aimed at HIV/AIDS impact (DeJong 2003).
6. Another aspect of the state's openness about AIDS is that it may be serving as a substitute for openness in other areas, particularly that of democratization and multipartyism. Until very recently, it was much more common to find frank and

conflict-ridden discussions about sexuality than about political transition in the Ugandan press.

7. The average Ugandan woman will bear 6.9 children during her lifetime: this is the second highest fertility level in sub-Saharan Africa after Niger, and third highest in the world after Yemen (Macro 2001 cited in Ministry of Finance 2002).

8. The percent of married Tanzanian women who reported ever-use of family planning increased from 25.6 in the 1991/92 DHS to 35.6 by the 1996/97 DHS. Uganda, despite its persistently high fertility, shows similar trends in contraceptive use; 21.5 percent of married women reported that they had ever used a contraceptive method in the 1988 UDHS, and the percentage jumped to 33.9 percent in the 1995 survey and 44.1 percent by the 2000/01 UDHS.

9. The DHS shows that 88.5 percent of all married Tanzanian women know a contraceptive method (1996), and the figure is even higher, 93.4 percent, for Ugandan women (1995).

10. These donors include UNFPA, WHO, DFID, UNICEF, USAID, and GTZ.

11. Parkhurst argues that the data on which claims for a national success were initially based were actually not nationally representative. For example, the famous claim that overall rates of HIV–1 have been reduced from 30 percent to 10 percent (a statement he cites to the Government of Uganda, Uganda AIDS Commission, and UNAIDS' "National Strategic Framework for HIV activities in Uganda: 2000/1–2005/6" and mass media) was based on data from a few urban government antenatal clinic surveillance sites. Furthermore, he argues that the claims of such a rapid decline were based on prevalence rates (the overall proportion of women who test positive for HIV–1), not on incidence rates (the number of new infections). The slippery terminology of "HIV rates" was used to suggest that a decline of incidence was taking place at a time when there was no evidence of this.

12. Partners contributing to Uganda's health sector budget support are: Belgium, Denmark, European Union, Ireland, Netherlands, Norway, Sweden, United Kingdom, and the World Bank (Orinda and Mbonye 2003).

13. An issue of the Uganda Health Bulletin from the Ministry of Health was published on the theme "The Paradox of Uganda's Poor and Worsening Health Indicators in the Era of Economic Growth, Poverty Reduction and Health Sector Reforms" (Health Policy Analysis Unit 2001).

14. Other risk factors were nonuse of family planning (arguably also an indication of health system failure), use of traditional medicine, and mothers aged 15–19 or 30–50 (Mbonye 2001).

15. The case of Botswana, where AIDS drugs have been provided to everyone for free by the government, Merck Pharmaceutical, and the Gates Foundation, has refocused attention on the health care system and its human resources. As Botswanan health staff go to work in Europe, the drugs distribution program is struggling for sufficient skilled labor (Hale 2003). For other examples of successful and unsuccessful public-private partnerships on public health issues, see Reich 2002.

16. "Poor" was defined as the entire population in poor countries (countries with gross

national product per capita of less than $1,200 [in 1999 U.S. dollars] plus all of sub-Saharan Africa) and the poorest groups in middle-income countries (Hanson et al. 2003).

17. The variable on government effectiveness was taken from World Bank data, which include polls of experts and surveys of firm managers or citizens (Kaufmann et al. 1999) and combines "perceptions of the quality of public service provision, the quality of the bureaucracy, the competence of civil servants, the independence of the civil service from political pressures, and the credibility of the government's commitment to policies" (Ranson et al. 2003).

18. Challenges to the development of a capable state in Africa involve strengthening the components of democracy, facilitating the role of civil society organizations in development, rebuilding the capacities of failed states, and strengthening economic governance through enhanced institutional and human capacity for sound and efficient public management (ECA 1999).

References

Abdool-Karim, Q. 1998. "Women and AIDS. The imperative for a gendered prognosis and prevention policy." *Agenda* 39: 15–25.

AHF Global Immunity. 2003. Media release, September 10. www.ahfgi.org/newsroom/press/PR091003a.htm.

Allen, A. 2002. "Uganda v. Condoms: Sex Change." *New Republic* May 16. www.thn.com.

Askew, I., and M. Berer. 2003. "The Contribution of Sexual and Reproductive Health Services to the Fight against HIV/AIDS: A Review." *Reproductive Health Matters* 11(22): 51–73.

Barnett, T., and A. Whiteside. 2002. *AIDS in the Twenty-First Century: Disease and Globalization*. New York: Palgrave Macmillan.

Baylies, C. 2001. "Safe Motherhood in the Time of AIDS: The Illusion of Reproductive 'Choice.'" *Gender and Development* 9(2): 40–50.

Berkovitch, N. 1999. "The Emergence and Transformation of the International Women's Movement." In J. Boli and G. M. Thomas, eds., *Constructing World Culture: International Nongovernmental Organizations since 1875*, 100–126. Menlo Park: Stanford University Press.

Bessinger, R., P. Akwara, and D. Halperin. 2003. *Sexual Behavior, HIV and Fertility Trends: A Comparative Analysis of Six Countries (Phase I of the ABC Study)*. Chapel Hill, N.C.: USAID MEASURE Evaluation Project.

Birungi, H. 1998. "Injections and Self-Help: Risk and Trust in Ugandan Health Care." *Social Science and Medicine* 47(10): 1,455–1,467.

Boonstra, H. 2003. "U.S. AIDS Policy. Priority on Treatment, Conservatives' Approach to Prevention." *Guttmacher Report on Public Policy* 6(3). http://www.agi-usa.org/pubs/journals/gr060301.html.

Brewer, D. D., S. Brody, et al. 2003. "Mounting Anomalies in the Epidemiology of HIV in Africa: Cry the Beloved Paradigm." *International Journal of STD and AIDS* 14(3): 144–147.

Center for Health and Gender Equity. 2004. *Debunking the Myths in the US Global*

AIDS Strategy: An Evidence-Based Analysis. Takoma Park: Center for Health and Gender Equity.

Contact Group on Accelerating Access to HIV/AIDS-Related Care. 2001. Report of the Third Meeting. Geneva: UNAIDS.

Dabis, F., and R. Ekpini. 2002. "HIV–1 and Maternal and Child Health in Africa." *The Lancet* 359 (June 15): 2,097–2,104.

DeJong, J. 2003. *Making an Impact in HIV and AIDS: NGO Experiences of Scaling Up.* London: ITDG Publishing.

De Waal, A. 2003. "How Will HIV/AIDS Transform African Governance?" *African Affairs* 102: 1–23.

DISH (Delivery of Improved Services for Health). 2003. Project on adolescent sexual and reproductive health in Uganda. www.ugandadish.org/resources/aa/aa6.shtml.

Ebanyat, F.A.O. 2002. *The Reproductive Health Programme in Uganda.* Kampala: Ministry of Health, Uganda.

ECA (Economic Commission of Africa). 1999. *The ECA and Africa: Accelerating a Continent's Development.* New York: United Nations.

Erickson, S. 2003. "Maternal Mortality Background Paper." Paper presented at National Reproductive Health Symposium, Kampala, May.

Freedman, L. P. 1999. "Reflections on Emerging Frameworks of Health and Human Rights." In J. M. Mann et al., eds., *Health and Human Rights,* 227–252. New York: Routledge.

Gisselquist, D., and J. J. Potterat. 2003. "Heterosexual Transmission of HIV in Africa: An Empiric Estimate." *International Journal of STD and AIDS* 14 (March 1): 162–173.

Gisselquist, D., J. J. Potterat, et al. 2003. "Let It Be Sexual: How Health Care Transmission of AIDS in Africa Was Ignored." *International Journal of STD and AIDS* 14 (March 1): 148–161.

Goetz, A. M. 1998. "Women in Politics and Gender Equity in Policy: South Africa and Uganda." *Review of African Political Economy* 76: 241–262.

———. 2003a. "Introduction: Women in Power in Uganda and South Africa." In A. M. Goetz and S. Hassim, eds., *No Shortcuts to Power: African Women in Politics and Policy Making.* London: Zed Books.

———. 2003b. "The Problem with Patronage: Constraints on Women's Political Effectiveness in Uganda." In A. M. Goetz and S. Hassim, eds., *No Shortcuts to Power: African Women in Politics and Policy Making.* London: Zed Books.

Government of Uganda. 1999. *The NCSD Sustainable Development Report.* www.ncsdnetwork.org/global/reports/ncsd1999/uganda/cap1.htm.

Government of Uganda et al. 2000. The National Strategic Framework for HIV/AIDS Activities in Uganda: 2000/1–2005/6. Kampala: Government of Uganda.

Green, G., R. Pool, S. Harrison, G. J. Hart, J. Wilkinson, S. Nyanzi, and J.A.G. Whitworth. 2001. "Female Control of Sexuality: Illusion or Reality? Use of Vaginal Products in South West Uganda." *Social Science and Medicine* 52 (4): 585–598.

Hale, B. 2003. "The Missing Medics in Botswana's AIDS Battle," http://newsvote. bbc.co.uk/mpapps/pagetools/print/news.bbc.co.uk/2/hi/business/3280735.stm.

Hanson, K., M. K. Ranson, V. Oliveira-Cruz, and A. Mills. 2003. "Expanding Access to Priority Health Interventions: A Framework for Understanding the Constraints to Scaling Up." *Journal of International Development* 15: 1–14.

Harrison, G. 2001. "Reform: Reflections on the Cases of Uganda and Tanzania." *Development and Change* 32(4): 657–679.

Hartmann, B. 1995. *Reproductive Rights and Wrongs: The Global Politics of Population Control*. Boston: South End Press.

Health Policy Analysis Unit, Ministry of Health. 2001. "The Paradox of Uganda's Poor and Worsening Health Indicators in the Era of Economic Growth, Poverty Reduction and Health Sector Reforms." Special Issue of *Uganda Health Bulletin* 7(4) October–December.

Hogle, Janice A. 2002. *What Happened in Uganda? Declining HIV Prevalence, Behavior Change, and the National Response*. Project Lessons Learned Case Study. Washington, D.C.: U.S. Agency for International Development.

IRIN News. 2003. "Uganda: Leading User of Antiretrovirals." Kampala, February 13. www.irinnews.org/AIDSreport.asp?ReportID=1750.

Jeppsson, A., P. O. Ostergren, and B. Hagstrom. 2003. "Restructuring a Ministry of Health—an Issue of Structure and Process: A Case Study from Uganda." *Health Policy and Planning* 18(1): 68–73.

Karanja, L. 2003. "Just Die Quietly: Domestic Violence and Women's Vulnerability to HIV in Uganda." Special Issue of *Human Rights Watch Report* 15(15).

Kaufmann, D., A. Kraay, and P. Zoido-Lobatón. 1999. *Governance Matters*. World Bank policy research working paper 21. Washington, D.C.: World Bank Development Research Group, Macroeconomics and Growth, and the World Bank Institute, Governance Regulation and Finance.

Kawamara-Mishambi, S., and I. Ovonji-Odida. 2003. "The 'Lost Clause': The Campaign to Advance Women's Property Rights in Uganda 1998 Land Act." In A. M. Goetz, and S. Hassim, eds., *No Shortcuts to Power: African Women in Politics and Policy Making*. London: Zed Books.

Kirumira, E. K. 1996. "Familial Relationships and Population Dynamics in Uganda: A Case Study of Fertility Behavior in the Central Region." Ph.D. dissertation, Institute of Sociology, University of Copenhagen.

———. 1998. "Developing a Population Policy for Uganda." In H. B. Hansen and M. Twaddle, eds., *Developing Uganda*, 185–193. Oxford: James Curry.

———. 2001. "HIV/AIDS Incidence and Prevalence: Reality or Myth?" Paper presented at conference on Gender, Sexuality and HIV/AIDS: Research and Intervention in Africa, Copenhagen, April 23–24.

Kivumbi, G. W., and F. Kintu. 2002. "Exemptions and Waivers from Cost-Sharing: Ineffective Safety Nets in Decentralized Districts in Uganda." *Health Policy and Planning* 17(suppl. 1): 64–71.

Knudsen, L. 2003. "Limited Choices: A Study of Women's Access to Health Care in Kiboga Uganda." Special Issue on Women and Development: Rethinking Policy and Reconceptualizing Practice, *Women's Studies Quarterly* 31(3): 251–258.

Lane, S. D. 1994. "From Population Control to Reproductive Health: An Emerging Policy Agenda." *Social Science and Medicine* 39(9): 1,303–1,314.

Lewis, S. 2003. Speech by the UNV Special Envoy on HIV/AIDS in Africa at the conference of the Centre for the AIDS Programme of Research in South Africa. http://allafrica.com/stories/200308030120.html.

Lloyd, C. B., C. E. Kaufman, and P. Hewett. 1999. *The Spread of Primary Schooling in Sub-Saharan Africa.* New York: Population Council.

Macro ORC. 2001. *Nutrition of Young Children and Mothers in Uganda—Findings from the 2000–01 UDHS.* Calverton: Macro.

Mbonye, A. K. 2001. "Risk Factors Associated with Maternal Deaths in Health Units in Uganda." *African Journal of Reproductive Health* 5(3): 47–53.

Ministry of Finance, Planning and Economic Development. 2002. *Infant Mortality in Uganda 1995–2000: Why the Non-Improvement?* Discussion paper no. 6. Kampala: Ministry of Finance, Planning and Economic Devleopment.

Ministry of Health. 2001. "The National Policy Guidelines and Service Standards for Reproductive Health Services." Kampala: MOH Community Health Department, Reproductive Health Division.

Mpagi, J. 2003. "Gender and Reproductive Health: Involvement of Men." Paper presented at the National Reproductive Health Symposium: Raising the Profile of Reproductive Health in Uganda. Kampala, June 17–19.

Nuwagaba, A. 1997. "Population Crisis in Sub-Saharan Africa: Who Is Responsible? An Illustrative Analysis of Population Trends in Uganda." *Eastern Africa Social Science Research Review* 13(2): 75–88.

Okidi, J. A., and G. K. Mugambe. 2002. *An Overview of Chronic Poverty and Development Policy in Uganda.* Working paper 11. Kampala: Chronic Poverty Research Centre.

Omomuhangi, N. 2002. Interview, 7 March. Associate programme officer of Reproductive Health Programme, UNFPA.

Orinda, V., and A. Mbonye. 2003. "Putting EmOC in the SWAPs Process: Experience from Uganda." Paper presented at the AMDD Network Conference, Kuala Lumpur, October 21–23.

Parkhurst, J. O. 2001. "The Crisis of AIDS and the Politics of Response: The Case of Uganda." *International Relations* 15(6): 69–87.

———. 2002. "The Ugandan Success Story? Evidence and Claims of HIV–1 Prevention." *The Lancet* 360 (August 15): 78–80.

Pillai, V., T. S. Sunil, and R. Gupta. 2003. "AIDS Prevention in Zambia: Implications for Social Services." *World Development* 31(1): 149–161.

Pitts, J. R. 2003. "The ABCs of Hope." *Washington Times*, March 26. http://www.washingtontimes.com/commentary/20030326–5461378.htm.

Presser, H. B. 2000. "Demography, Feminism, and the Science-Policy Nexus." In H. B. Presser and G. Sen, eds., *Women's Empowerment and Demographic Processes: Moving beyond Cairo,* 377–412. Oxford: Oxford University Press.

Ranson, M. K., K. Hanson, V. Oliveira-Cruz, and A. Mills. 2003. "Constraints to Expanding Access to Health Interventions: An Empirical Analysis and Country Typology." *Journal of International Development* 15: 15–39.

Reich, M. R. 2002. *Public-Private Partnerships for Public Health.* Cambridge: Harvard University Press.

Reproductive Health Division, Ugandan Ministry of Health. 2001. *Annual Report July 2000–June 2001.* Kampala: Ministry of Health.

Richey, L. A. 2002. *Is Overpopulation Still the Problem? Global Discourse and Reproductive Health Challenges in the Time of HIVAIDS.* Working paper series 02.1. Copenhagen: Centre for Development Research. www.cdr.dk.

Shuey, D. A., B. B. Babishangire, S. Omiat, and H. Bagarukayo. 1999. "Increased Sexual Abstinence among In-School Adolescents as a Result of School Health Education in Soroti District, Uganda." *Health Education Research Theory and Practice* 14(3): 411–419.

Singh, S., J. E. Darroch, and A. Bankole. 2003. *The Role of Behavior Change in the Decline in HIV Prevalence in Uganda.* New York: Alan Guttmacher Institute.

Stein, Z. 2000. "International Women's Health." In M. Goldman and M. Hatch, eds., *Women and Health,* 379–389. San Diego: Academic Press.

Tallis, V. 2002. *Gender and HIV/AIDS Overview Report.* Bridge: Development and Gender, Institute of Development Studies.

Tripp, A. M. 1999. *Women and Politics in Uganda.* Oxford: James Currey.

———. 2000. "Rethinking Difference: Comparative Perspectives from Africa." *Signs: Journal of Women in Culture and Society* 25(3): 649–675.

———. 2001. "The Politics of Autonomy and Cooptation in Africa: The Case of the Ugandan Women's Movement." *Journal of Modern African Studies* 39(1): 101–128.

UAC (Uganda AIDS Commission). 1997. "Inventory of Agencies with HIV/AIDS Related Activities in Uganda 1997." Kampala: UAC.

Uganda Bureau of Statistics and ORC Macro (2001) Uganda Demographic and Health Survey 2000/2001. Calverton, MD: ORC Macro.

UNAIDS/WHO. 2003. Joint press statement, March 14, Geneva. www.unaids.org.

Vaughan, M. 1991. *Curing Their Ills: Colonial Power and African Illness.* Cambridge: Polity.

Vavrus, F., and U. Larsen. 2003. "Girls' Education and Fertility Transitions: An Analysis of Recent Trends in Tanzania and Uganda." *Economic Development and Cultural Change* 51(4): 945–976.

Walker, D., H. Muyinda, S. Foster, J. Kengeya-Kayondo, and J. Whitworth. 2001. "The Quality of Care by Private Practitioners for Sexually Transmitted Diseases in Uganda." *Health Policy and Planning* 16(1): 35–40.

Wendo, Charles. 2003. "Uganda Agrees to Increase Health Spending Using Global Fund's Grant." *The Lancet* 361 (February 5, 2003): 319. http://www.aegis.com/news/ads/2003/AD030240.html.

Whyte, S. R. 2002. "Subjectivity and Subjunctivity: Hoping for Health in Eastern Uganda." In R. Werbner, ed., *Postcolonial Subjectivities in Africa,* 171–190. London: Zed Books.

Whyte, S. R., and H. Birungi. 2000. "The Business of Medicines and the Politics of Knowledge in Uganda." In L. M. Whiteford and L. Manderson, eds., *Global Health Policy, Local Realities: The Fallacy of the Level Playing Field.* Boulder: Lynne Rienner.

Mapping the Contours

Reproductive Health and Rights and Sexual Health and Rights in India

Radhika Chandiramani

The Paradox in India

> My husband has a touring job. I know that he has sex with other
> women when he is away. I have heard of AIDS and am fright-
> ened. But I cannot refuse to have sex with him when he returns. I
> know about condoms but if I tell him to use one he will suspect
> me of infidelity and will beat me. I dare not confront him about
> his having sex with others. What should I do?
> —Woman caller on the TARSHI sexuality help line[1]

This woman, like many others, cannot exert control over what is done
to her body. She does not have the right to refuse to have sex. For her, as for
many others, safety from infection is confounded by the need to ensure safety
from accusations of infidelity as well as safety from physical violence. Sexuality, for her, is an area of compromise, resignation, and danger, and, ultimately, one that clearly marks out her lack of choices. This woman lives in
India, a country in which she can use contraceptive and abortion services. In
principle, she has some choice about the reproductive consequences of acts
of sex. However, without social and cultural change that will allow her to
encourage her husband to use condoms or get tested for HIV, her choices are
limited.

Despite her problems, this woman is more privileged than many other
Indian women. She lives in a city, speaks English, has access to information,
and is able to call a help line to share her fears about HIV. In contrast, 72
percent of the Indian population lives in rural areas, most of which lack the

basic amenities of electricity, piped drinking water, and toilet facilities. Of India's 1.2 billion people, 37 percent over the age of six are illiterate. The rates of illiteracy are higher in rural populations and among girls and women (Registrar-General of India 2001).

Like this woman, most women in India are aware of contraception because of the Indian government's emphasis on population control. As the second National Family Health Survey (National Family Health Survey–2 2001) revealed, 99 percent of currently married women know of at least one modern method of contraception; the majority knows about female (98 percent) and male sterilization (89 percent). However, 52 percent of currently married women do not use contraception. Among those who do, most women use irreversible methods, with female sterilization accounting for 71 percent of all contraceptives used. On the other hand, male sterilization accounts for only 4 percent of contraceptive use. The median age at sterilization is 25.7 years for women. Sterilization rates are higher in rural areas, and rates of reversible methods are higher in urban areas. Many factors, including lack of information about reversible contraception, dissatisfaction with reversible methods, provider bias toward sterilization, and incentives for sterilization, account for the large numbers of women undergoing sterilization (Visaria 2000).

Abortion is another popular "family planning" method in India. Pregnancy may be terminated as long as it is done by a trained doctor within twenty weeks of gestation in an institution recognized by the government. Abortion has never been a controversial issue in India, and was legalized in 1971 through the Medical Termination of Pregnancy Act. This was not motivated by the government's commitment to women's autonomy, but rather by its intention to defuse the "population bomb." Though abortion is not a moral or rights issue in India, access to *safe* abortion is still not available to the majority of women. Although abortion was legalized thirty years ago and most women support the right to have an abortion, not many are aware that it is legal. For instance, a community-based study found that 70 percent of women supported abortion as a right, but only 18 percent knew that it was legal (Gupte et al. 1997). Indian society's negative attitude toward sexuality means that abortion providers are often judgmental and moralistic about sex before marriage, and it has resulted in the mushrooming of unregistered and backstreet abortion clinics. Unsafe abortion contributes to 12 percent of maternal deaths every year (Government of India 1990). The number of reported induced abortions is around 670,000 annually (Chhabra and Nuna 1994). However, unqualified practitioners at unrecognized facilities conduct an estimated additional 5 to 6 million abortions every year. These go unreported because they are illegal. They result in an estimated 15,000 to 20,000 abortion-related deaths annually (Khan et al. 1999).

Abortion is viewed as a way of controlling family size when contraception fails. Because of the pressure to have sons in India, prenatal diagnostic techniques are misused to detect the sex of the fetus, and sex-selective abortion has become a way of planning a family with the desired number of male offspring (Ganatra 2000, Mallik 2003). In the community-based study quoted above, though almost all the women were aware that prenatal tests were being used to detect the sex of the fetus, fewer than 10 percent of them knew that they were intended to detect fetal anomalies. Further, 45 percent approved of aborting a female fetus, mainly because of economic reasons, fear of domestic violence, and social pressure (Gupte et al. 1997). Other reasons cited for not wanting daughters included huge dowry and wedding expenses, lack of personal security for women, women's inability to look after their parents, family violence and wife-beating, and the ill treatment of mothers of female infants (Nayar 1995). Sex-selective abortion poses a dilemma in terms of the right to choice in a country where women are pressured to bear male children (Menon 1995).

The paradox in India therefore is this: Despite the availability of contraceptive and abortion services, women lack control over their own bodies and are unable to exercise their sexual and reproductive rights. This is because India has a history of coercive population control policies, an absence of progressive policies, and conservative social norms. Consequently, women are not able to make choices about their own bodies and sexual and reproductive lives.

Population Control Activities in India

The Government of India began its family planning program in 1952 to deal with the burden of a large population. It viewed family planning not as the right of individuals and couples to decide how many children they might want but rather as a mechanism to stabilize population growth to reduce poverty. This antinatalist policy, coupled with the subordinate status of women, led to a top-down family welfare program that targeted women, offered incentives and disincentives to health care workers to meet contraceptive targets, and used sterilization as the key instrument to control population. The excesses of the program peaked in the 1970s when, in its zeal to achieve demographic targets, the Congress party (then the ruling party in the country) forcibly sterilized millions of men.[2] The resulting backlash forced subsequent governments to promote voluntary family planning. In a major program shift in the early 1980s, the government promoted reversible methods of contraception but, unfortunately, also emphasized a time-bound, target-oriented approach to family planning that led to the violation of women's rights. The baggage of coercive policies still accompanies the government on its journey toward more women-centered policies and programs in a country marked by highly conservative social norms.

Conservative Social Norms

India is a complex country characterized by diversity in geography, language, religion, and social practices and customs. Common to the whole country is an unwillingness to openly address issues of sexuality. This is ironic, given that marriage is early and almost universal in India. Of women between 15 and 19 years old, 30 percent are married, as are 94 percent of 25- to 29-year-old women. The average age at marriage for men is five years later than that for women. For women, the median age at first birth is 19.6 years (National Family Health Survey–2 2001).

Families arrange most marriages in India. Partner choice and consensual sex are the privilege of urban, educated populations. A married woman's sexuality is viewed as part of her husband's proprietary right, over which the woman herself has little control. These views are perpetuated and reinforced by the nonrecognition of marital rape (Section 375) and the provisions on adultery (Section 497) and assault (Section 354) under the Indian Penal Code of 1861 (Indian Penal Code). These laws make justice conditional upon protectionist and moralistic value systems, thus restricting the unqualified right of all women to their bodily integrity (National Alliance of Women's Organizations 2000).

It is not just women who are oppressed in a patriarchal society that allows sexual attraction and activity only in a heterosexual context. Anyone who doesn't conform to heteronormative standards is penalized. However, sexuality is not easily categorized into simplistic hetero and homo categories. In India, for example, not all men who have sex with other men classify themselves as "gay." They may choose a local label (such as *ali, kothi, panthi, giriya,* and so on) or not give themselves any label at all. This is because in many cases they themselves consider only peno-vaginal sex with a woman as "real sex" and refer to sex with another man as *masti* or play (Chan et al. 1998, Chandiramani 1998). Men who have sex with men are viewed as sexually deviant and perverted, and are discriminated against in their families and in inheritance and benefit rights, and they risk social ostracism and ridicule.

Because of this, they agree to enter into heterosexual marriages arranged by their families but may continue to have sex with other men.

Lesbianism is even less visible. Lesbians also suffer violations of their right to privacy, to nondiscrimination, to safety, and to sexual expression and association (Campaign for Lesbian Rights 1999). The premium on heterosexual relationships and marriage, combined with the discrimination against lesbians and the ensuing pressure to "pass" as heterosexual, push many women into relationships with men. The violations of people who are transgender are only now beginning to be documented (People's Union for Civil Liberties—Karnataka 2003). Sexuality is thus contested terrain for anyone who dares to transgress societal norms. However, conforming to norms does not make sexuality any less fraught, as we see in the case of the woman who called the help line: Married and monogamous, she still cannot assert control over her own sexuality.

Indian society is also racked by its inability to let go of class hierarchy and an archaic caste system and is easily divided into opposing religious camps. Religion and caste issues differentially affect the sexual and reproductive rights of both men and women. The class order is usually based on education, income, and professional status and permits mobility across levels. The caste system, on the other hand, is rigid and allows for no mobility. People are born into the caste of their family and remain in that caste until death. Marriages are arranged among families of the same or similar castes.

In the caste hierarchy, Dalits are at the lowest level, are considered "untouchable," and therefore are denied equal access to public spaces and services. Though Article 17 of the Indian constitution abolished "untouchability," it remains a hurdle for millions of people in the country. Dalit women are stuck at the bottom of caste, class, and gender hierarchies. They are cheated of a fair income, sexually exploited, raped, and abused with impunity (Human Rights Watch 1999).

Religion further jeopardizes women's right to bodily integrity. Despite being a secular state, India has witnessed increasingly violent upsurges of hatred and violence between different religious communities. These have taken the form of communal riots that include mass beatings, killings, arson, looting, and other forms of violence. In many cases the state has been either complicit with or actively supportive of this violence (Human Rights Watch 1996, Sarkar 2002). The most recent and horrific example is the genocide in the state of Gujarat in 2002, when Muslim women's sexuality and bodies were a battleground for mobs of Hindu men (Citizen's Initiative 2002, Khanna and Shah 2002). Sarkar (2002) points out that the abuse, rape, mutilation, killing, and burning of Muslim women and their children and fetuses by Hindu men (often encouraged by Hindu women) followed a pattern: Women's bodies were a site of violence, women's sexual and reproductive organs were the special focus of attack, and their children and fetuses were attacked and killed before them. Sarkar interprets this against the backdrop of Hindu fears of Muslim men's virility, Muslim women's fecundity, and the Muslims' attributed ability to outnumber Hindus, combined with a right-wing Hindu ideology of revenge and violence.

Like any other complex society, India is also in transition. Though the majority of people live in villages, Indian cities are developing at a fast rate and attracting thousands of migrants in search of better living conditions. This has led to changes in traditional family structures and ways of life. For example, it is now easier for single women to find jobs and housing in major cities than it was even ten years ago. Sexual conservatism is being challenged from many different quarters—there is more allusion to sexuality in the media, including popular soap operas in regional languages; lesbian and gay groups are emerging; and there is more out-of-marriage sexual activity. In fact, the cover story in the September 15, 2003, issue of *India Today*, a highly respected national weekly, focused on "Sex and the Indian Woman" (Vasudev 2003) and on how she is escaping the confines of conservatism. Similarly, a special feature on sexuality in *Outlook*, another national weekly, focused on how the urban Indian woman is challenging patriarchal control of her sexuality (Wadhwa 2003).

No Sex Please, We're Indian

Young People and Sexuality

Young people are particularly disadvantaged in a conservative society that refuses to acknowledge their sexuality. Because parents as well as school teachers are embarrassed to talk frankly about sexuality, schools refuse to provide sex education for fear that parents might object—although they do not concern themselves with parents' views on the curriculum or the syllabi when it comes to other subjects.

The Convention on the Rights of the Child (1989) states in Article 13 that the child (defined as any human being below the age of eighteen years) "shall have the right to freedom to seek, receive and impart information and ideas of all kinds." Article 19 addresses violence and protects children from physical and mental violence and sexual abuse, as well as from neglect and negligent treatment. Might keeping information on sexuality and safety from adolescents be construed as negligence? Information about sexuality can protect young people from HIV/AIDS and unsafe abortions, for example. What are young people learning about sexuality, especially given that a new generation is growing up in the shadow of HIV/AIDS?

Girls grow up with the message that they must exercise restraint in sexual expression to uphold family honor (Abraham 2000, Sodhi 2000). This translates into restricted social mobility for girls when they reach puberty. Though sex before marriage is a sensitive topic, some studies conducted in different parts of India have shown that sexual activity outside of marriage is common among young people in both urban and rural communities (Joshi et al. 1998, Pelto 1999). A review of the reproductive behavior of adolescents suggested that 20 to 30 percent of young men, and up to 10 percent of young women, mainly from the urban areas, are sexually active before marriage (Jejeebhoy 1996).

The taboos around talking about sexuality in India leave young people without an adequate understanding of their own bodies and uncomfortable with sexuality. Even college students in urban areas know little about the body and sex (Sachdev 1997, Sharma and Sharma 1998). In Mumbai, only 16 percent of adolescent girls and 54 percent of adolescent boys knew that sexual intercourse could result in pregnancy (Bhende 1994). Similarly, Jejeebhoy (1996) found that up to 88 percent of unmarried young women seeking abortions did not know that pregnancy resulted from sex. They are more likely than older women to delay seeking abortion and hence to undergo second-trimester abortions, which have greater clinical risks. Trikha (2001) found that 90 percent of adolescent girls undergoing abortion were unmarried and that incest accounted for pregnancy in 16 percent of them; 11 percent were undergoing abortion for the second or third time, 42 percent sought abortions in the second trimester, and 56 percent of the abortions were carried out at unapproved centers by unqualified personnel. For these young women, safety was less important than confidentiality and cost. Notions of chastity and family honor, coupled with the lack of information about pregnancy, ignorance of services, cost, and fear of social stigma make it difficult for young women to seek sexual and reproductive health services.

HIV/AIDS in India

In this complex scenario in India, HIV/AIDS is yet another factor that poses a huge threat to sexual and reproductive health. According to the latest estimates, there are between 3.82 and 4.58 million people, age fifteen to forty-nine, who are infected with HIV (NACO 2003). The fifteen- to forty-four-year age group account for 90 percent of cases; this is the age group considered to be most sexually active and economically productive. By the end of May 2004, there were 70,453 people (of all ages) with AIDS in India. Among those with AIDS, about 85 percent of the transmission occurred through the sexual route, 2 percent through blood transfusion, and 2 percent through injecting drug use. One in every three cases reported is a woman (NACO 2004). HIV infection is prevalent in almost every part of the country and is increasingly spreading into the general population. Awareness has increased in urban areas but remains quite low in rural areas. The lowest awareness rates are among rural women.[3]

The first case of AIDS in India was reported in 1986. The government set up the National AIDS Control Committee the same year and a National AIDS Control Programme a year later to monitor and control the spread of HIV. In 1992 the government formulated a multisectoral strategy for the prevention and control of AIDS through the National AIDS Control Organization (NACO). The government's efforts are not enough, and nongovernmental organizations (NGOs) are attempting to meet the challenges that HIV/AIDS poses to a country characterized by traditional social ills, cultural myths on sex and sexuality, and a huge population of marginalized people.

In spite of these efforts, understanding of how sexuality is connected to HIV/AIDS remains abysmally low. Even health care professionals are ill informed about the diversity of sexual practice, and provide services based on heterosexist assumptions. Because most doctors ignore or are unaware that married men in India may also have sex with other men, male-to-male sex tends to be overlooked, putting these men and their partners at increased risk. Thus, all men who attend sexually transmitted disease (STD) clinics are asked, "When did you last visit a woman?" (UNAIDS 2001).

AIDS is still perceived as a disease of "others"—of people living on the margins of society, whose lifestyles are considered "perverted" and "sinful" (UNAIDS 2001). This results in discrimination, stigmatization, and denial, because of which there is a lack of appropriate policies. A case in point is the Supreme Court of India's controversial ruling in 1988 that suspended the right of HIV-positive people to marry. This case is known as *Mr. X vs. Hospital Z* (1998).[4] The court decided that the law imposes a duty on a person living with HIV/AIDS (PLWHA) "not to marry, as the marriage would have the effect of spreading the infection of his own disease, which is obviously dangerous to life, to the woman he marries."

According to the judges, "AIDS is the product of undisciplined sexual impulse." The judges did add that PLWHAs "deserve full sympathy and are entitled to all respects as human beings. They should not be discriminated against." However, they also said that "sex with them or possibility thereof has to be avoided as otherwise they would infect and communicate the dreadful disease to others." That members of the highest court in the country were seemingly unaware that safer sex techniques allow for the possibility of people who are HIV positive to have sex without transmitting the virus to others is shameful. This was the first time in judicial history anywhere in the world that a court took away the fundamental right of an individual to marry (Grover 2001). The right to marry and found a family is a fundamental human right recognized internationally.[5] In India, the right to marry and found a family is part of the "right to life and liberty" under Article 21 of the constitution.

This case illustrates how public health arguments are used to curtail sexual activity, even when their moralistic bases are very clear. Marriage was seen as a "sacred union" for the purposes of procreation by the two Supreme Court judges. The Supreme Court judgment restrained HIV-positive people from marrying even if they had obtained full, free, and informed consent from their prospective spouses. Further, the effect of the judgment was such that the attempts of HIV-positive people to marry would make them criminally liable.[6] The judgment provoked widespread protests by NGOs and other groups. The Lawyers Collective HIV/AIDS Unit, an NGO that provides legal services, filed a case challenging the judgment of the Supreme Court. In December 2002, the Supreme Court passed an order restoring the right of people who are HIV positive to marry (*Mr. X vs. Hospital Z* 2002).

Though the court restored the right to marry, its earlier judgment continues to have negative effects. The court in its 1998 judgment had said that the hospital authorities, by keeping the complainant's HIV status confidential, would have become "participant criminals." In keeping with the court's stand, official policies encourage partner notification; in cases of positive test results, the person's partner or spouse is notified.[7] This means that doctors disclose HIV test results to the family and/or spouse of the person arbitrarily and without following proper procedures for obtaining consent. These are violations not only of the right to privacy but also of the right to life in a country where extreme discrimination costs people their jobs, homes, and even their lives.

The absence of appropriate policies also affects access to HIV tests in the case of young people. In India there are no guidelines and statutes empowering minors to consent to confidential HIV testing without parental involvement. That HIV testing is a sensitive issue and that young people might not want their parents or guardians to know about their sexual activity or concerns about HIV seems not to matter. In fact, the official guidelines state, "in case of minor, the consent should be obtained from the parents" (NACO 2001).

Even though the government program supports HIV prevention efforts among men who have sex with men, NGOs in the country are finding that a law that criminalizes sex between men hampers their HIV prevention efforts. Although being homosexual is itself not a crime in India, Section 377 (Unnatural Offenses) of the Indian Penal Code (IPC) has been used to criminalize male homosexual behavior and reads thus: "Whoever voluntarily has carnal intercourse against the order of nature with any man, woman or animal, shall be punished with imprisonment for life, or with imprisonment of either description for a term which may extend to ten years, and shall also be liable to fine. Explanation—Penetration is sufficient to constitute the carnal intercourse necessary to the offence described in this section." The police use this law together with other provisions on obscenity (Section 292 of the IPC) to harass NGOs working on HIV and sexual health issues among men who have sex with men (Human Rights Watch 2002). These provisions on obscenity are often justified under Article 19 (2) of the Indian constitution on the grounds of preserving public decency and morality. They have been used to restrict the dissemination of sexual health information and the distribution of literature and material, including condoms (Human Rights Watch 2002).

Apart from restricting sexual plurality and violating the rights of men who have sex with men, Section 377 has the effect of pushing same-sex behavior underground and leading to risky sexual practices. The absence of safe private spaces makes men seek male partners in public spaces (parks, roadsides, public toilets, and so on). Groups such as the AIDS Bhedbhav Virodhi Andolan (1991) and the People's Union for Civil Liberties—Karnataka Chapter (2000) have documented how the police have misused Section 377 to harass, physically and sexually abuse, and blackmail men who have sex with men. The fear of criminal law in this context implies that for men who have sex with other men in parks or public toilets, sex is often hurried and furtive, leaving partners without an option to consider or negotiate safer sexual practices. Prison authorities have also used Section 377 to deny prison inmates access to condoms despite evidence of homosexual activity. This law actually results in increasing the vulnerability of a population to HIV (Menghaney 2003).

The Lawyers' Collective on behalf of the Naz Foundation (India) Trust (an NGO based in New Delhi) filed a petition in the Delhi High Court in

2001 challenging the constitutional validity of Section 377 and seeking to decriminalize private consensual adult sexual behavior.[8] The case is pending.

That policies and programs are planned and implemented in a piece-meal fashion is also illustrated by the latest development in the field of HIV/AIDS in India. The Indian government has decided to provide antiretroviral therapy to people with HIV and AIDS. The government promised that by April 2004 it would begin providing free antiretroviral therapy to all HIV-positive new parents and all children under fifteen in the six states (Tamil Nadu, Andhra Pradesh, Karnataka, Maharashtra, Manipur, and Nagaland) with the highest rates of HIV and AIDS. Eventually, all people in those states with full-blown AIDS are to be treated (Waldman 2003).

At the same time, the government moved away from what Sushma Swaraj, the minister for health and family welfare, called a "condom-centric" public education campaign to a more "holistic" one. The minister is averse to condom advertisements on television, believing that they lead people to have more sex. Government-sponsored public messages now read, "If there is loyalty and fidelity between husband and wife, there is no space for HIV/AIDS." This message reinforces the burden on women and men to prove mo-nogamy, even while in nonmonogamous relationships. In India, because of the double standards that exist around what men and women may do sexu-ally, this burden falls disproportionately on women.

The urgent need to provide adequate sexual and reproductive health ser-vices and to tackle HIV/AIDS requires that interventions incorporate prin-ciples of sexual rights and that state agencies function in a cohesive manner to affirm the promises made at the Cairo and Beijing Conferences.

The Paradigm Shift: More Rhetoric Than Action

Ten years ago, the government of India agreed at the International Con-ference on Population and Development at Cairo that reproductive rights (in-cluding the right to reproductive and sexual health) are part of the larger body of human rights. In 1995, at Beijing they agreed that the right to control over matters of sexuality was part of human rights. The concepts endorsed at the Cairo and Beijing conferences are based on the notion of gender equity. They recognize that without gender equality and equity, there is no possibility of choice or autonomy in decision making in sexuality and reproduction. They therefore imply that for individuals, societies, and communities to attain sexual and reproductive health and rights, gender equality must prevail in econom-ics, law, education, employment, and so on.

These two international conferences also emphasized that human rights are reciprocal and indivisible—that women could not realize their reproductive rights if their other rights were violated, such as rights to education, information, freedom of movement, and of association. Policies and programs not only about sexuality and reproduction are required but also about a range of other conditions that affect one's ability to make meaningful choices. Sexual and reproductive rights will have meaning only when the enabling material and social conditions are in place (Correa and Petchesky 1994). For example, no amount of information about menstrual hygiene is useful to a woman who does not have clean water with which she can wash. Or women constrained by economic dependence and the cultural preference for sons may "choose" abortion as a means of sex selection.

Three issues from the International Conference on Population and Development in Cairo in 1994 and the Fourth World Conference on Women in Beijing in 1995 are important in resource-poor settings like India: first, acknowledging that population is an aspect of human development and is related to other areas of development such as governance, education, livelihood, security, and social justice; second, the notion that individuals have sexual and reproductive rights that governments must uphold and protect; and, third, understanding that empowering women is key to enabling individuals and communities achieve sexual and reproductive well-being.

These developments represented a significant paradigm shift for countries like India that had long followed a population control model. In October 1997, partly in response to Cairo and partly because of evidence that method-specific contraceptive targets had failed, the Indian government made two complementary policy decisions that support the principles of reproductive health and rights. It abolished the widely criticized contraceptive targets that had been in place for more than three decades, and it introduced a more women-centered Reproductive and Child Health (RCH) program in the public-sector health delivery system all over the country (Visaria 2000, Santhya 2003). The RCH program added elements of safe motherhood and child survival and the prevention and management of reproductive tract infections and STDs to what was essentially a family planning program. The National Population Policy adopted in 2000 further legitimized the shift away from a target-based approach and affirmed the government's commitment to a reproductive health approach.

Though the shift to a reproductive health approach was a welcome change, its full impact is yet to be felt. Reproductive health services have developed as if fertility regulation and safety from reproductive ill health have little, if anything, to do with sexuality. The Indian program continues to operate with an underlying assumption that the only people in need of services are procreating heterosexuals, especially married women, in the reproductive years, as is clear from the lack of access to safe abortion, of sex education for young people, and of coherent and complementary policies around HIV/AIDS as well as the violations of people's sexual and reproductive rights. Sexual health is subsumed under reproductive health, which results in programs that merely add on some elements of sexual health, such as the prevention and management of STDs. Related sexual and reproductive health and rights issues, such as safe abortion, adolescents' needs, violence against women, and the concerns of single or older men and women and those of nonheterosexual people, continue to be ignored. In practice, the "sexual" goes largely missing (Ramachandran 1999), and reproductive and sexual rights are still not recognized as women's rights and human rights.

There also appears to be an alarming regression to earlier antinatalist policies. Some states (including Andhra Pradesh, Madhya Pradesh, Maharashtra, and Rajasthan) have incorporated several open or "veiled" disincentives. The population policy of Madhya Pradesh, for example, advocates that individuals who marry before the legally permissible age be debarred from seeking jobs, being admitted to educational institutions, and applying for loans (Pachauri 2001 cited in Santhya 2003: 5). The Supreme Court has recently upheld a Haryana state law that prohibits a person from contesting or holding a leadership position in the panchayat institutions if he or she has more than two children (Venkatesan 2003).[9]

Reproductive health thus appears to have three different meanings in India: for health professionals, as stated in the Cairo Programme, "it is a state of complete physical, mental, and social well-being and not merely the absence of disease or infirmity in all matters related to the reproductive system and its functions and processes"; for women's rights advocates, the emphasis is on rights; and for policy makers, reproductive health is an instrument to stabilize population growth (Datta and Misra 2000).

Clearly the reproductive health approach alone, especially as it is practiced in India, is not sufficient to address sexual and reproductive ill health, HIV/AIDS, and violence against women. Adopting a sexual rights approach is more promising not only because it offers more scope for addressing these issues but also because it further advances gender equity and women's autonomy.

The Potential of Sexual Rights

Going beyond Reproduction

As illustrated above, the various government programs and policies appear to function in isolation and sometimes even in opposition to each other. For instance, had the Supreme Court acknowledged that people living with HIV/AIDS may want to have sex and that they may want to have children, it might have considered other, less intrusive and restrictive methods for reducing infection rates, such as more effective safer sex education and emotional and social support to encourage voluntary disclosure to partners or spouses, rather than suspending the right of HIV-positive people to marry.

Adopting a sexual rights approach means acknowledging that people experience and express their sexuality in diverse ways. Given the multiple meanings and manifestations that occur at the intersections of gender, class, ethnicity, and sexual orientation, sexuality cannot be confined to a singular notion. The expression and understanding of sexuality are specific to a particular place, time, and group of people. They change, as do the factors that govern the regulation of sexuality. Sexuality is not a given, it is a product of negotiation, struggle, and human agency (Weeks 1986). These struggles to define, regulate, and resist have most often occurred around such nonnormative practices as nonheterosexual and nonprocreative sexuality.

Sexual rights include the right to diverse forms of sexual expression, identity, and practice and therefore apply to all people. They include the right to consensual sexual relations and therefore to partner choice. They also include the right to appropriate information about sexuality for all people of all ages. They can be used to regulate age of marriage and sexual activity depending on the evolving capacities of young people. Clearly, young people's rights to information and access to health care, privacy, and nondiscrimination in terms of their sexuality are not being met if they do not have access to sexual and reproductive health services (sex education and safe abortions, for example) and cannot even choose to have an HIV test. Because the notion of sexual rights includes the right to safety from violence as well as the right to pleasure, it goes beyond a violations-based approach that only protects from negative conditions to an approach that affirms positive and life-enriching experiences. This view portrays women as active agents capable of making decisions and not just as passive victims of sexual horrors and abuses (Miller 2000).

In a rights-based approach, marital status cannot be the yardstick for provision of services. According to a newspaper report, some government hospitals provide abortion services only if the woman is married.[10] A single woman must provide the hospital with either a written statement that she was not raped or, if she was raped, with a copy of the statement made to the police (Tewari 2002). As Jesani and Iyer (1993) point out, for a liberalized abortion law to be effective, it has to be backed by good infrastructural support and accompanied by a full range of other functional social services including health, prenatal care, sex education, and protection from abuse.

Women's needs vis-à-vis HIV/AIDS will continue to be inadequately addressed until their sexual rights are affirmed. Women as a group are more vulnerable to HIV infection than are men (Ramasubban 1995). Sexual transmission of the virus is two to four times more efficient from men to women than vice versa. Compounding this is the fact that unequal relationships make it difficult for women to negotiate safer sex.

HIV prevention messages emphasize safer sex, as of course they need to. However, the emphasis was and still is on the element of "safer" without understanding the context in which safety is prescribed as a regular practice. Because sex is more than a matter of simply inserting a part of one's body into a part of another person's body, people's emotions, fantasies, roles, and expectations have to be addressed. Sexual relationships between people occur in the context of social and cultural structures that are based on inequitable gender and power relations. In keeping with this, paragraph 98 of the Beijing Programme recognizes that "social vulnerability and the unequal power relationships between women and men are obstacles to safe sex."

Most HIV prevention efforts in India address women either as sex workers or as wives. As sex workers they are targeted as a "high-risk group" and considered "vectors" of the infection. Prevention efforts are made to educate female sex workers about HIV and the need for condoms to protect their clients from contracting the infection. (Male sex workers receive almost no attention.) There are very few efforts to protect sex workers themselves from contracting the infection from their clients. Support and care for sex workers who are infected with HIV hardly exist. As wives, women are expected to be monogamous and to ensure that their husbands do not "stray." As we saw in the vignette at the beginning of this chapter, women cannot insist on condom use for fear of being accused of infidelity, even though non-monogamous men may transmit infections to their monogamous wives.

In dealing with the issues of vulnerability, transmission, care, and support, the rights and health dimensions that affect women cannot be separated (Correa 1994). Cultural silence and unequal power relations serve as barriers to discussions about sex between men and women, leaving women unable to adopt HIV prevention strategies. Condom use and women's negotiation skills are meaningless terms in a context in which women have very little actual power (George and Jaswal 1994). HIV is much more than a health issue, and an effective response to it must be firmly anchored in an affirmation of both sexual and reproductive rights.

Keeping safe also involves working to reduce the risks associated with certain sexual activities and learning about others that are pleasurable. This requires an approach that validates sexuality as an integral and rewarding part of each person's life. Without such an approach, policies and programs run the risk of not affirming people's sexual rights. Further, they might marginalize certain groups of people based on difference in their sexual/gender identities, roles, preferences, and practices. Below is an example of how an Indian NGO has used an approach based on sexual rights to address concerns of reproductive and sexual health.

Sexual Rights in Practice

Believing that all people have the right to sexual well-being and a self-affirming, enjoyable sexuality, Talking about Reproductive and Sexual Health Issues (TARSHI) works toward expanding sexual and reproductive choices in people's lives. TARSHI is an NGO based in New Delhi that, among its various other programs, runs a telephone help line that provides information, counseling, and referrals on sexuality and reproductive health in Hindi and English (UNAIDS 2002). The TARSHI help line guarantees anonymity and confidentiality to its callers. TARSHI has responded to more than 54,000 calls since 1996. Callers range from seven to more than seventy years of age and are from diverse socioeconomic backgrounds. Callers speak about wide-ranging concerns, including body image, masturbation, contraception, abortion, STDs, HIV/AIDS, sexual abuse, emotional and relationship problems, and so on (Chandiramani 1998). Trained counselors respond to calls. Counseling on the help line is premised on the belief that all people are able to make choices, however insignificant those choices might seem to anyone else, and helps callers discover what it is that they want to do. Through the counseling process, people find ways that feel right to them, ways that "fit" their lives.

The help line counselors are trained to not give advice or assume responsibility for other people's decisions. They use gender-sensitive and nonheterosexist language so that callers are not marginalized by assumptions made about their sexual preferences. For example, the counselors do not use words like husband, wife, girlfriend, or boyfriend, or masculine and feminine pronouns, but use the gender-neutral term "partner" instead. This allows callers to freely express their concerns and does not further violate or negate those who have experienced discrimination because of their sexuality.

Consistently following the principle that all people have a right to sexual pleasure means helping them find ways to enhance pleasure when they call the help line. This raises the question: What about safety from infection, unwanted pregnancy, and harm? The debate on balancing pleasure and safety is unending. As all practitioners know, it is not easy to advocate condom use 100 percent of the time; women and especially men ask "but, what about skin-to-skin?" Sexual interactions are influenced by desire, fantasy, passion, and even fear. People report their inability to use safer sex techniques because of intimacy and trust, because of fear that it might signal the presence of more than one sexual partner, because these techniques actually restrict the full range of pleasure that they or their partners wish to experience, and diverse other reasons. Thus it is essential to acknowledge and address two facts: one, that asking people to change their sexual behavior might require them to give up certain pleasures; two, it means addressing complex gender and power issues because these are what affect decisions about and the ability to use safer sex techniques.

TARSHI records reveal that men find it easier to demand information about sexual acts, techniques, and positions that enhance sexual pleasure than women do. The help line counselors provide this information, in addition to information about sexual and reproductive health. However, this can be a double-edged sword. In the case of oral sex, for example, many women find fellatio repulsive and refuse to perform it, citing reasons of hygiene, or saying "it is not a normal way of having sex." Once callers learn from TARSHI that there is nothing that is normal or abnormal in sex, male callers use this information to pressure their unwilling partners to perform fellatio. Not giving men information on pleasure enhancement is denying them information. But giving them this information gives them an additional tool of power to use against women who cannot refuse to engage in sex. Following a sexual rights approach, TARSHI counselors resolve this issue by giving men the information they request while also emphasizing that for sex to be pleasurable, it must be consensual. Not giving men information about sexual pleasure because women are not able to refuse sex is paternalistic and protective of women.

In addition to working at the individual level, TARSHI also tries to take the message of the Cairo and Beijing Conferences to diverse audiences to build awareness and change public attitudes about sexuality. Its staff writes a weekly advice column on sexuality for a national newspaper to reach out to as many people as possible so that sexual rights become the rights of all. Sexual rights apply to everyone, not only to people who identify as belonging to a marginalized group. The absence of this understanding not only reduces the potential impact of work on sexuality but sometimes also leads to programs, advocacy initiatives, and actions that ultimately do not further well-being and the assertion of rights. In order to deepen the understanding of the conceptual and theoretical underpinnings of the fields of sexuality and rights and to encourage activists and others to critically examine the assumptions on which they base their work, TARSHI conducts an annual Sexuality and Rights Institute in collaboration with Creating Resources for Empowerment in Action.

To scale up programs that incorporate sexual and reproductive rights is a challenge that can be met if there is sufficient political will and commitment. It also requires the support and legitimization of these efforts through further development and use of sexual rights language in the international arena.

Legitimizing Sexual Rights Internationally

Concepts of reproductive and sexual rights have evolved in the last decade and are increasingly considered as part of the larger body of human rights. The term "reproductive health" became popular in the 1980s and was widely accepted after the Cairo Conference. It challenged population-control-based family planning programs that are based on the belief that population was the cause of poverty rather than that factors such as poverty exacerbated population growth. A reproductive health approach means that individuals should be able to have a satisfying and safe sex life and the freedom to make decisions about if, when, and how often to reproduce.[11] Reproductive health includes sexual health, according to the definition developed in Cairo.

Reproductive rights are meant to create the conditions under which reproduction can be controlled by women and men. Reproductive rights "rest on the recognition of the basic right of all couples and individuals to decide freely and responsibly the number, spacing, and timing of their children and to have the information and means to do so, and the right to attain the highest standard of sexual and reproductive health. It also includes the right of all to make decisions concerning reproduction free of discrimination, coercion and violence as expressed in human rights documents" (United Nations 1994).

The Fourth World Conference on Women in Beijing in 1995 reaffirmed reproductive rights and introduced the notion of the right to control one's sexuality in Article 96 of the Platform for Action: "The human rights of women include their right to have control over and decide freely and responsibly on matters related to their sexuality, including sexual and reproductive health, free of coercion, discrimination, and violence. Equal relationships between women and men in matters of sexual relations and reproduction, including full respect for the integrity of the person, require mutual respect, consent and shared responsibility for sexual behavior and its consequences" (United Nations 1996).

Though the Beijing Platform does not use the term "sexual rights," it is understood to refer to the rights of all people to control their sexuality. The term is gaining currency and being used by bodies that have a large international presence and weight. The World Health Organization (WHO) is one such body. WHO sets standards of health care internationally. It has moved toward a more comprehensive definition of sexuality that allows for variations in the way that people express and experience their sexuality.[12] It has recently also revised its definition of sexual health and also defined sexual rights.[13] WHO's draft working definition of sexual rights is as follows:

> Sexual rights embrace human rights that are already recognized in national laws, international human rights documents, and other consensus documents. These include the right of all persons, free of coercion, discrimination and violence, to:
> - the highest attainable standard of health in relation to sexuality, including access to sexual and reproductive health care services;
> - seek, receive, and impart information in relation to sexuality;
> - sexuality education;
> - respect for bodily integrity;
> - choice of partner;
> - decide to be sexually active or not;
> - consensual sexual relations;
> - consensual marriage;
> - decide whether or not and when to have children; and
> - pursue a satisfying, safe, and pleasurable sexual life.
>
> The responsible exercise of human rights requires that all persons respect the rights of others. (World Health Organization 2002)

Recognizing sexual and reproductive rights as women's rights and human rights provides an exciting opportunity for constructive dialogue and partnership among state and nonstate actors to promote policies and programs that advance gender equity and women's autonomy.

Conclusion

The vignette at the beginning of this chapter illustrates the paradox of how reproductive health programs give women the ability to choose the reproductive consequences of sexual behavior but do not in themselves allow for choice regarding the sexual aspects of their lives. Unless societal attitudes about sexuality are changed (through public education and the government's willingness to accept the reality of sex) and women are able to control their own sexuality, there will be very little that women can do to protect themselves.

That social conditions have to change in order for women to be able to have as well as refuse sex in accordance with their own desires is irrefutable. Meanwhile, women are going about living their lives and having to make difficult decisions. The woman caller whose dilemma is quoted at the beginning of this chapter cannot wait for enabling conditions to materialize—she has to find ways to protect herself from possible HIV infection as well as from abuse *now*. Even if the counselor feels that the woman can confront her husband, leave the relationship, or give him an ultimatum of "no condom, no sex," the reality is that the consequences of each of these acts are unacceptable to the caller. This woman has to find her own ways of dealing with the situation. On the TARSHI help line, she begins to find small ways of resisting demands for sex (pleading tiredness, the heat, her period, and so on) and also becomes better informed about risks associated with different kinds of sexual acts. She gets practical tips (such as using lubricants so that her vaginal lining is not torn during intercourse) and discusses how she might be able to identify occasions when she might get away with not having sex with her husband. Over a number of calls, the counselor also speaks with her about her (the caller's) own perceptions of women's status in society, gender-power relations, abusive relationships, and safety plans.

Social norms change with concerted social action that includes public education as well as individual empowerment and action. This then may spiral into demands for government accountability and provision of adequate services that include basic amenities of water, electricity, and education as well as conditions of health and safety. Effective strategies for public education include information dissemination during festivals and fairs, street theater, peer education programs, and representation in local governance bodies. For example, Sampada Grameen Mahila Sanstha (SANGRAM), an NGO based in Maharashtra, uses all the above techniques to educate the community about

HIV. Through this program, women in prostitution are now able to insist that their clients use condoms. They are also empowered as a collective to resist police harassment and violence (SANGRAM undated).

There are positive signs in India. Though characterized by conservative social norms that in many cases denigrate women and penalize those who engage in nonheterosexual practices, Indian society is in transition, at least in the urban areas, resulting in gains in power and status for women. The government, in its rhetoric at least, is committed to a reproductive health approach and to supporting prevention and care in terms of HIV/AIDS. The Health Ministry has launched a serious effort to reorient the family welfare program from a demographic to a client- and women-centered reproductive health approach. These positive signs in government functioning have been accompanied by an increased willingness on the part of civil society to engage with the government regarding needed changes in the objectives, scope, and implementation of government programs to translate the rhetoric of Cairo and Beijing into action. For meaningful change to occur, work on reproductive health must be accompanied by work on sexual rights. Reproductive health work entails the provision of a range of health services, whereas a sexual rights approach entails working toward changes in social norms.

A health-based approach alone does not guarantee women the ability to control their own lives because it focuses on curing ills without regard to the underlying social, cultural, economic, and other factors that cause or exacerbate ill health. It does not focus on gender and systemic inequities that contribute to sexual and reproductive ill health and does not work toward positive social change. It treats the ills caused by unequal gender power relations, but does not work toward ensuring that these do not happen. For example, it provides treatment services to a battered woman but does not uphold her right to safety from violence. Similarly, it might provide for sterile conditions under which traditional genital cutting procedures could occur but would not get to the roots of preventing this form of female subjugation. The same arguments can be made against a sexual health approach that does not include components of rights. Sexual health does not situate sexuality in a context of power relationships and inequitable systemic factors and therefore does not address the reality of coercion, violence, abuse, and exploitation. Sexual rights add the notions of bodily integrity and gender equity to sexual health. The ability to freely enter into sexual relationships, to refuse sex, and to choose one's partner are only partly health concerns. They are also about dignity and autonomy that lie at the heart of sexual rights. Information about sexuality, the questioning of traditional gender and sexual roles, critiques of government policies as well as government inaction need to accompany health-based interventions.

Sexual rights also offer advocacy groups a tool they can use to hold governments accountable and can be used to build alliances across movements and groups. For instance, a people's movement group in India joined forces with a sexual minorities group to document violations against sexual minorities and the transgender community on the grounds of discrimination and police harassment (People's Union for Civil Liberties—Karnataka 2000, 2003). The Rainbow Planet, a coalition of groups of sex workers, members of groups oppressed because of their sexual or gender preference, people living with HIV/AIDS, and activists from other movements, made the issue of discrimination against sexual minorities visible during the World Social Forum in Mumbai in January 2004 (Murthy 2004). The Rainbow Planet effectively used slogans like "Judge Not, Support Sexual Preference" and "Our Rights, Human Rights" to create awareness about the marginalization of people who do not conform to gender and sexual norms. Voices Against Section 377, a forum composed of representatives of different movements—women's rights, gay rights, health and human rights, and children's rights—is demanding that the government repeals Section 377 and make a separate law for child sexual abuse (Narrain 2004). These groups offer inspiring examples of coalition building across movements to demand sexual rights for all.

For continued movement toward gender equity and women's autonomy in India, sexual rights offer a promising avenue for change because sexuality need not be an area of compromise, resignation, and danger; after all, women's autonomy ultimately hinges on women's control of their own sexuality.

Notes

1. TARSHI is an acronym for Talking about Reproductive and Sexual Health Issues. A nonprofit organization in New Delhi, it believes that all people have a right to sexual well-being and to a self-affirming and enjoyable sexuality. Among its other programs, TARSHI operates a telephone help line that offers information, counseling, and referrals on sexuality.
2. Close to 7.6 million vasectomies were performed in less than two years, accounting for 49 percent of all "acceptors" of family planning during that period (Ministry of Health and Family Welfare 1996).
3. Awareness rates are lowest among rural women in the most developmentally backward states in the country: Bihar, 21.5 percent; Gujarat, 25 percent; Uttar Pradesh, 27.6 percent; and Madhya Pradesh, 32.3 percent.
4. The complainant (who was engaged to be married and who had voluntarily do-

nated blood in a hospital) had filed a case alleging breach of confidentiality by hospital authorities about his HIV status. He discovered his positive status in this roundabout manner and not directly from the hospital, and called off his engagement and subsequent marriage himself. The matter before the judges was one of compensation by the hospital for breach of confidentiality. However, the judges wrote a decision on the right to marry, treating it as a "public interest matter."

5. Article 23 of the Universal Declaration of Human Rights (United Nations 1948) and Article 16 of the International Covenant on Civil and Political Rights.

6. Section 269 of the Indian Penal Code on Negligent Act Likely to Spread Infection of Disease Dangerous to Life and Section 270 of the Indian Penal Code on Malignant Act Likely to Spread Infection of Disease Dangerous to Life.

7. Section 5.6.4 of the NACO policy states that test results "should be given out to the person and with his consent to the members of his family. Disclosure of the HIV status to the spouse or sexual partner of the person should invariably be done by the attending physician with proper counseling." Section 5.6.5 states, "In case of marriage, if one of the partners insists on a test to check the HIV status of the other partner, such tests should be carried out by the contracting party to the satisfaction of the person concerned" (NACO undated). The *HIV/AIDS Handbook for Counselors* (NACO 2001) states: "In accordance to the decision of the Supreme Court, the National AIDS Committee decided to include partner notification as a policy. In this regard, all HIV positive individuals should be encouraged to disclose the HIV status to their sexual partner. However, it is imperative for the attending physician to disclose the status to the spouse or sexual partner with proper counseling."

8. The petition argues this unconstitutionality on several grounds, including: 1. the prohibition of private, consensual relations violates the right to privacy, which is guaranteed "within the ambit of the right to liberty" in the Indian constitution; 2. a distinction between procreative and nonprocreative sex is unreasonable and arbitrary and undermines the equal protection provision of the constitution; 3. the right to life guaranteed in the constitution is violated by Section 377's jeopardizing HIV/AIDS preventive efforts, as it is a tangible threat to individuals and NGOs who wish to work with men who have sex with men or with the gay community as part of HIV interventions; and 4. Section 377 effectively violates the prohibition of discrimination on the grounds of sex because it criminalizes predominantly homosexual activity.

9. A panchayat is an elected body of representatives at the village level that carries out village administration.

10. The Guru Teg Bahadur Hospital in New Delhi provides an abortion only if the woman is married and agrees to have a tubal ligation or insertion of an intrauterine device. At the Lady Hardinge Medical College, single women seeking abortions must make written statements that they were not raped, and if raped, must provide a copy of the First Information Report made to the police. Safdarjung Hospital prefers to have the woman come with her husband or father and seek the husband's or in-laws' written consent for the procedure. According to the Medical Termination of Pregnancy Act, the presence of a guardian is mandatory only for minors (Venkatesan 2003).

11. "Reproductive health is a state of complete physical, mental, and social well-being and not merely the absence of disease or infirmity, in all matters relating to the reproductive system and its functions and processes. Reproductive health therefore implies that people are able to have a satisfying and safe sex life and that they have the capability to reproduce and the freedom to decide if, when, and how often to do so. Reproductive health care is defined as the constellation of methods, techniques, and services that contribute to reproductive health and well-being by preventing and solving reproductive health problems. It also includes sexual health, the purpose of which is the enhancement of life and personal relations, and not merely counseling and care related to reproduction and sexually transmitted diseases" (United Nations 1994).

12. "Sexuality is a central aspect of being human throughout life and encompasses sex, gender identities and roles, sexual orientation, eroticism, pleasure, intimacy, and reproduction. Sexuality is experienced and expressed in thoughts, fantasies, desires, beliefs, attitudes, values, behaviors, practices, roles, and relationships. While sexuality can include all of these dimensions, not all of them are always experienced or expressed. Sexuality is influenced by the interaction of biological, psychological, social, economic, political, cultural, ethical, legal, historical, and religious and spiritual factors" (World Health Organization 2002).

13. "Sexual health is a state of physical, emotional, mental, and social well-being related to sexuality; it is not merely the absence of disease, dysfunction, or infirmity. Sexual health requires a positive and respectful approach to sexuality and sexual relationships, as well as the possibility of having pleasurable and safe sexual experiences, free of coercion, discrimination, and violence. For sexual health to be attained and maintained, the sexual rights of all persons must be respected, protected, and fulfilled" (World Health Organization 2002).

References

Abraham, L. 2000. "True-love, Time-pass, Bhai-bahen . . . Heterosexual Relationships among Youth in a Metropolis." Paper presented at the workshop on Reproductive Health in India: Evidence and Issues, Pune, February 28–March 1.

AIDS Bhedbhav Virodhi Andolan. 1991. *Less Than Gay: A Citizen's Report on the Status of Homosexuality in India.* New Delhi: AIDS Bhedbhav Virodhi Andolan.

Bhende, A. 1994. "Study of Sexuality of Adolescent Girls and Boys in Underprivileged Groups in Bombay." *Indian Journal of Social Work* 55(4): 557–571.

Campaign for Lesbian Rights. 1999. *Lesbian Emergence: A Citizens' Report.* New Delhi: Campaign for Lesbian Rights.

Chan, R., A. R. Kavi, G. Carl, S. Khan, D. Oetomo, M. L. Tan, and T. Brown. 1998. "HIV and Men Who Have Sex with Men: Perspectives from Selected Asian Countries." *AIDS* 12(suppl B): S59–S68.

Chandiramani, R. 1998. "Talking about Sex." *Reproductive Health Matters* 12: 76–86.

Chhabra, R., and S. C. Nuna. 1994. *Abortion in India: An Overview.* New Delhi: Veerendra Printers.

Citizen's Initiative. 2002. *The Survivors Speak: How Has the Gujarat Massacre Affected Minority Women? Fact Finding by a Women's Panel.* Ahmedabad: Citizen's Initiative.

Convention on the Rights of the Child. 1989. Published for the Government of India by UNICEF Country Office, 1994.

Correa, S. 1994. "Sexual and Reproductive Health and Rights." In Correa, *Population and Reproductive Rights: Feminist Perspective from the South*, 57– 97. London: Zed Books.

Correa, S., and R. Petchesky. 1994. "Reproductive and Sexual Rights: A Feminist Perspective." In G. Sen, A. Germain, and L. C. Chen, eds., *Population Policies Reconsidered: Health Empowerment and Rights*, 107–123. Cambridge: Harvard University Press.

Datta, B., and G. Misra. 2000. "Advocacy for Sexual and Reproductive Health: The Challenge in India." *Reproductive Health Matters* 9(16): 24–34.

Ganatra, B. 2000. "Abortion Research in India: What We Know, and What We Need to Know." In R. Ramasubban and S. J. Jejeebhoy, eds., *Women's Reproductive Health in India*. New Delhi: Rawat Publications.

George, A., and S. Jaswal. 1994. "Understanding Sexuality: An Ethnographic Study of Poor Women in Bombay, India." In *Report-in-Brief, International Center for Research on Women*. Washington, D.C.: International Center for Research on Women.

Government of India. 1990. *Survey of Census of Death, (Rural) Annual Report, 1990*. New Delhi: Registrar-General of India.

Grover, A. 2001. *HIV/AIDS Persons' Right to Marry Suspended: Supreme Court Judgement Needs Reconsideration*. New Delhi: Lawyers Collective.

Gupte, M., S. Bandewar, and H. Pisal. 1997. "Abortion Needs of Women in India: A Case Study of Rural Maharashtra." *Reproductive Health Matters* 9: 77–86.

Human Rights Watch. 1996. "Communal Violence and the Denial of Justice." *Human Rights Watch* 8(2) (April). http://hrw.org/reports/1996/India1.htm.

———. 1999. "Broken People: Caste Violence against India's "Untouchables." *Human Rights Watch* (March); http://www.hrw.org/reports/1999/india/.

———. 2002. "Epidemic of Abuse: Police Harassment of HIV/AIDS Outreach Workers in India." *Human Rights Watch* 14(5) (July): 19–27.

Indian Penal Code. http://www.indialawinfo.com/bareacts/ipc.html#_Toc496765260.

Jejeeboy, S. 1996. *Adolescent Sexual and Reproductive Behavior: A Review of the Evidence from India*. Working paper 3. Washington, D.C.: International Center for Research on Women.

Jesani, A., and A. Iyer. 1993. "Abortion—Who Is Responsible for Our Rights?" *Studies in Family Planning* 24(2): 114–129.

Joshi, A., M. Dhapola, and P. Pelto. 1998. *Male Involvement in Seeking Abortion Services in Rural Gujarat*. Gujarat: Operation Research Group.

Khan, M. E., S. Barge, N. Kumar, and S. Almroth. 1999. "Abortion in India: Current Situation and Future Challenges." In S. Pachauri and S. Subramanian, eds., *Implementing a Reproductive Health Agenda in India: The Beginning*. New Delhi: Population Council.

Khanna, R., and T. Shah. 2002. "Women and Violence in Gujarat." Paper presented at special plenary session at the Tenth National Conference of the Indian Association for Women's Studies, October 17–20.

Mallik, R. 2003. "Negative Choice." *Seminar* 532 (December): 30–35.

Menghaney, L. 2003. "Youth and HIV/AIDS." *The Lawyers*. http://www. lawyers collective.org/lc-hiv-aids/magazine_articles/may_2003.htm.

Menon, N. 1995. "The Impossibility of 'Justice': Female Foeticide and Feminist Discourse on Abortion." *Contributions to Indian Sociology* 29(1&2): 369–392.

Miller, A. M. 2000. "Sexual but Not Reproductive: Exploring the Junction and Disjunction of Sexual and Reproductive Rights." *Health and Human Rights* 4(2): 69–109.

Ministry of Health and Family Welfare. 1996. *Family Welfare Programme in India, Yearbook 1993–94*. New Delhi: Government of India.

Mr. X vs. Hospital Z. 1998. 8 SCC 296. http://www.lawyerscollective.org/lc-hiv-aids/ index.htm.

———. 2002. 2002 SCCL. COM 701. http://www.lawyerscollective.org/lc-hiv-aids/ index.htm.

Murthy, L. 2004. "Rainbow Planet Lands at WSF." http://www.infochangeindia.org/ features151.jsp.

NACO (National AIDS Control Organization). Undated. *National AIDS Prevention and Control Policy*. http://www.naco.nic.in/nacp/ctrlpol.htm.

———. 2001. *HIV/AIDS Handbook for Counselors*. New Delhi: NACO. http:// www.naco.nic.in/nacp/coun.htm.

———. 2003. *HIV Estimates in India*. http://www.naco.nic.in/indianscene/esthiv.htm.

———. 2004. *HIV/AIDS Surveillance in India*. http://www.naco.nic.in/indianscene/ overv.htm.

Narrain, S. 2004. "Sexuality and the Law." *Frontline*, January 2, 2004. http:// www.frontlineonnet.com/fl2026/stories/20040102002209500.htm.

National Alliance of Women's Organizations. 2000. *Alternative NGO Report on CEDAW*. New Delhi: NAWO.

National Family Health Survey–2. 2001. *India 1998–99*. Mumbai: Indian Institute of Population Studies.

Nayar, U. 1995. *Doomed before Birth–Study of Declining Sex Ratio in the Age Group 0–6 Years in Selected Districts of Punjab and Haryana*. Delhi: Department of Women's Studies, National Council for Education, Research and Training.

Pelto, P. 1999. "Sexuality and Sexual Behavior: The Current Discourse." In S. Pachauri and S. Subramanian, eds., *Implementing a Reproductive Health Agenda in India: The Beginning*. New Delhi: Population Council.

People's Union for Civil Liberties–Karnataka. 2000. *Human Rights Violations against Sexuality Minorities in India: A PUCL-K Fact-Finding Report about Bangalore*. Bangalore: PUCL-K.

———. 2003. *Human Rights Violations against the Transgender Community: A Study of Kothi and Hijra Sex Workers in Bangalore*. Bangalore: PUCL-K.

Ramachandran, V. 1999. "Shying away from Sexuality: Government Reproductive Health Programme." *Voices for Change* 3(1): 19–21.

Ramasubban R. 1995. "Patriarchy and the Risks of STD and HIV Transmission to Women." In M. Das Gupta, L. C. Chen, and T. N. Krishnan, eds., *Women's Health In India—Risk and Vulnerability*. Bombay: Oxford University Press.

Registrar-General of India. 2001. *Provisional Population Totals, Census of India 2001*. New Delhi: Office of the Registrar-General. http://www.censusindia.net/resultsmain. html.

Sachdev, P. 1997. "University Students in Delhi, India: Their Sexual Knowledge, Attitudes and Behavior." *Journal of Family Welfare* 43(1): 1–12.

SANGRAM (Sampada Grameen Mahila Sanstha). Undated. *Of Veshyas, Vamps, Whores and Women*. Sangli: SANGRAM.

Santhya, K. G. 2003. *Changing Family Planning Scenario in India: An Overview of Recent Evidence*. South and South East Asia Regional Working Paper Series no. 17. New Delhi: Population Council.

Sarkar, T. 2002. "Semiotics of Terror: Muslim Children and Women in Hindu Rashtra." *Economic and Political Weekly* July 13, 2002. http://www.mnet.fr/aiindex/ TanikaSarkarJUL02.html.

Sharma, A., and V. Sharma. 1998. "The Guilt and Pleasure of Masturbation: A Study of College Girls in Gujarat, India." *Sexual and Marital Therapy* 13(91): 63–70.

Sodhi, G. 2000. "Seeking Gratification: Study of Sexual Behavior Patterns of Adolescents in an Urban Slum." Paper presented at the workshop on Reproductive Health in India: Evidence and Issues, Pune, February 28–March 1.

Tewari, M. 2002. "Abortion for Single Women: No Children Ever." *Pioneer*, May 9. http://www.dailypioneer.com/archives1/default12.asp?main_variable= front%5 Fpage&file_name=story8%2Etxt&counter_img=8&phy_path_ it=%5C% 5C1u%5Cdailypioneer%5Carchives1%5Cmay902.

Trikha, S. 2001. "Abortion Scenario of Adolescents in a North India City–Evidence from a Recent Study." *Indian Journal of Community Medicine* 26(1): 48–55.

UNAIDS. 2001. *India: HIV and AIDS-Related Discrimination, Stigmatization and Denial*. Geneva: UNAIDS.

———. 2002. "HIV/AIDS Counselling, Just a Phone Call away: Four Case Studies of Telephone Hotline/Helpline Projects." *Best Practice* Collection. Geneva: UNAIDS.

United Nations. 1948. Universal Declaration of Human Rights. http://www.un.org/ Overview/rights.html.

———. 1994. *Report of the International Conference on Population and Development, Cairo*. UN Doc No A/CONF. 171/13, October 18.

———. 1996. *The Beijing Declaration and the Platform for Action*. New York: United Nations.

Vasudev, S. 2003. "Sex and the Indian Woman." *India Today*, September 15: 34–44.

Venkatesan, J. 2003. "SC Upholds Two-child Norm." *Hindu*, July 31. http://www. hinduonnet.com/thehindu/2003/07/31/stories/2003073105290102.htm.

Visaria, L. 2000. "From Contraceptive Targets to Informed Choice." In R. Ramasubban and S. J. Jejeebhoy, eds., *Women's Reproductive Health in India*. New Delhi: Rawat Publications.

Wadhwa, S. 2003. "Beyond the Bed." *Outlook*, November 24: 38–44.

Waldman, A. 2003. "India Plans Free AIDS Therapy, but Effort Hinges on Price Accord with Drug Makers." *New York Times,* December 1, page 6, column 1.

Weeks, J. 1986. *Sexuality*. London: Ellis Horwood/Tavistock.

World Health Organization. 2002. *Draft Working Definitions*. Geneva: WHO, Department of Reproductive Health and Research. http://www.who.int/reproductive-health/gender/sexual_health.html#3.

The Politics of Abortion in Mexico

THE PARADOX OF DOBLE DISCURSO

ADRIANA ORTIZ-ORTEGA

Paulina: A Story of Women Challenging Legal Boundaries

On July 31, 1999, in Mexicali, Baja California, just across the United States border, thirteen-year-old Paulina Ramírez Jacinto was stabbed, beaten, and raped in her older sister Janet's home during the course of a burglary. Her assailant, a local cocaine addict with multiple prior arrests, was apprehended a month later, tried for the crime, and put back in jail. His accomplice, who also participated in the sexual assault and in taking precious cash savings that Janet's husband had sent home from his job far away, was never caught.[1]

Paulina comes from a poor family. She and her mother had taken refuge with Janet because it was an especially warm night, and Janet was the only one who owned a portable fan. Paulina was raped in the same bed she had shared with her sister and her one- and six-year-old nephews, who were tied up on the floor nearby and made to witness the brutality. After the men left, Paulina lay comatose, covered in blood. Her family thought she was dead. Her mother, asleep nearby, woke up and screamed for help but failed to arouse neighbors. Only when a brother arrived some time later did anyone go to the police.

Subsequently, Paulina was sent by the police to a local physician, Sandra Montoya. She was found to be pregnant and advised to request an abortion. Abortion is legal in all thirty-two Mexican states in cases of rape, and public hospitals are required to have staff members available to perform the procedure free of charge when requested by the state attorney of justice. It was there at the Hospital General in Mexicali that the second half of Paulina's ordeal began.

A doctor on the hospital staff initially agreed to perform the operation but then changed his mind. Since the Baja California state law does not spell out how the law should be enforced, the doctor could not be taken to task. On October 1, Paulina was hospitalized for seven days while she waited for another willing provider. Callously, she was placed in a ward with women giving birth and caring for their newborns. Doctors ordered that she receive no solid food since her stomach had to be empty in order for the abortion to be performed. Still, nothing happened during that week.

Public Justice Agent Norma Velázquez ordered that the director of the hospital, Dr. Ismael Ávila Iñiguez, be placed under arrest for thirty-six hours for not complying with the law, and he was, in fact, detained for three hours. On October 14, two women who identified themselves as public servants from the Sistema Nacional para el Desarrollo de la Familia (National System for the Integral Development of the Family), but who in fact belonged to a local antichoice group, tried to persuade Paulina to carry the baby to term. That same day, Dr. Ávila Iñiguez met in private with Paulina's mother and insisted that her daughter might die or become infertile as a result of an abortion.[2] Confused and frightened, mother and daughter decided not to go ahead. Public Justice Agent Velázquez drafted an official statement documenting that the abortion had never been performed, while never detailing the delays and scare tactics that led mother and daughter to refrain from having the abortion performed.

Paulina and her mother then appealed to Juan Manuel Salazar Pimentel, the state prosecutor for Baja California. Salazar Pimentel, however, advised that Paulina carry to term and also drove her to a Catholic priest who, of course, echoed the same advice.

On October 16, a reporter wrote an article about Paulina in a local magazine, *La Voz de la Frontera* (Voice of the Frontier). Silvia Reséndiz, director of the local women's group, Alaide Foppa (named for a Guatemalan feminist who lived in Mexico and was killed by her government for her political involvement) learned about the case and began to lobby in favor of Paulina's rights, since Paulina was still within the twelve-week period permitted by the law to have an abortion. With the support of feminist groups, Paulina again sought legal recourse and secured an official recommendation from the state's attorney of human rights and citizen protection that she be financially compensated for her suffering and for the public hospital's failure to provide the abortion after her initial request. The recommendation also mandated that the state of Baja California provide financial support for education, health care, clothing, and housing for Paulina and her future child. On March 13, 2000, then Governor Alejandro González Alcocer responded to the state Ministry of Human Rights that neither the hospital nor the Public Ministry of Justice had denied Paulina's legal right to an abortion and that, in fact, mother and daughter had decided on their own to continue the pregnancy. Request for compensation was denied.

In April Paulina gave birth by Cesarean section to a son, Isaac. For more than a year after Isaac's birth, Paulina worked fourteen hours a day (for which she was paid six hundred pesos or approximately $54 per month) to provide for her son. But fatigue and health problems, including colitis and a post-Cesarean section hernia, forced her to leave her job.

Paulina's family is Catholic, but they no longer look forward to going to church. The bishop of Mexicali has threatened to excommunicate Silvia Reséndiz, the feminist activist who has advocated on behalf of Paulina and who the family asked to be Isaac's godmother. Paulina had trouble finding a priest who would baptize her child, because of the unfortunate circumstances of his birth.

Paulina has received support from women's groups in Baja California and all across Mexico. Alaide Foppa, along with Grupo de Investigación en Reproducción Elegida (GIRE) in Mexico City, publicly denounced the denial of Paulina's rights. GIRE commissioned Isabel Vericat, a feminist lawyer, to further investigate her case. Vericat argued before the president of the National Commission for Human Rights in Mexico, Dr. José Soberanes, that Paulina had been the victim of intolerance and an irregular application of the law. Dr. Soberanes recommended that Paulina receive a lump sum of $32,000 to buy a house, as well as ongoing financial support for education and medical care for her son. During a press conference in Mexico City in August 2003, Paulina reported that she had received the promised money for the house, but that the social welfare payments to cover her educational needs and medical care of her child never materialized.

Mexican feminists felt that they had exhausted all local channels, so women from Alaide Foppa and GIRE contacted sister organizations in New York for help. Lilián Sepúlveda, a lawyer with the New York-based Center for Reproductive Rights, is preparing to bring Paulina's case before the Interamerican Commission on Human Rights (CIDH) at the time of this writing.[3] Paulina, meanwhile, is back at work in a local shopping center.

Paulina's case illustrates the many barriers that continue to confront poor women in Mexico in gaining access to their limited rights to abortion care, despite a widely celebrated liberalization in recent years of the laws that expand those rights. Even when abortion is legal, as in the case of rape, it remains highly stigmatized, especially by the church and by many in the medical profession. In addition, abortion regulation does not exist in most Mexican states, except since 2000 in the Federal District and in Morelos. As a result, abortion services may simply be unavailable to the majority of women who are poor and cannot afford to pay an illegal provider.

In the years that followed Paulina's case, the Mexican media has reported on at least two similar cases of adolescent girls who have been denied abortion services by public hospitals although their cases complied with the conditions under which abortion can be practiced. These cases testify to the difficulties of translating liberalization measures into practical realities. Abortion has thus become one of the most recent arenas of contest in a long history of negotiation between church and state in Mexico for control over the lives of its people. For more than a century, the Mexican state has sought to differentiate itself from the church—and elevate its standing in the global community of secular nations—by liberalizing laws that govern family life, including divorce, inheritance, property, and most contentiously, sex and reproduction. This was especially true in the 1970s when, bending to both international and domestic concerns about population growth, Mexico made contraception a constitutional right of its citizens.

The price of this compromise on family planning, however, was a tacit agreement between church and state that abortion would remain illegal. Nonetheless, this process did not prevent progressive reforms from being gradually, though quietly, introduced into the body of state penal law that governs abortion. The entire process was surreptitious. The reform laws would not be repealed, as they had been with considerable controversy in the United States and elsewhere, and illegal provision of abortion services would continue for those women in the middle classes who could afford them, without overt interference by church or state. Thus a long-standing tradition of *doble discurso* on these highly charged matters continued, with laws and behaviors contradicting one another in many complex ways.

The compromise over abortion never really suited women, but it lasted for more than twenty years until developments of recent years called it into question. The first factor destabilizing the doble discurso tradition in Mexico is the growing power of Mexico's feminist movement, which early in the

1970s positioned reproductive rights—and particularly abortion—as an essential right, not subject to compromise, in the fight for women's equality. The second is the growing influence of the global discourse that equates women's rights and reproductive rights with essential human rights. This discourse was without doubt galvanized by the UN Conference on Population and Development in Cairo in 1994, and the Fourth World Conference on Women in Beijing in 1995. Mexico's enthusiastic participation in these landmark conferences was significant for several reasons.

First, strong feminists joined the official government delegations and returned home with renewed determination to bring questions about sexuality and reproduction back to renewed attention. Second, though the Cairo and Beijing accords do not call for the legalization of abortion, they do acknowledge illegal abortion as a public health problem, and this fueled the determination of Mexican advocates to address the disparity between legal rights and available service provision in their own country. This has brought the issue of service provision and not only legal reform as a big element in women's quest for social justice and democratization. Third, the success of feminists and liberal reformers spawned a backlash by grassroots conservatives in Mexico who have since gained considerable political power and now seek to undermine the meager progress on abortion reform that had been made in favor of an absolute denial of abortion rights.

Cairo and Beijing thus called into question the abortion compromise that had existed in Mexico for many years. They helped women open up a debate that had long been silenced by what I refer to as a gentleman's agreement between church and state. Extensive press coverage of Paulina's case and several others like it has kept this debate alive. But the abortion issue remains far from settled in Mexico and serves as a constant reminder of the great disparities that exist between laws and practices, many of which are rooted in century-old traditions and beliefs. This chapter will trace the long and complicated history of doble discurso on matters of sexuality and reproduction in Mexico as a way of demonstrating how difficult the local application of international and national norms can be, and as a necessary context for understanding contemporary policy constraints and for adjusting advocacy strategies for change in the future. So long as religion, politics, and public policy remain entangled in Mexico and elsewhere in Latin America and the Caribbean, doble discurso will prevail, laws and norms will not reflect behavioral practices, and individual women, especially from the poorest and most disenfranchised classes, will suffer.

Church, State, and Doble Discurso in Mexico

Legal Status of Abortion in Mexico Today

Abortion law varies widely throughout Latin America. Generally, access to abortion has come about incrementally through liberalization of laws rather than frank legalization. This is due in large part, particularly in the case of Mexico, to the tension to balance a desire for autonomy from the Catholic Church with recognition of the importance of having the church's political support in order to remain in power. Caribbean countries such as Cuba, Barbados, and Guyana, where abortion is legal and where the church plays a lesser role in public life, provide a striking contrast to Chile and El Salvador, where abortion is not permitted under any circumstances. Mexico, which has significantly liberalized its abortion laws by reforming criminal codes at the state level, lies somewhere in the middle of this spectrum.

Twenty-seven of the thirty-two Mexican states liberalized their abortion laws between 1970 and 2000. Local variation is considerable, and the range of circumstances under which the practice of abortion is justified is great. "Carelessness" (accidental injury resulting in spontaneous abortion) is an acceptable justification for abortion in twenty-nine states; so women desperate to end pregnancies are encouraged to throw themselves down stairs or otherwise sustain injuries that may appear accidental.[4] Provisions for abortion to protect the life of the woman exist in twenty-eight states, while those performed in order to protect the health of the woman are permitted in only nine states. Abortion is legal in case of fetal anomalies in thirteen states without any gestational age limit, though in practice terminations of pregnancy for this reason only take place up to twenty weeks of gestation.

Penal code provisions regarding abortion in Mexico can be divided into three categories.[5]

1. Moderate or Conservative Legislation. The most restrictive regulations are in Guanajuato and Querétaro, which permit abortion only in cases of rape and carelessness, with no provision for legal abortion if the woman's life or health is in danger (Barza and Taracena 2001). Six Mexican states (Aguascalientes, Campeche, Durango, San Luis Potosí, Sinaloa, and Sonora) allow legal abortion only in cases of rape, carelessness, or to protect a woman's life.

2. Intermediate Legislation. In thirteen states (Baja California Norte, Baja California Sur, Coahuila, Colima, Chihuahua, Chiapas, Estado de México, Morelos, Oaxaca, Puebla, Quintana Roo, Tabasco, and Vera-

cruz), the list of acceptable reasons for legal abortion includes the existence of a genetic malformation and pregnancy resulting from an assisted insemination that has taken place under coercion.

3. Progressive Legislation. In ten states (Federal District, Hidalgo, Jalisco, Michoacan, Nayarit, Nuevo León, Tamaulipas, Tlaxcala, Zacatecas, and Yucatán), abortion is legal to protect the health of the mother or in the case of economic hardship. Because danger to health and economic hardship are defined broadly, this legislation opens the door, at least theoretically, to including women's needs and the adverse circumstances they may face from carrying pregnancies to term. Yucatán allows abortion in case of economic hardship if the woman already has at least three children. To perform legal abortions in these states, providers must obtain approval from a medical committee composed of at least two other doctors, underscoring the fact that neither a physician's opinion nor a woman's request is considered sufficient grounds for abortion.

As the case of Paulina illustrates, however, legal reform does not guarantee that services are available. Only the states of Morelos and Federal District have promulgated rules of procedure that dictate how the laws must be translated into abortion practice in public hospitals. These rules excuse doctors from performing abortions if their conscience dictates that they not do so. If this is the case, however, the woman in question must be referred to another member of the medical staff willing to provide care. Abortions approved by the law and referred to public hospitals are supposed to be provided free of charge, with services complying with accepted standards of quality. Women are supposed to be properly informed about their rights to abortion services. Doctors must perform the abortion within five days of the request (Gobierno del Distrito Federal 2004).[6]

The penalties for abortion-related crimes are also a window into the doble discurso-entrenched culture. Medical personnel who perform illegal abortions can be sentenced to up to eight years in jail and may also lose their medical licenses, though the law here is rarely enforced. Women who abort illegally are rarely placed in jail, and if they are, endure a sentence of six months to five years in prison. Women very often have their sentences reduced by demonstrating compliance with three circumstances that constitute what has been long established in Mexico as a legacy of liberalism among elites who sought justification for termination of pregnancy. It is called honoris causa: 1. the woman must be married and of a socially acceptable background; 2. the pregnancy must be the result of an extramarital affair; 3. the woman must have concealed her pregnancy (presumably to safeguard her own reputation, as well as that of her husband and family) up until the moment that she sought an abortion.[7] If the honoris causa requirements can be met, the maximum punishment is only twelve months, as opposed to five years. Honoris causa provisions, which appear in many Latin American penal codes, make explicit that protections granted to the fetus are not absolute. Rather, they privilege male interests in maintaining family reputations over Catholic claims to fetal rights to life. These provisions have only been challenged recently by feminists in sophisticated communities like Mexico City on grounds that they fail to provide equal protection to women.

The Doble Discurso of Abortion Laws in Mexico

Despite comparatively moderate abortion laws, the policies of the Mexican state are still influenced by Catholic values. A doble discurso results— this term is widely used "to signify the art of espousing traditional and repressive socio-cultural norms publicly, while ignoring—or even participating in—the widespread flouting of these norms in private" (Shepard 2000). Thus one aspect of doble discurso is the disparity between public policy and private behavior.

A 1994 study carried out by Catholics for a Free Choice, for example, confirmed previous findings that contraceptive patterns in Latin America do not conform to Catholic teachings (Catholics for a Free Choice 1994). In Mexico, the same is now becoming true for abortion. Sandra Garcia recently conducted 3,000 interviews with a representative sample of the Mexican population. She found that 69 percent believe that abortion should be legal under certain circumstances; 48 percent think legislators should give greatest weight to the opinions of women when changing laws (14 percent think the opinions of doctors should be most important); and 29 percent think that the views of society should prevail. Eighty percent believe that it is "wrong" for legislators to act in accordance with their personal religious beliefs (García 2001).

The doble discurso system is most powerful in Latin American countries where local laws and policies most closely mirror repressive church doctrine. In these places, however, informal escape valves have developed to expand the private sexual and reproductive choices of citizens who are able to take advantage of them, while maintaining the public status quo. In the case of abortion in Mexico, for example, the doble discurso system allows for the existence of a large number of private clinics and doctors' offices that provide abortion services. The clinics are an open secret, raided by police from time to time, but for the most part allowed to operate without state interference. Because these clandestine abortion clinics function informally and involve illegal and irregular procedures, "neither availability, safety (in the case of services) nor protections of basic rights are guaranteed" (Shepard 2000).

Not surprisingly, poor women and marginalized populations bear the brunt of the burden of doble discurso in Latin America. In Mexico, as well as in other countries, although services can sometimes be difficult to find, liberal and humanitarian doctors provide illegal abortions to their patients in expensive private clinics. In public hospitals that provide free care to poor women, however, women rarely access these services, as they fear censorship or denial. According to some partial reports available in Mexico City in the last three years, no more than three or four abortions per month are performed in public hospitals in Mexico City. As a result poor women often resort to unlicensed or untrained providers, self-administered drugs or teas, or other unsafe practices to interrupt their pregnancies, while women who can afford to pay for services are generally able to obtain safe care.

Penal codes in Latin American countries, like those in Mexico, have evolved to allow the practice of abortion under limited circumstances (rape, for example), despite continued defense by public officials of the absolute rights of the fetus to life from the moment of conception. Perhaps to avoid confronting this contradiction, and certainly to avoid other more obvious political risks, changes in abortion law often take place quietly and covertly.

This has presented a special dilemma for many feminists and progressives. Gradual change has been achieved by working within the doble discurso system, however compromised this path may be. Yet for certain sectors of feminism(s) it is critical to denounce doble discurso. One key approach used by national and international organizations interested in increasing access to safe abortion has been to document the many human costs of doble discurso. It has been estimated that complications from an estimated 4 million abortions in Latin America every year result in 800,000 hospitalizations and nearly as many maternal deaths (Alan Guttmacher Institute 1996). Such data about the prevalence and characteristics of abortion practice in Latin America and the Caribbean, however, has only recently become available. The Alan Guttmacher Institute carried out national surveys on abortion in six Latin American countries in the mid-1990s: Peru, Chile, Brazil, Colombia, the Dominican Republic, and Mexico. Abortion rates were found to be highest in countries where abortion is outlawed completely, such as Chile, and lowest where abortion is legal under certain circumstances, such as Mexico, belying claims that legalization promotes the practice. AGI estimated approximately one-half million abortions in Mexico, although according to the National Population Council this figure is much lower and ranges from around 120–180,000. These numbers vary so dramatically because the state figures reflect estimations based on women who declare abortions, while the AGI numbers are based on surveys and qualitative research and include illegal procedures.

The tensions inherent in a doble discurso system are also revealed by the ways in which laws are conceived, implemented, and debated. Those who support liberal reproductive rights, as well as those who oppose them, have until recently tended to work within the framework of doble discurso.

Reproductive Rights in Mexico: An Historical Overview

The Earliest Gentleman's Agreements: 1500s–1800s

In order to understand the current paradoxes of abortion in Mexico and to strategize for the future, one must better understand the longer history of church-state relations within which reproductive rights have been negotiated in Mexico. Present realities are rooted in specific historical circumstances dictated by ever-evolving relations between secular and religious actors.

During the colonial period (1529–1836), when the church was most powerful, the punishment for women accused of abortion was death.[8] By 1857, however, church powers were actively limited under a new constitution that regulated the separation of church and state. Reforms introduced in 1873 restated these principles in strong terms, insisting that religion be practiced as a private matter. The church was not recognized legally; priests could not exercise political power; and no religious institution was allowed to acquire real estate or capital (Rabasa 1993). Changes in laws governing reproduction then followed. The first state penal codes were approved in 1871, sixty years after Mexico's independence from Spain. They permitted abortion only when the life of the woman was endangered, and shifted punishment for illegal abortion from death to jail time.

Still, the continued criminalization of abortion (abortion was only permitted when the woman's life was threatened) suggests that the state conformed in large part to Catholic values.[9] Secular ideas influenced the code as well, however, and it should therefore be considered the first of Mexico's gentleman's agreements. The code legalized abortion to protect the life of the mother, acknowledging advances in midwifery and in the developing professionalization of obstetrics in medicine. This willingness to treat fetal and newborn human life differently created an important legal distinction between infanticide and abortion. Punishment for infanticide in the 1871 penal code was twice as harsh as that for abortion, an indication that fetal life was accorded less significance than that of a newborn or infant (De la Barreda 1991).

Post-Revolution Mexico: 1900s

With the advent of the Mexican Revolution in 1910, the state became the central political actor, and the Catholic Church's role was further curtailed. The new constitution drafted in 1917 not only banned Catholic participation in public, political, and economic affairs but also made public education fully secular. This shift in the balance of church/state power was a product not only of liberal ideas but also of the influence of socialist-minded revolutionary leaders, who, a decade earlier, had also endorsed the organization of the first feminist congresses in Yucatan.[10]

In 1917, the newly elected president, Venustiano Carranza, drafted the first family law reform. This allowed women to sign contracts, take part in legal suits, serve as guardians, and exercise equal rights in the custody of children. More important, women were given equal authority to spend family funds and were allowed to divorce. The new law rejected the category of illegitimacy for children born out of wedlock and permitted the regularization of relationships by legalizing remarriage. It granted rights to concubines and to women in common-law relationships. Though the law did not address contraception or abortion directly, pamphlets on family limitation by the American reformer Margaret Sanger began to circulate in parts of Mexico at this time.

The most prominent feature of Mexican liberalism was thus anticlericalism. Early Mexican liberals were secular-minded, and the most significant ideological battles among them were fought over the intensity with which the powers of the Catholic Church would be curbed. As anticlericalism grew, however, Catholic sectors began to organize and fight back. In 1926, the Movimiento Cristero (Movement in defense of Christ) developed. It supported religiously inspired guerrilla actions, which originated in rural areas of Central Mexico and sought to overthrow the Mexican state.[11] The Movimiento Cristero became the first social movement to challenge the Mexican Revolution. Although it did not have the official endorsement of the Catholic hierarchy, many individual priests participated. Women from the urban classes, along with some from the working poor, also played a critical role in the Cristero Movement through the lay Catholic organization Acción Social (Social action), which *did* receive the endorsement of the Catholic hierarchy (Meyer 1978). Although la Cristiada, as it came to be known, failed to reverse the new constitution that limited religious influence in state affairs, the strength of the movement nonetheless enhanced the church's negotiating position with the state. To halt the grassroots Cristero offensive, the Mexican government collaborated with the hierarchy of the Mexican Catholic Church, the Vatican, and the U.S. government, which had an interest in stemming what was perceived as a tide of socialism. Gentlemen's agreements to end the conflict were signed by the government and religious leaders in December of 1929 (Meyer et al. 1978).

Between 1935 and 1960, the Mexican state and the Catholic Church reached an informal alliance that had anti-communist undertones, which placed the exaltation of motherhood at its core. This iteration of the gentleman's agreement was entrenched in doble discurso which, on the one hand, advanced the notion of the working mother and incorporated women into low-level state positions but, on the other, undermined women who sought the vote. Mexican women did not gain the right to vote until 1953.

Mexico could have chosen to make contraception and abortion legal back in the 1930s and 1940s, when many European countries did so.[12] Engaging in typical doble discurso, however, the Mexican state refrained from legalizing abortion in order to appease the church but, at the same time, maintained its anticlerical appearance by introducing a social program hostile to religion through its educational and mass communication programs. In practice, however, the state always left itself ample room to maneuver in its negotiations with the Catholic Church. Indeed, church leaders occupied a privileged role in closed-door negotiations and discussions with heads of state. Despite the state's seeming anticlericalism, a tacit truce between church and state always existed, subject to continuous renegotiation. In other words, despite claims of revolutionary secularism, governmental policy and action were considerably less radical than they may have appeared. Abortion rights thus remained subject to the vagaries of politically expedient gentlemen's agreements between church and state.

During these years of power struggle between church and state officials, however, another, grassroots Catholic presence was emerging. The conservative Partido Acción Nacional (PAN) movement was initiated in 1939, and began to gain strength during the 1990s. Now politically dominant in Mexico, with the recent election of its candidate, President Vincente Fox, the PAN movement is indicative of the difficulties that a conservative agenda has found in advancing its positions publicly. For example, although the ultraright wing of the PAN tried to ban abortion under all circumstances in 2000, President Fox had to stand in favor of a more moderate position. Similarly, although President Fox has endorsed a conservative proabortion position on different occasions, no actual reversals of abortion laws have taken place during his tenure. In fact, Mexico city's abortion laws were reformed with some fanfare in 2000, when Rosario Robles of Partido de la Revolucíon Democrátia (PRD) was in power there, and the reform bill was given the nickname "Ley Robles." It expands the acceptable motives for abortion to include risk to the health and life of the woman, congenital fetal malformation, and absence of consent to artificial insemination, while overturning honoris causa claims previously permitted to allow an "honorable lady" to protect the father's name.

Recently, a public scandal involving financial irregularities among prolife groups has further undermined their reputation and influence. The PAN party now stands firmly against abortion, without compromise, much as the Republican Party platform in the United States now does. But especially in light of these scandals, PAN does not have sufficient political power or will to overturn existing abortion reforms. Doble discurso thus remains a feature of public life, and abortion transformation and access to service are still difficult to achieve.

The same was true for family planning. At first, the Catholic Church did not actively oppose the introduction of family planning (the term "birth control" carries a more defined contraceptive meaning that the Church would have opposed) in Mexico. Indeed, dissent within the church all over the world on this and other issues had resulted in the organization of the Vatican Council (Vatican II) in 1965, but after considerable discussion, Rome reiterated its firm opposition to birth control in the encyclical *Humanae Vitae* of 1968. Despite its ideological rigor on birth control, however, for all practical purposes the church turned its attention away from birth control and focused instead on stopping abortion. In Mexico, both church and state followed suit. As was characteristic of its doble discurso system, while the government introduced family planning and quietly liberalized abortion laws in some states, it maintained strong antiabortion rhetoric in public.

By the early 1970s global support for publicly assisted family planning programs was well established, and fertility patterns began to change in many developing countries. A strong link between population decline and economic growth and opportunity was established. Pronatalist policies receded as Mexico pioneered the first family planning programs in Latin America, advocating responsible limitation and spacing of births. In 1972 the Mexican government announced its intentions to implement the Programa de Planeación Familiar Integral (Program on Integral Family Planning). Mexican bishops joined in what emerged as nearly unanimous support for this policy by issuing a congratulatory message on "responsible parenthood." Following the etiquette of past gentleman's agreements, the family planning program was officially called an initiative in Responsible Parenthood Action. The Mexican constitution was amended in 1974 to legitimize this policy and to make women equal under the law so that they would not need the approval of their partners or religious leaders to receive family planning from state clinics. The 1974 constitutional reform, however, neutralized conservative opposition by claiming to defend the family at the same time as it gave women freedom to make these decisions on their own. It represented yet another example of compromise between church and state in which sexual and reproductive rights are granted or restricted according to changing political exigencies. Sexual and reproductive rights proved again to be negotiable, and thus were treated as pawns to be exchanged for church support that the state could then use in pursuit of other agreed-upon political ends (Ortiz-Ortega 2000).

Feminist Struggle for Reproductive Rights in Mexico: Late 1900s–Present

A shift away from traditional *doble discurso* was first promoted by feminist groups and coalitions, which began to advocate strongly for uncompromised reproductive rights in the early 1970s as well as for the defense of sexual orientation. Newly formed feminist groups have challenged state positions on abortion and family planning on the grounds that they do not privilege women's bodily integrity or provide equal legal protection to women.

At first, the goal of feminist groups was to establish a radical critique of the state's family planning model, but in practice their actions served to strengthen the negotiating position of the state vis-à-vis the church. Indeed, the state used the feminists to justify its adoption of a "balanced" position between the growing antiabortion forces in Mexico and those demanding legal abortion. The years 1975 to 1981 were critical in building a feminist movement in Mexico—a time when feminist groups agreed on a strategy to advocate for legal and safe abortion, calling their efforts "voluntary motherhood campaigns." Feminists drew a connection between the fourth article of the constitution, which grants women the right to space and limit the number of children, and their demands for legal abortion. They also built campaigns around the biased application of the law, demanding in 1978, for example, that a woman who had been raped be allowed to have an abortion in a public clinic.[13]

Feminists then drafted a Voluntary Motherhood Bill, which made the demand for legal abortion more concrete by identifying all the provisions that would have to be removed from state penal codes, by including sanitary provisions, and by establishing limits on the gestational period for performing a legal abortion. Establishing a time limit on legal abortion, this demand was made by the Communist Party, when it formally presented the Voluntary Bill in the Chamber of Deputies, since feminists lacked formal political representation (Coalición de Mujeres 1979). Communists and feminists came to a tactical agreement (Grupo Parlamentario Comunista 1979), and in 1980 the Communist Party took a stand on legal abortion during its first electoral period in the Chamber of Deputies. In true doble discurso tradition, however, the demand was never endorsed by the allegedly leftist, progressive Partido Revolucionario Institucional (PRI), which supported reform in private but refused to take a public stand so contrary to the position of the church. In effect, the majority PRI partnered with the conservative PAN to defeat the bill.

The political reform of 1977 opened the door to greater participation of the Catholic Church in state affairs by allowing individual priests to participate more actively in politics and to lobby for their antichoice position. In addition, the PAN began to gain greater visibility in the political arena and thus was better able to promote an antiabortion agenda. Conservative factions of the Catholic Church under John Paul II also began to organize more aggressively in Mexico. The archbishop of Mexico City, Corripio Ahumada, became an inspirational force in the creation of the Comité Nacional Pro-Vida (National Pro-Life Committee), which remained, until its recent scandals, the most visible element of a conservative coalition of more than a hundred organizations (Muro and Gabriel 1991), most of them formed in the 1930s.[14] The Comité Nacional Pro-Vida, together with sister organizations like Vida y Familia (Life and Family), promoted the establishment of abortion prevention clinics, abstinence-only sex education programs, and adoption services. Nonetheless, it has still been difficult for the conservative opposition to persuade the public to demand a reversal of legal gains with respect to abortion. No one has a sufficient monopoly on power or public opinion to effect meaningful change.

During the 1980s, while both women's groups and conservative antiabortion forces expressed their views and demands explicitly, the state developed a new doble discurso strategy to straddle the chasm between its liberal and conservative allegiances: secrecy. The national government continued to differentiate itself from the Catholic leadership, and several abortion law reforms were introduced quietly in a number of states.[15] State officials never mentioned these modifications of penal codes; the new penal codes were not reprinted, reported to the local or national press, or disclosed to public hospitals, feminist groups, or women. The national government, in promoting this strategy, thus avoided opposition from the Catholic Church, but the obvious cost of this new gentlemen's agreement was that the reforms achieved could not be meaningfully implemented. When this quiet liberalization of abortion laws was opened up to public debate in Mexico City in 1981, the Catholic Church mounted a major offensive against it. As a result, that liberalization effort failed, and the law was reversed. Thus, this moderate and secretive liberalization of abortion laws was a low-cost strategy for the state; it implied increased tolerance of abortion but did not lead to actual provision of services or regulation of private practice, as feminists had demanded.

During the 1990s, under this veil of secrecy and continuing the tradition of doble discurso, some of the most comprehensive liberalization proposals for abortion were introduced. Reforms proposed in the state of Chiapas would have permitted abortion in cases of contraceptive failure. A newly reempowered Catholic Church, however, immediately demanded that the measure be withdrawn a few days after it was publicly announced, and the government conceded. The failure of this proposal nonetheless gave great visibility to feminist groups, which advocated for the reforms nationally and internationally. Feminists had been working closely with Teología de la Liberación (Theology of Liberation) and with the peace and human rights advocate Bishop Samuel Ruiz of Chiapas. The Catholic leadership responded by forbidding Ruiz's continued involvement (Fontanine and Damián 1995). This left Católicas por el Derecho a Decidir (Catholics for a Free Choice) as the only Catholic voice to oppose the position taken by the Vatican (Marcos 1994).[16] This event marked the start of this organization's work in Mexico and also led to the increased involvement of other international groups with an interest in abortion, such as the Population Council.

Despite this defeat, feminist visibility in Mexico expanded during the 1990s. The formation of several nongovernmental organizations provided for increased international funding, and strong mobilization efforts in favor of sexual and reproductive rights globally led to the inclusion of several Mexican feminist and NGO groups in the official delegations that attended the watershed Cairo and Beijing conferences. The Mexican government endorsed the Programme of Action that followed Cairo and the Platform for Action developed in Beijing. Following Cairo +5, the government expanded this commitment by agreeing to treat abortion complications as a public health problem. Finally, Mexico transformed its family planning programs into reproductive health programs that incorporate a more holistic approach, with increased attention given to quality of care and contraceptive choice.

Activists in Latin America have long relied on public health and epidemiological arguments to advance the legalization of abortion, since such arguments give a scientific basis to their demands as a counter to moral arguments against abortion. However, as others have observed, "epidemiological facts will not sway someone who is defending a sacred norm" (Sheppard 2000). These were advances made on paper, while in local communities the conservative PAN was gaining popularity and political clout. Conservative forces actively sought to block implementation of international agreements such as those reached at the Cairo and Beijing conferences.

Thus, a consequence of the Cairo and Beijing accords is increasingly explicit public debate, initiated by feminists, on sexuality and reproduction, rather than doble discurso. Cairo and Beijing have subtly eroded the dividing lines between the private and the public by calling attention to the importance of sexuality and reproduction in the constitution of gendered citizens. Conservatives and other political actors must now engage in dialogue and debate and contest the meanings attached to reproductive or sexual practices and discourses.

The national political victory of the PAN in 2000 marked a key political transition in Mexico. The July election brought the long-term political monopoly of Partido Revolucionario Institucional to an end. Women are very active politically in modern Mexico, often thriving in positions of leadership. Women played a key role in the 2000 election; more than half (51.8 percent) of those who voted were female, and many more women ran for Congress. Two of the three main political parties (PRI and PRD) have been headed by women, as have government agencies such as the secretariats of tourism and social development. However, these women do not necessarily speak in terms of gender issues. PAN, PRI, and PRD actively court women voters by supporting many political and economic rights for women. However, PAN remains adamantly opposed to a woman's right to choose abortion. Local sectors within the PAN actively seek to reverse abortion laws or to ban abortion services allowed under certain circumstances by Mexican law. Moreover, ultraradical conservative groups are being appointed to government positions through which they advance their antiabortion agenda, and antiabortion groups have received public funding to open maternity clinics in Mexico City.[17] The influence of religious conservatism is felt not only within the PAN but also among the leadership of the other parties, including the leftist Partido de la Revolución Democrática. At present Mexico's historic separation of power between church and state has tipped in favor of the church, as the PAN victory has given right-wing groups an important entry point within federal and state institutions. But even so, with respect to abortion the tradition of doble discorso prevails. There is simply not enough power—even in PAN—to effect extreme change in patterns of practice that have prevailed for decades.

Conclusion and Strategies for Future Advocacy

A liberalization tendency in abortion law has been present in Mexico since the inception of the penal code of 1871. This demonstrates that religious conservative influence does not translate automatically into legal procedures in Mexico, thanks to the liberal ideas that informed the constitution of the Mexican state. This liberal tradition has allowed the state to limit the political influence of the Catholic Church and has permitted the state to enjoy a significant degree of autonomy from religious influence.

Nonetheless, as the Paulina case demonstrates, a tradition of doble discorso continues to prevail even in terms of access to those abortion services that are protected by legal reforms of recent years, as well as in public debates about abortion more generally. As the Mexican case is paradigmatic in terms of the separation of church and state, as well as in terms of abortion liberalization in the region, we need to continue assessing alternative routes for exercising reproductive and sexual rights in all of Latin America. Also, we need to evaluate if and when unrestricted legalization of abortion will ever take place in Mexico, as well as the feasibility of relying on a human rights agenda to achieve this goal. Last, we need to ponder feasible routes for the advancement of reproductive rights and sexual rights in Mexico at a time when a conservative influence seems on the rise there, as well as in the United States, Mexico's influential neighbor

Given the historical circumstances described in this chapter, should activists support a strategy of continued, gradual liberalization of abortion laws—tolerating clandestine secret provision of additional services where necessary—or should we demand absolute repeal of all criminal penalties for abortion? What does it mean that ten years after Cairo, one of Latin America's most progressive countries can only accomplish partial and often inaccessible reforms of criminal abortion law?

My own view is that we must do both. We must actively support a nongovernmental sector that pushes back against the resurgent influence of religion in Mexican government and that takes two parallel courses with respect to abortion law and service provision. On the one hand, we must continue to demand enforcement of existing reforms, while on the other, we must try to expand public discourse further by calling for total decriminalization or repeal. These strategies can be complimentary, not contradictory.

Strategies

Need to Limit Religious Influence in Public Life.   Activists in Mexico are learning how to cope with the paradox that democracies in fostering rights to self-determination and freedom of speech allow different political points of view to coexist and thereby may enhance the influence of conservatives (Blancarte 2002). Religious groups often occupy a particularly privileged position in democratic politics, even though they often rely on fundamentally "undemocratic" mechanisms to wield their influence and to advance their agenda, including the use of moral and physical intimidation and even violence.

In Mexico, in view of the growing influence of conservatism in formal and informal political and policy settings, it is thus necessary to consider how to limit the influence of religious forces within state agencies and on public policy. More and more this strategy is critical to advance sexual and reproductive rights.

Promotion of Lay Human-rights Approach in Medical and Legal Contexts.   Conservatives seek to influence the definition of rights as well as constrain the discussion of sexual rights to assert their moral autonomy. As Hunter points out, "At root, the conflict between differing conceptions of moral authority is about power—a struggle to achieve or maintain the power to define reality" (Hunter 1991: 52). Thus, limiting the access of the church to institutional power by making the electorate more aware of the consequences of electing conservatives to power should be stressed. In addition, all secret negotiations made by religious groups should be made public. This should take place before it's too late, and these groups manage to reverse important laws, constitutional agreements, and rights. To these ends, advocates must more effectively mobilize informed constituencies of physicians, lawyers, and other professionals whose professional and personal rights are at stake. These are the very groups, however, that are being influenced by the success that conservatives, especially within the church, are enjoying as they hijack the human rights discourse on behalf of fetal rights and invert it to portray abortion advocates as baby-killers and criminals. Progressives must find ways to reclaim public opinion on these matters.

Aspire for a More United and Diverse Movement for Reproductive Rights. Feminists must be more united if they are to challenge the conservatives. Some believe in a more gradual approach to social change, one which works within (and perpetuates) the *doble discurso* culture, and others are more radical in their approach. The gradual incremental approach may be a more effective way to educate and organize in grassroots communities, but the radical approach is more direct and uncompromised in its means and message. In the post-Cairo and post-Beijing world, the coalition of actors in favor of legal abortion—including feminists, NGOs, international donors, progressive lawyers, committed doctors, and radical church members—must overcome differences and come together as a more powerful force, united in their conviction to protect social spending for family planning, sex education, and reproductive rights, which conservatives are trying to cut (Petchesky 2000, 2003).

Focus on Access to Services. As Paulina's case so clearly demonstrates, one of the greatest challenges that reproductive and sexual rights advocates face in Mexico is the institutionalization of abortion services. Because public opinion in Mexico overwhelmingly supports the decriminalization of abortion, conservative efforts to reverse abortion reforms have not yet succeeded.[18] However, efforts to limit women's access to abortion services, especially those supported by public funds, have been successful. Thus the greatest bottleneck in access to abortion in Mexico is at the level of service provision and not at the judicial or legal level.

Document the Impact of Doble Discurso and Lack of Access to Abortion. It is necessary to document cases of abuse within the system, attain resources, increase visibility, and create political momentum, as Paulina's case also illustrates. Progressive forces, however, seem to be somewhat divided on the matter of transparency and visibility. Some believe that "public debate can lead to increased repression and limits of the informal mechanisms that expand choice, creating ethical dilemmas for advocates of reform" (Shepard 2000). Others claim that conservative forces advance precisely because of the lack of visibility sought by progressive groups, and that this doble discurso and lack of visibility place reproductive rights and health advocates in fragile social positions, exposing them to greater risks (Hinojosa 2002).

In my view, advocates of sexual and reproductive rights must bear in mind the need to build social consensus and fight against the tendency of many individuals to remain silent on controversial matters, even when they tend to agree with progressive positions. Advocates must identify openings, assess risks, and work on making majority views prevail in public. Studies of social perceptions have shown that if a majority thinks it is a minority, it will tend to decline, and vice versa (Noëlle-Neuman 1995).

Many activists in Latin America find it difficult to advance their ideas as they become trapped in the mire of the doble discurso system. Documenting the costs of such a system is an important goal and one that should be accomplished within a human rights framework. Such a framework is important because it emphasizes that rights are indivisible and nonnegotiable, and it roots actions in principles that respect individual rights to privacy, personhood, freedom, and sexual and reproductive self-determination. These are views held by a majority of citizens, even as a determined conservative minority intimidates them into thinking otherwise (Correa and Petchesky 1994).

Notes

I thank my research assistant, Patricia Meza, for her help in organizing the bibliography and notes.

1. For this summary I consulted the following sources: Grupo de Información en Reproduccion Elegida (GIRE) 2000; Poniatowska 2000; CIMAC 2003; Lamas 2003; Vericat 2004; Chavarria 2000; del Valle 2000; Winocour 2003; and Cornejo 2003.

2. On March 29, 2000, Isabel Vericat and Elena Poniatowska interviewed Ismael Ávila Iñiguez, the director of the Hospital General in Mexicali. Vericat had traveled to Baja California to support Poniatoswka's efforts to gather information to write a book and document the case (Poniatowska 2000). During this interview, Ávila Iñiguez admitted that Paulina had a legal right to an abortion but that he had refused to provide the service, saying that the medical staff threatened to resign if he required them to perform or assist in Paulina's abortion. When Vericat and Poniatowska asked why he had exaggerated the risks associated with abortion, he stated that he had no memory of such an exchange. When asked about another offense, that he had allowed antiabortion activists from the Comité Nacional Pro-Vida to enter the hospital disguised as employees of the Department of Child Protection and show Paulina a copy of the video "The Silent Scream," he said he was unaware that this had occurred (Poniatowska 2003).

3. According to government sources quoted by Lilian Sepúlveda in an open letter to Martha Altoaguirre, president of the Interamerican Commission on Human Rights, rape ranked seventh in frequency of all crimes in 2002 and Baja California ranked fourth among states in which rape took place most often (Sepúlveda 2003).

4. "Carelessness" is defined as an accident that results in fetal demise. To avoid prosecution, the woman must be able to prove that she did not intentionally injure herself in an attempt to end her pregnancy.

5. The distinctions among progressive, intermediate, and moderate legislation were made according to the most progressive circumstance under which abortion is allowed by law. In this chapter the most progressive circumstance is defined as that which allows access to abortion due to economic hardship, thus suggesting that this circumstance would allow the largest number of women to access abortion services.
6. The cases of Federal District and Morelos prove that greater transparency and accountability emerged after the 2000 elections, thanks to feminist mobilization and increased feminist presence in decision-making bodies.
7. There is no evidence that this clause has ever been applied.
8. Historians have documented that women nonetheless used abortive herbs. I speculate that the use of abortificants (at least by Indian women) was further complicated by the fact that Indian women were frequently raped by the Spaniards. Further research on this subject is much needed to discover how the Catholic Church came to terms with these practices (Viqueira 1984).
9. The Catholic Church initiated an international offensive against abortion in the second half of the nineteenth century. In 1859 Pope Pius IX published the Apostolic Sedis encyclical, asserting that the soul enters the body at conception (Ibañez 1992). The Catholic Church did not attack the Mexican state in response to the 1871 Penal Code, however, perhaps because the church's economic and political power had been curtailed significantly.
10. General Salvador Alvarado became the governor of Yucatán in 1917 and supported feminist, anarchist, and socialist ideas (Macías 1982).
11. The movement was most active in the states of Jalisco, Michoacán, Colima, and Guanajuato and consisted of an armed force of 30,000 men (Meyer 1978).
12. Abortion was legalized in the Soviet Union in 1920, in Iceland in 1935, in Sweden in 1937, and in Denmark in 1938. During this period Mexico, Bolivia, Chile, and Colombia liberalized abortion laws with the introduction of honoris causa and/or endangerment to women's lives clauses. It is evident that the Mexican state was not only aware of legal abortion in the Soviet Union but also interested in exploring the possibility for Mexico. In 1929 the Mexican state commissioned Matilde Rodríguez Cabo, a doctor who worked for the Public Ministry of Health, to make recommendations based on her official trip to the Soviet Union. According to Dr. Cabo, abortion should be legalized and offered on demand to poor women during the first three months of pregnancy. She argued that these women bore the human costs of illegal abortion and could be counted in the thousands.
13. The Coalición de Mujeres helped to defend a girl who had become pregnant as the result of rape. When this young woman reported it, the police asked her to come another time because then "they were too tired." Also, the doctor declared that it was only "an attempted rape," although few weeks later it was clear that the woman was pregnant. Feminists met with the local authorities to demand the girl's right to an abortion. Some of the officials they visited suggested that they would overlook the case so "the woman could get away with her abortion." They also said that if she was detained they would help her "get out of the situation." It was only after considerable effort that feminists obtained the support of a high-ranking judicial official, who gave orders to a local judge to review the case. He

in turn directed a public hospital to perform the abortion. This case helped feminists understand that in Mexico it was necessary to fight for the practical implementation of the law in order to reduce the time of juridical deliberation and also provide women with access to public services (Brito de Marti 1981).

14. Most of the political actors I interviewed believe that prolife groups have received technical assistance and financial support from the Mexican Catholic Church as well as from the headquarters of Pro-Life International, which is located in Miami, Florida. This fact was confirmed by Serrano Limón, although he did not disclose the extent of the assistance (Ortiz-Ortega 1994).

15. No state debate took place regarding any of the penal code reforms. During confidential interviews, key political actors suggested that the president conceived of the reforms and made suggestions to his close collaborators, who implemented the changes. These penal code modifications started to circulate in government circles by the mid-1990s and were widely publicized by GIRE and other feminist nongovernmental organizations from 1998 onward.

16. Founded in 1994 in Mexico, this NGO is affiliated with the U.S.-based Catholics for a Free Choice. The group contends that there is more than one theologically and ethically defensible viewpoint on abortion within the Roman Catholic tradition. Internationally, the priests and theologians who support this organization have been threatened by religious superiors, church employees, and bishops. In Mexico, it is primarily a radical grass-roots group composed of lay people and has no real influence on the Catholic leadership.

17. The 2000–2003 legislature appropriated nearly $3 million for Pro-Life Group to build ten antiabortion clinics in Mexico (Rocha 2003).

18. During President Vincente Fox's first few months in office, antiabortion groups in alliance with the PAN sought to reverse liberalized abortion laws in the state of Guanajuato. Public opinion did not support these efforts, however, and President Fox declined to participate in the debate in public. It was during this time that the Population Council carried out its poll on public perceptions of abortion. As the results clearly show, the public is more influenced by liberal values than by orthodox Catholic teachings.

References

Alan Guttmacher Institute. 1996. "Panorama general del aborto clandestino en América Latina" [General View of Clandestine Abortion in Latin America]. Policy analysis. New York: Alan Guttmacher Institute.

Barza, E., and Taracena, R. 2001. "Leyes de aborto" [Abortion Laws]. Mexico City: Hoja Informativa.

Blancarte, Roberto, comp. 2002. "Laicidad y valores en un estado democrático" [Laicism and Values in a Democratic State]. Mexico City: El Colegio de México.

Brito de Martí, Esperanza. 1981. "El Aborto" [Abortion]. *Caballero* (Magazine), 11, 94, 95, 108. Mexico City.

Brito de Martí, E. 1981. "Una legislación insuficiente" [Insufficient Legislation]. *Revista Feminista* 4. 16: 73–78.

Catholics for a Free Choice. 1994. *Catholics and Reproduction: A World View.* Washington, D.C.: CFFC.

Communicacion y Informacion de la Mujer. 2003. "Rechaza resultados presentados a las autoridades" [Rejects Results Presented to Authorities]. Consultado 15 marzo. Mexico City: CIMAC (Communicacion y Informacion de la Mujer).

Coalición de Mujeres Feministas y Frente Nacional de Liberación de la Mujer. 1979. "Maternidad voluntaria Ante proyecto de Ley" [Coalition of Feminist Women and National Women's Liberation Front]. *Folletos Feministas.* Mexico City.

Cornejo, J. A. 2003. "Comparece ex Procurador de Justicia de Baja California por anomalías en el caso Paulina" [Former Attorney General of Baja California Appears in Court over Anomalies in the Paulina Case]. *La Jornada*, February 22.

Correa S., and Petchesky, S. 1994. "Reproductive and Sexual Rights: A Feminist Perspective." In G. Sen, Adrienne Germain, and Lincoln C. Chen, eds., *Population Politics Reconsidered: Health, Empowerment and Rights.* Cambridge: Harvard University Press. 123.

De la Barreda Solórzano, Luis. 1991. *El delito en el aborto, una carta de buena conciencia* [Abortion as Punishment, a Card of Good Consciousness]. Mexico City: Editorial Porrúa.

Del Valle, Sonia. 2003. "Se realizará función a beneficio de niña violada para celebrar sus XV años" [Fund-raiser to Be Held to Enable Girl to Celebrate Her 15th Birthday]. *La Jornada,* February 28, 2.

Fontanine, A., and Damián, D. 1995. "Chiapas: una mirada en retrospectiva" [Chiapas in Restrospective View]. In Adriana Ortiz-Ortega, *Razones y pasiones en torno al aborto.* Mexico City: The Population Council y Edamex, México.

García, S. 2001, *¿Qué piensan y qué opinan los mexicanos sobre el aborto? Resultados de una encuesta nacional de opinión pública sobre el aborto* [What do Mexicans Think and Say about Abortion?]. México City: Population Council.

Gobierno del Distrito Federal. 2004. "Decreto que reforma los artículos 145 y 148 del nuevo código penal para el Distrito Federal y se adicionan los artículos 16 bis y 16 bis 7 a la ley de Salud del Distrito Federal" [Decree Reforming Articles 145 and 148 of the Federal District New Penal Code and Adding Articles 16 bis and 16 bis 7 to the Federal District Public Health Law]. Mexico City: *Gaceta Oficial del Distrito Federal,* January 27.

Grupo de Información Elegida sobre el aborto [Group of Selected Information on Abortion]. www.gire.org.mx.

Grupo Parlamentario Comunista and Coalición de Izquierda. 1979. "Maternidad Voluntaria, Proyecto de Ley" [Voluntary Motherhood, Law Project]. Mexico City, December 29.

Hinojosa, C. 2002. "En busca de pistas para la construcción de los derechos sexuales como derechos humanos" [Searching for Ways to Construct Sexual Rights as Human Rights]. In I. Szasz and Guadalupe Salas, eds., *Los derechos sexuales en México.* México: El Colegio de México.

Hunter, J. D. 1991. *The Political Mobilization of Religious Beliefs.* New York: Praeger.

Ibáñez, José Luis y Garcia Velasco. 1992. *La despenalización del aborto en el ocaso del siglo XX* [Depenalizing Abortion at the End of the 20th Century]. Madrid: Siglo XXI editores.

Lamas, Marta. 2000. "Paulina: herida y cicatriz" [Paulina: Injury and Scar]. December 3. Amnesty International. http://www.puntog.com.mx/2000/081200/IDA081200. htm.

Macías, A. 1982. *Against All Odds: The Feminist Movement in México to 1940.* Westport, Conn.: Greenwood Press.

Marcos, Sylvia. 1994. *"Historia de una expropiación. Mujeres e iglesia"* [History of an Expropriation: Women and the Church]. Montevideo, Uruguay: Católicas por el Derecho a Decidir.

Meyer, L. 1978. *El conflicto social y los gobiernos del Maximato.* Vol. 13 of *Historia de la revolución mexicana* [Social Conflict and the Governments of the Maximato. Vol. 13 of History of the Mexican Revolution]. Mexico City: El Colegio de México.

Meyer L., R. Segovia, and A. Lajous, 1978. *Historia de la revolución mexicana.* Vol. 12, *Los inicios de la institucionalización;* vol. 14, *La política del Maximato* [History of the Mexican Revolution. Vol. 12, The Beginnings of Institutionalization; vol. 14 The Politics of the Maximato]. México City: El Colegio de México.

Muro, González, and Víctor Gabriel. 1991. "Iglesia y movimientos sociales en México." [Church and Social Movements in Mexico]. *Estudios Sociológicos* 9(27) (September–December), 541–556.

Noëlle-Neumann, E. 1995. "La espiral del silencio: una teoría de la opinión pública" [The Spiral of Silence: A Theory of Public Opinion]. In Centre National de la Recherche Scientifique, ed., *Le nouvel espace publique,* 2nd edition, 200–207. Barcelona: España,

Ortiz-Ortega, Adriana. 1987. "For Her Own Good: The Legitimization of State Family Planning in Mexico (1970–1976)," Paper presented at the Institute of Advance Study, Berlin.

———. 1994. *Razones y pasiones en torno al aborto* [Reasons and Passions around Abortion]. Mexico City: Population Council and EDAMEX.

———. 2000. "Si los hombres se embarazaran ¿el aborto sería legal?" [If Men Got Pregnant, Would Abortion Be Legal?]. Mexico City: Population Council and EDAMEX.

Petchesky, R. P. 2000. *Reproductive and Sexual Rights: Charting the Course of International Women's NGOs.* Geneva: United Nations Research Institute for Social Development.

———. 2003. *Global Prescriptions: Gendering Health and Human Rights.* London: Zed Books.

Poniatowska, E. 2000. "Las mil una . . . la herida de Paulina" [A Thousand and One . . . Paulina's Injury]. México City: Plaza and Janes.

———. 2003. "El caso Paulina. La niña a la que los médicos obligaron a tener el producto de una violación" [The Paulina Case. The Girl Doctors Forced to Have the Product of Rape]. *La Jornada,* Special Supplement, July 3. http://www.jornada.unam.mx/2000/may00/000510/poni_paulina1.htm.

Rabasa, E. 1993. "El artículo 14, estudio constitucional, y el juicio constitucional orígenes, teoría y extensión" [Article 14: Constitutional Study, and Constitutional Judgment, Origins, Theory and Extension]. Mexico City: Porrúa.

Rocha, R. 2003. "Nuestros impuesto para Provida" [Our Taxes for Pro-Vida]. *El Universal México* (Mexico City), A10.

Sepúlveda, L. 2003. Carta abierta a Martha Altoaguirre, Presidenta de la Comisión Interamericana de Derechos Humanos [Open Letter to Martha Altolaguirre, President of the Human Rights Inter-American Commission]. September 4.

Shepard, B. 2000. "The 'Double Discourse' on Sexual and Reproductive Rights in Latin America: The Chasm between Public Discourse and Private Actions." *Health and Human Rights Journal* 4(2): 110–143.

Viqueira, J. P. 1984. "Matrimonio y sexualidad en los confesionarios en lenguas indígenas" [Marriage and Sexuality in Confessionals in Indigenous Languages]. *Cuicuilco* 4(12) (January): 27.

Winocour, M. 2003. "Una historia de abandono" [A History of Abandonment]. *Reforma* (electronic version). September 7.

Sexual-Reproductive Health and Rights

What about Men?

Benno de Keijzer

A trucker, forty-two years old and weighing more than 200 pounds, is driving his wife to the local clinic in a small town in Veracruz, Mexico, for the birth of their fifth child. Before this pregnancy his wife had wanted to have bilateral tubal ligation surgery (sterilization), but he refused, fearing she might cheat on him. He was away for the four previous births, but this time he was home when the contractions started. They arrive at the rural clinic on a Saturday at ten o'clock to find that only the midwife is there. Although he wants nothing more than simply to hand over his wife and leave, the midwife insists he stay to help. He grows pale with fear, but can't refuse. He assists as best as he can while watching, for the first time, his wife experience labor. He almost faints when his fifth child is born. After the birth, he timidly approaches his tired wife and promises: "It's the last one, woman, the last one . . . "

What is the role of men in sexual and reproductive health and rights? The story above, told by a midwife during a Salud y Género training course in 1999, is just one of many possible examples in which men are confronted by situations that can become opportunities for change. This trucker was accidentally present at the birth of one of his many children. It was a moving experience for him in many senses, and it inspired his willingness to move toward accepting his wife's desire (and right) to limit further childbearing.

What helps some men change and learn to accept equity in reproductive, sexual, and family relations? What kind of results have various projects and approaches had in working with men? How are they contributing to equity? Under what conditions might work with men contradict or undermine work done with women? Won't funding men's programs take resources away from women's projects? Has work with men had any influence on public policy?

This chapter will attempt to address these questions, concentrating on men's current position and potential to contribute positively to the advancement of sexual and reproductive health and rights. This discussion is based on the work of three organizations: ReproSalud, which works with indigenous men and women in Peru; Salud y Género, which promotes alternative ways of working with men in Mexico; and Program H: Working with Young Men, a Latin American coalition-based initiative for gender equity and better health.

The Gender Transition in Latin America

The number of families with a single male breadwinner has decreased drastically throughout Latin America. More members of the family have to work outside the home, and both men and women have moved into the service and manufacturing industries in massive numbers.[1] Important markers of social change and gender transition also include an increase in female heads of households: Up to one-fifth of families in Latin America are headed by women (Valdés 1995). Second marriages, in which women tend to negotiate more equitable relationships, are also on the rise (Schmuckler 1996).

Women's employment, together with thirty years of family planning efforts, is associated with a significant drop in the total fertility rate (TFR) in Latin America, which fell from 5.9 to 3.1 children per woman from 1950 to 1995.[2] Mexico's TFR fell from 6.8 to 3.2 in the same period and to 2.6 in the year 2000. In 2000, more than 70 percent of Mexican couples were using some contraceptive method (Valdés 1995, and INEGI 2001).

Women have struggled for gender equity in all spheres of Mexican society for decades. As women have progressed in these struggles, their acceptance of the traditional male role of exclusive provider and family authority has eroded, leading to new tensions and conflicts. As with every crisis, these shifts in roles should be seen as both a risk and an opportunity for positive change. The expectations that women—and even children—have of men are changing rapidly, and men confront and negotiate with women and children in order to keep up. As one woman in a workshop in Nicaragua put it, "Men are looking for women who don't exist anymore, and women are looking for men who don't exist yet."

Increased opportunities for women with regard to education and the workplace and smaller family sizes have also fueled the gender transition in Mexico. Changing attitudes toward gender roles and inequalities have been gaining momentum since the 1950s, when women gained the right to vote. Traditional beliefs about what it means to be a man are increasingly influenced by changes in the sociocultural position of women and demands for gender equity both in the public and private spheres. These shifts were further fueled by work done by nongovernmental organizations (NGOs) and the impetus provided by the UN Conference on Population and Development in Cairo in 1994 and the Fourth World Conference on Women in Beijing in 1995. The gay rights movement has also actively contributed to destabilizing existing gender norms, and the HIV/AIDS epidemic has exposed the fact that many gay and bisexual men feel so stigmatized that they present themselves as straight.

Despite this shake-up in gender roles, however, significant inequities still exist. Although some men are involved in child rearing and domestic work, many remain closed to discussing this and other critical issues such as sex and contraception, financial power, domestic violence, alcohol abuse, and who has ultimate decision-making authority in the family. Latin American feminists sense that the hard core of gender-based power and discrimination is still alive and well.[3]

The gender transition is not a linear process—quite the contrary, it moves in different directions according to such variables as region, class, ethnicity, and the influence of conservative movements. Men's reactions to the gender transition range from open opposition to active promotion of equitable gender relations. Between these poles is a gamut of reactions, including passive resistance, adaptation, and even chameleonism, in which men adopt the discourse of equity but do not practice it.

Understanding Men's Socialization

Men's reactions to the gender transition that is taking place throughout much of the developed and developing world are complicated because the traditional constructs of masculinity that such transitions challenge are so deeply rooted. The principal traits of hegemonic masculinity include dominance, entitlement to autonomy and privilege, emotional detachment, and violence.[4] Traditional masculine socialization that values these traits can contribute to both male and female health risks.

Why does this model of hegemonic masculinity prevail? As socioculturally constructed beings, we function with a mixed array of representations, thoughts, and feelings. These are structured in what Pierre Bourdieu (1984 and 2001) calls the *habitus*. The habitus is conceived of as a system of perception, thought, and action, durable in time and adaptable to different situations. Such a system functions as a defining structure in society; it tends to be reproduced by pedagogic authority (parents, teachers, the church, the military). This habitus conditions the way we perceive the world, process it in thought, and act in it.

By the time boys arrive at adolescence, the habitus is formed; most have learned the main lessons that shape masculine behavior and identity. Many of these lessons limit certain forms of emotional expression and encourage others, such as anger and violence. These patterns have a clear influence on sexual behavior and reproductive health, often leading men to ignore or violate women's rights. The strength of the habitus makes it difficult for many men to be more flexible and sensitive once they develop couple and parental relationships. Privileged gender, class, and race differences falsely appear to those who possess them as essence, distinction, and personal attributes rather than the product of an unequal appropriation of cultural capital. Inequity thus becomes naturalized and therefore unconscious and automatic. Bourdieu sees habitus as the embodiment of male difference as power and privilege that appears as "natural" to men and even to most women. This has everything to do with the male sense of entitlement to differential rights, authority, and services from women, from cradle to grave. If women question or deny these rights and services, violence is frequently the response. Women are subject to the same forces; for them, "successful" socialization produces a subordinate identity that internalizes discrimination and forgets the original pedagogic process.

The habitus affects men's relationships with other men, which are often constrained or complicated by competition for power or attempts always to appear strong and invulnerable. Elizabeth Badinter (1995) describes men's socialization as a straight but very narrow path, with danger on both sides: fear of expressing feminine traits leads to active misogyny, and fear of being labeled gay leads to homophobia. Men are submitted to this gender straightjacket from early childhood into the adult years. Men must not only demonstrate masculinity continuously, but also actively reject femininity (Fuller 2001). It is still common for school children in Latin America to run quickly when someone screams: "The last one there is . . . *vieja*" (an old woman). Even girls run!

Kimmel (1997) has stressed the power of homophobia in the socialization of men in Western culture. A powerful example of this process in Mexico is "forty-one phobia." It is a popular belief in central Mexico that any man approaching his forty-first year is at great risk of becoming sexually attracted to other men. When a man is reaching that age, other men will joke, saying he is approaching "the difficult years." He may answer he is only turning "thirty eleven." Many men and even some boys fear and actively avoid the number forty-one: When groups of boys are numbered in school the one following number forty will yell, "I'm not it!" There is no forty-first division in the Mexican army. I've known men to change their bus tickets upon receiving number forty-one. Where does this phobia come from?

Few people know it today, but the origin is neither hormonal nor psychological, but historical: In 1906 Mexico City's police, under dictator Porfirio Diaz, raided a gay party at which forty-one men, some of them dressed as women, were feasting. Forty were captured, and one escaped. Most of the forty men were sent to prison under forced labor. The incident was widely covered by the press, and since then, the number forty-one is associated with being gay, and therefore most heterosexuals have to make it clear: *It's not me!*

Almost one hundred years later the number is still taboo, although it is losing force among contemporary adolescents. It is a clear demonstration of the presence of homophobia in the *habitus* of several generations that have lost track of the original historical facts, but continue to avoid anything to do with homosexuality. This avoidance leads to hypermasculine, transgressive, and dangerous behaviors linked with substance abuse, unhealthy or violent sexual initiation, violence, and being prone to accidents (Kimmel 1997). At the furthest extreme are homophobic crimes in which homosexuals are harassed, beaten, raped, and even killed by gangs of men.

A growing movement of men seeking gender equity, influenced both by the women's and gay rights movements in Latin America and globally, has begun to alter this habitus. Although key traits associated with hegemonic masculinity are prevalent in Mexico, where the term *machismo* was born, there is more than one way of being a man.[5] Sexual diversity among men in Mexico has challenged what once appeared as a uniform way of expressing maleness. Rather than focus on a singular type of masculinity, it is more accurate to describe varying masculinities, in order to capture important differences of class, ethnicity, sexual orientation, occupation, education, and other variables. Male identities also change throughout the life cycle. Many men adopt new behavior patterns when they become fathers and continue to change as their children grow up. Rigid or authoritarian fathers can become gentle grandfathers once they retire not only from work but also from the social constraints on male conduct to which they clung earlier in their lives. As one man explained at a Salud y Género workshop, "I have a right not to constantly have to prove my masculinity and not to have to respond hydraulically to what is expected from me as a man."

The strength of habitus explains the difficulty of changing gender norms embedded in culture and embodied in men and women. Changing habitus requires a secondary pedagogic process coming from a new pedagogic authority with sufficient time and intensity to produce shifts in collective representations and gender norms. Many times these lessons come from the consequences of life itself: losing a partner after repeated or excessive violence, negative sequelae of alcoholism or drug abuse, suffering a heart attack from overwork, or even becoming a father or grandfather.

Barker and Lowenstein (1997) have tried to understand why certain men emerge from violent settings with nonviolent and more gender equitable attitudes, while others perpetuate violent and inequitable relationships. Based on ethnographic research in Brazil and the United States, they note that many young men have observed the costs of traditional manhood or have been victims of or witnesses to domestic violence. However, those young men who have had positive influences, such as contact with positive male models, alternative peer groups (cultural, musical, church-related), and the experience of becoming fathers, and who have been able to reflect upon the violence in their childhood, are more likely to strive for more equitable relationships.[6] Barker and Lowenstein's research shows how gender equity can appear among men even in the midst of a violent and patriarchal context and pave the way for different possibilities of involvement. Men are a major part of the problem, but if they can interrupt or question the messages they receive about traditional masculinity and understand its costs, they also have the potential to become a significant part of the solution.

Men: Part of the Solution

Although researchers have been reflecting on and theorizing about masculinity since the 1960s and 1970s in Europe and North America,[7] in Latin America, they began to organize and respond to public and private initiatives from a gender-based perspective only in the late 1980s and early 1990s. Initiatives developed simultaneously yet independently among men in Mexico, Brazil, Argentina, Nicaragua, and Chile. Major UN agencies (World Health Organization, UNICEF, UNFPA, and others) and private foundations and institutions (MacArthur Foundation, Ford Foundation, International Planned

Parenthood Federation, EngenderHealth) promoted men's involvement in reproductive health initiatives during the 1990s, stressing the need for a gender equity approach in the projects they funded. Many of these agencies have been pioneers not only in promoting projects dealing with men and sexual reproductive health and rights but also in addressing sexual diversity among men and stressing links between reproductive health and gender-based violence.

Although early work on male involvement predates the Cairo and Beijing conferences, such work received a major boost from inclusion in the action plans that resulted. Men are identified as an important part of the problem in the Cairo action program, and are also included in its recommendations for change. The Cairo Programme of Action calls for emphasizing men's shared responsibility for and promoting their active involvement in responsible parenthood, sexual and reproductive behavior, control of and contribution to family income and children's education, recognizing the value of children of both sexes and educating them from the earliest ages in male responsibilities in family life, and preventing male violence against women and children.

A recent publication from the Alan Guttmacher Institute (2002) synthesizes and advances the vision of the role of men proposed at the Cairo and Beijing conferences: "Movement toward a more holistic and broad-based approach to sexual and reproductive health care for men should enhance their well-being, equip them to make responsible decisions, result in lower levels of STDs and unintended childbearing, and help make men better fathers. Thus, what is increasingly seen as good for men in their own right should turn out to be just as good for women—to the benefit of men and women as individuals, couples, families, and society as a whole."

Men are often identified as interfering with the success of health education, family planning, and development programs for women. Although men play a major role in public policy, establishing and enforcing laws and regulations governing sexuality, reproduction, and domestic violence, work to change men themselves is still a relatively unexplored strategy, despite the support gained for these efforts at Cairo and Beijing (de Keijzer 2000 and Kaufman 2003). However, several organizations, including Salud y Género, ReproSalud, and Program H are bucking this tide and working closely with men throughout Latin America.

Male participation is not always free of conflict: The idea of men's rights is threatening to many women struggling for their own rights. This is especially true when sexual and reproductive rights are at stake. In this case, men's rights are relational—they have to be thought out in the context of women's rights and with a clear understanding that most of the reproductive process occurs in female bodies.

Please Tell Our Husbands—ReproSalud in Peru

Many programs in Latin America have initiated work with men as a way to improve women's health and conditions. Take the example of ReproSalud, a decade-old cooperative project developed by the Movimiento Manuela Ramos (one of two major feminist organizations in Peru). The ReproSalud project is devoted to improving the reproductive health of low-income indigenous women living in rural and marginal urban areas of Peru whose health indicators are poorest. The project ensures that women themselves define their needs and assume leadership in the projects through community-based organizations (CBOs) (Movimiento Manuela Ramos 2003).

The men who participate in the various projects discussed below come to do so through a variety of channels: Some are related to women participants, some are "sent" by their partners, and some are curious or sincerely interested. Initiating work with men often results from women's own requests: "We already know, please tell our husbands" is a common rallying cry. The issue of working with men was taken up by the organization because many men opposed their wives' participation in ReproSalud projects and because of the obvious role men have to play in sexual and reproductive health. In some communities, a desire to reduce violence against women was key to the development of projects that integrate men. The impetus for including men in programming came primarily from women in the CBOs, however, rather than from the organizers of ReproSalud:

> Work with men was initiated following requests made by women—mainly women in rural Andean areas. After participating in the educational activities, they thought that men should receive the same information so they could understand what the women were doing and stop preventing them from going to the sessions. Another reason given was that men should know about the reproductive health problems that can affect women, and in that way the women could achieve more dialogue and understanding on the part of their partners. (Movimiento Manuela Ramos 2003: 22)

Many men encounter notions of women's sexual and reproductive rights for the first time through contact with ReproSalud's programs. Although evaluations of the programs that include men have shown improvements in men's lives, in working with men, ReproSalud focuses on bettering women's sexual and reproductive health and rights. Leadership in local programs is still assumed by women, and men understand that their participation in programming is a direct result of women's having requested their involvement.

Concepts of power and gender equity are clearly understood by the Peruvian indigenous women who participate in ReproSalud programs. They classify men into two types, those who "don't know" and those who "refuse to learn":

> Some recognized there were two types of men. Men who hit their wives or abuse them because they don't know. No one has ever told them, or they have not thought about it, but they are good people and it is necessary to make them understand. And the others are the ones who don't [want to learn] and it was funny because they said: "For them we have to call the priest, so that he can tell them it is a sin, we have to call the teacher, so that he can tell them that they should not act like that, that it is bad to hit a woman and it is bad for the children, and we have to call the police so that they can threaten them and take them to jail." (Movimiento Manuela Ramos 2003: 22)

This is a key distinction, separating men who are "teachable" from men who refuse to learn and only respond to pressure, coercion, and the assertion of a more powerful person's authority. It suggests that change not only requires strategies that focus on education and reflection but also calls for policy efforts that recognize power relations.

ReproSalud's programs for men provide education and consciousness-raising opportunities with regard to sexual and reproductive health. Professional facilitators from Lima first trained local professionals (who speak the indigenous language) to be health promoters. Then the health promoters began work with men at the community level. The health promoters lead three core sessions: My Body—Her Body (basic sexual and reproductive physiology), Women's Sexual and Reproductive Rights, and Sexual and Reproductive Health Problems (including sexually transmitted infections, genital cancer, pregnancy and birth complications, domestic violence). One of the most striking lessons indigenous men learn in these sessions is that a child's sex isn't determined by the mother, as many of them had believed. Aside from improving men's knowledge of the basic physiology of reproduction and introducing concepts like sexual and reproductive rights, these core sessions encourage men to take on specific tasks to better the health of their partners and of all women in the community, such as developing strategies to transport a pregnant woman in danger to the nearest health post.

Recruitment for these programs was not difficult: Many men were already interested in participating or curious about what the women in their families were learning. The number of men trained and sensitized in the community has soared. By the year 2001, ReproSalud's programs have benefited almost 150,000 women and more than 67,000 men. These men benefit not only from knowing more about their partners' bodies, sexuality, and reproductive health and rights but also from knowing more about their own health. As a result of the programs many of them start to review their roles in child care and domestic work.

Change is a difficult process: Men don't want to be labeled *macho* anymore, but lack an alternative model. *Saco largo* (long coat—a term used for a man who is supposedly dominated by a woman) remains a feared taunt. As in other countries, "gender fright" (the fear of inverted roles and of being controlled by women) often appears and must be confronted (Movimiento Manuela Ramos 2003: 31). Still, some men have learned to laugh it off, which becomes easier when there is a collective process occurring. As a male health promoter in Ucayali puts it, "They might see you cooking and they say 'Hey! *Saquito!*' [diminutive for *saco largo*]. Before men used to get mad, they could tell you to go jump in a lake, but not now, they all joke with each other" (ibid.).

The Campaign on Fathering—Salud y Género in Mexico

The medical and mental health professionals (both women and men, including this author) who founded Salud y Género began working together as a group to address specific health and gender concerns in 1993. The group formally organized as an NGO two years later in 1995. Salud y Género's work is grounded in the belief that biological and physical manifestations of health are inextricably linked to social factors and that social inequality interferes with the attainment of good health. Through dialogue, experience sharing, and reflection Salud y Género's programs aim to change negative consequences of gender inequity in sexual, reproductive, and mental health.

Salud y Género uses a number of approaches to lessen the negative effects of male socialization on health: consultative services, including sensitization and training workshops for NGOs, donors, and others; gender education programs with men, women, mixed groups; adolescent boys and professionals in the public and private sectors; and advocacy for sexual and reproductive rights, enhanced male participation, and prevention of gender-based violence. From 1998 to 2001 Salud y Género's educational activities reached almost 5,000 people, approximately 40 percent of whom were men.

In Salud y Género's educational programs, men analyze the construction of male subjectivity as a way to understand and modify it. The programs engage with men in a group setting to share experiences, question ideas of hegemonic masculinity, and expose its affects on male attitudes and practices in sexual and reproductive health and family relations. Workshop groups have reflected on the beliefs men grow up with: that men hold essential "authority" over women; that they are entitled to services from them; that violent responses are acceptable and a legitimate "correction" of female behavior; and that emotions, especially ones like fear or sadness, are more appropriately expressed as anger. Salud y Género's programs also encourage men to look closely at the steep toll hegemonic masculinity extracts in different aspects of their own health, sexuality, and family lives.

We have learned that discussing fathering is a good entree with men who otherwise might feel threatened by topics such as violence, alcohol, or sexuality (Salud y Género 2003).[8] Fathering is a socially respectable part of manhood and is central to male self-esteem. Sharing in child care also serves as a point of intervention for strengthening equitable relationships. Inquiries into fathering can lead men to question their beliefs about authority and negotiation, domestic work, discipline and violence, emotions, and reproduction.

A starting point for such male participation is the father's presence at the birth of his children. Thus Salud y Género is also committed to consciousness raising in the health sector, with the goal of defending men's reproductive rights, including a man's right to be present during labor and birth. In Mexico, this is a long-term advocacy process, as men are currently not allowed to witness the births of their children if they take place in public hospitals.

The "How My Daddy Looks to Me" campaign, launched in 1998 by Salud y Género in collaboration with Colectivo de Hombres por Relaciones Igualitarias (CORIAC, Men for Equality in Relations Collective) from Mexico City, fosters fuller paternal responsibility for and emotional commitment to both male and female children. A request for drawings of fathers yielded 500 drawings from primary and preschools in three cities. The same campaign was conducted nationally in 2000 with full government and UNICEF support and produced more than a quarter of a million pictures. The drawings were displayed widely with the help of local, state, and national governments. Posters, calendars, and a book published by the Instituto Nacional de las Mujeres and UNICEF (2001) have been produced using these pictures.

In their drawings, children emphasized what fathers do in their work and what they do with children in their free time, afternoons, weekends, or vacations. Many depicted love and respect, and a striking number revealed authoritarian attitudes and even violence. Few of the drawings were about fathers' presence in domestic life, except for helping with homework. Finally, there were dramatic drawings criticizing fathers' abuse of alcohol and tobacco, as well as of absent fathers—migrant, divorced, dead, or simply disappeared—including a drawing full of question marks and one completely black with the caption "I never knew my father."

In an effort to celebrate Father's Day in a different, more reflective way, Salud y Género has promoted the same exercise in schools, asking fathers, mothers, and children (in separate groups) to draw a life-size father with children and to write down anonymously what they like and dislike about fathers. The exercise culminates with the exhibition of three mega-drawings created and viewed collectively. In Brazil, a city program addresses fathering through initiatives like "Fathers' Week" and slogans like "World peace begins at home" (Branco 2003).

Where and how does one learn to be a father? Often only through the experience of having been our father's sons.[9] Salud y Género asks men to reflect on their experiences as children as a way to understand their attitudes as fathers. This exercise has led to some of the most provocative and transformative workshop experiences. Different kinds of fathers are evoked: the close and friendly guide, the sometimes (or often) authoritarian father, and the absent father. This is a profound opportunity for men to reflect on the way we wish to be or are being fathers—are we repeating a negative model or can we struggle toward a more flexible and democratic family life?

A striking difference was revealed between women's and men's priorities in Tijuana, Mexico. Men considered the issue of time as the major obstacle to improved family relations: "Not enough time for my kids." Women however, identified lack of communication as the major barrier to improving family relations, citing screaming and other authoritarian styles, but also fathers' and husbands' silence about their feelings and their inability to express love.

Finally, research has identified some of the benefits of being more involved in fathering (USAID 2002): better communication and stronger bonding in the couple and family, better role modeling for children, increased commitment to contraceptive use and disease prevention, increased support for women during pregnancy, and reduced violence in the home. Of course, more involvement is important, but it is the quality of this involvement that can enrich the lives of men, their partners, and children. The presence of excessively authoritative or violent men can have the opposite effect.

Working with Boys and Young Men:
Program H in Brazil and Mexico

Another key issue of male involvement in reproductive and sexual health has to do with the health and rights of youth—a key agenda in a youthful country. Nearly a quarter of the Mexican population is between ten and nineteen years old (INEGI 2001). It is a youth boom never seen before (Barker 2003). It is crucial to work with younger men and adolescents on sexual and reproductive rights, while their perceptions and practices of masculinity are still crystallizing. Barker (2003) stresses the need to approach young men in order to encourage them to question traditional gender norms, learn new communication skills, and promote more flexible attitudes toward sexual diversity and the construction of emotional intimacy.

Too often campaigns targeted to young men and boys are narrowly focused on the short-term goal of increased condom use; such programs could also incorporate key issues of gender equity, as Program H does. Program H was initially developed by a small coalition of organizations whose leaders first began working together during a Latin American seminar in 2000 that addressed working with young men, including health, sexuality, gender, and violence prevention.[10] The coalition (called Program H because the word for "men" in both Spanish and Portuguese starts with H: *hombres* and *homens*) now includes the support of an array of national and international organizations.[11]

Program H creates empirically designed and rigorously evaluated interventions to engage young men internationally in the promotion of gender equity and to address problems like sexuality and reproduction, preventing HIV/AIDS, gender-based violence, mental health, and good fathering. We have designed a set of manuals for educators and health workers entitled "Working with Young Men." The five manuals (Sexuality and Reproductive Health, Paternity and Care Giving, Reason and Emotions, From Violence to Peaceful Coexistence, and Preventing and Living with HIV/AIDS) are accompanied by an animated videotape with no words, "Once upon a Boy," which focuses on issues of gender socialization, health, and gender equity. Each manual includes background information on the theme and outlines concrete educational activities. Both the manuals and video were field tested widely in Latin American and the Caribbean and were developed in collaboration with the International Planned Parenthood Federation/Western Hemisphere Region and the Pan American Health Organization. These materials are available in Spanish, Portuguese, and English.

Program H is developing interventions that target a variety of youth, ranging from impoverished youth in Brazilian *favelas* to university students and health professionals across the region (Program H 2003):

- Participatory group educational workshops (including the "Once upon a Boy" cartoon video) that encourage young men to reflect on the costs of traditional masculinity and what it means to be a man, in order to promote HIV/AIDS prevention, and changed attitudes toward young women;
- The H Hour: a lifestyle social marketing campaign to promote more equitable attitudes, including condom use, greater involvement as fathers, and negotiation and respect instead of violence against partners;
- Campaigns to engage young men more effectively in public health services (including HIV/AIDS testing and sexually transmitted infection counseling and treatment) by making services more youth-friendly;
- A program evaluation model developed specifically for working with young men.

All four programs have been implemented in Brazil and are being implemented in Mexico. The programs have been developed locally in both countries and are in the process of scaling up and seeking incorporation in public programs directed to youth at the state level. The evaluation in Brazil shows that the program has had an impact on both gender attitudes and condom use. Within the next three years Program H will expand its work to seven states in Mexico and begin work in India, Central America, and several African nations.

Masculinity as a Risk or Limiting Factor

> We courted death in order to call ourselves brave and hid like
> thieves from life.
> —Toni Morrison, *The Bluest Eye*

Typical characteristics of hegemonic masculinity, such as dominance, entitlement to autonomy and privilege, emotional detachment, and violence, are often health risk factors. Although it is often clear to both men and women that hegemonic masculinity can have a negative impact on women's health, its negative impact on men's own health such as early deaths and disability for men due to accidents, AIDS, alcohol and other drugs, suicide, violence, lung and prostate cancer, is less well recognized (de Keijzer 1997).

Understanding the connection between hegemonic masculinity and male mortality and morbidity could be an important motivating factor for social and cultural change. Policy makers and activists invest enormous resources in battling the consequences of public health problems associated with hegemonic masculinity and concomitant gender inequality, while too little attention (and money) is directed toward prevention of such problems.

Kaufman (1987) has proposed a violence triad in which the three sides represent violence directed by men toward women, toward other men, and toward themselves. Borrowing from this model, we can hypothesize a health risk triad that accounts for health risks directly related to hegemonic masculinity. The three sides would represent men's contributions to women's health risks (this would be the longest side), to the health risks of other men, and finally, to their own.

For example, men in Mexico can expect to live up to 6.5 fewer years than women do. That gap has grown during the last century, even though women face unique risks related to reproduction.[12] The mean gap in life expectancy in Latin America is 5.2 fewer years of life for men (Valdés 1995).[13] Sex differences in the distribution of age and cause of death are also revealing. Men accounted for 62 percent of deaths among all 5- to 19-year-olds in Latin America from 1950 to 1955, but this increased to more than 70 percent in the 1990s. The proportion of male deaths in the next age group (20–59) increased from 55 percent to 60 percent in the same period (Valdés 1995). Violent deaths among men, including homicide, accidents, and suicide, many linked to hegemonic masculinity, account for these differences.

The costs of the AIDS epidemic are also part of this toll; the ratio of AIDS cases in men and women was 1.8:1 in Bolivia, 6:1 in Mexico, and a staggering 16:1 in Paraguay during the 1990s (INEGI 2001). In the last decade the proportion of women infected with HIV has grown because of heterosexual transmission. Men who present themselves as heterosexual but who have sex with other men without using condoms (and often under the influence of alcohol) have contributed in large part to the increase in heterosexual transmission (INEGI 2001).

Homophobia, another characteristic of hegemonic masculinity, leads many men to risk prostate cancer rather than seek help or screening, out of fear that the digital rectal exam performed by a male physician (as part of screening for the disease) might somehow be understood as a homosexual act.

Men and traditional masculine behaviors can also be seen as limiting or risk factors in terms of sexuality and reproduction, if they are studied at all; however, only rarely do demographers ask men how many children *they* have. A review of demography texts and statistics makes it look as if only women reproduced (Figueroa 1998, Greene and Biddlecom 2000). Fears and misunderstanding surrounding vasectomy and the social meanings men commonly ascribe to it reveal one way in which hegemonic masculinity and women's reproductive health are intertwined. The trucker from the vignette at the beginning of this essay, so moved by witnessing the birth of his child, could decide to have a vasectomy, a much simpler and safer surgery than that for female sterilization. As a consequence of that choice, however, he would have to face potential ridicule or criticism from other men and also worry about whether his family would imagine a loss of his sexual potency. Although a man may agree to vasectomy as an egalitarian act, research has also shown that some men may use it to control their partner's sexuality ("If she gets pregnant I will be sure it was not me") (Viveros, 2002).

On Working with Men: Lessons Learned in Promoting Reproductive Health and Rights

How can we include men in sexual and reproductive health and rights programming and policy making? The traditional perspective is not to do so. Another view is to include them only as allies for women's health and rights. As we saw in the ReproSalud example, men find benefits even with this kind of limited approach as they learn more about women's health and start treating women with more respect. The Salud y Género perspective, on the other hand, is that men need and deserve to be integrated into all reproductive health programs and that an integrated approach will generally have benefits for both men and women. Men should not be addressed only as gatekeepers of women's health but also as sensitive, concerned subjects with their own rights and concerns.

The experience of Salud y Género demonstrates that to be effective, projects must investigate the emotions that accompany or are suppressed by hegemonic masculinity (Kaufman 1999 and Salud y Género 2003). Facilitators and professionals must reflect on their own socialization and current attitudes and practices. We must offer men mirrors in which they can be witnesses not only to their current behavior but also to their enormous potential. Programs should help men question power relationships with women and other men (Kaufman 1999). Group norms supporting equity or less tolerance of violence against women build a strong framework to support the individual process. This is why so much effective work with men is done in group settings with a participatory and self-reflective focus. Though some men flee rather than confront the results and consequences of their socialization, in our experience, many men undergo a positive process of questioning that can lead to the gradual inclusion of a different discourse and new practices.

Assessing the costs of hegemonic masculinity on men's own health and lives (and on those of others) and emphasizing the possible rewards for changing is another key element in supporting new behaviors (Salud y Género 2003). Change occurs with greater ease if the individual's process is not resisted but supported collectively, not only by the family but also by other men. Individual change has to happen as part of cultural change in networks, institutions, policies, and the media; otherwise men in the process of changing may be isolated and ridiculed and the desire for further or sustainable change crushed.

Projects should be culture based and culturally appropriate, precisely because culture is often seen as an obstacle to change.[14] Drawing from tradition, men tend to defend the need to "correct" their wives violently. As Barker (2003) stresses, however, the most effective and sustainable change takes place in the local culture itself—within the individuals and networks that are already promoting change.

Much of what is being done in the field of men and sexual and reproductive health and rights was presented at the Interagency Gender Working Group event, "Reaching Men To Improve Reproductive Health for All," held in Washington, D.C. in 2003.[15] This event focused on interventions from all over the world and demonstrated a clear evolution from the narrow family planning (demographic) focus to a more integrated approach including gender, sexuality, and fathering. The more successful programs used a relational approach with men and women and a participatory methodology. An impressive array of original initiatives deals with work with men in new contexts like trade unions, religious movements, traditional authorities in indigenous communities, truck drivers, police departments, and armed forces, as well as men in prisons and boys in sports. As Michelle Bograd (1991) puts it in a book on therapy with men: "This process can be angry, confusing, self-righteous, and painful, but it is not without many moments of exhilaration and promise."

Education and Activism for New Policies

Many of the initiatives directed to men emerge from the experience of civil society and still have a long way to go before they turn into public policy.

There are hundreds of projects aimed at men waiting to be thoroughly evaluated in order to select successful ones for scaling up and replication in other contexts. The domains to be evaluated have to expand from participation in contraception to other variables, including sexuality, violence, homophobia, and participation in child care and the domestic sphere. Qualitative research must consider the similarities and differences among men and their individual problems and needs in order to avoid generalizations about men with respect to issues like violence, sexuality, and fathering.

We have learned much about how to work with men in groups and institutions, and organizations are increasingly applying these approaches in promoting sexual and reproductive rights.[16] The experiences of ReproSalud in Peru, Salud y Género in Mexico, and Program H in Brazil point the way toward some of the most promising policy changes.

Salud y Género's interventions have revealed that policies limiting male participation in important moments like birth and caring for newborns or sick children must be altered. Although male presence at childbirth has started to become the norm in Chile, in Mexico and most of Latin America the right to be present at the birth of their children exists only for men whose children are born at home or who can pay for delivery in a private hospital. By contrast, in most European countries and in the Unites States men can count on witnessing the birth of their children and are entitled to paternal leave to care for newborns or sick children (Badinter 1995). Male involvement at birth can be increased by formally encouraging male participation in programs such as UNICEF's Mother and Child Friendly Hospitals initiative and the Safe Motherhood Initiative, a program of the Safe Motherhood Inter-Agency Group, a partnership of international and national agencies working since 1987 to reduce the burden of maternal death and ill-health in developing countries.

UNICEF's Mother and Child Friendly Hospitals (as their name accurately reflect) have left the father out completely at a time when he might be extremely motivated to reflect on the type of life he might be willing to construct with his partner and child. Although the campaign attempts to improve hospital conditions for mothers and babies, it does not include advocating for the rights of fathers to be witness the births of their children. Likewise, the Safe Motherhood Initiative has often overlooked the potential of men (especially husbands) as allies. In a study reviewing maternal deaths in Tlaxcala, Mexico Elu (1994) showed that monetary resources are often not made available for health care or transportation when pregnant women have symptoms that might indicate deadly complications. If the woman dies, however, monetary resources are then made available and spent on her culturally "proper" funeral. Elu concludes that men lack a basic understanding of danger signs during pregnancy and delivery and that an attitude of fatalism prevails in which intervention is often seen as futile. Even when evidence like this suggests the importance of involving men to increase understanding and change attitudes, few policy initiatives consider the potential role of men in reducing maternal mortality.

A further policy challenge is to redefine the messages we send to men in positive and creative ways. The H Hour (In the heat of the moment or The moment of truth, part of Program H), in Brazil has come up with the message:
The attitude marks the difference:

- *a man with a capital M*[17] *listens, accepts, takes care* (of himself and his partner)
- *a man with a capital M converses, respects, and takes care* (in sexuality)
- *a man with a capital M assumes, shares, and takes care* (of his children).

This is just one example of the innovative work that can be done and deserves full support from government institutions and the media. All elements of Program H are in the process of scaling up; securing their incorporation into public programs directed to youth at the local, state, and country level throughout Latin America would be a major policy victory.

ReproSalud's successful experiences with CBOs suggest another method for scaling up and policy innovation. The CBOs that direct the work of ReproSalud have provided a powerful model of community-driven health education services, from which work targeted at men evolved organically. Such CBOs, or groups modeled on the participatory structure on which the CBOs rely, could be formally linked to the Peruvian Ministry of Health. Currently there is support for the CBOs from the ministry, but more formal linkages would guarantee the long-term sustainability of the ReproSalud work and provide a successful model for increased community-based relationships in other countries.

If initiatives directed to men are implemented on a larger scale, how will they be funded when resources for women's programs are so scarce? Funding shortfalls require difficult choices, but the simplest cost-benefit analysis demonstrates the importance of investing much more in preventive strategies for men. Major public health costs are associated with the results of hegemonic masculinity in our societies: alcohol and other substance abuse, violent deaths (accidents, homicide, suicide), domestic violence, HIV/AIDS epidemic, and unwanted pregnancies. The potential for significant health care savings garnered by prevention of these risk behaviors is clear. Funding programs for women and for men should not be viewed as a zero-sum game. Savings realized through prevention efforts can be used to fund programming that benefits both women and men.

Stubbornly, however, we remain on the curative side of the problem; we attend to the symptoms without being able to link the causes to a common starting point: hegemonic masculinity. Family planning professionals working internationally have grown aware of how gender, sexuality, violence, and alcohol affect reproductive health outcomes, but too many others still separate physical, reproductive, sexual, and mental health. We need to reunite what we tend to view as separate manifestations. Only a radical multisectoral (health, education, justice, and so on) approach can modify gender roles and create the possibility of preventing a large percentage of these problems.

What have our governments learned and incorporated from the Cairo and Beijing conferences? How can they develop public policies and programs seeking men's participation and respect for women's sexual and reproductive rights? Though policies are slowly changing and limited programs are being implemented, we are still very far from including a relational gender and sexual-reproductive rights perspective in official health programs. Some controversial initiatives have been successful in reaching men, but lack a gender perspective that cares about women's empowerment. The long-term impact of slogans like those directed to men in the Zimbabwe campaign ("You are in control!") or in Mexico ("Are you really so macho? So plan your family!") are questionable. Although they may motivate men to participate in fertility control, they also reinforce hegemonic gender norms. Men's participation should be achieved from a gender equity perspective.

While gender and rights transitions are taking place in Mexico and other countries, the conservative movement is represented in the current administration in Mexico, as well as in the United States and many Islamic countries. The goal of these movements is to impose a renewed religion-based hegemony over sexual, gender, and political relations (Clatterbaugh 1997, Brusco 1995). Despite conservative attempts to block progress, however, the overall tendency in Latin America is toward new forms of masculinity and family relations, moving closer to equal rights and family democracy.

Men play a critical role in the reproduction of gender inequity, both as individuals and as part of a gender hierarchy, and this inequity results in lost rights and consequences for women in sexual and reproductive health. I have argued here that men *also* suffer the consequences of hegemonic masculinity in their health and lives and would benefit from equitable relations. The programs directed to men in Mexico, Peru, and Brazil show that many men are interested in and able to move from being part of the problem to being part of the solution. From the intimacy of a particular couple or father-child relationship to the sphere of public policy, men have to be present, sensitive, and active in seeking a better life for women, children, and themselves.

Notes

I wish to thank the Open Society Institute and the Mailman School of Public Health at Columbia University team for their support during the fellowship. Special thanks to Judith Helzner and Marjorie Marcieira for their encouragement and to Michael Kaufman, Michael Kimmel, and Richard Parker and the numerous reviewers of the different versions of this chapter. Last but not least, to the Salud y Género team for the rich discussion and learning process over the past decade, as well as the MacArthur Foundation for its continued support.

1. Despite the promises of progress through free trade, the number of people in poverty in Mexico has actually increased during the past decade, leading to the acceleration of urbanization and to increased migration of the rural poor to the United States (INEGI, 2001).
2. The drop was smaller in Guatemala (to 5.4) and much larger in Cuba (to 1.9).
3. Teresita de Barbieri, personal communication.
4. The concept of hegemony, coming from Antonio Gramsci's *Prison Notebooks* (1929–1935) implies more than mere domination, because it tends to include the active (or passive) acceptance of such dominance.
5. Together with the words "chile" and "chocolate," *machismo* is probably the most internationally known Mexican word. It originated in the 1940s when presidential candidate General Avila Camacho's campaign publicity geniuses separated the second part of Ca-*macho*, and used *macho* as a way to underscore his masculinity. *Macho* is used to refer to male animals, especially horses.
6. Studies in Chile have shown that becoming a father can be a legitimate excuse for a young man to leave the *barra brava* (aggressive gangs that follow their soccer teams) (Abarca and Sepúlvada, 2000).
7. See Seidler 1994, Kaufman 1987, Kimmel 1997, Connel 1995.
8. We name this social link fathering as opposed to biological fatherhood, thus including the social role many men play with children who may or may not be biologically theirs.
9. Curiously there is no equivalent word for the unique experience of having been our father's sons: "sonhood"?
10. The organizations involved were Instituto PROMUNDO in Rio de Janeiro, Brazil; ECOS in São Paulo, Brazil; PAPAI in Recife, Brazil; and Salud y Genero, in Mexico. The International Planned Parenthood Federation/Western Hemisphere Region (IPPF/WHR) and its affiliate in Mexico, MEXFAM, in collaboration with PROMUNDO from Brazil organized the seminar entitled: Working with Young Men: Health, Sexuality, Gender, and Prevention of Violence. The seminar took place in Querétaro, Mexico, on May 28–31, 2000. For more information on the conference see: http://www.ippfwhr.org/publications/serial_article_e.asp?SerialIssuesID=38&ArticleID=155.

11. The International Planned Parenthood Federation/WHR, Pan American Health Organization, World Health Organization, UNFPA, Ford Foundation, Horizons/Population Council, EngenderHealth, Program for Appropriate Technology in Health, World Education, Durex Condoms/SSL International, John Snow Brasil, and the MacArthur Foundation.

12. In the 1930s women's life expectancy was only 1.5 years longer than that of men (de Keijzer, 1997).

13. The country with best life expectancy in Latin America is Costa Rica, with 79 years for women and 74 for men, and the worst is Bolivia with 61 female/58 male. It is striking that the life expectancy difference between Bolivian and Costa Rican men is 16 years! Rural/urban differences among men also show three years more for the latter (Valdés 1995).

14. See essays by Horn and Imam in this volume that explore in greater depth the issue of a "cultural defense" of practices that harm women.

15. The Bush administration lobbied for and eventually succeeded in having the word "sexual" removed from the title of the event. A year before, the same word was eliminated from an announcement for the event on Power and Sexual Relationships held at the Center for Strategic Studies. After all, what does sexuality have to do with reproduction and gender relations?

16. Many of these efforts are described and analyzed in Michael Kaufman's "The AIM Framework: Addressing and Involving Men and Boys to Promote Gender Equality and End Gender Discrimination and Violence."

17. A man with a capital M is a translation of "Un hombre con H," promoting new ways of considering masculinity.

References

Abarca, H., and M. Sepúlveda. 2000. *El feo, el sucio y el malo. Un estudio exploratorio sobre masculinidad y violencia entre varones de dos barras del fútbol en Chile*. Rio de Janeiro: Fundación Carlos Chagas.

Alan Guttmacher Institute. 2002. *In Their Own Right: Addressing the Sexual and Reproductive Needs of American Men*. Washington, D.C.: Alan Guttmacher Institute.

Badinter, E. 1995. *XY: On Masculine Identity*. New York: Columbia University Press.

Barker, G. 2003. "The status of men in sexual and reproductive right since Cairo: Obstacles, partners or subjects of rights?" Paper presented at the conference on Reaching Men to Improve Reproductive Health for All, Interagency Gender Working Group, Dulles, Va., September.

Barker, G., and I. Lowenstein. 1997. "Where the boys are: Attitudes related to masculinity, fatherhood and violence toward women among low income adolescent and young adult males in Rio de Janeiro, Brazil." *Youth and Society* 29(2): 166–196.

Bograd, M. 1991. *Feminist Approaches for Men in Family Therapy*. New York: Harrington Park Press.

Bourdieu. P. 1984. *Distinction: A Social Critique of the Judgement of Taste*. London: Routledge and Kegan Paul.

———. 2001. *Masculine Domination*. Menlo Park: Stanford University Press.

Branco, V. 2003. "Masculinities, reproductive health and public policies." Paper presented at the conference on Reaching Men to Improve Reproductive Health for All, Interagency Gender Working Group, Dulles, Va., September.

Brusco, E. 1995. *The Reformation of Machismo: Evangelical Conversion and Gender in Colombia*. Austin: University of Texas Press.

Clatterbaugh, K. 1997. *Contemporary Perspectives on Masculinity: Men, Women and Politics in Modern Society*. Denver: Westview.

Connel, R. W. 1995. *Masculinities*. St. Leonards, Australia: Allen and Unwin.

De Keijzer, B. 1997. "El varón como factor de riesgo." In E. Tuñón, ed., *Género y salud en el sureste de México*. Villahermosa: ECOSUR UJAD.

————. 2000. "Reaching men for health and development." In UNESCO Education Institute, *Questions of Intimacy: Redefining Population Education*. Hamburg: UNESCO Education Institute.

Elu, M. 1994. *La luz enterrada*. Mexico City: Fondo de Cultura Económica.

Figueroa, J. G. 1998. "La presencia de los varones en los procesos reproductivos: algunas reflexiones." In S. Lerner, ed., *Varones, Sexualidad y Reproducción*. Mexico City: El Colegio de México.

Fuller, N. 2001. *Masculinidades: cambios y permanencias*. Lima: Pontificia Universidad Católica del Perú.

Green, M., and M. Biddlecom. 2000. "Absent and problematic men: Demographic accounts of male reproductive roles." *Population and Demographic Review* 26(1): 81–116.

Instituto Nacional de Estadística Geografía e Informática. 2001. *Mujeres y hombres en México*. Aguascalientes: INEGI.

Instituto Nacional de las Mujeres and UNICEF. 2001. *¿Como veo a mi papá? Por una paternidad mas padre*. Mexico City: INMUJERES and UNICEF.

Kaufman, M., ed. 1987. *Beyond Patriarchy: Essays by Men on Pleasure, Power and Change*. New York: Oxford University Press.

————. 1999. "Men, feminism and men's contradictory experiences of power." In J. Kuypers, ed., *Men and Power*. Halifax: Fernwood Books.

————. 2003. "The AIM framework: Addressing and involving men and boys to promote gender equality and end gender discrimination and violence." Paper prepared for UNICEF. http://www.michaelkaufman.com/articles/index.html.

Kimmel, M. 1997. "Masculinity as homophobia: Fear, shame and silence." In H. Brod and E. Brod. *Dialogue among Reproductive Health Professionals*. New York: Population Council.

Movimiento Manuela Ramos. 2003. *Opening Our Eyes: A Work Experience with Men on Gender Issues and Sexual and Reproductive Health*. Lima: Movimiento Manuela Ramos.

Program H. 2003. *Working with Young Men to Promote Health and Gender Equity*. Executive folder. Rio de Janeiro.

Salud y Genero. 2003. "Constructing new gender-equitable identities: Salud y Genero's work in Mexico." In IGWG *Involving Men to Address Gender Inequities*. Washington, D.C.: Population Reference Bureau.

Schmuckler, B. 1996. "Negociaciones de género y estrategias femeninas en familias populares." *Revista Paraguaya de Socología* 74: 7–42.

Seidler, V. 1994. *Unreasonable Men.* London: Routledge.
USAID. 2002. *Involving Men in Sexual and Reproductive Health.* Orientation guide. CD-Rom. Washington, D.C.: USAID, International Gender Working Group, Men and Reproductive Health Subcommittee.
Valdés, T. 1995. *Mujeres latinoamericanas en cifras. Tomo comparativo.* Santiago de Chile: Instituto de la Mujer and FLACSO.
Viveros, M. 2002. *De quebradores y cumplidores.* Bogotá: Universidad Nacional de Columbia.

Maximizing the Impact of Cairo on China

EDWIN A. WINCKLER

In the early 2000s, China is abuzz with local experiments at reforming its birth limitation program. By mitigating past abuses and improving future services, most of these reforms promise to significantly advance international principles of reproductive health and rights, at least as the People's Republic of China (PRC) has adapted those principles to "Chinese circumstances." Though short of international ideals of full reproductive freedom, the gradually deepening reforms of the 1990s and 2000s have been adapting birth limitation to the market-oriented and law-based society into which China has been evolving.[1]

A main model for experiments at this adaptation is Mudanjiang, a middle-sized city governing a scenic metropolitan area of Heilongjiang province in northeast China. Despite an only modest level of economic and social development, Mudanjiang has a long record of outstanding performance in state-enforced birth limitation. In the mid-1990s it was not one of the few localities that the national government chose for experiments in moving from harsh enforcement of state birth limits toward "quality of care" in reproductive health services. Nevertheless, the man who took charge of birth planning in Mudanjiang in 1998 resolved to pursue such reforms anyway. He obtained a Chinese translation of the Cairo program and related materials, such as Judith Bruce's classic article on "quality of care." Aspiring to international standards of project design, the Mudanjiang birth commission formulated detailed plans for raising its birth work toward international ideals (Mudanjiang 2002).

As a result, in 2001 national program leaders chose Mudanjiang as one of sixteen pilot localities for eventual nationwide "Comprehensive Reform" of the PRC birth program. That reform is "comprehensive" in several senses: It obligates the whole city government to support improvement of the birth program, it requires the birth program to renovate itself in order to deliver better quality services, and it allows some public participation in running the program (Wang 2001). In 2002, because Mudanjiang had done such a good job in so many aspects of Comprehensive Reform, national program leaders chose it as the site for a September national conference (Zhang Weiqing 2002). As the best example from sixteen pilot projects, clearly Mudanjiang is not typical of China as a whole. Nevertheless, it does show the direction in which national policy makers would like the whole country to move.

The main reason Mudanjiang was chosen as a national model is that the birth program there has achieved high levels of public satisfaction with its services, at least according to its own surveys. In the early 2000s, national political leaders set achieving public satisfaction—really reducing public dissatisfaction—as a main standard for evaluating birth work (Zhang Weiqing 2000 and 2001). Mudanjiang exemplifies a transition from "birth-according-to-plan" to "birth-according-to-law." In other words, a couple can have its first legally authorized child without having to obtain a personal birth quota in a local population plan. Mudanjiang also exemplifies an ongoing revision of the criteria for evaluating local political and program leaders. Whereas formerly those criteria emphasized limiting population and enforcing birth control, now they include quality service and public satisfaction. This shift in evaluation goes a long way toward guaranteeing that local officials will actually implement reforms. Finally, Mudanjiang also exemplifies a shift from purely top-down administration toward incorporating some bottom-up supervision through "village self-government." The elected village council can make minor adaptations of national and provincial birth regulations, and it can supervise both birth work and public compliance. Ordinary villagers can participate in both the selection and supervision of village birth workers (Alpermann 2001). Much of public satisfaction with these reforms is probably genuine. However, much of it may amount to saying that if there must be birth limits it is better if they are more sensitively administered and accompanied by some reproductive health benefits.

In November 2003, I visited Mudanjiang to learn more about its reforms. Urban districts were improving coordination between the local birth system and health system, in order to make optimal use of expensive medical resources. Similarly, urban districts were merging birth work with other community social services into "one-stop shopping" service windows within large residential blocks, for administrative efficiency and client convenience.

Urban districts were also strengthening the control and servicing of migrants, now a highly mobile tenth of China's population that is difficult to reach with social services. Rural counties were gradually extending village self-administration of birth planning to more communities, along with competitive selection and evaluation of birth workers, designed to recruit good performers and to remove poor ones.

One of Mudanjiang's rural counties, Muleng, was beginning a three-year term as one of a new cycle of local demonstration experiments by the United Nations Population Fund (still known by its old acronym UNFPA). A particular focus of UNFPA's 2003–2005 work in China is, within its project counties, "gradually to reduce and eventually to eliminate" the steep "social compensation fee" that the PRC levies on couples who do not comply with birth regulations. Muleng is a propitious place for such an experiment, because Muleng already has virtually universal compliance with birth rules, not having levied a birth fee in two years. That is possible because Muleng is a relatively sparsely populated county on China's border with Russia, and therefore national policy permits Muleng to allow all of its couples to have two children. Thus Muleng constitutes a de facto experiment at shifting toward a universal two-child policy, which most ordinary Chinese would prefer and which some reformers have long advocated.

During my visit to Muleng, the county birth program arranged a meeting for me with several dozen women of reproductive age in one rural village. Seated near the front of the group, sitting side by side, were two women village officials. One was a rather hard-bitten older woman who had run village birth work from 1975 through 1995 during the difficult transition to strict birth limits. She was now the village's first female head of government. The other was a pleasant-looking younger woman who had succeeded her in charge of birth work. I asked the other women in the room to compare their past and present experiences with birth planning. They quickly erupted into harsh criticism of the past, complaining bitterly about how their elder female relatives had been treated. I was quite surprised that young rural Chinese women would criticize a village official to her face, particularly at a public meeting with a foreigner present. These young women did not know what the Cairo conference was, but they exemplified at least some of its principles. They were remarkably forthright in discussing reproductive matters, and they seemed in no doubt about their right to an informed choice of contraceptive method and to quality reproductive health care. As people remarked to me throughout China, the new young generation is "different" from older generations. As I remarked in return, ultimately this "difference" is the surest guarantee of better reproductive health and rights throughout China.

The local story of Mudanjiang reflects a national story of recent evolution in the PRC birth program, which in part reflects an international story of increasing foreign advocacy of reproductive health and rights in China.

At the national level, birth planning had gradually intensified during the 1970s. Around 1980 national political leaders adopted the one-child limit. A cycle followed of harsh over-enforcement, popular backlash, some adjustment of policy, and much relaxation of implementation. Around 1990 national political leaders installed personnel evaluation systems that required local political leaders to again strictly enforce the revised birth limits. This resulted in a new round of harsh enforcement. Thus in both the early 1980s and again in the early 1990s, local officials conducted mass campaigns in which women with out-of-plan pregnancies were required to abort them and couples who had already produced their permitted number of children were required to have one member sterilized. The early 1990s reenforcement was *not* followed by either revision of birth limits or relaxation of their implementation. However, it *was* followed by progressively deepening reforms. The earlier reforms attempted to improve state-centric birth planning by professionalizing its services, codifying its procedures, adapting it to marketization, and integrating it with antipoverty efforts. The later reforms began moving toward a more client-oriented approach, mostly through experiments at improving quality of care. By the early 2000s, PRC leaders were convinced that China had largely achieved the low fertility they desired. In a 2000 party decision and 2001 national law they issued new reproductive policies for the coming decade, instructing the birth program to maintain low fertility while reforming itself to deliver better services.

Meanwhile, at the supranational level, between the 1980s and 2000s, foreign intervention in the PRC birth program also progressively deepened. During the 1980s, there were only a few international actors, and they were focused mostly on upgrading the PRC's technical capabilities, in line with international preoccupations at the time. During the 1990s, a series of international conferences provided PRC birth leaders with a new human rights language for reevaluating their program and with new ideas for initiating experiments at client-oriented reforms. The Rockefeller Foundation, Ford Foundation, Population Council, UNFPA, and other international organizations assisted these experiments. Gradually the agenda expanded to include empowering women, educating adolescents, and involving men. Meanwhile, the

PRC began sending delegations of program leaders abroad to learn more about current international thinking and practice. In the early 2000s foreign funding has declined, but the pace of change has nevertheless accelerated. Not least among outside inputs, scores of foreign delegations, both governmental and nongovernmental, have inspected the PRC birth program and UNFPA intervention in it. Virtually all have concluded that the PRC is reforming significantly and that UNFPA has contributed greatly to that reform.

Problems

If things have begun to change for the better in China, what is the problem? One problem concerns difficulties and dilemmas that PRC programs have encountered. Another problem is the limits to the reforms that the PRC has undertaken. A third problem is that some American politicians want to use UNFPA involvement in China as an excuse to suspend U.S. funding for UNFPA.

Regime Dilemmas

A first problem is that, in promoting its version of reproductive health and rights, the PRC has encountered difficulties, some of them inherent in the regime's own ideals, some of them resulting from collision of ideals with reality. From the beginning, the PRC advanced some health and reproductive rights while trampling others.[2]

Since its founding in 1921, the Chinese Communist Party (CCP) has stood for many progressive ideals, including liberating Chinese women from Confucian patriarchy, achieving equality between genders, and protecting women against violent abuse. In addition to pursuing those objectives, after the founding of the PRC in 1949, the CCP began modernizing maternal and child health services (MCH) and, after some hesitation, promoting birth control. From the beginning, the MCH tradition of the PRC's Ministry of Health included the ideal that there should be a range of contraceptive methods available, that methods must be adapted to individual women, and that all relevant medical procedures must be safe. As of the early 2000s, PRC national political and program leaders very much want to participate in the international elaboration and implementation of the Cairo program—as they put it, "to have a seat at the table." However, in trying to realize their progressive ideals, PRC leaders have encountered at least three kinds of difficulties, some of which they themselves have compounded.

First, by the late 1970s PRC leaders believed they had identified a con-

tradiction between increasing economic production and increasing population reproduction. After the stagnation of the Maoist period, post-Mao leaders wanted to accelerate China's modernization. Internally, they wanted to
provide most Chinese with a "modestly comfortable" standard of living by
the end of the century, in order to preserve the CCP's position in power. Externally, post-Mao leaders wanted to catch up with the rest of the world in
economic and military power, in order to fulfill the CCP's historic mission
of restoring China's independence (Greenhalgh 2003b). Facing a tall peak of
new young childbearing couples in the last two decades of the twentieth century, post-Mao leaders decided to ask that generation of Chinese to make the
huge sacrifice of having only one child. National political leaders' goal of
drastic limits on childbearing overrode MCH ideals, with devastating effects
on adult women's physical health, reproductive autonomy, and self-esteem.
The decline in childbearing lowered maternal mortality, but the vast increase
in poor-quality birth control operations increased women's morbidity (ill
health). Tight birth limits had even more devastating effects on the life prospects of unwanted girls and out-of-plan children. In the long term, inadvertently but predictably, drastic birth limits decimated the traditional Chinese
family, skewed sex ratios, and accelerated population aging. In the early 2000s,
with socialist provision of retirement pensions and elder care still only an
aspiration for most Chinese, the PRC state is again turning to the family, particularly women, to provide those services. But to a significant extent the family—
and the women—are no longer there.

Second, in 1949 China was a poor country with virtually no modern
rural health services, not to mention modern reproductive health care. Under Mao, the PRC made some progress toward delivering some elementary
health care to most citizens, including training a few people within each community to perform modern birth control operations. Nevertheless, when the
PRC was tightening control of population growth (from the late 1970s through
the early 1990s), rural medical infrastructure remained inadequate for con-
ducting mass birth control operations or for delivering other mass reproductive health services. Therefore initially the PRC enforced the one-child rule
through periodic crash campaigns of mass abortion and sterilization, supervised by generalist local political leaders who were amateurs at health administration. Birth program leaders fervently wished to progress from such
emergency measures to continuous professional work (summarized as the
"three basics" of education, contraception, and routinization). By the early
2000s, the resources that national leaders have insisted that subnational governments spend on local birth programs probably have made them more

professional, providing a significant supplement to the MCH services offered by the less-favored Ministry of Health. However, still more resources and training are now required to achieve "informed choice" of "quality care." Moreover, by now China has entered a crisis of health care affordability and provision comparable to that in the United States. The financial calamity of catastrophic illness has become the leading cause of rural families falling into poverty. Government finances are so strapped that localities have difficulty keeping basic contraception free of charge, let alone adding more reproductive health care.

Third, despite decades of "propaganda-and-education" and socioeconomic change, Chinese society has been slow to abandon traditional patriarchy, largely because of the real practical need for male labor in rural areas. Already in the late 1950s, during the establishment of rural communes, PRC leaders found it necessary to compromise with male authority over the family. In the early 1980s, as the one-child rule was introduced, PRC leaders again found it necessary to compromise, allowing rural families with "real difficulties" to have two children, where "real difficulties" meant that the first child was a daughter. Subsequently, despite significant effort, the PRC has been unable to prevent couples from using ultrasound to identify female fetuses for abortion, particularly so that a permitted second child will be a son. Against its own principles, state birth policy has imposed most of the physical and emotional costs of fertility reduction on women. Against its own intentions, birth policy has not only institutionalized discrimination between male and female children but also has inadvertently intensified that discrimination (Greenhalgh 2001b, 2003a).

Overall, feminist activists from other parts of the world may wonder where in this narrative is female agency. The truth is that there has been very little of it. Some early women CCP leaders did help call attention to the need for modern childbearing and contraception. Aside from that, women, like men, have had to act within instructions from the CCP Central Committee. At the elite level, distinguished women officials have helped found and reform the PRC birth program. At the mass level, the main role prescribed for women activists has been to implement official birth policies, as village representatives of the official All China Women's Federation. Those policies often took an approach to birth control operations that some knowledgeable foreign observers have disparagingly called "veterinary." Such policies have provoked much covert individual resistance, but it has had to remain largely unorganized and inarticulate. The PRC's discourse on liberating women has always been as much about incorporating women into state management of production and reproduction as it has been about freeing women from caricatures of feudal superstition and Confucian patriarchy. By the early 2000s, government-organized nongovernmental organizations perform some useful functions, but empowering civil society against the state is not one of them. This despite current national political leaders' nominal commitment to "small state, big society" and despite China's desperate need for more social initiative in such fields as adolescent sex education and combating HIV/AIDS.

Reform Limits

A second problem is that the PRC's reforms to its birth program have distinct limits and that those limits continue to impose growing social costs. Again, regime reforms have advanced some rights while infringing others.[3]

Evidently most Chinese political leaders still believe that continuing to limit China's population growth is necessary for China's future economic prosperity, social stability, and environmental viability. They believe that these, too, are ethical concerns that require some tradeoff with other public policy objectives, including citizen's rights. In their view, managing the largest population in the world requires continuing to discipline citizens' reproductive behavior. Evidently China's new younger leaders now wish to promote citizens' social rights. They have begun shifting the birth program from exclusive preoccupation with limiting quantity toward also improving quality—better population-related programs in health, education, employment, and retirement. Nevertheless, the politics of elite succession in China probably make it difficult to loosen birth limits. Any younger would-be reformers are vulnerable to attacks by rival would-be successors, supported by senior leaders who are only ostensibly retired. As a result, policy goals have remained "equifinal," enforcement has become more ineluctable, and some adverse social consequences have gradually intensified.

Equifinality is a condition in which any route always leads to the same result. Because PRC policy making remains autocratic, PRC reproductive policy has been equifinal in several ways. Some policy reorientation became possible only after national political leaders became convinced that they had largely met their goal of low fertility. As the 2000 decision stated, the main goal of policy then became "stabilizing" that low fertility by "strengthening" the birth program: continuing old methods where they still worked and substituting new methods where they didn't. National political leaders remain cautious in their demographic assumptions and policy decisions. Reform experiments must not raise fertility. New methods must be successfully phased in before old methods are gradually phased out. For individuals, informed choice does not include the option of not contracepting. Maintaining low fertility remains the bottom line. If PRC leaders wanted only public satisfaction, they could obtain more of it more readily by allowing all couples to have two children than by marginally improving reproductive health care. A two-child rule would also ease the growing social problems of sex ratio imbalance and old-age support. However, because PRC political leaders have not yet been persuaded that a two-child rule is prudent, improving reproductive health care serves as an interim compromise, making some contribution both to stabilizing low fertility and to easing public dissatisfaction. Obviously the equifinality of PRC birth policy places quite narrow constraints on external intervention to promote reform. In this context, improving reproductive health care largely extends long-standing PRC efforts to improve contraceptive services whose use remains mandatory.

Ineluctability of compliance has been increased by institutionalization, the main general process of the past decade. Institutionalization specifies state goals, constrains implementers' behaviors, and clarifies citizens' rights. It has curbed past abuses, improved technical services, and opened opportunities for further reform. However, institutionalization also entrenches the program, authorizes enforcement, and imposes duties on citizens. For policy makers, the 2001 law and associated regulations finally established a national legal basis for a program that had been running for three decades but that remains intensely controversial. For administrators, early 2000s policy documents reduce uncertainty that might inhibit implementation, by providing a legal basis for enforcement, clear policies to obey, and detailed instructions to follow. For citizens, those documents establish still more officially and in still greater detail that compliance with birth limits is mandatory. Neither the initiation of strict birth limits around 1980 nor their legalization around 2000 was done democratically. Although compliance may be increasingly voluntary, that willingness has resulted from two to three decades of ideological education, administrative enforcement, and economic development. Usually the most that program leaders have claimed is that most people "accept" birth limits, though expressing the hope that "if we do our work well enough" eventually most people will "support" them.

Intensification of adverse social consequences has been occurring in several ways. First, birth limits continue to deny many Chinese their reproductive aspirations. In many places substandard but mandatory "technical services" continue to adversely affect reproductive health. This continues to raise issues of reproductive freedom and reproductive health. Second, sex ratios at birth continue to deteriorate, having become more skewed in each year since

1987, when strong enforcement of birth limits resumed (from 107.6 in 1982 to 117.8 in 2000; Cai and Lavely 2003). Already many men cannot find brides, creating individual hardship and social instability, such as kidnapping of young women, which is on the rise. These rights issues of gender discrimination and gendered violence are side effects of state birth limits. Finally, already many couples are entering old age with inadequate or no support from children, and this problem will grow. In 1980 the Open Letter announcing the one-child rule promised a series of public programs to substitute for private old-age support. Such social programs have proven difficult to finance, however, particularly because the national government relies on subnational governments to finance them. Here the rights issue is this: If the state could not guarantee alternatives, couples should have remained free to make their own arrangements. In 2003 the new Hu Jintao–Wen Jiabao administration addressed many of these problems; for example, launching a program to compensate couples who have suffered from birth limits (particularly the one hundred thousand whose only child has died). Nevertheless, these problems are likely to remain intractable.

What does it mean, in practice, to say that the PRC birth program is advancing from simply limiting births to also delivering better reproductive health services? Overall, it is entirely credible that the PRC birth program should now be attempting to upgrade the quality and scope of its services, because for so long the quality of those services was so abysmal and their scope was so limited. By the early 2000s, most programs' community "service stations" did offer a choice of at least three to five methods of contraception. However, only 6 percent had added any other reproductive health services (SFPC 2002, preliminary report on 2001 survey). Providing more comprehensive reproductive health care will depend on cooperation between the birth system and health system to construct a local service network, as national political leaders have instructed them to do. By the early 2000s, the birth system is more enthusiastic than the health system about promoting reproductive health, because the birth system has a more focused mission, greater political support, and wider international interaction. However, the health system continues to have most of the relevant medical capacity, to control the certification of practitioners, and to regulate the provision of technical services. In this context, the national birth program is attempting to impose the following agenda on local birth programs.

First, in its own core birth control services, the birth program must stop harming women while "helping" them. It must depoliticize service delivery and include doctors among its supervisors, from top to bottom. All service providers must be medically competent, for example, to recognize contra-indications that particular women should not use particular methods. Any clinical procedures that the birth system performs must be competent and safe, with minimal risk of injury or infection. Second, again in its own core services, the birth program must actually help women. It must continue to upgrade the technical quality of the birth control methods it provides and it must insist that local governments pay the premium that better methods cost. It must offer more alternatives, educate women about them, and allow women themselves to choose. It must provide follow-up services such as screening for side effects. Third, the program must take the opportunity of purveying birth control to provide other minimal elements of reproductive health care (Kaufman, Zhang, and Fang 1997). It must contribute more to MCH services surrounding childbearing. Beyond MCH, the birth system should diagnose the most common reproductive tract infections and gynecological problems, referring most patients to the health system for cure. Birth workers must recognize symptoms, educate the public in the importance of reproductive health, and persuade the public to use relevant services.

UNFPA Role

A third problem is that some right-wing American politicians want to use these problems with the PRC birth program and its reform as an excuse for denying UNFPA a role not only in helping solve these problems in China but also in delivering family planning and reproductive health services around the world. UNFPA has had to endure PRC infringement of some rights in order to advance others.[4]

UNFPA was established in 1969 at the initiative of the United States and other Western countries to help developing countries address population issues, including how to slow their rapid population growth. Any UN member that is a developing country has the right to request assistance, and UNFPA is obliged to provide specific types of assistance appropriate to specific stages of demographic transition. At the PRC's request, UNFPA entered China in 1979 and, by the early 2000s, is in its fifth multiyear cycle of projects. As international thinking evolved and as China developed, these projects have gradually progressed from demography and contraception toward reproductive health and rights. UNFPA is governed by an international board that initially approves and regularly reviews all UNFPA activities. On that board, in the early 2000s, the United States has been a minority of one in its strenuous criticism of UNFPA's presence in China. Some critics convey the impression that UNFPA endorses or condones PRC birth limits and enforcement methods and that UNFPA is helping or allowing the PRC to maintain them. In fact, UNFPA objects to them and is actively working to demonstrate to PRC leaders that China can maintain its already low fertility without birth limits and coercive enforcement, largely by delivering better reproductive health services. Of course, UNFPA cannot encourage violations of PRC laws (though the PRC has waived some local regulations to facilitate UNFPA demonstration projects).

One of the goals of UNFPA's first two program cycles in China (1980–1984 and 1985–1989) was to help the PRC conduct its first modern census, to train modern demographers, and to establish population science curricula. In the long run, better demographic data and analysis have helped moderate extreme policies. Some of the demographers that UNFPA trained became important advocates of reform. For example, it was UNFPA's very first 1980s fellowship grantee, Chinese demographer Gu Baochang, who in the mid-1990s translated the Cairo materials that Mudanjiang used to transfer Cairo ideals into its reform plans. Another main goal of UNFPA's early cycles was helping China to improve its contraceptives, so that they did less damage to women's health and became more reliable, thereby avoiding unnecessary abortions. Thus during its third cycle (1990–1995), UNFPA supported a study that recommended switching from steel to copper IUDs, which the PRC immediately did, thereby averting millions of unwanted pregnancies and unnecessary abortions (41 million and 26 million, respectively, according to UNFPA estimates). In the early 1990s UNFPA collaborated with UNICEF to improve MCH care in three hundred poor counties, pioneering a model for reducing mortality rates that was then adopted by the World Bank and extended to another nearly three hundred counties. The third UNFPA program cycle also promoted other aspects of reproductive health and education, including raising the status of women.

In the early 1990s, as international attention began shifting from target-driven population limitation toward client-centered services, UNFPA lobbied increasingly strenuously for the PRC to begin experiments with less coercive methods of limiting population. UNFPA even delayed beginning a new program cycle for two years (1995–1997) until the PRC agreed to begin trying more voluntary approaches. During the resulting fourth program cycle (originally 1998–2000, extended to 2002), at UNFPA insistence the PRC abolished population targets and birth quotas in thirty-two counties in which UNFPA conducted quality care demonstrations. To complement the PRC's experiments in advanced counties, UNFPA deliberately placed its experiments in less advanced counties, to demonstrate that quality care could work there too. Both kinds of experiments were quite successful at increasing informed choice of quality care while maintaining low fertility and reducing abortions. Moreover, as intended, those demonstrations contributed to the spread of reforms beyond official pilots to some eight hundred other counties, about a third of China. Furthermore, all of these experiments contributed to the confidence of PRC leaders that they could embark on the nationwide Comprehensive Reform that the birth program launched in the early 2000s.

Building on all of this, a major objective of the fifth cycle of UNFPA programs in China (2003–2005) is to demonstrate to the PRC that it can maintain low fertility without the remaining enforcement mechanisms, particularly the social compensation fee. UNFPA is urging a new round of thirty experimental counties toward three levels of aspiration: first, applying the mildest methods possible within existing regulations; second, asking superiors for exceptions to make enforcement milder than stipulated by regulations; third, changing regulations to make them milder. In addition to reform of birth planning, UNFPA is addressing several other challenges: uncovered groups (adolescents, migrants, men, remote areas), AIDS (prevention through education), gender (violence against women), monitoring (building local capacity for self-analysis), reproductive health (improving coordination between birth system and health system), and aging (an important effect of declining fertility).

In all of this, using human rights to promote reproductive health is a main theme. As Siri Tellier, the UNFPA representative in China, said to a November 2003 human rights training session for subnational officials:

> The fact that a client in a village receives a green letter in her home explaining her rights; when she goes to the clinic, sees the law posted on the wall, also informing about rights; sees a clinic which has been improved to be clean and well stocked; sees the photographs and titles of all the clinic staff on the wall, and the staff have been trained to be courteous and respectful; sees a list of services available, and their price, on the wall; sees a list of the five contraceptive choices with advantages and disadvantages, on the wall; sees the suggestion box and knows there is a hotline if she has any complaints or suggestions—all of this conveys the message that the clinic respects the client's need for information, choice, and quality service.

Such concrete indicators facilitate both training and monitoring. Using rights concepts to promote reform increases the rights consciousness of both clients and cadres. Nevertheless, informed choice of quality care does not deliver the whole international bill of reproductive rights, at least under the definition that PRC policy allows. PRC leaders are well aware of that, not least because of UNFPA advocacy of still deeper change (Zhang and Sun 1999).

Evidence

If these are the problems, what are the solutions? In particular, on what terms might the United States be persuaded to resume its contribution to UNFPA? To be of any practical use, any reframing of that issue must address the most recent terms of discussion between the participants themselves, particularly any movement toward common ground between them. The evidence is that most people, when informed about current reproductive policy in China and the current UNFPA role in reforming it, quickly converge toward practical solutions to American concerns. Evidently, across cultures and ideologies, human beings share much moral common sense. Here we note three areas where at least some participants have already reached at least some convergence.

U.S. Preconditions
The 1985 Kemp-Kasten amendment to U.S. foreign aid legislation prohibits U.S. funding of any organization that, as determined by the president, "supports or participates in the management of a program of coercive abortion or involuntary sterilization." Invoking this provision, in the late 1980s the Reagan and Bush administrations suspended U.S. contributions to UNFPA because of UNFPA's presence in China. During the 1990s, the Clinton administration again funded UNFPA. In 2001 the new Bush administration initially approved a continuation of U.S. funding, the State Department praising UNFPA accomplishments. However, after right-wing allegations of continued coercion in the PRC birth program, the administration put a hold on funds for UNFPA, pending a review. To gather information, in May 2002 the State Department sent an Independent Assessment Team to China, consisting of two former State Department officers and a Chinese-American professor of public health. The team found evidence that PRC birth limitation was still somewhat coercive, but found no evidence that UNFPA "knowingly" abetted that coercion. Noting UNFPA contributions to reform, the team recommended that the U.S. resume funding UNFPA. The State Department forwarded that recommendation to the White House. However, the White House ruled that the social compensation fee and other PRC enforcement

measures were coercive. An interagency legal review then concluded that the Kemp-Kasten amendment therefore prohibited refunding (Boucher 2002).[5]

During the second half of 2002, State Department officials who had previously handled these issues (most seeking some way for the United States to resume funding UNFPA) were transferred to other assignments and replaced by more ideologically committed officials eager to take a harder line with both the PRC and UNFPA. As a condition for even considering the funding of UNFPA, these new officials instructed the PRC to abolish all enforcement measures immediately, at least within UNFPA experimental counties, *before* UNFPA could begin work there. As of late 2004, that remained official U.S. policy. Meanwhile, however, the Bush administration has encountered more support for UNFPA than it expected: In Congress even moderate Republicans have joined efforts to fund UNFPA once again. This broad support has led at least some within the administration to begin seeking some compromise. Evidently at least some U.S. officials would settle for the PRC's eliminating just the social compensation fee in UNFPA counties. Multilateral negotiations then further narrowed disagreement. At least some U.S. officials would settle for the objective jointly defined by the UNFPA and PRC, which is "gradually to reduce and eventually to eliminate" the fee in UNFPA counties. However, as with the earlier Independent Assessment Team, evidently this field-based recommendation was overturned on review by political superiors in Washington.

One thing that U.S. assessments do not report is that PRC policy itself involves ethical considerations. The main mismatch between U.S. and PRC ideas concerns whether PRC enforcement is or should be "coercive." Birth limits are PRC state policy, and enforcement of any policy by any state involves some coercion. It is not necessary to send an assessment team to China to ascertain that PRC birth limits are mandatory: PRC laws say so quite clearly. When PRC officials say they are eliminating coercion they mean eliminating enforcement that is unauthorized, clumsy, or abusive. They also mean that they hope that compliance with birth rules will eventually become entirely voluntary, because of education, economics, or other factors. They do not mean that, in the meantime, violation of birth rules should go without cost to the violators. Moreover, if birth limits are mandatory, and some citizens comply with them, the PRC actually has an obligation to enforce them equally on everyone. Such fairness is a practical and ethical precondition for quasi-voluntary compliance by citizens with laws.

Here a minor mismatch concerns the fact that PRC law subjects public officials and state employees to more severe punishments for violating birth rules than it does ordinary citizens. The conservative Republican Bush administration even objects to communists losing their party memberships for violating CCP policies! The United States cites such provisions as evidence of coercion. For its part, the PRC regards public leadership and state employment as privileges and therefore expects the beneficiaries to set a good public example. Nothing would undermine public compliance with birth planning faster than official noncompliance, particularly by party leaders. Moreover, sanctioning official noncompliance is part of vigorous PRC anticorruption efforts, which address the fact that growing public outrage at official privilege is one of the main underlying ethical issues in post-Mao Chinese politics.

UNFPA Complicity?

A second area of some convergence concerns alleged UNFPA complicity in PRC conduct, particularly as defined in the Kemp-Kasten amendment. Moderates in Congress are trying to add "directly" to "supports or participates" to provide more latitude for intervention. Evidently that change in wording is the solution that is politically most feasible within the U.S. Congress. However, it does not entirely clarify the underlying issues. Obviously there is a continuum of possible involvements and effects. At the bad extreme is major negative impact from deliberate support for obnoxious policies. In the middle is knowing intervention to produce at least mixed results. At the good extreme is major positive impact from engaging the host country in dialogue with the explicit goal of modifying practice and policy. On this continuum, during the 1980s, UNFPA may have slipped toward the "bad" side of the middle, allowing the appearance of support for policies whose obnoxiousness presumably UNFPA did not fully realize. For example, in 1983 UNFPA awarded its first population prize to China (and India), just at the height of harsh overenforcement of the new one-child rule. However, by the late 1990s UNFPA was well to the "good" side of the middle, actively advocating the deepening of already ongoing reforms, while having at most inadvertent and minor negative impact.[6]

A concrete form of the "support or participation" issue concerns potential PRC misuse of UNFPA resources. The main answer here is that the PRC spends a hundred times more on birth planning than UNFPA provides, so the PRC can do what it wants with or without UNFPA. The purpose of UNFPA resources is not to supplement PRC resources but to demonstrate how PRC resources can be better used. A direct version of this concern is whether vehicles and computers that UNFPA has given project localities to improve reproductive health services might also be used to enforce birth limits. However, UNFPA needs such equipment to implement and monitor UNFPA programs and claims that UNFPA monitoring ensures that the equipment is limited to those uses. An indirect variant of the concern about resources involves fungibility: Even if no UNFPA resources go directly to any use that can be construed as coercive, UNFPA resources free PRC resources that can then be applied to coercive purposes. However, such transfer seems unlikely, because UNFPA does not actually give the PRC government any fungible resources. Instead, again, UNFPA supplies its own programs with what they need to operate, leaving PRC resources largely unaffected. In fact, if there is any transfer-of-resources effect it is probably in the opposite direction, diverting PRC resources from existing PRC uses to provide counterpart funds to support UNFPA demonstration projects.

A less concrete form of the "participation" issue concerns the PRC's systems for evaluating programs and personnel. Abolishing plan targets, revising evaluation criteria, and promoting quality care are inextricably interrelated because, if programs and personnel continue to be evaluated on the old "birth-according-to-plan" model even though policy has moved on to the new "birth-according-to-law" model, birth workers will continue to operate in the old mode. For example, birth workers cannot implement informed choice of contraceptive method if the criteria by which they are evaluated continue to require that a certain high proportion of contraception be sterilization. This is the sort of point that the UNFPA and reformist Chinese are trying to get across to local political and program leaders through local demonstration experiments. PRC program leaders are well aware of these interrelations, and in the early 2000s they are redesigning evaluation systems in order to promote more nearly Cairo-compliant birth work. Extraordinarily, PRC program leaders have even invited UNFPA to participate in that redesign, to check whether the new evaluation system meets international standards.

China Situation

By the early 2000s, one thing on which at least some U.S., UNFPA, and PRC officials agree is that the answers remain uncertain to some crucial factual questions about conditions in China that affect the feasibility of abolishing enforcement mechanisms. The social compensation fee is the main remaining legal measure for enforcing birth rules on ordinary citizens. Nominally it is a one-time up-front payment of as much as several times a couple's annual disposable income. In practice, local officials often allow poorer couples to make installment payments, often of lesser amounts. Formerly called a fine, the fee continues to be intended as a strong disincentive—just enough, in relation to couples' incomes, to dissuade them from violating birth rules. Nevertheless the PRC now presents the fee as a sort of tax paid to society to help cover the public cost of raising unauthorized children (even as a sort of social savings account on the child's behalf). Some have suggested that the fee would be more ethically acceptable if formally converted into a tax. In the long run, the PRC may well be willing to do that. In the short run, however, the PRC considers it not yet feasible, because in China the institution of paying personal taxes is not yet well established.

As already noted, the United States simply wants the fee and all other coercive enforcement mechanisms abolished outright and immediately. UNFPA believes that, through a few years of local experiments, it can demonstrate that the fee is unnecessary to the PRC's goal of maintaining low fertility. The PRC believes that the fee is still necessary in practice in order to deter illegal pregnancies in less-developed areas and still necessary in principle out of fairness to those who have complied with birth limits. Nevertheless, the PRC is willing to consider at least minimizing the amount and incidence of the fee where possible. Actually, it is amazing that the PRC—having spent more than a decade narrowing legal enforcement mechanisms down to the fee, and then having just institutionalized that relatively flexible and marketlike method in its 2001 population law—would so soon even consider modifying it.[7]

A first set of questions relevant to the feasibility of abolishing the social compensation fee concerns fertility in China as of the early 2000s. How many children is the average woman actually having (the total fertility rate, or TFR)? How many children, of which gender, do people still want? What is the relationship between either of these and the number of children that PRC birth regulations permit them?

As regards the number of children that women in China actually do have, the plain fact is that nobody knows. The PRC now uses sophisticated methods for censuses, surveys, and statistics, but these are all compromised by the serious underreporting of births that PRC birth limits induce. Estimates of fertility range from 2.3 to 1.2, with the most plausible range between 1.8 and 1.5. PRC leaders use 1.8 as the official figure for public announcements, population projections, and policy decisions. Although 1.8 is below "replacement" (2.1), it is above the "policy rate" (about 1.6, the average number of children that couples would have if all couples had exactly the number of children that birth regulations allow them). Moreover, since

1.8 is a national average that includes some localities with quite low fertility, in some other localities fertility must be higher than birth rules allow. To PRC policy makers, this suggests a need to strengthen enforcement in backward localities. It also suggests a need to be cautious about reform experiments, lest they spread "prematurely." Lower estimates of TFR would allow more room for reform experiments and for gradual movement toward a two-child rule.

A closely related and equally basic question is how many children of what sex Chinese couples want. Under any circumstances, asking people about their ideal fertility aspirations is an inherently problematic exercise, because the number of children that couples actually have depends on their eventual circumstances. Moreover, in China those circumstances have long included strict legal limits and strong public education, making it difficult for people to imagine what they themselves might ideally prefer. Nevertheless, most studies suggest that ideally most Chinese couples would now like two children: one son and one daughter. Many rural couples probably would like two sons and a daughter. If restricted to one child, many urban couples will accept either a son or a daughter. Most rural couples feel they need at least one son. To PRC policy makers, this means that some gap still remains between what people would ideally like and what policy permits. However, most studies also suggest that, as a result of factors such as the high cost of raising children and a desire to live their own lives, many couples now choose to have fewer children than they might ideally prefer. Some couples now choose to have fewer children even than birth regulations would allow them. Low limits—whether state imposed or self-imposed—result in sex-selective abortion by couples determined to have at least one son.

A second set of questions concerns the actual working of the social compensation fee. On what proportion of couples is the fee actually levied, in what amounts, and for what violations? To what extent does the PRC actually need this disincentive to achieve or maintain low fertility? To what extent can positive reproductive health services and client empowerment substitute for negative sanctions? The PRC birth system itself has long been monitoring problems associated with birth fines or fees. For example, in the 1990s some communities were using birth fines as a cash cow for financing community government (township and village). In 2002 the birth program issued regulations for levying such fees that reduced incentives for overcollection by separating the collector from the user and by requiring that fees be deposited with the county-level branch of the national ministry of finance for closer auditing and control. Meanwhile, the birth system is working with the finance system to secure, in all localities, funding through the regular state budget for birth personnel and birth work. However, ongoing reforms of other aspects of local finance make this difficult.

In order to discover relevant facts, quite constructively the U.S. Embassy in Beijing helped UNFPA to commission a leading Chinese university to do some field studies of how the fee is actually administered (Renmin University 2003). Those studies found that, overall, nearly all couples comply with birth regulations and therefore only a small proportion of couples are subject to such a fee. Remarkably, in one locality, three-quarters even of those fined say that birth rules are reasonable and enforcement justifiable (report on Qianjiang, Hubei, page 15). Moreover, within the small proportion levied a fee, only about a third are fined because they have more children than permitted. (The other two-thirds contravene rules about marital status, age of marriage, or spacing between children.) Furthermore, within the third that do have unauthorized children, it is not clear that all couples were determined to do so. For example, in some cases the woman became pregnant by accident and then was afraid to terminate the pregnancy for fear of health effects. Thus the upshot is that only a small fraction of fees are levied because couples have more children than birth limits permit. (Of course, that is because, given birth limits, many couples choose to abort girl children that they might otherwise prefer to have.) At least some national program leaders believe that the fee should be limited only to couples who produce unauthorized children, because other violations of birth rules do not actually add children to society. Moreover, on just that ground, some provinces are beginning to drop timing requirements, such as spacing a second child. Evidently there is much room for narrowing the application of the fee without jeopardizing low fertility.

Conclusion

At least some actors have come close to at least some agreement on how to allay U.S. concerns about UNFPA involvement in reforming PRC birth planning. What remaining reframing is needed? On the basis of what common ground might more consensus be achieved? What are the implications of this case for other issues?[8]

Constructive Engagement

Our main question has concerned "constructive engagement": Assuming that the PRC is wrong to impose birth limits, should one support UNFPA's efforts to reform that policy? As we have seen, most foreigners, including

UNFPA, do assume that it is wrong for the PRC to limit births. Moreover, some foreigners believe, reasonably enough, that UNFPA should not, by its presence, lend the PRC's ethically flawed birth program legitimacy, which PRC leaders then use to justify the program to themselves, their citizenry, and the world. Nevertheless, most foreigners, once they learn about the direction and pace of PRC reforms and about UNFPA's contribution to those reforms, conclude that UNFPA's role should be supported.

There are at least three main dimensions to the issue of constructive engagement. First, under what circumstances is moral ostracism versus constructive engagement appropriate? The answer depends in part on one's preference for maintaining one's own moral purity versus one's commitment to producing positive change. However, the answer also depends in part on a second main dimension: How bad are things in the host country and in what direction are they moving? Where things are bad and getting worse, moral ostracism may be the best strategy. However, this does not mean that constructive intervention should be delayed until things are perfect: Then there will no longer be any need to intervene. Accordingly, it is not necessary to minimize problems in China to make the case for UNFPA involvement. A third dimension is the crucial one: What impact is intervention likely to have on the host country, and how can that impact be shown? It is relatively easy to measure the impact of demonstrations externally, in terms of number of imitators and degree of policy change. It is more difficult to demonstrate impact internally, within project counties themselves, because of the many possible causes of outcomes.

The main difference between the Bush and UNFPA approaches to further reforming PRC birth policy is understanding and patience. As in other foreign policy areas, having disavowed a multilateral approach, the Bush administration is pursuing its own unilateral approach: Simply tell the PRC it must abolish the social compensation fee and other enforcement measures immediately, meanwhile holding UNFPA hostage. As we have seen, UNFPA believes that in a few years it can demonstrate to the PRC that coercive enforcement is not necessary to maintain low fertility. UNFPA understands that reformers at the national level within the PRC birth program must bring along many kinds of doubters. Reformers must persuade other national program leaders and most national political leaders, from whom the birth program receives its instructions. Reformers must convince subnational political and program leaders, to whom they cannot issue orders. Reformers must bring along the nearly half million birth administrators and workers in fifty thousand townships and three-quarters of a million villages, who must be retrained for the transition from simply limiting births to delivering quality care. Simply abolishing existing procedures would produce chaos within both the birth system and society, not an orderly transition to better reproductive health and rights.

The still more basic problem with Bush policy toward the UNFPA issue is that it is part not only of a "stealth coup" that the administration has been staging in U.S. domestic and foreign reproductive policy but also of a "stealth revolution" that the Bush administration has launched in basic American political principles and political practice. Classically, public policy has rested on public principles that have been publicly debated and democratically adopted, not simply on private morality or professional ethics. It has not been the Western democratic tradition that, once elected to public office, public officials should adopt policies based on their own private moralities. Yet that is what the Bush administration has been doing, not only on the UNFPA-PRC issue but also in American foreign and domestic policy in general. Thus the sort of analysis conducted in this chapter has unfortunately wide application. In many matters besides the UNFPA issue it is necessary to ascertain in exactly what terms issues are currently being debated, toward what common ground participants are moving, and what remaining issues separate them.

Limiting Births

There are, in fact, some additional issues that concerned people should face. Even a "comprehensively reformed" PRC birth program will continue to pose ethical challenges to the international community. Future elaboration of Cairo would benefit from addressing those challenges, whether the conclusion is to justify PRC policies or not.

Is it so obvious that it is wrong for the PRC to impose birth limits on its citizens? If, under some extreme demographic circumstances such limits were legitimate, why would it be illegitimate for the PRC to enforce them? Of course, by Western standards, the processes through which the PRC has adopted, managed, and reformed its birth program have been altogether undemocratic. Nevertheless, how can such limits and enforcement be absolutely illegitimate if most Chinese now accept them as reasonable? The purpose of raising these questions here is not to argue that PRC birth policy is correct and that therefore it is okay for the United States to fund UNFPA "participation" in the PRC birth program. Instead, the purpose is to establish that these are legitimate and complex questions over which reasonable people and countries can respectfully disagree. PRC adoption and enforcement of mandatory birth limits may or may not be the wisest public policy for China, but such a policy is not ipso facto immoral and should not automatically subject the PRC to absolute moral condemnation. Public policy on complex issues often requires making moral tradeoffs between competing values. Current PRC leaders deserve some respect as they grapple with the difficult practical problems and ethical issues posed by China's huge population and by the policies and methods that previous PRC leaders put in place.

Of course, any state-imposed limit on births violates the international principle, dating from the 1968 Tehran human rights conference, that couples should be free to choose the number and spacing of their children. However, it is relevant to recall that when that principle was introduced, in a world still reluctant to endorse birth control, the principle's main intended meaning was that couples should be free to have as *few* children as they want, not as *many*. It is not obviously unreasonable for the PRC to insist that this principle may require some adaptation in situations of evident overpopulation. Moreover the principle does say "decide responsibly," implying that the couple must consider more than their own whim. The PRC, although endorsing the Tehran principle, interprets "responsibly" to mean "in light of national circumstances and national policy," in China's case the fact of overpopulation and what the PRC views as the need to limit births. Again, there can be no absolute principle of individual freedom that does not require tradeoffs against other public policy objectives. The Bush administration itself affirms the need for such tradeoffs in some policy areas (such as post-911 tradeoffs between liberty and military security) while denying it in reproductive policy (such as PRC tradeoffs between liberty and population stability). In fact, American public policy itself intervenes in reproductive behavior—for example, on the one hand subsidizing middle-class childbearing with tax deductions while on the other hand urging lower-class female welfare recipients to limit their fertility.

Strategic Lessons

What then are some strategic lessons from international efforts to maximize the impact of Cairo on China?

First, the overall lesson is that propagating attractive ideals can be powerfully effective, even toward such an apparently unpromising interlocutor as the post-totalitarian PRC. Actually, such an idealistic strategy is quite similar to the Chinese approach to guiding social action, which begins by getting everyone to understand the relevant ideas. As a wise UN official has observed, once Chinese catch on to human rights, it will spread like wildfire. As of the early 2000s, that has begun to happen, from national leaders in Beijing to ordinary women in remote provinces.

Second, in this process of propagation, criticism has a constructive role, but critics should not mistake it for the whole process of promoting change. As common sense suggests, criticism is more effective if it conveys positive ideals along with negative censure, if the critics interact with the country being criticized instead of ostracizing it as a pariah, and if the "push" of criticism is accompanied by the "pull" of help. (PRC birth program leaders complain that the U.S. approach is all push and no pull.) Critics cannot promote positive change if they cannot, or will not, recognize positive change when it occurs. The prospects for success in positive intervention are particularly promising in China, where there is desire to achieve international standards, belief in state intervention to achieve them, and manpower and funding to replicate reforms once they have been demonstrated to be feasible.

Third, PRC reproductive reform illustrates another common observation, that external pushes and pulls can only point the way. Fundamental policy change requires, in addition, an internal crisis that creates the need and provides the opportunity to adapt and actualize external ideas. In the course of the 1990s, PRC birth policy faced multiple crises: increasingly urgent need to adapt birth planning to marketization and legalization, growing recognition of the side costs of unnecessary regulations and over-harsh enforcement, and growing realization that, politically, the CCP could no longer afford the resulting mass disaffection. In the early 2000s, new younger national political leaders still want low fertility, but they want to further reduce public dissatisfaction, particularly at unnecessary public interference in private lives and at accompanying maladministration (coercion and corruption).

Fourth, ideals like Cairo must be made understandable and appealing to the subnational political leaders who must authorize and fund reform and to the subnational program administrators who must supervise the reform process and take responsibility for the outcomes. Although China is formally a unitary political system, its large size and decentralization make it de facto federal, particularly in social policy. The main means available to national program leaders for promoting reform is to propagate attractive ideals to subnational leaders. That is one main function of UNFPA local demonstration projects and one main reason they involve counties in all provinces.

Fifth, intervention strategies that include rights ideals have greater impact in the long run than interventions that focus simply on technical upgrades. Actors preoccupied with improving technique can have difficulty moving on to expanding their ideas. China illustrates that at several levels. For example, the PRC public health tradition tends to translate socially acceptable "quality care" into technically adequate "quality service." Some localities that have improved their physical infrastructure therefore think they have nothing more to learn. In the early 2000s, a main purpose of continuing local demonstrations of informed choice is to get rights ideals across to local and community administrators.

Sixth, in propagating ideals of health and rights, obviously international civil society must address not only the national state but also domestic civil society. Unfortunately in posttotalitarian China, civil society remains weak because the state still dominates most social organizations. Also, the legal infrastructure for large-scale philanthropy and for genuinely voluntary associations remains underdeveloped. Outsiders face a dilemma of whether to channel resources through official mass organizations under strong state control or through unofficial voluntary associations that the state remains determined to keep weak. Civil society is perhaps the weakest front in China's reproductive reforms.

Seventh, promoting health and rights obviously is easier if the public itself already embraces similar ideas. In China it is an epochal change in public attitudes that birth program leaders say defines the "new situation" to which PRC reproductive policy must adapt in the early 2000s. The young people whose reproductive behavior the program must regulate no longer defer to either state or family, but instead are more individualistic, wanting both consumer power and personal independence. Regardless of whether they articulate this as "human rights," the effect is similar—a sense of entitlement to both benefits and respect. This change has resulted in part from state instruction, in part from domestic socioeconomic modernization, and in part from increasing interaction with the outside world.

Eighth, having recognized and reported such complexities, anyone aspiring to reframe international issues can identify common principles that most parties share. This is relatively easy for the UNFPA issue, first because most participants do, in fact, share many basic principles, and second because the argument for constructive engagement is so persuasive. Unfortunately there is no obvious way to include in this consensus the minority of American religionists who claim that U.S. reproductive policy, domestic and foreign, must reflect their private morality, regardless of the cost to others around the world.

Ninth, in practice, a would-be "reframer" would do well to observe the extent to which some of the participants themselves are moving toward some common ground. On the UNFPA issue the pattern has repeatedly been one of skeptics sweeping into China to censure misdeeds and leaving as converts to constructive engagement. Bushism in America now faces the same dilemma that Maoism in China faced before: In the long run, familiarity with the facts tends to produce pragmatic moderation, even among the most ideologically reliable of agents. A policy that prefers moral purity to practical results must eventually fail, in America as in China. Or so progressives must hope.

Notes

For the general reader, on each topic, these notes emphasize recent publications of general interest that are widely available in English. In addition, this chapter is based on extensive reading of documents and interviewing of participants, mostly in Chinese. For the opportunity to discuss these issues with five delegations of Chinese birth planners visiting the United States from 1998 through 2002, I thank the Advanced Leadership Program of the Public Media Center and Center for Social Policy (both in San Francisco). For assistance during my November 2003 research visit to China, I thank the National Population and Family Planning Commission, the China Population and Information Research Center, UNFPA in Beijing, and the U.S. Embassy in Beijing. For financial support in writing this chapter I thank the Soros Reproductive Health Fellowship. For other support I thank Herb Gunther, Axel Mundigo, Judith Bruce, Jason Wang, and the 2003 Soros fellows and staff. For scathing criticism I thank Soros reviewers Joan Kaufman and Barbara Pillsbury and, particularly, my own reviewers G. William Skinner and Susan Greenhalgh.

1. Introduction. On Comprehensive Reform in general and on Mudanjiang in particular, see Greenhalgh and Winckler 2005. On reforms, see also Kaufman et al. 2003 and White Paper 2000 (by PRC). For recent local studies of PRC birth planning, see Merli, Qian, and Smith 2004; Yan 2003; Gu, Simmons, and Szatkowski 2002; Zhang Wei-guo 2002 and 1999; and Smith et al. 1997. For much "local color," see Interfaith Delegation to China 2003.

2. Regime dilemmas. For comprehensive accounts of PRC birth planning, see Greenhalgh and Winckler 2005, and Scharping 2003. The most recent updates on PRC birth policy are Kaufman 2003, Winckler 2002, Greenhalgh and Winckler 2001, and Winckler 1999; see also White Paper 2000 (by PRC). Recent retrospectives include Greenhalgh 2003b, White 2000, and Xie 2000. Earlier studies include Milwertz 1997 and Wang and Hull 1991. Most of the rest of the best previous work on earlier PRC reproductive policy has been done by Tyrene White and Susan Greenhalgh, many of whose articles most other works cite (for example, Greenhalgh and Winckler 2005 or Scharping 2003). On adverse effects of PRC birth planning on women, see Part Two of Greenhalgh and Winckler 2005; Johnson 2004; Greenhalgh 2001b; Johnson, Huang, and Wang 1998; and Zhu et al. 1997. On Chinese women's health, see Yu and Sarri 1997, and Pearson 1996. For other adverse social effects see Greenhalgh forthcoming and 2003a (on unplanned persons); Cai and Lavely 2003 and Chu 2001 (on sex ratios); and Du and Tu 2000 (on aging). English materials on PRC health history include Lawrence 2002, Chen 1984, and Lampton 1977; on the political formulation of early PRC MCH work, see Goldstein 1998. On the development of human rights in China, see Svensson

2002. On PRC domestic reproductive rights policy, see Keith and Lin 2001 (49–92) or Keith 1997. On human rights in PRC foreign policy, see Kent 1999 and 1993. On Chinese women and "women's work," see Judd 2002, Hsiung, Joshok, and Milwertz 2001, Evans 1997, Gilmartin et al. 1994, Wolf 1985, Johnson 1983, Stacey 1983, Davin 1976. For Chinese feminist views of PRC birth planning, see Greenhalgh 2001a, and Greenhalgh and Li 1995.

3. Reform limits. On the balance between stability and change in early 2000s PRC birth policy, see Winckler 2002. On unsolved problems, see again Part Two of Greenhalgh and Winckler 2005.

4. UNFPA role. For a sympathetic overview of the UNFPA in general, see Sadik 2002. Again, a good early 2000s report on UNFPA work in China and the issues surrounding it is Interfaith Delegation to China 2003. Other major recent reviews include Independent Assessment Team 2002 (from United States), an April 2002 mission by members of Parliament (from United Kingdom), and an October 2001 international team (for UNFPA). My sketch of UNFPA's five cycles of programs in China draws on conversations with both past and present UNFPA officials and on in-house UNFPA documentation of both past and present programs.

5. U.S. preconditions. The Web site planetwire.org follows U.S. foreign reproductive policy; see particularly "Legislative background: The Kemp-Kasten Amendment" and "Timeline of US funding of UNFPA." The classic American critique of the PRC birth program is Aird 1990; for field details see Mosher 1993.

6. UNFPA complicity? Treatments of the issues between the United States, UNFPA, and PRC include Cohen 2000 and 1999, and Crane and Finkle 1989. For recent diverse testimony see Congressional-Executive Commission on China 2002.

7. China situation. On PRC population dynamics and birth policy, see Peng and Guo 2000, Peng 1991, and Banister 1987. On the dynamics of Chinese fertility aspirations, see Skinner and Yuan 1998. For an advanced sociospatial analysis of China's recent transition to low fertility, see Skinner, Henderson, and Yuan 2000.

8. Conclusion. A wise summary of ethical preconditions for imposing birth limits is Isaacs 1995. The most sophisticated discussion of seeking common ground between Chinese and Americans on human rights issues is Angle 2002.

References

For the general reader, these references emphasize recent publications of general interest that are readily available in English.

Aird, J. 1990. *Slaughter of the Innocents: Coercive Birth Control in China.* Washington, D.C.: AEI Press [American Enterprise Institute].

Alpermann, B. 2001. "The post-election administration of Chinese villages." *China Journal* 46: 45–67 (54–59, Case study 1: Birth planning).

Angle, S. C. 2002. *Human Rights and Chinese Thought: A Cross-Cultural Inquiry.* New York: Cambridge University Press.

Banister, J. 1987. *China's Changing Population.* Stanford: Stanford University Press.

Boucher, R. 2002. "Daily press briefing for July 22 (transcript)." http://www.state.gov/r/pa/prs/dpb/2002/12036.htm.

Cai, Yong, and W. Lavely 2003. "China's missing girls: Numerical estimates and effects on population growth." *China Review* 3(2): 13–29.

Chen, Haifeng, ed. 1984. *Chinese Health Care: A Comprehensive Review of the Health Services of the People's Republic of China.* Lancaster, Pa.: MTP Press.

Chu, Junhong. 2001. "Prenatal sex determination and sex-selective abortion in rural central China." *Population and Development Review* 27(2): 259–281.

Congressional-Executive Commission on China. 2002. *Women's Rights and China's New Family Planning Law.* Washington, D.C.: U.S. Government Printing Office. Also www.cecc.gov.

Cohen, S. 1999. "The United States and the United Nations population fund: A rocky relationship." *Guttmacher Report on Public Policy* 2(1). http://www.agi-usa.org/journals/toc/gr0201toc.html.

———. 2000. "Abortion politics and US population aid: Coping with a complex new law." *International Family Planning Perspectives* 26(3). http://www.agi-usa.org/journals/toc/ifpp2603toc.html.

Crane, B., and J. L. Finkle. 1989. "The United States, China and the United Nations Population Fund: Dynamics of US policymaking." *Population and Development Review* 15(1): 23–59.

Davin, D. 1976. *Woman-work.* Oxford: Clarendon Press.

Du Peng, and Tu Ping. 2000. "Population aging and old age security." In Peng and Guo, eds. *The Changing Population of China,* 77–90. Oxford: Blackwell.

Evans, H. 1997. *Women and Sexuality in China: Dominant Discourses on Female Sexuality since 1949.* New York: Continuum.

Gilmartin, C. K., G. Hershatter, L. Rofel, and T. White, eds. 1994. *Engendering China: Women, Culture, and the State.* Cambridge: Harvard University Press.

Goldstein, J. 1998. "Scissors, surveys, and psycho-prophylactics: Prenatal health care campaigns and state building in China, 1949–1954." *Journal of Historical Sociology* 11(2): 153–184.

Greenhalgh, S. 2001a. "Fresh winds in Beijing: Chinese feminists speak out on the one-child policy and women's lives." *Signs* 26(3): 847–886.

———. 2001b. "Managing 'the missing girls' in Chinese population discourse." In C. M. Obermeyer, (ed.), *Cultural Perspectives on Reproductive Health.* 131–152. Oxford: Oxford University Press.

———. 2003a. "Planned births, unplanned persons: Population in the making of Chinese modernity." *American Ethnologist* 30(2): 196–215.

———. 2003b. "Science, modernity and the making of China's one-child policy." *Population and Development Review* 29(2): 163–196.

———. Forthcoming. "Making up China's 'black population.'" In S. Szreter, A. Dharmaligam, and H. Sholkamy, eds., *Categories and Contexts in Population Studies.* Oxford: Oxford University Press.

Greenhalgh, S., and Li Jiali. 1995. "Engendering reproductive policy and practice in peasant China." *Signs* 20(3): 601–641.

Greenhalgh, S., and E. A. Winckler. 2001. *Chinese State Birth Planning in the 1990s and Beyond.* Washington, D.C.: Resource Information Center, Immigration and Naturalization Service, U.S. Department of Justice.

————. 2005. *Governing Population in China: From Leninist to Neoliberal Biopolitics*. Stanford: Stanford University Press.

Gu, Baochang, R. Simmons, and D. Szatkowski. 2002. "Offering a choice of contraceptive methods in Deqing County, China: Changing practice in the family planning program since 1995." In N. Haberland and D. Measham, eds., *Responding to Cairo: Case Studies of Changing Practice in Reproductive Health and Family Planning,* 58–73. New York: Population Council.

Hsiung, Ping-chun, M. Joshok, and C. Milwertz, eds. 2001. *Chinese Women Organizing: Cadres, Feminists, Muslims, Queers*. Oxford: Berg.

Independent Assessment Team. 2002. *Report of the China UN Population Fund (UNFPA) Independent Assessment Team.* Washington, D.C.: Bureau of Population, Refugees and Migration, U.S. Department of State. May 29.

Interfaith Delegation to China. 2003. *The United Nations Population Fund in China: A Catalyst for Change.* Washington, D.C.: Catholics for a Free China.

Isaacs, S. L. 1995. "Incentives, population policy, and reproductive rights: Ethical issues." *Studies in Family Planning* 26(6): 363–367.

Johnson, K. A. 2004. *Wanting a Daughter, Needing a Son.* St. Paul: Yeong and Yeong Book Co.

Johnson, K. A. 1983. *Women, the Family, and Peasant Revolution in China*. Chicago: University of Chicago Press.

Johnson, K. A., Huang Banghan, and Wang Liao. 1998. "Infant abandonment and adoption in China." *Population and Development Review* 24(3): 469–510.

Judd, E. 2002. *The Chinese Women's Movement between State and Market.* Stanford: Stanford University Press.

Kaufman, J. 2003. "Myths and realities of China's population program." *Harvard Asia Quarterly* 7(1): 21–25.

Kaufman, J., Kaining Zhang, and Jing Fang. 1997. "Rural Chinese women's unmet need for reproductive health services." In *23rd IUSSP General Population Conference, Symposium on Demography of China,* 485–490. Beijing: China Population Association. October.

Kaufman, J., Zhang Erli, and Xie Zhenming. 2003. "Quality of care in China: Scaling up a pilot project into a national reform program." Paper prepared for a workshop on "scaling up," in Bellagio, Italy, March-April.

Keith, R. C. 1997. "Legislating women's and children's rights and interests in the PRC." *China Quarterly* 149 (March): 29–55.

Keith, R. C., and Zhiqiu Lin. 2001. *Law and Justice in China's New Marketplace.* Houndsmill, Basingstoke, Hampshire: Palgrave.

————. 1993. *Between Freedom and Subsistence: China and Human Rights.* Hong Kong: Oxford University Press.

————. 1999. *China, the United Nations and Human Rights: The Limits of Compliance.* Philadelphia: University of Pennsylvania Press.

Lampton, D. M. 1977. *The Politics of Medicine in China: The Policy Process, 1949–1977.* Boulder: Westview.

Lawrence, S. V. 2002. "The sickness trap." *Far Eastern Economic Review* 165(23): 30–33.

Merli, G., Zhenchao Qian, and H. F. Smith. 2004. "Adaptation of a political bureaucracy to economic and institutional change under socialism: The Chinese state family planning system." *Politics and Society* 32(2): 231–256.

Milwertz, C. N. 1997. *Accepting Population Control: Urban Chinese Women and the One-Child Family Policy.* Surrey: Curzon Press.

Mosher, S. 1993. *A Mother's Ordeal: One Woman's Fight against China's One-Child Policy.* New York: Harcourt, Brace, Jovanovich.

Mudanjiang. 2002. *Collection of Documents for National Conference on Comprehensive Reform, Mudanjiang, September 2002.* Beijing: China Population Press.

Pearson, V. 1996. "Woman and health in China: Anatomy, destiny and politics." *Journal of Social Politics* 25(4): 529–543.

Peng, Xizhe, 1991. *Demographic Transition in China: Fertility Trends since the 1950s.* Oxford: Clarendon Press.

Peng, Xizhe, and Zhigang Guo, eds. 2000. *The Changing Population of China.* Oxford: Blackwell.

Renmin University, Population and Development Studies Center. 2003. *Investigation Project on Social Compensation Fee.* Beijing: Renmin University. Five papers.

Sadik, N. 2002. *Agenda for People: The UNFPA through Three Decades.* New York: New York University Press.

Scharping, T. 2003. *Birth Control in China 1949–2000: Population Policy and Demographic Development.* London: Routledge-Curzon.

SFPC (State Family Planning Commission). 2002. "National family planning and reproductive health survey (2001)." On commission Web site at www.sfpc.gov.cn under Fresh News, March 4, 2002.

Skinner, G. W., M. Henderson, and Yuan Jianhua. 2000. "China's fertility transition through regional space." *Social Science History* 24(3): 613–652.

Skinner, G. W., and Yuan Jianhua. 1998. "Reproductive strategizing in the face of China's birth-planning policies." Paper prepared for the Center for Chinese Studies Seminar, University of Michigan, April 14.

Smith, H. L., Tu Ping, M. G. Merli, and M. Hereward. 1997. "Implementation of a demographic and contraceptive surveillance system in four counties in North China." *Population Research and Policy Review* 16(4): 289–314.

Stacey, J. 1983. *Patriarchy and Socialist Revolution in China.* Berkeley: University of California Press.

Svensson, M. 2002. *Debating Human Rights in China: A Conceptual and Political History.* Lanham: Rowman and Littlefield.

Wang Guoqiang. 2001. Speech to meeting initiating experiments at Comprehensive Reform, February 2001. In *China Birth Planning Yearbook 2002,* 117–118. Beijing, 2002. In Chinese.

Wang Jiye, and T. H. Hull, eds. 1991. *Population and Development Planning in China.* Sydney: Allen and Unwin.

White, T. 2000. "Domination, resistance and accommodation in China's one-child campaign." In E. J. Perry and M. Selden, eds., *Chinese Society: Change, Conflict and Resistance,* 102–119. London: Routledge.

White Paper. 2000. [State Council, Information Office]. *China's Population and Development in the 21st Century.* Beijing: State Council. www.sfpc.gov.cn/en/whitepaper.htm.

Winckler, E. A. 1999. "Re-enforcing state birth planning." In E. A. Winckler, ed., *Transition from Communism in China,* 181–203. Boulder: Lynne Rienner.

———. 2002. "Chinese reproductive policy at the turn of the millennium." *Population and Development Review* 28(3): 1–40.

Wolf, M. 1985. *Revolution Postponed.* Stanford: Stanford University Press.

Xie, Zhenming. 2000. "Population policy and the family-planning program." In Peng and Guo, eds., *The Changing Population of China,* 51–63. Oxford: Blackwell.

Yan, Yunxiang. 2003. *Private Life under Socialism: Love, Intimacy, and Family Change in a Chinese Village, 1949–1999.* Stanford: Stanford University Press.

Yu, Meiyu, and R. Sarri. 1997. "Women's health status and gender inequality in China." *Social Science and Medicine* 45(12): 1,885–1,898.

Zhang, Hanxiang, and Sun Jiahai. 1999. "Human rights questions in the area of birth planning: A question that is worth serious attention." In *China Birth Planning Yearbook 1999,* 256–259. Beijing, 1999. In Chinese.

Zhang Wei-guo. 1999. "Implementation of state family planning programmes in a northern Chinese village." *China Quarterly* 157 (March): 202–230.

———. 2002. *Economic Reforms and Fertility Behavior: A Study of a North China Village.* London: Taylor and Francis.

Zhang Weiqing. 2000. Speech to national birth planning work conference, December 2000. *China Birth Planning Yearbook 2000,* 60–68. Beijing, 2001. In Chinese.

———. 2001. "The 'three represents' and the party's population policy and practice." *People's Daily* July 11. FBIS–CHI–2001–0711, in World News Connection.

———. 2002. Speech to national conference on experiments in comprehensive reform. Mudanjiang, September 2002. In *China Birth Planning Yearbook 2003,* 74–81. Beijing, 2003. In Chinese.

Zhu Chuzhu, Li Shuzhou, Qiu Changrong, Hu Ping, and Jin Anrong. 1997. *The Dual Effects of the Family Planning Program on Chinese Women.* Xian: Xian Jiaotong University Press.

International Human Rights from the Ground Up

The Potential for Subnational, Human Rights-Based Reproductive Health Advocacy in the United States

Martha F. Davis

The origins of the Kensington Welfare Rights Union (KWRU) could hardly be more local: The KWRU was started in 1990 by six welfare mothers struggling to establish a new playground in Philadelphia's Kensington district (N. Davis 2000). Headed by Cheri Honkala, a thirtyish welfare mom with a flair for dramatic and confrontational tactics, the organization expanded both its membership and support by focusing on housing and community needs of low-income residents of North Philadelphia. Today, the KWRU headquarters distributes food and clothing and provides advocacy assistance, taking calls twenty-four hours a day from low-income people whose homes have been condemned, whose children have been taken by foster care, or who are simply hungry. All we ask in return, says one KWRU activist, is that our callers "join the struggle to help other people to fight for an end to poverty" (Thul 1997).

KWRU's tactics are aggressive. Their slogan—"you only get what you're organized to take"—reflects a commitment to both grassroots organizing and taking what one needs to survive. Many KWRU members were arrested throughout the 1990s for taking over abandoned, city-owned buildings to use as residences—homes that they called "human rights houses." When they could find no housing, KWRU created strategically located tent cities to house the homeless, effectively keeping the needs of Philadelphia's poor community in the public eye (Zucchino 1997).

KWRU had some success in securing legal residences for its members, several dozen of whom were given vouchers for affordable housing in a government effort to placate KWRU. But by 1995, KWRU's persistent confrontations became counterproductive. According to one observer, the government "was taking a stand. There would be no more exceptions. Cheri's people had to go through the shelter system like everyone else" (Zucchino 1997).

Frustrated, KWRU members began looking for new approaches. They found the answer in a training program conducted by the People's Decade of Human Rights Education, an international human rights education organization.[1] KWRU decided to shift the organization's focus from domestic legal frameworks to international human rights, based specifically on the Universal Declaration of Human Rights (UDHR) (Gilbert and Masucci 1998; Ford Foundation 2004). According to Executive Director Honkala, a change was necessary because KWRU had "exhausted our ability to get our needs met" (Honkala 2003). Although the underlying issues facing KWRU members have not changed, the UDHR has the potential to produce a "paradigm shift" in the public discussion of poverty (N. Davis 2000).

Implementing its new vision, KWRU organized the Poor People's Economic Human Rights Campaign, a coalition of more than forty grassroots organizations nationwide committed to bringing international human rights law to bear on poverty in the United States (Poor People's Economic Human Rights Campaign 2003). The campaign's member organizations focus on economic justice, low-wage work, and housing issues. Like KWRU, many of the campaign's members find that an international human rights perspective contributes to their organizing efforts. As Sandra Robertson of the Georgia Citizens Coalition on Hunger says, "It just caught us on fire. Sometimes it's hard to talk about economic justice because it has so many facets to it. The human rights framework really allows you to tie it all together" (N. Davis 2000).

Within a few months, the Kensington activists moved the international strategy to the center of their agenda. In 1997, they organized a successful March for Our Lives from the Liberty Bell in Philadelphia to the United Nations in New York City. The same year, they began an Economic Human Rights Documentation project to document violations of the UDHR; the project serves as an organizing tool as well as a vehicle for developing materials to submit to the United Nations. When visiting welfare offices, KWRU activists regularly initiate conversations with waiting recipients by asking them to complete the Human Rights Violations Survey, which asks about their housing situation and treatment by the welfare bureaucracy (Thul 1997).[2]

KWRU staged a second march on the United Nations in 1998, and in November 1998, Mary Robinson, then the United Nations High Commissioner for Human Rights, presented KWRU's economic campaign in her report on the state of human rights in the world to the General Assembly (Gilbert and Masucci 1998). More marches followed: in 1999, the March of the Americas; in 2000, the March for Economic Human Rights during the Republican National Convention in Philadelphia; and in August 2003, the Poor People's March for Economic Human Rights (KWRU 2003).

KWRU's international work also encompasses law and policy advocacy. In 1999, members collaborated with lawyers from the Center on Economic and Social Rights in New York. Together, they filed a petition with the Inter-American Commission on Human Rights, an arm of the Organization of American States, challenging U.S. welfare policy under the International Covenant on Civil and Political Rights (ICCPR) and international customary law (KWRU 2003). More recently, Kensington members worked in coalition with the National Association of Social Workers to promote domestic adoption of international human rights standards. As a result of this advocacy, a select committee of the Pennsylvania House of Representatives held a series of unprecedented hearings in the fall of 2002 to investigate "the integration of human rights standards in Pennsylvania's laws and policies" (General Assembly of Pennsylvania 2002). KWRU used these hearings as a powerful vehicle for organizing members and as a high-profile forum for sharing KWRU's message about ending poverty.

KWRU's initial decision to use international human rights principles to organize on the *local* level required a shift away from the usual paradigm that identifies human rights as a purely national issue. International human rights activism and advocacy in the United States has generally centered on the obligations that international agreements impose on the federal government. Because the United States has not ratified human rights treaties such as the Convention for the Elimination of All Forms of Discrimination against Women (CEDAW) and the International Covenant on Economic, Social and Cultural Rights (ICESCR), activists' attention has necessarily focused on threshold issues of ratification. For example, human rights activists may try to persuade the executive branch to make ratification of a particular treaty a priority or may lobby the Senate Foreign Relations Committee to vote in favor of ratification, thus putting the issue of ratification before the entire Senate—

the final arbiter of treaty ratification. Once agreements are ratified, activists often continue their federal focus in monitoring U.S. compliance with the agreements. If the United States has taken reservations under the treaty—that is, if it has formally identified areas of the treaty that it does not fully accept—advocates may urge elimination of these reservations (Center for Reproductive Rights 1999).

This attention to federal adoption and implementation is necessary: Only the federal government can bind the nation as a whole to international obligations (*Crosby v. National Foreign Trade Council* 2000). But in the face of federal recalcitrance in implementing human rights norms, international human rights groups are increasingly looking beyond purely federal issues to examine state and local implementation of international human rights (Human Rights Watch 2002). At the same time, faced with a hostile federal judiciary, a shrinking federal safety net, and an increase in state autonomy, domestic civil rights and economic justice groups are looking to both state law and international human rights law as potential means for shoring up domestic rights (NOW Legal Defense and Education Fund et al. 2002). Finally, community-based activists like KWRU are increasingly aware of their own place in the global struggle and see human rights paradigms as an effective basis for organizing constituents and expanding rights on the state and local levels. As the Internet and ease of travel connect activists worldwide, globalization blurs the lines between local, national, and international and reinforces the relevance of international law to local struggles (M. Davis 2000; Resnik 2001).

This chapter examines the status of this emerging local human rights movement in the United States and its particular potential for addressing the reproductive health and rights of low-income women. This potential has remained largely unexplored, in part because reproductive health and poverty have historically been reserved for state and local regulation at the same time that international human rights activism has been largely focused on federal policies.[3] Developments at the subnational level have moved forward under the human rights radar. But particularly after the devolution of welfare reform to the states in 1996, the choices that the states and localities make have a profound effect on low-income women's reproductive health and well-being; the lens of international human rights provides an important perspective on these policies. At the same time, a human rights framework has the potential to influence domestic conceptions of the scope of reproductive rights and health—to encompass issues such as the right to bear children and the right to health education.

Domestic activists have a rich palette from which to draw as they move forward with local human rights advocacy on reproductive health and rights. The ICCPR, ratified by the United States in 1992, explicitly addresses privacy rights and has been applied to reproductive health and rights (Center for Reproductive Rights 2002b). Review documents prepared at the International Conference on Population and Development (Cairo) in 1994 and the UN Fourth World Conference on Women (Beijing) in 1995, both of which the United States has endorsed, articulate a basis for significant protections for low-income women's reproductive health. Other international agreements not ratified by the United States, such as CEDAW, may articulate customary international law protecting women's reproductive health that has domestic legal force.

The campaigns described below—addressing a range of issues and drawn from other nations as well as the United States—illuminate the ways in which these international human rights obligations to support low-income women's reproductive health might be successfully translated to the local level, and what sorts of appeals may convince local policy makers to take action in the absence of federal directives.

Rationales for State and Local Obligations under International Human Rights Law

State and local policy makers are rarely aware of their critical role in human rights implementation in the United States. Indeed, they may see local human rights advocacy as misdirected—representing an agenda that is purely the province of the federal government. Local activists working on these issues must articulate the connection between international human rights and state and local policies. Three basic arguments support the proposition that state and local policy makers in the United States should always take international human rights norms into account—and in some instances are obligated to implement them.

International Treaties, Covenants, and Customary Law Bind State and Local Governments

First, when the United States assents to a treaty or other international agreement or is bound by customary law, the federal system itself demands implementation on the state and local as well as the federal level. The U.S. federal system is categorical: States have primary regulatory responsibility for social welfare and health, among other things, and the federal government regulates commerce and international relations (Resnik 2001; Spiro 1997). Because international human rights agreements often address health and welfare, and customary law may also arise in these areas, federal implementation alone is doomed to fall short of international standards. Thus, the categorical nature of U.S. federalism necessitates implementing human rights standards at the state and local level.

The federal government has acknowledged this issue and, through the treaty ratification process and other public representations, has recognized the obligations of individual states to meet U.S. human rights commitments.[4] For example, each time the Senate has given its advice and consent to ratify a major human rights treaty, it has done so with the following understanding:

> the United States understands that this Covenant shall be implemented by the Federal Government to the extent that it exercises legislative and judicial jurisdiction over the matters covered therein, and otherwise by the state and local governments; to the extent that state and local governments exercise jurisdiction over such matters, the Federal Government shall take measures appropriate to the Federal system to the end that the competent authorities of the states or local governments may take appropriate measures for the fulfillment of the Covenant. (U.S. reservations, declarations, and understandings—ICCPR 1992, CERD 1994, and Convention Against Torture, 1990)

Additionally, when the United States issued its first report in 1994 to the United Nations Human Rights Committee regarding its compliance with the ICCPR, the federal government stated that the "United States will implement its obligations under the Covenant by appropriate legislative, executive and judicial means, federal or state, and that the federal government will remove any federal inhibition to the abilities of the constituent states to meet their obligations in this regard" (U.S. reservations, declarations, and understandings 1992).[5]

In more recent testimony before the Committee on the Elimination of Racial Discrimination, Assistant Attorney General for Civil Rights Ralph Boyd further acknowledged the relevance of state laws to U.S. compliance with the International Convention on the Elimination of All Forms of Racial Discrimination (CERD). According to Boyd, a governmental working group had "been entrusted with the task of developing proposals and mechanisms for improving the monitoring of actions at the state level." Boyd stated that even in preparing the report under review, "the Government had requested local and state officials to provide the necessary information to determine the extent to which the Convention was being implemented at the local level" (CERD Summary Record 2001).

In sum, the federal system necessitates—and the U.S. government has itself acknowledged—shared responsibility for human rights implementation among federal, state, and local authorities.[6] This is powerful support for the relevance of human rights frameworks on the state and local levels and for subnational governments' obligation to implement international human rights norms.

International Human Rights Norms Provide Models for State and Local Policies

Second, international human rights law offers a persuasive source of law and policy ideas to state and local policy makers. The importance of this resource is particularly clear when state courts are called on to construe state constitutions—many of which have positive guarantees of rights that mirror international human rights obligations and for which there are no analogs in the federal system.

State constitutions have legal force independent of federal law and have often been separately construed by states' high courts. These departures may be based on different perceived values of the state or may be dictated by textual differences between state and federal law. Unlike the federal constitution, many state constitutions contain express affirmative obligations (Hershkoff 1999). Positive rights to welfare and education are among the most common in state constitutions (M. Davis 2002b; Andres 1995). Affirmative rights to health are also found in some state constitutions. For example, the Alaska constitution, adopted at the time of statehood in 1959, Louisiana's 1974 constitution, and Article XVII of the New York State constitution, as amended in 1938, all speak directly to the issue of public health (Friesen 2000; Hershkoff 1999).

State policy makers or courts should always examine relevant international treaty and customary law in developing policy or rendering decisions because of the state's obligations to implement human rights treaties. But there is a particularly good reason for a judge to examine international human rights norms when a state constitution is closer in content to international agreements than to the federal constitution: International law may provide persuasive guidance on how to interpret the provision at issue.

The New York State constitution provides a clear example. Article XVII, s. 3 of the constitution provides that "The protection and promotion of the health of the inhabitants of the state are matters of public concern and provision therefore shall be made by the state and by such of its subdivisions and in such manner, and by such means as the legislature shall from time to time determine." The federal constitution does not mention health at all, much less mandate that "provision therefore *shall* be made by" the government. In contrast, the ICESCR, though not ratified by the United States, provides a blueprint for how the New York State constitution might be construed and implemented. Article 12 provides that:

1. The States Parties to the present Covenant recognize the right of everyone to the enjoyment of the highest attainable standard of physical and mental health.
2. The steps to be taken by the States Parties to the present Covenant to achieve the full realization of this right shall include those necessary for:
   (a) The provision for the reduction of the stillbirth-rate and of infant mortality and for the healthy development of the child;
   (b) The improvement of all aspects of environmental and industrial hygiene;
   (c) The prevention, treatment and control of epidemic, endemic, occupational and other diseases;
   (d) The creation of conditions which would assure to all medical service and medical attention in the event of sickness.

Government's obligation to address health is also specifically addressed in CEDAW and the Convention on the Rights of the Child (CRC). Provisions of international law giving content to economic and social rights should provide useful and persuasive authority to state policy makers implementing affirmative state constitutional obligations.

Consistency with States' Economic Role Internationally

Third, in today's interconnected world, taking account of international human rights norms is also in the states' own economic interests. In some ways, talking about purely state and local actors is misleading, because virtually all governmental entities are now involved extensively in foreign trade and foreign economic relations. Domestic activists have begun to exploit states' international economic interests to promote human rights at home. For example, antideath-penalty advocates are now embarked on a campaign to link foreign trade opportunities with individual states' death penalty policies. Capitalizing on the strong international sentiment against the death penalty, particularly in Europe, as well as on the growing movement for corporate responsibility, advocates are urging corporations and foreign governments to use their economic relationships with states to increase the pressure to cut back or eliminate the death penalty (Hawkins 2003; Ford Foundation 2004). Similar economic boycotts have been used to pressure national governments such as South Africa to adopt domestic policy changes.

Given their extensive economic dealings with other nations, states have an independent practical interest in ensuring that their social policies are in line with international human rights norms. This economic interest, along with the other factors outlined above, augurs strongly that states should take appropriate responsibility for implementing international human rights norms under the federal system.

A Sampling of Domestic Advocacy that Incorporates International Human Rights Law: Three Approaches

Examples of domestic activists using international human rights to influence state and local policies demonstrate the rich possibilities this approach has for organizing and educating constituents, persuading policy makers, and enforcing rights.

Using International Human Rights Law to Organize and Educate

Kensington Welfare Rights Union, Philadelphia, Pennsylvania. One of KWRU's three basic goals is to "organize a broad-based movement to end poverty" (KWRU 2003). In pursuit of this goal—through campaigns ranging from surveys to housing takeovers to marches—KWRU has successfully used an international human rights approach to shore up its organizing efforts and expand its public education about the breadth of poverty's impact in the United States.

Significantly, in the process of promoting an international human rights framework for its local struggles, Kensington has built a stronger, more cohesive organization with a national and international reputation. This credibility has increased its ability to gain local, national, and international attention for its message. For example, KWRU's Inter-American Commission petition alerted sister groups in other nations as well as other governments to the situation facing the poor in the United States. A number of groups and individuals worldwide have used the Internet to share messages of solidarity and support (KWRU 2003). This international dialogue contributes directly to KWRU's goal of organizing a broad-based movement to end poverty.

Further, the public education derived from KWRU's international human rights work has been considerable. Another of KWRU's principal goals is to "speak to the issues that directly affect our lives." The higher profile that the organization has gained through a combination of its tactics and message makes it more likely that KWRU's message will be heard. KWRU activists are regularly quoted in media outlets around the country and the world, often speaking directly about human rights abuses. Similarly, KWRU and its members have been the subject of a traveling photo exhibit, a book by a Pulitzer Prize-winning author, and a documentary (KWRU 2003).

Finally, KWRU's third basic goal is to "help . . . all poor people get what we need to survive" (KWRU 2003). In the long run, public education and a stronger organization will contribute to achieving that goal. In the short run, tangible victories for KWRU members are sometimes incremental and hard to achieve. But even in the short run, KWRU's international human rights approach may maximize its local influence. In the summer of 2003, for example, flanked by KWRU's Honkala and other affordable housing advocates, Philadelphia City Council members proposed an additional $10 million to provide affordable housing (Fleming 2003). Temple University researchers attribute KWRU's ability to spur such local initiatives to its adoption of an international human rights framework: "One of the results of the successful UN strategy is that local officials, including [the Mayor] . . . have begun to identify KWRU as a legitimate voice of the poor in Kensington, one of Philadelphia's poorest neighborhoods. . . . Although KWRU's Director has testified about the plight of the poor in Congress on two previous occasions, it is the UN strategy that has given KWRU increased local legitimacy" (Gilbert and Masucci 1998). Honkala echoes this point, noting that the term "'welfare' just has so much baggage," but when she talks about human rights, "legislators are more willing to sit down and listen" (Honkala 2003). KWRU's international human rights focus has proven to be an effective tool even in its most locally based advocacy.

SisterLove, Inc., Atlanta, Georgia.   Like KWRU, SisterLove has found that an international human rights approach enhances mobilization, which in turn increases the organization's overall effectiveness in promoting social change.

Founded in July 1989, SisterLove began with a group of volunteers interested in educating women of color in Atlanta about AIDS prevention, self-help, and safer sex techniques (SisterLove 2003). Shortly after the Beijing Conference in 1995, the group began using a human rights framework in its work, much of which involves local AIDS advocacy before city and county agencies. According to founder and director Dazon Diallo, the human rights approach now permeates every part of SisterLove's program (Diallo 2003).

Diallo has identified three primary advantages to the international human rights approach. First, the human rights framework transcends the baggage of identity politics in the United States. Historic tensions between white women's and black women's approaches to civil rights—the latter reflecting the lived experience of being both black and female and the intersections of race and sex discrimination—are deeply rooted and can be traced back to Reconstruction. A human rights framework diffuses these old tensions. The framework creates a "safe space for women of color" to take action on women's issues despite their discomfort working within explicitly feminist frameworks, says Diallo (Diallo 2003).

Second, like KWRU, using a human rights approach has given Sister-Love "more credibility internationally" (Diallo 2003). Recognizing the global challenges posed by AIDS, SisterLove initiated a formal program in South Africa in 1999, actively collaborating with established South African AIDS service organizations to provide training, technical assistance, and capacity-building assistance. SisterLove's involvement in human rights issues in the United States facilitates these cross-border collaborations, because South Africa's nongovernmental organizations share a human rights agenda.

Finally, SisterLove's local advocacy has been directly furthered through its human rights approach. According to Diallo, human rights "is not just the same old, same old argument," and SisterLove is better positioned to shape the issues because these concepts are new to their audience and empowering to their constituency (Diallo 2003).

SisterLove's experience with the countywide Ryan White Planning Council, which sets the Atlanta area's agenda for AIDS policy and services, is a good example of how the "surprise" of the human rights approach can yield beneficial results. Atlanta's council has an open review process for its grant allocations. Diallo was increasingly frustrated because, as a straight black woman, she found it difficult to get her voice heard by an AIDS committee run largely by gay white men. She wrote a letter to the council describing how the experience had marginalized her, including very specific references to the international human rights involved. As a result of the letter, the entire 145-person council underwent mandatory training on human rights and diversity. Diallo believes that a more traditional—and expected—framing of the issues would not have prompted such an immediate and direct response (Diallo 2003).

Women's Economic Agenda Project, Oakland, California.   The Women's Economic Agenda Project (WEAP) is a twenty-one-year-old organization that advocates for the well-being of low-income women and their families, provides community-based services such as food distribution and day care in its Oakland community, and runs technology and job readiness training classes for low-income people in downtown Oakland.

WEAP's social justice work has always been an integral part of its overall program. In 1998, after years of addressing civil rights and poverty rights in a domestic framework, WEAP was introduced to—and embraced—the UDHR as a centerpiece of its social justice work (Long Scott 2003).

Like SisterLove, WEAP found human rights to be a unifying principle in its organizing efforts. According to Executive Director Ethel Long Scott, "it is encouraging for people to learn that we have rights as humans, that we have common ground, and we are not necessarily always separated in our rights by race, gender, and so on" (Long Scott 2003). People who are exposed to this approach through WEAP's workshops, classes, rallies, and literature are often energized to get more involved. As one student wrote, "This month-long Human Rights class at WEAP was the most practical experience I have ever received. I am truly inspired to begin working and educating others" (WEAP 2003).

Further, using a human rights framework has been an effective means to educate the broader public about poverty. Says Long Scott, "human rights codifies the view that poor people have rights in a way that the mainstream can become accustomed to" (Long Scott 2003). WEAP's methods take a page from the 1960s civil rights movement—in recent years, WEAP has sponsored a series of bus tours, including the Freedom Bus Tour of 2000 and the Save the Soul of America Bus Tour of 2002. The purpose of these tours has been "to protest, educate, and document that poverty is an economic human rights violation." For example, during the "Save the Soul" tour, each day was designed to highlight one of the UDHR articles that address economic justice. Long Scott believes that promoting the "life-affirming framework" of human rights is an effective way to build new alliances between working and poor people (Sabir 2002).

Using International Human Rights Law to Change Policies on the State and Local Level

A number of local advocacy groups have used international human rights law to request specific policy changes from state and local policy makers, with some significant success.

Women's Institute for Leadership Development of Human Rights, San Francisco.   In 1998, San Francisco did what no other U.S. city or state had done before: It codified CEDAW into its own municipal law. The organization that spearheaded the effort, Women's Institute for Leadership Development of Human Rights (WILD), was founded by women who attended the Beijing Conference and were committed to "bringing human rights home." San Francisco's CEDAW was their first project.

WILD's decision to adopt a human rights approach to its work was strategic, according to Executive Director Krishanti Dharmaraj, and enabled WILD to move beyond single issues or identity-based politics. In the wake of the divisive debate over Proposition 209, which barred government-sponsored affirmative action in California, activists were looking for holistic, unifying approaches to their work. "This was the only framework that encompassed it all," says Dharmaraj (Dharmaraj 2003).

Working closely with the local Amnesty International and the San Francisco Women's Foundation, WILD conducted numerous human rights training sessions to organize community groups in support of a local CEDAW. Further, working with a core group of activists committed to the project, WILD began the process of crafting the CEDAW measure. In order to make the project politically viable, this group agreed to focus on three issues: violence, economic justice, and health. The group also agreed that San Francisco's CEDAW would not create a reactive complaint mechanism, but would require government to take affirmative measures to address discrimination against women.

In building a base of support for the local CEDAW, WILD reached out to potentially friendly governmental groups, such as the San Francisco Commission on the Status of Women, and to individual members of the Board of Supervisors. According to Sonia Melara, former executive director of the Commission on the Status of Women, "there was initial skepticism. The President of the Board of Supervisors did not want San Francisco to be laughed at" (Melara 2003). But once the legislation was reworked to focus on economic needs, the president joined in support (Melara 2003), and the measure passed unanimously (Sappenfield 2003).

Implementation of the measure has been phased in in six city departments, each of which is required to conduct a gender analysis of its work and develop an action plan to address any discrimination. According to Ann Lehman, a policy analyst at the Commission on the Status of Women and the individual primarily responsible for the implementation phase, departments were at first concerned about "one more group looking over their shoulders and telling them what to do" (Lehman 2003). "You've got to be kidding," was a common reaction when human rights issues were raised.

Five years later, after numerous training sessions, gender analyses, and even policy changes, Lehman reports that the departments still "aren't really using human rights language" (Lehman 2003). However, Lehman believes that examining city practices through a gender lens has resulted in a permanent change in city government's culture.[7]

Further, the departments' gender analyses led to a number of tangible results. At the Arts Commission, for example, the analysis revealed that the street artist program held its lottery for street sites very early in the morning, making it inaccessible to people with children (Ford Foundation 2004). The commission changed the program (Lehman 2003). At the Department of Public Works, the analysis indicated that work hours made it difficult for women with small children to find child care; the department took steps to assist with child care. The Public Utilities Commission moved street lights closer together after learning of the impact on women's safety after dark (Dharmaraj 2003). In short, San Francisco's CEDAW has been woven into the fabric of city policy. According to the city's chief juvenile probation officer, San Francisco's CEDAW "has been an inspiration and a watchful eye to keep us moving forward" (Sappenfield 2003).

Kensington Welfare Rights Union/National Association of Social Workers, Pennsylvania Chapter.   The UDHR forms the basis for a policy initiative in Pennsylvania designed to draw connections between international human rights and domestic law. Inspired by the human rights work of KWRU and assisted by members of the statewide National Association of Social Workers (NASW), in 2001 Pennsylvania legislators introduced resolutions in both houses to establish a select committee to study the integration of human rights standards in Pennsylvania's laws. The House of Representatives resolution HR 473 was passed in June 2002 without opposition.

Representative Lawrence Curry, primary sponsor of the resolution, proposed the measure after participating in a march to Harrisburg with Cheri Honkala and other KWRU members. As someone who had participated in Dr. Martin Luther King's 1965 March to Freedom, Curry has long been active in social justice campaigns. Curry began this legislative effort by sending House colleagues a cosponsorship memo explaining the resolution. Because of a conservative majority in the legislature, he was careful to "tread lightly" and use "innocuous language" (Curry 2003). For cosponsorship,

Curry targeted those who were already generally supportive of social justice, using the proposal to educate them about international human rights.

Bipartisan support was important. According to Curry, the NASW's lobbying efforts were essential to getting Republican members on board. KWRU's tactics, although attention grabbing, were not the right approach for the legislature. Asks Curry rhetorically, "Do I think that Kensington, the group that barricaded the legislature and camped on the steps could have gotten it done alone . . . no, you can't be militant. To pass a law, you must gently, lovingly, and patiently teach the opposition" (Curry 2003).

Following the resolution's passage, the select committee held hearings around the state and must produce a report with its findings and recommendations. The report may lead to more legislative activity and, potentially, policy changes that would integrate human rights and domestic law. Although policy change is one possible outcome, Mary Bricker-Jenkins, a social work professor who coordinated NASW's activities in support of the measure, sees the campaign's trajectory differently. "Legislation is not the solution," she says, "the goal of the effort is to build a movement" (Bricker-Jenkins 2003). On that score, the resolution has already been a success: The hearings created an occasion for KWRU to deliver its organizing and educational message across the state.

Court-based Strategies

Strategic litigation has been a component of social justice campaigns at least since the 1920s (Tushnet 1987). In the past few years, activists interested in broadening domestic recognition of international human rights have also looked to the courts—if not for leadership in the area, then at least for support.

Consideration of international human rights law has proved controversial in the federal courts. Supreme Court Justices Ginsburg and Breyer, supporting international dialogue, argue that other nations have grappled with similar problems—such as the death penalty, affirmative action, and federalism itself—and that the Court can learn from the approaches that they have taken (Ginsburg and Merritt 1999; *Printz* 1997). In the other camp, Justices Scalia and Thomas and Chief Justice Rehnquist assert that because the United States is unique and no other nation shares its history, values, and specific constitutional language, international comparisons are irrelevant (*Printz* 1997).[8]

Despite this split, a majority of justices recognize the relevance of international law to domestic policy, at least in some circumstances. In *Atkins v. Virginia,* striking down the death penalty for mentally retarded defendants, the majority acknowledged worldwide opinion against imposing the death penalty in such circumstances (*Atkins* 2002). Likewise, in *Lawrence v. Texas,* striking down a Texas sodomy law, the majority acknowledged the strength of international opinion supporting privacy rights of gays (*Lawrence* 2003).[9] Most recently, a five-justice majority looked to international law to support its decision to strike down the juvenile death penalty in the United States (*Roper* 2005).

State courts in the United States have not typically viewed the relevance of international law to domestic legal issues as controversial. As one among fifty, each state is accustomed to looking outside its own borders to sister states for jurisprudential and policy ideas. Thus, state courts have often invoked international law for reasons similar to their sister courts in other nations—to stress universal values or to acknowledge the persuasive logic of an argument adopted by a foreign court.[10] In addition, state courts have sometimes cited international instruments as evidence of the existence of fundamental rights beyond those enshrined in the federal Constitution, such as the right to education, using international law to elucidate values inherent within the state system (*Pauley* 1979).

Recognizing the potential for state courts to develop a domestic human rights jurisprudence, a number of advocacy groups have advanced human rights arguments in state court litigation. The case outcomes have been mixed, but each effort contributes to the long-term goal of judicial education on human rights issues.

Using International Human Rights to Establish Customary Law.   Many state courts have cited international standards as persuasive authority that influences, or even controls, interpretations of domestic law. The use of international human rights law to support state court challenges to the juvenile death penalty is an example of this trend.

In recent years, considerable litigation centered on the issue of the juvenile death penalty. The CRC, the most widely ratified human rights convention (though not by the United States), specifically condemns the juvenile death penalty. In 2003, Professor Victor Streib reported that "Every other nation in the world has joined international agreements prohibiting the execution of juvenile offenders, with only the United States refusing to abandon its laws permitting the juvenile death penalty" (Streib 2003).

Litigators capitalized on this virtual unanimity to argue that there was no longer the "national consensus" legally required to sustain the juvenile death penalty in the United States. In 2003, the Missouri Supreme Court struck down the state's juvenile death penalty, positing that the U.S. Supreme Court would agree if it were presented with the issue. In reaching its conclusion, the state court specifically cited international standards as persuasive: "We also find of note that the views of the international community have consistently grown in opposition to the death penalty for juveniles. Article 37(a) of the United Nations Convention on the Rights of the Child and several other international treaties and agreements expressly prohibit the practice" (*State ex. rel. Simmons v. Roper* 2003).

Two years later, acknowledging the "overwhelming weight of international opinion against the death penalty" and specifically citing the CRC, the United States Supreme Court affirmed the Missouri court's ruling and found that the juvenile death penalty is unconstitutional (*Roper* 2005).

These courts' acceptance of the CRC as establishing the principles and practices of the international community are significant. Indeed, in other contexts such as child custody and immigration, domestic courts have accepted the CRC's provisions as indicative of customary international law. As such, all levels of government are obliged to comply with the convention's provisions unless they are specifically overridden by an act of Congress. Under this formulation, the United States's failure to ratify the convention does not undermine its relevance to domestic law on either the state or federal level. The Missouri state court recognized this principle when it took the initiative to reevaluate the state's juvenile death penalty rather than wait for the United States Supreme Court to revisit the issue.

Using International Human Rights Law to Establish Affirmative Governmental Obligations. International human rights conventions and many state constitutions share language that imposes affirmative obligations on government. Litigators have tried to use international law to expand these obligations to address poor women's reproductive rights and health—to date, with mixed success.

As an initial matter, a number of state courts have already distanced their states from the hands-off approach to reproductive choice adopted by the federal courts in *Harris v. McRae* (1980). In that case and others, the Supreme Court determined that the federal constitution did not require the government to fund abortion for low-income women. However, a growing number of state courts have opined that their state constitutions require such funding to ensure the full range of reproductive choices and to shore up women's equal participation in society (*Doe v. Maher* 1986; *Valley Hospital Ass'n v. Mat-Su Coalition for Choice* 1997; *New Mexico Right to Choose/NARAL v. Johnson* 1999).

To date, the cases attempting to extend this principle to state welfare programs—and to challenge the states' "family cap" policies—have been largely unsuccessful. The family cap, first introduced in Wisconsin in 1992 and now adopted in more than twenty states, denies welfare benefits to children born to mothers on welfare. The Indiana Supreme Court, the New Jersey Supreme Court, and a Massachusetts trial court have concluded that their respective state constitutions do not require the same government neutrality with respect to a decision to carry to term as is accorded the decision to terminate a pregnancy; that is, a government may disfavor the decision to bear a child. As a result, there is no affirmative obligation that the state fund the decision to have a child, even where the state is obligated to fund abortion under its state constitution.

Litigators challenging the state's family cap in New Jersey submitted an international human rights amicus brief to support their claim, relying on CERD's prohibition of race discrimination, the ICCPR's guarantee of equality, and customary international law regarding children's well-being (Center for Economic and Social Rights 2002). The brief argued that in accordance with international law, the state had an affirmative obligation to provide subsistence support to all children, regardless of the circumstances of their birth. The New Jersey Supreme Court did not address these claims in any detail, but simply upheld the family cap policy as an appropriate exercise of government discretion under the state constitution (*Sojourner* 2003). To date, no judge has acknowledged the relevance of international human rights law to this issue.

Addressing the Limits of International Human Rights Law

As these examples illustrate, domestic activists using international human rights law face challenges that arise from the differences between domestic and international law. For example, the enforcement mechanisms in the international sphere are different from those employed domestically. Similarly, definitions of equality or the approaches to presenting claims may be quite distinct. The following section enumerates three of the most significant challenges and describes the approaches activists have taken to dealing with them.

International Human Rights Law Is Not Binding; State and Local Governments Are Not Held Accountable under International Law

According to one commentator, formal international human rights agreements rely only on the good will and good faith of existing governments for implementation; there is no effective international enforcement mechanism (Petchesky 1998). The enforcement issue inherent in international law is compounded by the domestic politics of the United States. In ratifying the ICCPR and CERD, the United States reiterated its long-standing position that international human rights treaties are non-self–executing and that ratified treaties cannot be used directly by U.S. litigants absent additional implementing legislation (International Covenant on Civil and Political Rights 1992; International Convention on the Elimination of All Forms of Racial Discrimination 1994). Treaties that have not been ratified by the United States are even less likely to be viewed as binding on state and local governments unless the principles in the treaty are, like some provisions of the CRC, found to be matters of customary international law.

The most innovative and ambitious way to sidestep the issue of whether international law is binding in the United States is to make international law "our law." This was the project undertaken by WILD. In San Francisco—admittedly one of the most progressive cities in the United States—CEDAW is now a matter of law, which is indisputably binding on San Francisco. Inspired by WILD's success, activists are mounting similar efforts to promote local adoption of both CEDAW and CERD in a number of other cities. These efforts, in Los Angeles, New York, Boston, and Milwaukee, will test the efficacy of "incorporation" strategy in more politically diverse communities. But given that twenty-three states and dozens of cities already support federal ratification of CEDAW (Milani 2001), the federal government's failure to ratify the convention is not likely to deter these governmental units from looking to CEDAW as a model for local legislation.

Strategic litigation may also move the issue of local implementation and enforcement. On the state level, judicial findings construing state law consistently with international human rights law or finding the existence of customary law make that law binding on the state or locality—and enforceable through domestic judicial channels. However, some litigators remain concerned that relying on international law sends a subtle message that domestic claims are weak. Because of this, international human rights arguments are often set out in amicus briefs rather than briefs filed by the parties (Post 2003). Even so, the international human rights discussions contained in these friend-of-the-court briefs serve incrementally to expose judges to the concepts of international human rights law (Albisa 2003). And despite their relative novelty in a domestic setting, a number of state courts have been willing to rely on human rights instruments to construe domestic law.

International Human Rights Is Not Relevant in the United States

Closely related to the claim that international law is not binding is the assertion that it is not even relevant to the United States. This is a common refrain in virtually every domestic forum in which human rights concepts are introduced, from the Senate to the classroom. In response, it is worth reiterating that human rights law is not external to state law, but reflects values generally shared by the United States—in part because of the U.S. government's active role in negotiating many of these international agreements. Moreover, in some instances, international human rights instruments share specific language and concepts with state constitutions.

Advocacy groups have dealt with this resistance by pursuing a course that makes the domestic connections with international human rights struggles indisputably real, at least to those active in the movement. In particular, although many advocates such as KWRU, SisterLove, and WEAP primarily focus their efforts on educating and organizing, this education is not limited to learning about the formal provisions of human rights. Rather, it extends to the interconnections between nations and people that make global conceptions of human rights necessary and relevant.

For example, KWRU has been active in opposing NAFTA and curbing actions of the World Trade Organization, arguing that it "destroy[s] millions of American jobs and allow[s] for the exploitation of workers in the third world" (KWRU 2003). In 2000, a delegation from KWRU visited El Salvador to connect with poor people's struggles in that nation; the organization also maintains contacts with groups elsewhere in Latin America and Canada. WEAP has worked directly with activists in Brazil, and SisterLove provides technical assistance to AIDS advocates in South Africa through its satellite office there. Indeed, a recent report surveying the practices of twenty "people's movements and NGOs" around the world, including KWRU, found that "All groups recognize the value of national as well as international outreach and alliances to their work, and have a wide range of partners across continents" (Hijab 2000). These individual connections across borders serve to confirm the common struggle of poor people worldwide and demonstrate by example that international human rights law is relevant to the U.S. experience.

Concerns about Unfamiliar Methodologies

Although international human rights principles are slowly gaining acceptance subnationally, international human rights methodologies have sometimes been more controversial. Such methodologies include extensive fact gathering by nongovernmental organizations, public hearings (sometimes called tribunals), and wide publication of the results. Because statistics and rigorous data are often not available—and may be in the control of the particular governmental entity under scrutiny—international human rights methodologies rely heavily on the cumulative weight of anecdotal evidence.

The Battered Mother's Testimony Project of the Wellesley Centers for Women used such human rights methodologies in developing a report on the treatment of domestic violence victims by the Massachusetts Family Courts. The report was a "multi-year, four-phase study using a variety of research approaches in which human rights fact finding was complemented by qualitative and quantitative social science research methodologies" (Wellesley Centers for Women 2002). The authors primarily relied on interviews with forty women across the state and forty-five victims' advocates, judges, and other court personnel; court records and other documentation confirming the information obtained in the interviews were reviewed in 25 percent of all cases. Based on this data, the study found that officials at nearly every family court in Massachusetts regularly commit "human rights violations" against battered women, that is, giving custody to batterers, ignoring women's claims of abuse, or denying them access to documents. The report included a number of recommendations for reforming the system, ranging from specific changes to the guardian ad litem system to increased funding for court interpreters.

According to Carrie Cuthbert, one of the report's coauthors, the reaction from family court judges was "universally negative" (Cuthbert 2003). Sean Dunphy, chief justice of the Massachusetts Family and Probate Courts, publicly asserted that a human rights approach "may work well for systems in Third World countries, but not for a court in the United States" (Lombardi 2003). As Dunphy later elaborated, he has no principled objection to the application of international human rights law domestically; his objections are to the traditional human rights methodologies that employ qualitative approaches. As he explained, unlike situations in which data are not readily available or sanctions may be attached to their use, researchers in Massachusetts had full access to the court records necessary to conduct a more rigorous statistical study of the courts' procedures. Under these circumstances, says Dunphy, "the human rights model doesn't seem appropriate" (Dunphy 2003). A study of the Arizona family courts that replicated the Massachusetts project's methodology and analysis has been similarly criticized by judges in that state (Cuthbert 2003; Post 2003; Arizona Coalition against Domestic Violence 2003).

Methodological critiques, often well founded, are an occupational hazard of social science research. But not all U.S. reports employing human rights fact-finding approaches have been subjected to these critiques. For example, Human Rights Watch used such an approach in its report on abstinence-only education in Texas (Human Rights Watch 2002). There, investigators interviewed staff and affiliates of four Texas-based federally funded abstinence-only programs, students in the programs, school officials in several districts, officials from relevant state and federal agencies, and a range of activists. The debate on the report has centered on the merits of abstinence-only education, rather than on methodology (Schleifer 2003). However, unlike the Wellesley Report, which criticizes state-level courts for deep-seated biases, the Human Rights Watch report takes aim at a federal policy, without assigning culpability to—or directing advocacy toward—state actors.

Further, because courts themselves are regularly engaged in fact finding, a report such as Wellesley's that scrutinizes courts may be particularly likely to raise methodological hackles. Similar debates have cropped up in other domestic contexts and even between coordinate branches of government. For example, in ruling on the constitutionality of the Violence against Women Act, the majority of the Supreme Court criticized Congress's fact-finding approach—an approach that is much more anecdotally based and cumulative than the formal evidentiary process of a courtroom setting (*United States v. Morrison* 2000).

Depending on activists' goals, a human rights approach to fact finding may still be the most effective, even if the methodology is subject to criticism from certain sectors. First, a "story-telling" approach can be a powerful tool for personalizing human rights issues. The media are particularly interested in how policies and practices affect individuals. If the goal is education and mobilization, individual stories will be more effective than cold statistics. Second, individual stories and anecdotes are the stock in trade of legislatures, the policy makers with ultimate authority over almost all state laws and policies. If the ultimate audience is the state legislature, a human rights fact-finding approach may be particularly appropriate and effective. Significantly, although the Arizona family court report met with hostility and criticism from judges, it nevertheless appears to have succeeded in promoting policy change: According to Diane Post, the report's author, many Arizona legislators have expressed interest in introducing legislation to address the report's recommendations (Post 2003).

Conclusion: Relevance of International Human Rights to Reproductive Rights and Reproductive Health in the United States

How might low-income women facing challenges to their reproductive health and rights use international human rights law at the state and local levels to expand their opportunities and choices? Three areas of potential advocacy emerge from these examples of international human rights activism: using human rights paradigms to broaden and energize coalitions; using human rights approaches to establish affirmative governmental obligations at the state and local levels; and expanding local gains to national fora.

Broadening Coalitions

Lawyer-activist Theresa McGovern has observed that in order to survive in a hostile political climate, "advocates for reproductive choice need to build a broader constituency and agenda . . . acknowledging and attempting to redress the larger disasters resulting from a lack of access to health care that many women face" (McGovern 2000). This observation is consistent with emerging understandings of human development work worldwide. Indeed, one nongovernmental organization in India argues that "activists focused on single issues are out of touch with people's concerns and cannot bring the multiple forces necessary to impact on the mainstream" (Hijab 2000). Likewise, Cheri Honkala argues that, particularly for poor women, "the right to choose includes the right to have children, intertwined with literacy, housing, domestic violence, you name it. All of these go into her choice" (Honkala 2003). A human rights approach to organizing, public education, and defining substantive rights is well suited to the task of expanding reproductive rights advocates' frame of reference.

One of the attractions of a human rights framework is its universal quality—not only does this paradigm unify people globally around a single expansive idea but it also encompasses and links a wide range of rights, from political to economic and social. In the U.S. context, employing a human rights paradigm also has the potential to break down—or at least not reinforce—ideological divisions that have sometimes hindered social movements (Diallo 2003; Ford Foundation 2004). There are strategic reasons for activists interested in building a broader constituency for reproductive health and rights to work in coalition with organizations that have a more comprehensive focus.

On the other hand, reproductive rights issues should not just be "swallowed up" by a larger human rights movement. Although a broad human rights agenda facilitates coalition building, there is also room within this agenda for specific, focused work to protect and expand reproductive health and rights. Organizations should strive to preserve their particular expertise and programmatic depth while broadening the scope of their work to reflect a human rights framework and to acknowledge the connections between reproductive health and other issues faced by low-income women. Approached in this way, reproductive health and rights can continue to serve as both an organizational focal point and as a gateway to a more comprehensive approach.

WEAP provides an example. Founded as a low-income women's rights organization, WEAP was well into its second decade when it deliberately shifted focus from specific health issues facing women of color to the larger context of human rights. Its goal was to avoid polarization and enhance effective coalition work. As a result of using more universal language, WEAP is now "more engaged with broader constituencies," including the Poor People's Economic Rights Campaign (Albisa 2003). In particular, WEAP has redefined its mission as fighting for universal health care, including the full range of reproductive care from health insurance to breast cancer treatment to support for the choice to have a child (Long Scott 2003). This new approach has required a realignment to accommodate new allies and new goals, but it has not compromised WEAP's substantive expertise on women's health issues.

The Institute of Women and Ethnic Studies in New Orleans, founded in 1994 to address the sexual and reproductive rights disparities facing women of color, has similarly found that the human rights framework allows it to be "part of a larger social change movement, and to work collectively, with more force and numbers," without compromising effectiveness (August 2003). Euna August, director of the institute, describes the process as an "evolution" that encouraged group members to take a much more holistic approach to reproductive rights. Instead of looking at health in isolation, they began to appreciate the "intersections between health, the economy, and education" (August 2003). This approach has informed their organizing and education work. For example, one of the institute's key organizing tools, the Reproductive Health Bill of Rights for Women of Color, uses the UDHR as a model to situate reproductive health in a larger context.

Significantly, the human rights framework provides a bridge to other reproductive rights advocates worldwide in addition to broader social movements within the United States. Advocates around the globe have adopted the human rights framework for their local reproductive health and rights advocacy. For example, during a campaign to address reproductive health issues in small towns, the Romanian Coalition for Reproductive Health successfully argued that providing family planning training at a local medical dispensary was a human rights issue (Draghici 2003). Taking up the human rights framework and employing a more inclusive human rights language would link local, U.S.-based activists directly with this international movement.

Expanding Affirmative Obligations

International agreements often speak directly to low-income women's reproductive health and rights, providing a normative grounding for targeted activism. As Rosalind Petchesky has noted, feminists "hav[e] achieved significant success at the level of theoretical visions and United Nations rhetoric" (Petchesky 1998), and that success is reflected in the specific language of a series of international agreements. As early as the UDHR (1948), international law accepted the proposition that states parties must act affirmatively to ensure equality and basic access to fundamental rights.

More recently, the Cairo agreement expressed a global consensus that population control should be approached from a perspective of empowerment. In particular, "[Cairo] achieved worldwide consensus that population is a top-ranking issue worthy of consideration at the highest level by all governments; it placed the discussion of population firmly in a development context; and it identified women and their status as central to sustainable global development efforts" (Cohen and Richards 1994). As the preamble to the Cairo Programme of Action notes: "The 1994 conference was explicitly given a broader mandate on development issues than previous population conferences, reflecting the growing awareness that population, poverty, patterns of production and consumption and other threats to the environment are so closely interconnected that none of them can be considered in isolation." As a result of this broad mandate, the Cairo Programme urges governments to provide "universal access to a full range of safe and reliable family planning methods and to related reproductive health services" and calls for an unprecedented commitment of funds devoted to implementing the reproductive-health-related aspects of the document in developing countries (United Nations 1994).

The principles set out in the Cairo Programme of Action were reaffirmed in July 1999 at the five-year review of the 1994 agreement (Center for Reproductive Rights 2000a). These same insights were reiterated at the World Conference for Women, held in Beijing in 1995, and in the Beijing + 5 conference in New York in 2000 (Center for Reproductive Rights 2000a).

Significantly, Beijing + 5 also incorporated the agreements reached in Cairo into the final review document, including specific time frames for addressing maternal mortality, provision of safe and effective contraception, and reduction of young people's risk to HIV/AIDS (Center for Reproductive Rights 2000b). This same education- and empowerment-centered approach to women's reproductive health and rights is reflected in international conventions, including CEDAW and the ICESCR.

Local and state activists should take particular advantage of the existing international frameworks to expand obligations of state and municipal governments to address reproductive rights and health. San Francisco's CEDAW, which mandates that the city actively review policies and procedures through a gender lens, provides a model. Further, the existence in many state constitutions of affirmative obligations to provide abortion funding for low-income women or to provide for the public health or welfare of state citizens more generally lays the conceptual groundwork for requiring that states affirmatively address reproductive health and rights. As state court rulings in the area of Medicaid-funded abortion indicate, these affirmative obligations extend to providing funding to enable exercise of rights.

One policy in which such affirmative obligations might be particularly helpful is in legislative efforts to address the family cap, adopted by more than twenty states. Although court cases challenging family caps have kept the issue in the public eye, their impact on policy has been at the margins.[11] Successful lawsuits have, for example, required that excluded children in Indiana and California be eligible for child support payments and mandated that the family cap program in Nebraska exempt families headed by disabled parents (Levin-Epstein 2003). However, advocates in Illinois recently succeeded in securing repeal of a family cap that had been implemented in 1995. According to attorney Wendy Pollack, who led the effort, convincing legislators that repeal was the "right thing to do" was critical to their success. A broad coalition, including the Catholic Conference, contributed to the repeal effort (Center for Law and Social Policy 2003).

Although international human rights law was not an explicit factor in the Illinois repeal, advocates seeking to replicate this result elsewhere should include a human rights component as part of the strategy. Not only would such a framework enlist a broader coalition to oppose the cap but it would also highlight the underlying assault on human dignity—recognized world-wide—of denying welfare benefits to certain children because of the circumstances of their birth. Further, unlike arguments that are particular to the politics of an individual state such as budget constraints or implementation issues, a human rights rationale is universal and can be readily extended to other states as well as to efforts to bar the family cap through national legislation.

International human rights law could also be brought to bear on a number of other reproductive health issues. For example, current iterations of abstinence-only education, which deny children access to comprehensive information about contraception, run afoul of both CEDAW and the CRC. Both of these international instruments—neither of which has been ratified by the United States—have been interpreted to require sex education that addresses HIV/AIDS prevention, adolescent pregnancy, and family planning. In addition, the ICCPR, to which the United States is a signatory, has been interpreted to require access to reproductive health education (Center for Reproductive Rights 2002b; Human Rights Watch 2002).

Litigation alone is unlikely to be successful as a strategy to attack the implementation of abstinence-only education on the state level; the international conventions that speak most directly to the issues have not been ratified by the United States and would be difficult to enforce directly. Instead, activists might begin by combining constituent organizing centered on international human rights and sex education with a public information campaign underscoring state constitutional provisions that establish a state-level right to education.[12] The language of international human rights, which views sex education as an issue of individual empowerment, could aid in repositioning such education as an aspect of the fundamental right to education under state law. Under that analysis, a state could not hide behind federal funding restrictions that limit federal abstinence-only money to certain restricted initiatives. Rather, the state would have an affirmative obligation to support its own programs that offer unbiased comprehensive education, including education on reproductive health.

In using international human rights law to directly influence subnational policies concerning reproductive rights and health, domestic advocates would be joining a vibrant worldwide movement working to implement human rights at the local level, often to benefit low-income people. Such efforts are particularly important in federal systems, in which implementation must occur at every level of government in order to be effective.

The Centre for Equal Rights in Accommodation (CERA), based in Canada, provides an example. Canada has a categorical system of federalism comparable to that of the United States, with provinces primarily responsible for health, social services, and education (United Nations [Canada] 1998). CERA has focused its human rights work on the provincial level. For example, in 2003, CERA challenged an Ontario policy of removing rent control for welfare recipients—a policy that makes it almost impossible for a single mother with children to find affordable housing. In its briefs, CERA argued that Ontario's policy violated the ICESCR, which Canada has ratified, quoting a United Nations committee's statement criticizing Ontario's policy (Goba 2003).

On the local level, CERA recently succeeded in convincing the Ottawa city council to adopt the principles of the ICESCR as part of its twenty-year city plan. The plan now obligates the city to "[p]romote the full realization of the right to housing of Ottawa's residents as articulated in Article 11(1) of the United Nations Covenant on Economic, Social and Cultural Rights, which was ratified by the Government of Canada and all provincial governments" (Goba 2003). Such provisions, which put the onus on government to recognize basic human rights, can be important tools for local advocates of reproductive rights as well as other social needs.

Bottom-up Strategies

Professor Catherine Powell has posited that state and local governments can serve as catalysts and leaders in ensuring that governmental policies at all levels conform to human rights norms (Powell 2001). In the reproductive health arena, for example, a groundswell of states repealing family cap policies on human rights grounds might trigger renewed criticism of the caps on the federal level—a hypothetical example of the "dialogic federalism" that Powell envisions, in which the international, federal, and subnational governments are in a constant back and forth about appropriate policies to promote social welfare. Operating within Powell's paradigm, state and local entities have considerable influence over federal policy, particularly when a number of states unite around a particular approach. However, state and local policy makers must have a better appreciation of their role in the federal system to more effectively use their leverage to promote national change—understanding both their control over substantive policies and their role in implementing human rights norms.

San Francisco's CEDAW experience provides a sobering example of the existing gaps in understanding. Reproductive rights and health fall squarely within the health care prong of the city's CEDAW. But even the sympathetic bureaucrats of San Francisco have not taken steps to address these rights under the city's law. Says Sonia Melara, former executive director of the Commission on the Status of Women, "There has not been anything actively done under the ordinance concerning reproductive rights because it is such a federal issue" (Melara 2003). Ann Lehman, the analyst responsible for overseeing CEDAW's implementation in San Francisco, agrees: "Though you could have a more human rights approach to restrictions on reproductive rights, that is really at the federal level" (Lehman 2003).

In fact, many aspects of reproductive health and rights are subject to state and local regulation. Compounded by the 1996 devolution of welfare to the states, very little reproductive health policy aside from *Roe v. Wade*, foreign aid, and military medical care is purely federal. Nearly two dozen states provide for at least some government-funded abortions, despite federal denial of funds. Almost thirty states have refused to adopt family cap laws, despite federal permission to do so (Center for Law and Social Policy 2003). California and several localities have refused federal abstinence-only education funds because restrictions undermine a responsible public health message to teens. Marriage promotion programs proposed as part of federal welfare reform would be largely crafted and implemented on the state and local levels. In short, were San Francisco to fully exercise its mandate under CEDAW, it could have a significant impact on the reproductive rights and health of low-income women in San Francisco.

By broadening coalitions, energizing existing constituencies, and addressing a new set of governmental actors, subnational activism to address reproductive health issues in the United States has the potential to make a real difference for women. And as states and localities begin to address human rights explicitly and affirmatively through their policies and enlist a range of global allies, the national dialogue on women's reproductive health and rights will necessarily respond by engaging these issues.

Such a "trickling up" of rights from the local to the national level is not unprecedented. Women were permitted to vote in many state and local elections before they secured the federal right to vote; when *Roe v. Wade* was decided, one-third of states had already paved the way by liberalizing their abortion statutes (*Roe v. Wade* 1973). Efforts to mandate contraceptive equity in employment-based health insurance seem to be following a similar path, with states currently taking the lead in enacting new laws while the federal government moves more slowly (Roos 2002).

International human rights obligations have not previously been implemented in this way. But using international human rights as a framework for local advocacy has the potential to produce a "paradigm shift" in the public discussion of low-income women's reproductive health and rights, just as KWRU's Cheri Honkala predicts it will with respect to their economic rights. The Cairo Programme could well be implemented in the United States from the ground up.

Notes

1. Founded in 1988, the People's Decade of Human Rights Education is an international service organization that works primarily with women's and social justice organizations to develop and advance human rights education in the context of struggles for social and economic justice. More information on its trainings can be found at www.pdhre.org.
2. The questionnaire is now available on line at www.kwru.org.
3. From colonial times, the United States' poor laws reflected Elizabethan presumptions of community control and responsibility (Katz 1986). After a six-decade period from 1935 to 1996, when the federal government exercised somewhat more authority over these issues, the Personal Responsibility and Work Opportunities Reconciliation Act of 1996 returned primary authority to the states and their subdivisions (Personal Responsibility and Work Opportunities Reconciliation Act 1996). Because of this welfare "devolution," states, counties, and even local governments once again have increased responsibility for establishing and enforcing the laws that govern poor women's reproductive choices. Exercising these prerogatives, West Virginia now awards a $100 bonus to welfare recipients who marry, twenty-two states deny welfare benefits to children born to women on welfare as a means to deter these births, and almost every state has responded to federal carrots and designed a program to administer restricted federal funds to promote "abstinence-only until marriage" (M. Davis 2002a; NOW Legal Defense and Education Fund 2003). In the early 1990s, activists fought hard to maintain federal authority over these programs, recognizing that historically the federal government was less likely to be captured by extreme political or religious political forces that might impose punitive measures on women who failed to conform to supposed social norms. Having lost that battle with the 1996 demise of a federal welfare entitlement, however, activism has continued at the state and local levels (Abramovitz 1996; Bhargava 2002). As federal authority in the area recedes, activists may increasingly seek to enlist international law to support their cause.
4. I am indebted to Cathy Albisa and Rhonda Copelon for this argument and references.
5. The treaty obligations, however, remain in effect on the federal government. The Human Rights Committee noted "with satisfaction the assurances of the [U.S.] Government that its declaration regarding the federal system is not a reservation and is not intended to affect the international obligations of the United States" (Concluding Observations/Comments). The Senate's approach to human rights treaties "merely displaces the primary implementation burden from the national government to each of the states . . . encourag[ing] unique enforcement solutions tailored to each state's specific situation" (Thomas 2002).
6. This is fully consistent with the approach adopted by other federal systems participating in the United Nations. For example, Canada, which has a categorical federal system that leaves certain areas of policy making to the provinces, explicitly acknowledges the levels of governmental accountability in its reporting to the United Nations. Canada's most recent report on CEDAW implementation included specific appendices on the state of implementation in each province (Fifth Report of Canada). In its consideration of Canada's report, the CEDAW Committee addressed a number of issues of provincial implementation while reiterat-

ing that the national government was the responsible signatory to the convention (CEDAW Committee).

7. The CEDAW task force implementing the ordinance officially expired in June 2003. However, the San Francisco Commission on the Status of Women incorporated human rights principles into its five-year action plan, approved in February 2003. Among other things, the plan creates a new CEDAW committee and calls for linking compliance with CEDAW principles to the city budget and performance evaluations (Ford Foundation 2004; Lozner 2004).

8. The United States House of Representatives has also entered the fray. House Resolution 568, under consideration by the House Judiciary Committee, would discourage federal judges from citing international and foreign authority when rendering constitutional decisions (U.S. House of Representatives 2004).

9. Although this issue has polarized the U.S. Supreme Court, high courts of other nations regularly cite international and comparative law. For example, members of South Africa's Constitutional Court addressing the constitutionality of the death penalty examined decisions from India, Zimbabwe, Jamaica, Germany, Canada, the United States, the European Court of Human Rights, Hungary, the United Nations Committee on Human Rights, Botswana, Hong Kong, and Tanzania (L'Heureaux-Dube 1998). The Israeli, Canadian, and Indian supreme courts also have long traditions of looking for wisdom from sister jurisdictions in other nations (Epp 1998; M. Davis 2000). A recent commentator identified five quite substantial justifications offered by judges for this practice: 1. concern for the rule of law, 2. desire to promote universal values, 3. reliance on international law to uncover values inherent within domestic regimes, 4. willingness to invoke logic of judges in other jurisdictions, and 5. concern to avoid negative assessments within the international community (Bahdi 2002).

10. See, for example, *New Hampshire v. Robert H.* (1978) (citing ICCPR and ICESCR to support the assertion that parental rights are natural and inherent under the state constitution in action to terminate parental rights); *Commonwealth v. Edward Sadler* (1979) (citing the UDHR to support the holding that the state had an obligation to educate juveniles in custody).

11. *Williams v. Humphreys* (2000), which challenged Indiana's family cap in federal court, required that the state modify the policy to permit pass-through of child support to otherwise excluded children.

12. Forty-nine state constitutions provide for a right education in some form (Andres 1995). Six states provide for a constitutional right to public health.

References

Abramovitz, M. 1996. *Under Attack, Fighting Back: Women and Welfare in the United States.* New York: Monthly Review Press.

Albisa, C. 2003. Personal communication, April 5. Director of U.S. Programs, Center for Economic and Social Rights, New York, N.Y.

Andres, G. D. 1995. "Private School Voucher Remedies in Education Cases." 62 U. Chi. L. Rev. 795.

Arizona Coalition against Domestic Violence. 2003. *Battered Mothers' Testimony*

Project: A Human Rights Approach to Child Custody and Domestic Violence.
Phoenix, Arizona: Arizona Coalition against Domestic Violence.

Atkins v. Virginia, 536 U.S. 304 (2002).

August, E. 2003. Personal communication, May 30. Executive director, Institute of Women and Ethnic Studies, New Orleans.

Bahdi, R. 2002. "Globalization of Judgment: Transjudicialism and the Five Faces of International Law in Domestic Courts." 34 Geo. Wash. Int'l L. Rev. 555.

Bhargava, D. 2002. "Progressive Organizing on Welfare Policy." In Gary Delgado, ed., *From Poverty to Punishment: How Welfare Reform Punishes the Poor,* 199–208. Oakland, Cal.: Applied Research Center.

Bricker-Jenkins, M. 2003. Personal communication, June 4. Professor, School of Social Administration, Temple University, Philadelphia.

CEDAW Committee. 2003. Consideration of Reports of States Parties: Canada. CEDAW/C/2003/I/CRP.3/Add.5/Rev.1.

Center for Economic and Social Rights. 2002. Amicus brief, *Sojourner v. N.J. Dep't of Human Services.* 177 N.J. 318, 828 A. 2d 306 (Aug. 4, 2003). http://cesr.org/node/view/459.

Center for Law and Social Policy. 2003. "Repealing the Family Cap in Illinois: An Interview with Wendy Pollack." CLASP *Newsletter* 16(9): 5–6. www.clasp.org.

Center for Reproductive Rights. 1999. *Cairo + 5: Assessing U.S. Support for Reproductive Health at Home and Abroad.* New York: Center for Reproductive Rights.

———. 2002a. *Beijing + 5: Assessing Reproductive Rights.* New York: Center for Reproductive Rights.

———. 2002b. *Bringing Rights to Bear.* New York: Center for Reproductive Rights.

CERD (International Convention on the Elimination of All Forms of Racial Discrimination). 1994. 140 Cong. Rec. S7634–02 (daily ed., June 24).

———. Summary Record. 2001. CERD/C/SR.1474, August 22, paras. 3, 22.

Cohen, S. A., and C. L. Richards. 1994. "The Cairo Consensus: Population, Development and Women." *International Family Planning Perspectives* 26(6): 150–155.

Commonwealth v. Edward Sadler, 3 Phila. Co. Rprtr. 316, 330 (Pa. Com. Pl. 1979).

Concluding Observations of the Human Rights Committee: United States of America. 1995. CCPC/C/79/Add.50; A/50/40/paras. 266–304. March 10.

Convention Against Torture and Other Cruel, Inhuman or Degrading Treatment or Punishment. 1990. 136 Cong. Rec. S17486–01 (daily ed., October 27).

Crosby v. National Foreign Trade Council, 530 U.S. 363 (2000).

Curry, L. 2003. Personal communication, June 4. Representative, Pennsylvania General Assembly, Harrisburg, Pa.

Cuthbert, C. 2003. Personal communication, July 14. Founding co-director, Women's Rights Network, Wellesley Centers for Women, Wellesley, Mass.

Davis, M. 2000. "International Human Rights and United States Law: Predictions of Courtwatcher." 64 Alb. L. Rev. 417.

———. 2002a. "Legislating Patriarchy." In Gary Delgado, ed., *From Poverty to Punishment: How Welfare Reform Punishes the Poor,* 147–154. Oakland, Cal.: Applied Research Center.

———. 2002b. *Women's Rights in Theory and Practice: Employment, Violence and Poverty.* Washington, D.C.: Woodrow Wilson Center.

Davis, N. 2000. "Welfare Organizing at the Grassroots." *Colorlines.* www.arc.org/C_lines/CLArchives/story3_3_08.html.

Dharmaraj, K. 2003. Personal communication, July 17. Executive director, WILD for Human Rights, San Francisco.

Diallo, D. 2003. Personal communication, May 28. Executive director, SisterLove, Inc., Atlanta.

Doe v. Maher, 40 Conn. Supp. 394, 515 A.2d 134 (Conn. Super. 1986).

Draghici, D. 2003. Personal communication, May 30. Coordinator, Romanian NGO Reproductive Health Coalition, Bucharest.

Dunphy, S. 2003. Personal communication, August 1. Chief judge, Massachusetts Family and Probate Courts, Boston.

Epp, C. R. 1998. *The Rights Revolution: Lawyers, Activists and Supreme Courts in Comparative Perspective.* Chicago: University of Chicago Press.

Fifth Report of Canada. Covering the Period April 1994–March 1998, Convention on the Elimination of All Forms of Discrimination against Women. CEDAW/C/CAN/5 and Add. 1.

Fleming, L. N. 2003. "Plan to Aid Affordable Housing." *Philadelphia Inquirer,* June 3, B1.

Ford Foundation. 2004. *Close to Home: Case Studies of Human Rights Work in the United States.* New York: Ford Foundation.

Friesen, J. 2000. *State Constitutional Law: Litigating Individual Rights, Claims and Defenses.* New York: LEXIS Publishing.

General Assembly of Pennsylvania. 2002. House Resolution no. 473.

Gilbert, M., and M. Masucci. 1998. *Pilot Program to Develop a Community-Based Information Technology Use Service Learning Course between Temple University and Kensington Welfare Rights Union.* Philadelphia: Philadelphia Network for Neighborhood Development.

Ginsburg, R. B., and D. J. Merritt. 1999. "Fifty-first Cardozo Memorial Lecture: Affirmative Action: An International Human Rights Dialogue." 21 Cardozo L. Rev. 253.

Goba, R. 2003. Personal communication, September 10. Staff attorney, Centre for Equal Rights in Accommodation, Toronto.

Harris v. McRae, 448 U.S. 297 (1980).

Hawkins, S. 2003. Personal communication, November 7. Executive director, National Coalition to Abolish the Death Penalty.

Hershkoff, H. 1999. "Welfare Devolution and State Constitutions." 67 Fordham L. Rev. 1,403.

Hijab, N. 2000. *Human Rights and Human Development: Learning from Those Who Act.* Human Development Report 2000 Background Paper. New York: United Nations Development Program. www.hdr.udnp.org/docs/publications/background_papers/Hijab2000.html.

Honkala, C. 2003. Personal communication, May 30. Executive director, Kensington Welfare Rights Union, Philadelphia.

Human Rights Watch. 2002. *Ignorance Only: HIV/AIDS, Human Rights and Federally-Funded Abstinence-Only Programs in the United States: Texas: A Case Study.* New York: Human Rights Watch.

ICCPR (International Covenant on Civil and Political Rights). 1992. 138 Cong. Rec. S4781–01 (daily ed., April 2).

Katz, M. B. 1986. *In the Shadow of the Poorhouse: A Social History of Welfare in America.* New York: Basic Books.

KWRU (Kensington Welfare Rights Union). 2003. Philadelphia. www.kwru.org.

Lawrence v. Texas, 123 S.Ct. 2472 (2003).

Lehman, A. 2003. Personal communication, July 17. Policy analyst, Commission on the Status of Women, San Francisco.

Levin-Epstein, J. 2003. *Lifting the Lid off the Family Cap: States Revisit Problematic Policy for Welfare Mothers.* CLASP Policy Brief, Childbearing and Reproductive Health Series no. 1. Washington, D.C.: Center for Law and Social Policy.

L'Heureaux-Dube, C. 1998. "The Importance of Dialogue: Globalization and the International Impact of the Rehnquist Court." 34 Tulsa L.J. 15, 38.

Lombardi, K. 2003. "Custodians of Abuse (Continued)." *Boston Phoenix*, January 9–16. www.bostonphoenix.com.

Long Scott, E. 2003. Personal communication, June 20. Executive director, Women's Economic Agenda Project, Oakland, Cal.

Lozner, S. 2004. "Diffusion of Local Regulatory Innovations: The San Francisco CEDAW Ordinance and the New York City Human Rights Initiative." 104 Colum. L. Rev. 768.

McGovern, T. M. 2000. *Building Broader Women's Health/Reproductive Healthcare Coalitions in the States: A Look at Idaho, Texas, and Florida.* New York: Open Society Institute.

Melara, S. 2003. Personal communication, July 17. Former executive director, Commission on the Status of Women, San Francisco.

Milani, L. R., ed. 2001. *Human Rights for All: CEDAW: Working for Women around the World and at Home.* Washington, D.C.: Working Group on Ratification of the U.N. Convention on the Elimination of All Forms of Discrimination against Women.

New Hampshire v. Robert H., 393 A.2d 1387 (N.H. 1978).

New Mexico Right to Choose/NARAL v. Johnson, 126 N.M. 788 (1999).

NOW Legal Defense and Education Fund. 2003. *Welfare and Poverty: State Marriage Initiatives.* New York: NOW Legal Defense and Education Fund. www.nowldef.org/html/issues/wel/statemarriage.shtml. N.B. NOWLDEF has changed its name to Legal Momentum.

NOW Legal Defense and Education Fund et al. 2002. Amicus curiae brief, *Grutter v. Bollinger, Gratz v. Bollinger*, Nos. 02–241 & 02–516, 2002 U.S. Briefs 241.

Pauley v. Kelly, 162 W.Va. 672, 255 S.E.2d 859 (1979).

Personal Responsibility and Work Opportunities Reconciliation Act of 1996. Pub. L. No. 104–193 (1996), 110 Stat. 2105 (1996).

Petchesky, R. P. 1998. "Introduction." In R. P. Petchesky, and K. Judd, *Negotiating Reproductive Rights: Women's Perspectives across Countries and Cultures.* London: Zed Books.

Poor People's Economic Human Rights Campaign. 2003. www.economichumanrights.org.

Post, D. 2003. Personal communication, July 15. Executive director, Arizona Coalition against Domestic Violence, Phoenix.

Powell, C. 2001. "Dialogic Federalism: Constitutional Possibilities for Incorporation of Human Rights Law in the United States." 150 U.Pa. L. Rev. 245.

Printz v. United States, 521 U.S. 898 (1997).

Resnik, J. 2001. "Categorical Federalism: Jurisdiction, Gender, and the Globe." 111 Yale L.J. 619.

Roe v. Wade, 410 U.S. 113 (1973).

Roos, B. 2002. "Note: The Quest for Equality: Comprehensive Insurance Coverage of Prescription Contraceptives." 82 B.U. L. Rev. 1289.

Roper v. Simmons, 73 U.S.L.W. 4153 (March 1, 2005).

Sabir, W. 2002. "Bus Tour Campaigns for Right to Work and Living Wage." *Oakland Tribune.* August 26. www.weap.org/press/pdfs/2002/oak_trib_8_02.pdf.

Sappenfield, M. 2003. "In One US City, Life under a UN Treaty on Women." *Christian Science Monitor.* January 30. www.csmonitor.com/2003/0130/p01s03_ussc. html.

Schleifer, R. 2003. Personal communication, June 11. Researcher, HIV/AIDS and Human Rights Program, Human Rights Watch, New York, NY.

SisterLove. 2003. Atlanta. www.SisterLove.org.

Sojourner v. N.J. Department of Human Services, 177 N.J. 318, 828 A.2d 306 (Aug. 4, 2003).

State ex rel. Simmons v. Roper, Mo. LEXIS 123 (Aug. 26, 2003).

Spiro, P. 1997. "The States and International Human Rights." 66 Fordham L. Rev. 567.

Streib, V. L. 2003. *The Juvenile Death Penalty Today: Death Sentences and Executions for Juvenile Crimes, Jan. 1, 1973–June 30, 2003.* www.law.onu.edu/faculty/ streib.

Thomas M. 2002. "Rogue States within American Borders: Remedying State Noncompliance with the International Covenant on Civil and Political Rights." 90 Cal. L. Rev. 165, 173.

Thul, L. 1997. "A Week in the Life with the Kensington Welfare Rights Union: Day 5, July 25, 1997." kwru.org/kwru/dayfive.html.

Tushnet, M. V. 1987. *The NAACP's Legal Strategy against Segregated Education, 1925–1950.* Chapel Hill: University of North Carolina Press.

United Nations. 1994. *International Conference on Population and Development. Programme of Action.* New York: United Nations.

United Nations (Canada). 1998. International Human Rights Instruments, Core Document forming part of the reports of States Parties: Canada. 12/01/98, at para. 66.

United States v. Morrison, 529 U.S. 598 (2000).

U.S. House of Representatives. 2004. House Resolution 568.

Valley Hospital Ass'n v. Mat-Su Coalition for Choice, 948 P.2d 963 (Alas. 1997).

Wellesley Centers for Women. 2002. *Battered Mothers Speak Out: A Human Rights Report on Domestic Violence and Child Custody in Massachusetts Family Courts.* Wellesley: Wellesley Centers for Women.

Williams v. Humphreys, 125 F. Supp.2d 881 (2000).

WEAP (Women's Economic Agenda Project). 2003. Oakland, Cal. www.weap.org.

Zucchino, D. 1997. *Myth of the Welfare Queen.* New York: Scribner.

Conclusion

WENDY CHAVKIN

"Where, after all, do universal human rights begin? In small
places, close to home—so close and so small that they cannot be
seen on any map of the world . . . unless these rights have meaning there, they have little meaning anywhere. Without concerted
citizen action to uphold them close to home, we shall look in vain
for progress in the larger world"
(Roosevelt 1958).

Where is a small place close to home
today? Is it an office in India where women answer telephone queries from
complaining customers in Indiana? A room where women watch Michael
Jackson on TV in Peru? Where they answer a cell phone in rural Botswana?
And what is home? Algeria or the suburbs of Paris? A council flat in London where a woman lives with her two children? Or an apartment in
Stockholm where a Swedish man spends his "daddy months" of paid leave
caring for his baby?

Many forces destabilize the realities today's adults knew as children:
the globalization of the world's economy and ascendance of transnational corporations, the post-Soviet unipolar hegemony of the United States, together
with massive migrations spurred by economic imperatives and war—all ren-
der the construct of the nation-state, the rules of international relations, and
the role of the United Nations contested and murky. Global media present
images of wealth and extravagant consumption to those living in extreme poverty. Fundamentalist movements have arisen around the world. Wars and terrorism assault daily stability, while governmental security responses raise civil
rights concerns. Long-term shifts in women's and men's participation in employment and childrearing have accelerated, and the resulting questions about
the meaning of gender and family contribute to a sense of profound disloca-

tion. The meaning of so many components of identity are no longer fixed—gender, ethnicity, religion, citizenship.

There had been such hope after the 1993, 1994, and 1995 Vienna, Cairo, and Beijing conferences. The World Conference on Human Rights in Vienna affirmed women's rights as integral to all human rights and accorded priority to women's participation in every aspect of life, free from discrimination. At the International Conference on Population and Development (ICPD) in Cairo and the UN World Conference on Women in Beijing, the strength and efficacy of popular activism, in the form of NGOs, shone clearly on the world stage. There, 179 nations had formally acknowledged profound changes in paradigms for economic growth, stabilizing population, and sustaining the environment. The new paradigm specified that advancing women's status was a prerequisite for reducing poverty, achieving sustainable development, and improving public health, and it advanced fertility control as a human right rather than for the sake of its social utility. The world community, under the umbrella of the United Nations, agreed to advance women's welfare and agency and thus made a commitment to reproductive and sexual rights. Ten years ago, we celebrated this international consensus as a major advance.

In the decade since then, transnational corporations and nonstate institutions, such as the World Bank and International Monetary Fund, have ascended to new levels of dominance, propelling forward neoliberal economic policies, with the consequent widening of economic disparities, and challenging the capability and meaning of the nation-state. Other transnational forces have also grown, including both global civil society and terrorist networks and alliances. Wars and ethnic conflicts abound, creating vast refugee populations in their wakes and draining resources from economic development. The United States has increasingly acted unilaterally, both militarily and by sidestepping multilateral and UN agreements, although in contrast, formal creation of the European Community represents a step toward international cooperation.

Infectious diseases have surged, with international travel and migration fueling global transmission. The HIV epidemic is poised to explode in new continents. The development of antiretroviral medications offers the potential to convert death sentences to chronic illness, but also raises questions for prevention strategies and highlights staggering disparities in access to treatment and care. Other major scientific breakthroughs—from genomics to stem cells to assisted reproductive technologies—open doors of thrilling therapeutic possibility at the same time that they underscore inequity in access.

In 2000, 156 heads of state gathered at the United Nations for a Millennium Summit and issued a Millennium Declaration, a statement of principles and objectives for the twenty-first century that affirmed human rights. Civil society participated through a separate Millennium Forum. The declaration established measurable goals and targets for reducing poverty, hunger, disease, illiteracy, environmental degradation, and discrimination against women, and charted a roadmap focused on implementation of eight Millennium Development Goals (MDGs). The United Nations collaborated with the International Monetary Fund (IMF), World Bank, and Organization for Economic Cooperation and Development to establish targets and indicators to measure progress, with task forces of scholars and UN staff also participating (Millennium Development Goals 2000).

Women's groups have actively critiqued these developments. They point to the paradox that the Millennium Project assigned responsibility to the nation-state for provision of key educational and health services by the very transnational players whose economic policies undermine the capacity of the nation-state to do so. They express grave concern about the omission of combating racism and militarism in the list of MDGs. They have been profoundly upset that reproductive and sexual health and rights are not explicitly on the list. Many consider this to be a fundamental retreat from the gains of Cairo and Beijing, reflecting the upsurge in power of religious fundamentalism. Key insights of the Cairo and Beijing meetings were that reproductive and sexual health and rights were essential in order to make progress on all of those fronts enumerated in the MDGs. Promoting gender equity (#3), reducing child mortality (#4), improving maternal health (#5), and combating HIV/AIDS (#6) all have reproductive and sexual health and rights as obvious lynchpins, but the other MDGs—reducing poverty, promoting primary education, environmental sustainability and development—also require advancing reproductive and sexual health and rights and women's status. It was the integration of these that made the Cairo–Beijing paradigm such a profound advance.

The 179 countries at the ICPD in 1994 signed on to a twenty-year Programme of Action. We are now at a halfway point—a key moment for taking stock. According to the recently published report card on reproductive and sexual health and rights ("Countdown 2015" 2004), important progress has been made in improving girls' enrollment in secondary school, in increasing women's share of parliamentary seats and participation in non-agricultural employment, as well as in increased use of contraception. On the other hand, women are still profoundly underrepresented in education and elected positions, and gender wage gaps prevail, as does unmet need for contraception. Maternal mortality has stagnated at appallingly high levels and while many abortion laws have become more liberal, 13 percent of pregnancies (19 million per year) still end in unsafe abortions. Teenage pregnancy rates have barely budged, and the HIV pandemic has both worsened in general and for women specifically. In real money, international donors are honoring approximately 40 percent of their ICPD commitments (with the Scandinavian countries in the lead), with the largest share of the money going to HIV/AIDS and declining shares going to family planning, basic reproductive health services, and research and policy.

In this past difficult decade, our attention has been pulled to the dislocations and the political struggles convulsing the world. Disputed gender roles have been flashpoints in the turmoil. It is critical at such a moment that activists and scholars dedicated to women's rights pause from the demanding and riveting concerns of the immediate in order to develop a long-term perspective. By bringing together in this book eight examples of local activism, we hope to contribute to such an assessment and thus inform strategies to further reproductive and sexual rights and health globally. Each of these chapters tells the story of a particular effort to implement the Cairo agenda and reflects on the utility of a human rights approach. Although we need to learn from each story's specificity, there are several crosscutting themes that can inform future strategies to advance the Cairo principles in this increasingly complicated world.

Relativity versus Universality: Tensions between Religion, Culture, and Rights

Religion has proven to be among the toughest arenas for advancing reproductive and sexual health and rights. Fundamentalist religious proponents have increasingly resisted the implementation of the Cairo-Beijing principles both locally and at the United Nations. In fact, many couch their resistance to the economic dominance of the developed world and the changes attendant upon "globalization" in terms of culture or religion. Some frame their defense of traditional gender roles in a meld of religious and nationalist-style terms, and label ideas about reproductive and sexual rights as encroaching Western values. This stance has, in turn, generated opposition from critics who have tried different strategies: to unpack the conflation of distress against the economic dominance of the developed world and the fast pace of change with adherence to fundamentalist religion; to analyze whose ends are served by casting the struggle within this framework; to demonstrate internal inconsistencies or interpretations of cultural and religious practices; and to appeal to secular national and international law. Although this tension runs through many of the chapters, three tackle it head on and delineate several of the varied situations and approaches in which this issue is currently in play. In varied fashions, all repudiate the idea that reproductive and sexual health and rights present conflicts with culture and religion, and explore diverse tactical approaches to advance both.

Ortiz-Ortega examines the long-term multipronged effort by the Catholic Church to make its teachings and behavioral proscriptions the law of the land in Mexico. She examines the Mexican version of the Latin American phenomenon of *doble discurso*, which she describes as widespread private flouting of publicly espoused conservative behavioral norms, particularly regarding sexuality and reproduction. The church-influenced conservativism of the public discourse has enabled the government to avoid providing reproductive health services. This informal balancing act has the harshest consequences for the poor, who are least able to negotiate this extralegal system and lack resources to purchase private care, as those with money do. She explains that the Mexican state's recent quiet liberalization of abortion laws appeased growing demands for such change, while neither challenging doble discurso nor providing services or regulation. This omission of services flouts the Cairo–Beijing insight that access to care is an essential component of rights.

Imam's chapter also locates the conflict between a rights model and a religious/nationalist identity model within the context of struggle between a secular state apparatus and religious domination of the public consensus. The situation she describes in northern Nigeria is starker than that in Mexico, as several Nigerian states have adopted a parallel system of religiously determined Sharia law, which proscribes many behaviors and punishes them severely, rather than solely denying services, as in Mexico's case. Imam attributes the rise of the contemporary version of Sharia in Nigeria, at least in part, to structural adjustment programs required by international financial institutions that mandate reductions in state social expenditure, which result in worsened conditions and popular loss of faith in a discredited, corrupt national government and legal system.

Several authors here concur with other Muslim feminists that it is strategically wiser to debate the interpretation of Islamic law than to focus on the concept of the secular state.

Both Imam and Horn argue that giving credence to a debate over the universality of rights versus culture/religion is neither nuanced nor necessary, as the very construction implies that both rights and culture/religion are static.

They line up with those who refute this essentialism as they say that both rights and culture are fluid, internally contested, and always undergoing reformulation. In fact, the concepts of human rights have not remained static in the half century since codification. During the Cold War, there was tension between the immediate post-Holocaust concern about protecting the individual from the state and the obligations of the state to its members, with increasing recognition of collective social and economic rights and even the right to culture itself.

However, according to some scholars, human rights groups often fail to perceive and challenge their own essentialist vision of religion (Merry 2001, Freedman 1996, Sunder 2003). Sunder maintains that this derives from the origin of the idea of rights in the European Enlightenment and the concept that all propertied men were free and equal and could be governed only by agreement. This "contract" separated the public world, in which men agreed to be governed by the state and rational laws, from the private extrarational sphere, which includes religion and is not subject to state interference. She argues that human rights legal advocates have failed to update this compromise and that such wholesale sequestering of religion effectively cedes it to those who currently hold power within religions.

Horn and Imam are among those who reject this binary division between rights and culture as simplistic, insisting instead that both are fluid, and contested, and comprise diverse visions and actors. By choosing to work within religion and culture, these two authors emphasize that women are players within both, and that concentration on their concerns is legitimate from this inside perspective. Ortiz-Ortega reports a similar phenomenon of internal dissension among Mexican Catholics and cites the involvement of liberation theology Catholics and Catholics for a Free Choice in supporting abortion reform in the state of Chiapas. De Keijzer, Horn, and Chandiramani expand the discussion of internal debate to include men as potential dissenters from within. They discuss the strategic significance of enlisting men in redefining religious practices, such as female genital mutilation, and redefining the culture of family responsibilities, sex roles, and violent constraints on women's behavior.

Imam concentrates on a different strategy, rather than relying solely on international rights models. She argues that since Nigeria has a long history of multiple parallel legal systems, it will be more persuasive to debate the interpretation of Muslim laws, along with reclaiming human rights discourses, than to focus only on the supremacy of the secular state. She refuses to cede Islam to those with constraining visions of women's roles and options, and she calls attention to those aspects of Islam that fundamentalist/sharianization forces neglect, such as obligations to develop the welfare of the poor. Her strategy is to include those with deep religious concerns and to respect local determination to protect identity against cultural and economic incursions of the West, building common platforms among those working on women's human rights in diverse communities in Nigeria and internationally. Imam contends that frequently the language and protest model adopted by Western feminists' and human rights organizations in their outrage against some of the Sharia courts' sentences have not helped locally. In fact, they have distracted from the Nigerian debate by providing pro-Sharia supporters a handle for rejecting criticism in the name of fending off Western assaults on Muslim identity. Imam suggests it would be more helpful for Western-based advocates for women's and reproductive rights to call attention to the contradictory stances of their own governments, rather than merely decry the Nigerian scene.

For example, United States–based feminists could insist that the United States fulfill promises to provide money and security to make girls' education a reality in Afghanistan before claiming to have liberated Afghan women from the Taliban. Also, they could pressure the United States government to use its influence in the IMF, the World Bank, and World Trade Organization for international economic policies that support development for poor countries. Davis uses a complementary approach in underscoring the applicability of human rights accords to the United States.

In her work against female genital mutilation/cutting (FGM/FGC), Horn also refuses to agree that there is an inevitable dichotomy between universality and locally rooted cultural and/or religious values. She shares Imam's concerns that accepting such polarity both fuels locally based resistance to perceived Western cultural hegemony and plays into Western notions of African "barbarism and exoticism." She corroborates Imam's conclusion that reinterpretation of local culture by its members can be a useful way to proceed. Put simply, she insists that women are "culture makers," just as Imam insists that they are valid interpreters of religion. Horn's strategy is to reveal the gender bias within culture, to reveal the links between limited possibilities for women, violence, and economic and social inequities. She stresses attention to gender inequity as a way to make inroads into a reexamination of culture.

Both Imam and Horn are concerned about the ways in which calling attention to practices harmful to women in Africa is dominated and structured by the "orientalist gaze" of those in the West (Said 1979). This well-founded anxiety can be somewhat assuaged by turning the Western gaze upon itself to see similar forces at play in the United States. In the United States, the fundamentalist movement is aligned primarily with evangelist Protestant groups, the Catholic Church, and the far right wing of the Republican Party. Such forces have been successful in making cumulative inroads into the secular state apparatus. They have had notable success in public education, in which creationism has gained equal footing with evolution in the science curricula of at least a dozen states. Abstinence is offered as the only option for unmarried people in more than a third of public school districts—despite research findings that this approach increases risk for sexually transmitted infections (Union of Concerned Scientists 2004, Waxman 2003, "Facts in Brief: Sexuality Education" 2003). Another example is Bush's "faith-based initiative," a program that provides government funds to religiously sponsored service providers, despite the constitutional principle of separation of church and state. Davis also calls for Western self-scrutiny when she reports on efforts to hold the United States accountable to international human rights standards inside its own borders.

France, another Western birthplace of the construct of church-state separation, is also riven by these tensions. The French government, however, has taken a position opposite to that of the United States, and aggressively defended the secular state, as illustrated by the recent ban on religious symbols and clothing in public hospitals and schools ("Chirac: Ban Headscarves in School" 2003). French Muslims were initially divided; some opposed the ban as discriminatory but a group of French Muslim women—Ni Putes Ni Soumises (Neither Whores nor Doormats)—supported it as protecting women against self-styled local religious authorities whose interpretations of religious doctrine they disputed. As of this writing, an Islamist group in Iraq has taken two French journalists hostage, demanding that France reverse the ban. The French government has refused and has been supported by leading French Muslim clerics, who have repudiated this violent and coercive intervention into French internal affairs ("France's Ban on Islamic Headscarves Passes First Test" 2004). The Canadian province of Ontario is exploring how a secular state committed to both gender equality and cultural tolerance can accommodate the religious practices of minorities—by allowing religious authorities to arbitrate civil matters as long as the parties participate voluntarily and can appeal decisions in Canadian court (Krauss 2004). This third approach has not fully satisfied either side.

Approaches to Human Rights Implementation:
The Role of the State, Donors, and International Accords

When Nigerian women ask whose interests are served by particular renditions or explications of Sharia, or when Amanitare members raise similar questions about FGC, they reveal the political struggle underlying these contests over interpretation. Analogously, human rights accords have been invoked selectively and inconsistently to achieve political ends since their formal codification at the start of the Cold War. Both sides in the Cold War saw the state as the principal actor, with the Western nations focused on constraining the power of the state and the socialist countries stressing the obligations of the state to provide the ingredients necessary for an adequate standard of living. However, such nonstate actors as transnational corporations and international economic institutions like the World Trade Organization, International Monetary Fund, and World Bank are playing starring roles in the post-Cold War era. These institutions limit the power of the state by imposing the shape and conditions for economic restructuring. They require states to privatize the public sector; reduce public provision of services such as health, education, social security, and subsidies; and open doors to foreign investment. All of these have profound implications for economic, social, and political arrangements and for accountability.

Therefore, many in developing countries are wary when human rights and international standards are used to criticize them unilaterally, and one response has been to point out the contradictory positions of the accusing countries. Countries that emphasize economic, social, and collective rights contend that Western insistence on the primacy of the individual is manipulative and converts the human rights paradigm into an ideological tool to preserve Western hegemony. The conflict among China, the UNFPA, and the United States over funding is one such example.

The Chinese effort to limit population growth had complex motivations; it was initially intended to spur development, deal realistically with a huge population and limited arable land, and redress gender inequities. The harshness of the implementation had the opposite effect, however, and has aggravated gender discrimination, with such serious sequelae as a significant imbalance in the sex ratio at birth, not registering girl babies, and relinquishing them for adoption. The one-child policy coincided and acted synergistically with a decline in fertility that accompanied increasing development, leading to a dramatically rapid decline in China's birth rate, which is now below replacement at about 1.8 (World Health Organization, 2000). Winckler attributes popular resentment of the one-child policy primarily to the harshness of implementation and the difficulties experienced by individuals, not to popular disagreement with the goal of limiting births. This underscores the varied facets of human rights as, according to Winckler, much of the Chinese public agrees that there is collective need to limit population growth in order to balance development and resources.

China has responded to internal discontent and international criticism by significantly modifying its population policies. After Cairo, the Chinese government endorsed individual choice and quality of health care as priorities, while maintaining the goal of limiting births. Winckler asserts that UNFPA involvement has consistently been supportive of these changes and concretely helpful in enabling the Chinese to implement them. The U.S. government's refusal to fund UNFPA, claiming that the agency abetted coercive abortion and sterilization in China, is not grounded in fact, but rather is meant to placate the American right wing. In fact, this represents a cynical manipulation of a rights paradigm by conservative U.S. politicians who themselves subvert women's rights consistently by defunding and undermining reproductive health programs in the United States and abroad (Jacobson and Mallik 2002).

The details of contradictions in the U.S. position merit attention both because of its role on the world stage and because they illustrate why the notion of human rights comes under suspicion. The United States has objected to the Chinese social compensation fee, which is levied on people who have more children than allowed. According to Winckler and others, the fee is intended both to deter births and to acknowledge the social costs of raising children. Many Chinese accept this last construct as legitimate. Although a flat fee is inequitable in principle, as it presents more hardship for those of lower income, in practice, Winkler reports, many local administrators do not try to collect it from the very poor. Analogously, Davis describes various provisions of U.S. welfare reform legislation intended to deter poor women from having more children, including financial penalties and disincentives for teenagers, unmarried women, and all who give birth while receiving public assistance (this last is known as the family cap). Some argue that these measures are effectively taxes, as welfare recipients who have subsequent children now have to care for them without additional monies (Chavkin, Romero, and Wise 2002, Levin-Epstein 2003).

Applying international human rights standards to the United States itself further reveals the contradictions in the U.S. position. At the same time that the United States offers political asylum to Chinese seeking refuge from the one-child policy, twenty-four states have passed versions of family cap legislation. Advocates for women on welfare say that the family cap violates international rights treaties on numerous grounds, including children's well-being, the state's affirmative obligation to provide subsistence level support to all children (regardless of the circumstances of their births), and guarantees of equal treatment and prohibitions against racial discrimination.

Among the many advantages Davis describes in applying international human rights law to the United States is to bring United States reproductive and sexual health and rights advocacy in line with the rest of the world, where rights discourse in general, and specific reference to the Cairo and Beijing principles have been on the rise.

The tension between nation-states and nonstate globalization forces has specific consequences for U.S. reproductive and sexual health and rights. The case of Uganda reveals these. Richey discusses the seeming paradox in Uganda between impressive success in lowering HIV transmission rates and poor reproductive health outcomes. She argues that the success of Uganda's famed ABC approach (Abstinence, Be faithful, use Condoms) to HIV prevention has been misinterpreted by those who claim it vindicates a moralistic emphasis on abstinence. Rather, it reflects the utility of a multipronged approach, both because each component of ABC resonates with different subgroups and because ABC itself is but one part of Uganda's multifaceted efforts to contain the epidemic. Richey further ascribes the popularity of ABC among Western donors to its low cost and to its focus on individual behavior, rather than to the systemic provision of services. This accords with these same donors' imposition of structural adjustment policies, which limit the state role and capacity to supply services, as Imam and Chandirimani describe in Nigeria and India.

The two other developing nations that have also reduced HIV transmission—Brazil and Thailand—have both made condom distribution and frank sexual education central components of their prevention campaigns. The Brazilian government, which cosponsors the manufacture of generic versions of many antiretroviral drugs, has negotiated reduced prices for others with international pharmaceutical companies and distributes antiretroviral medications (Teixeira, Vitoria, and Barcarolo 2003).

In fact, the troubling state of reproductive health in Uganda reflects the lack of health infrastructure associated with International Monetary Fund–imposed austerity measures following the colonial legacy of underdevelopment, compounded by the economic hardships resulting from decades of civil war. Uganda is still primarily rural and very poor, and total life expectancy is about forty years (partly due to AIDS). More than a third of Ugandan men are illiterate and two-thirds of women are, with low rates of female employment and wide male-female wage gaps. Although demographic data are sparse, it its estimated that about half the female population becomes pregnant before the age of eighteen, with an associated high rate of maternal mortality, due both to inadequate provision of basic emergency obstetric care and to illegal abortion. Uganda's success in reducing HIV transmission is remarkable, given these circumstances. Yet, Richey raises the sobering point that as attention shifts to HIV treatment rather than prevention, the lack of health infrastructure is likely to affect efficacy in this domain as well. It is only possible to dispense antiretroviral medication and medically monitor large numbers of people within a functional health care system.

This argument is bolstered by the Thai experience. Thailand's initial success in reducing HIV transmission was significantly undercut by the Asian financial crisis of the latter 1990s. The 1998 Thai budget for AIDS prevention and control cut funds for medical treatment and for condom distribution, and HIV rates rose (Kanabus and Fredrikson 2004).

All of these examples make clear the critical importance of focusing as much attention on the ICPD's concern with health infrastructure as on any other dimension of sexual and reproductive health and rights. This is obviously easier to pronounce rhetorically than to make real, as local ability to do so is increasingly constrained by the global economy.

The United Nations is currently working with the International Monetary Fund and World Bank to advance development and reduce poverty, but these are the very institutions that are imposing structural adjustment policies that do the converse and curtail the capacity of states to provide services. This fundamental contradiction has specific consequences for reproductive and sexual health and rights and for women, who both go without needed services and pick up the slack by privately, personally providing child, elder, and sick care. Several of the U.S.–based groups Davis describes have argued that failure to provide specific reproductive health services violates the Convention on the Elimination of All Forms of Discrimination against Women (CEDAW), International Convent on Civil and Political Rights (ICCPR), Convention on the Rights of the Child (CRC), and other rights accords.

New Possibilities for Advancing Sexual and Reproductive Health and Rights

Although many of the developments of the past decade pose serious setbacks for reproductive and sexual health and rights, some contain seeds of change within them. HIV is one such example, as the urgency of the pandemic has forced societies to examine sexual practices, gender roles, and inequities of power and resources. Richey points out that the "love faithfully" component of Uganda's ABC campaign may be harmful to those women caught in violent relationships or married to unfaithful men. Recognition that sexual and gender power inequalities fuel the epidemic has led to understanding that efforts to contain it must tackle women's empowerment and deconstruct sexuality as a given.

Chandiramani addresses sexuality and HIV within the Indian context, illustrating that legal availability of contraception and abortion does not suffice to guarantee reproductive rights if women cannot decide whether or not to have sex or with whom. India promoted access to contraception and abortion in order to curtail population growth, not to expand women's opportunities. Although the government has somewhat repudiated this population control model, conservative sexual norms still prevail, with many resulting harms, especially given the HIV epidemic. The Indian government has chosen to emphasize treatment rather than to promote condoms or public awareness of the consequences of unsafe sexual behaviors and power inequities. However, India is also in the midst of economic and social transition, and Chandiramani sees the construct of sexual rights as offering an important route forward. She considers sexual rights to be an expansive concept that can tackle such profound underlying issues as diversity of sexual choice and power differentials between sex partners based on gender and social inequalities.

The scrutiny of gender, sexuality, and power propelled by the HIV epidemic coincides with the new visions implicit in the Cairo consensus. All of these strands inexorably lead to questions about men—their roles, resistance, needs, and potential regarding reproductive and sexual rights. DeKeijzer discusses how female employment, solo parenthood, urbanization, decreased birthrates, and other social and economic transformations of the latter twentieth century have dramatically affected notions of traditional masculinity in Mexico. He sees men's vulnerabilities in health as providing a point of entry for engaging them in changing gender constraints. His strategy is to reveal to men the ways in which traditional gendered masculine behaviors imperil their own health. DeKeijzer fully acknowledges the threat of male nostalgia for gender roles, which clearly worked to their advantage. Nevertheless, he is hopeful that the irrevocability of the changes underlying men's current discomfort will lead them to view gender equality as in their own interest.

Changing Context, Changing Ground Rules:
Where Do We Go from Here?

The economic and social changes DeKeijzer cites include rapid urbanization, female employment, and a host of associated changes in family formation and stability and women's roles. These developments are not limited to Latin America, but have accompanied a cluster of profound demographic changes that transpired over the course of the last century, affecting both developed and developing countries, albeit at different rates (the lowest being in sub-Saharan Africa). The pace and global sweep of these changes accelerated dramatically in the last few decades and comprise reduced mortality and childbearing and an increased lifespan. These shifts have been so dramatic in the developed world that most European and "Asian tiger" countries now have total fertility rates well below the replacement level of 2.1 births per woman. Although in the developing world fertility rates are still above replacement, the pace and slope of the decline follows a similar trend.

In the developed world, this trend has led to a proportional shrinking of the working-age segment of the population available to support both children and older, retired people. This age shift in the population structure will determine the future size and productivity of the labor force and affect population-based disease patterns, with profound implications for pension and health systems. As women still earn less than men, are more likely to work in jobs without benefits such as pensions, and live longer, they will constitute the majority of the post-employment–age population, and face longer lives with inadequate income.

In both developing and transitional economies, women participate in the paid labor force, have entered the economic migrant streams, and often provide domestic care for employed women in the developed world. Global immigration complicates demographic patterns. Immigrants can attenuate shortages in the working-age population of host countries in the short term, both by their own labor and by adding their children to the future workforce, especially since many immigrants come from countries with higher fertility patterns (although many immigrants rapidly assume the host country's fertility profile) (Brucker 2002, United Nations 2000). This is a complicated phenomenon, as emigration deprives the country of origin of a productive labor force even as the monies sent home contribute to that economy. This loss of both wage earners and parents due to emigration is compounded in some sending countries by deaths due to AIDS, which, in turn, affects the demographic profile. Thus, via distinct pathways, both the developed and developing worlds face proportional shortages in their workforces.

Women's participation in both public and private spheres has been both liberating and exhausting. The persistence of gendered role divisions and the decline of traditional family norms, with increased divorce and single motherhood, have left women doubly burdened. Several scholars ascribe the very low fertility rates characterizing the countries of Mediterranean Europe to the conservative familial, governmental, and employer norms, which leave all domestic responsibilities to women who are simultaneously employed in circumstances that do not accommodate parenthood (McDonald 2000). In contrast, the Scandinavian countries have pioneered in social support to enable both men and women to work and raise children simultaneously. Sweden provides childcare and extensive parental leave, which can be shared by both parents. As De Keijzer points out, the cultural destabilization resulting from these shifts in work and family arrangements also opens possibilities for men to escape limiting roles—they too could participate in both domains, assume much more significant parental and domestic roles, and advocate for work conditions that accommodate these.

With the advent of modern contraception more than three decades ago, sex without reproduction became easily achievable. With the recent introduction of assisted reproductive technologies in some developed countries, reproduction without sex is now also an option. Assisted reproductive technologies (ARTs) have become widely used in developed countries because so many have deferred childbearing until ages at which it is harder to become pregnant. Yet the deconstruction of reproduction implicit in ARTs turns notions of these biological and social relationships upside down and inside out, and raises questions as to who and what constitutes parenthood. Developed world governmental responses reflect competing pressures and conflict over the meanings of these basic human activities and relationships as well as over the allocation of health care resources. For example, Italy recently passed a bill limiting ARTs and restricting their use to married heterosexual couples: alternatively, Sweden provides public funds for their use.

Such ethical debates contrast starkly with the realities of developing countries, however, where infertility is likely to result from lack of access to such basic health care as safe abortion and treatment for sexually transmitted infections (STIs). Although almost half of the developing countries recently queried by UNFPA reported new inclusion of family planning services in their primary health care systems, increased demand has left more than 200 million women without desired modern contraception, with a consequent 60 million unintended pregnancies annually. An estimated 19 million abortions per year take place under unsafe conditions, and more than half a million women die every year from complications of pregnancy and delivery. The global annual number of STIs is sky-high—about 340 million, with 38 million HIV infections ("Global Prevalence" 2004, UNAIDS 2004).

New reproductive technologies in settings of profound gender inequality are not necessarily liberating for women; witness the use of ultrasound for sex selection in India. Interestingly, one such development—emergency contraception—could be readily available at low cost even in resource-poor settings. The globalization of information, technology, and immigration guarantee that new reproductive technologies and related social questions will present complicated issues in both developed and developing settings for reproductive and sexual health and rights advocates.

The demographic trends and associated social and economic changes both reflect and portend seismic shifts in family constellations and in women's roles, options, and contributions to national development. Since they involve such intimately experienced matters as family, sex, birth, and childrearing as well as work and roles, it is no wonder that there is profound tumult over these fast-paced and dramatic shifts. The Vienna, Cairo, and Beijing conferences asserted the indivisibility of rights. Feminist theorists have articulated the critical insight that this indivisibility encompasses economic and reproductive labor or, put differently, that the concept of reproduction includes reproductive care taking and domestic labor. This unacknowledged and uncompensated work done by women is essential to societies and is also the source of the gender wage gap, which perpetuates women's economic vulnerability, even as they increasingly work in paid employment. Redressing this situation requires either compensation or public provision of domestic services and equalization of gendered salary structures.

Conclusion

Given the changes of the past decade, we have to think carefully about how our previous approaches fit the current tumultuous moment. The insight that reproductive and sexual health and rights are of central importance to these many domains of social and economic life is ironically confirmed by the backlash against them. Our understanding of their centrality should lead us to anticipate such resistance and to be poised to respond analytically and strategically. How can we use the notion of reproductive and sexual health and rights skillfully and sensitively to better people's lives? What have we gleaned from these chapters to guide us? We have shown how scholars and activists can frame the issues in order to stimulate public dialogue and engage participants. We have seen the utility of various points of entrée and of strategic diversity. Some work with the United Nations, some with civil society and with "street heat," some inside religion, some with secular law, some with men, and some concentrate on reframing popular ideas and practices. The next step is to translate these insights into actions that positively change the lives of women and men. The following outline provides some suggestions for action.

First, it is profoundly important to refute the notion that respect for culture and religion is necessarily in opposition to reproductive and sexual rights. When we question who benefits by positioning these in opposition, we can reveal the underlying political struggles for power and thus clarify local dynamics. That said, this is difficult terrain. The chapters here do not provide blueprints for action but, rather, they illustrate negotiation on the ground of local responses to those global forces that manipulate religion to advance social controls disadvantageous to women. Activists employ different strategic approaches because they acknowledge the complexities involved: that women are sometimes agents and sometimes victims or targets of fundamentalist repression; that religion is profoundly important to many; that religion is often manipulated to advance particular political and economic ends. Those who work "inside" to develop alternative interpretations of religious and cultural practice, and those who work in the secular and legal arenas can complement, rather than clash, with each other.

Second, it is important to engage with the United Nations and to work on multinational accords, but it is simultaneously essential to critique them and to understand the political forces buffeting and shaping them. Many women's organizations have critiqued the retreat from the Cairo-Beijing commitment to reproductive and sexual health and rights, and expressed ambivalence about spending time and resources participating in both the Beijing +10 review conference and the MDG process ("Seeking Accountability" 2004). Many concur that there should be no renegotiated text of the Beijing consensus at this political moment, but rather a focus on implementing the Cairo and Beijing accords, and that gender-related indicators should be developed for all of the Millennium Development Goals (not just #3), as well as alternative country reports. Reproductive and sexual rights and health advocates can also work with other UN and multilateral agreements such as CEDAW, the war crimes tribunals, and the International Labor Organization's Decent Work Initiative, and with regional bodies such as the African Union, the Inter European Parliamentary Forum, Population and Development, and so forth.

In addition to engaging with formal multinational accords, reproduc-

tive and sexual health and rights activists could contribute the gendered perspectives missing from both the antiglobalization and peace movements. Mass
transnational activism—both against globalized macroeconomic policies and
the war in Iraq—galvanized significant numbers in many countries. They have
been, however, notably silent on the specific impact of these economic developments and of war on women. Work on the transnational level—both the
formal and the grassroots—offers opportunities for cross-national strategic
discussions and for connecting local issues with a human rights framework.

Third, focus on public health offers a variety of entry points to underscore the Cairo/Beijing insight that access to health services is essential for
reproductive health and sexual rights to become reality. For example, the HIV
epidemic raises many reproductive and sexual health and rights questions:
gender roles, sex, and power; woman's value for her own sake, not merely as
a vector of infection, mother, or caretaker; the need for integrated methods
to control fertility and prevent STIs; the urgent need for health care infrastructure.

Working to assure access to Highly Active Antiretroviral Therapy
(HAART) immediately engages the question of the obligations and capabilities of nation-states to provide health services and of transnational pharmaceutical corporations to price lifesaving medications to address a global health
crisis. The international concern with prevention of vertical transmission of
HIV is another key arena in which to forward the paradigm of women's value
as women, not solely as mothers. As of this writing, recent studies have shown
that administering a single dose of neveripine during labor reduces newborn
infection but also increases maternal resistance to the drug ("Fact Sheet"
2002). This means that these infected women will derive less benefit from it
when their own disease advances and they need it. The alternative would be
to provide pregnant infected women with the full HAART regimen. Many
are proposing to continue with the cheaper single shot of neveripne, despite
the consequences for women, because the full HAART regimen is expensive
and requires the presence of a health care infrastructure. The urgency of containing the HIV epidemic and the widespread understanding that sex, gender roles, power, and violence are inextricably bound up with its spread, make
this a fruitful area for reproductive and sexual health and rights activists to
focus their work.

Reproductive and sexual health and rights activists can concentrate on
promoting recent technological developments in reproductive health, with
emergency contraception one of the most promising, because it offers the
opportunity to sidestep the abortion impasse, is cheap, and does not require

much health care infrastructure for distribution and use. Reproductive and sexual health and rights activists need to address how to use emerging medical technologies to reduce, rather than exacerbate, disparities and to usefully challenge traditional understandings of reproduction and familial roles and arrangements.

Fourth, reproductive and sexual health and rights advocates need to figure out how to work with men who are working to change gendered roles and possibilities. Women hold up half the sky but the other half remains in need of support. Those men's organizations contesting gendered constraints head on, as De Keijzer describes, are likely allies, as well as those whose focus on HIV has led them to understand how sexual roles, gendered economic circumstances, and violence propel the epidemic. Both women's and men's activists have urged vigilance to ensure that funders and multinational agencies not divert attention away from women's to men's groups. Profound changes in reproductive and sexual health and rights clearly require transformation and participation of both women and men.

Fifth, it is critical to try for an informed long-term perspective at the same time as work on immediate goals moves forward. The cluster of economic, social, and demographic trends associated with declining fertility will continue to alter the most private aspects of life with major public ramifications. Those working to advance reproductive and sexual health and rights should become informed and ready to anticipate the range of policies that can facilitate work, childrearing, and the needs of an increasingly longer-living older population. These encompass a wide range of social and economic policies, such as parental leave, child care, gender wage gap, tax structure, pensions and social security, housing, and elder care, as well as health insurance, immigration, and sustainable development policies. Many politicians and professionals in these arenas are unaware of the long-term trajectories here and their widespread impact. Infusing the development of these policies with gendered perspectives would significantly advance reproductive and sexual health and rights and profoundly reduce the constraints gendered opportunities impose on people's lives.

Finally, it is imperative to promote the understanding that reproduction includes the domestic work involved in rearing children and maintaining families and households. The Vienna, Cairo, and Beijing conferences achieved international agreement on the indivisibility of economic, social, political, and reproductive and sexual rights. The insight that reproduction encompasses postbiologic care and labor and thus is inextricably bound up with the gender wage gap expands this in a critically important way.

And so we come full circle to "human rights begin in small places close to home." Historical and theoretical developments have necessarily widened our notion of small places close to home from what may have been Eleanor Roosevelt's notion of the individual, to include these many aspects of gendered, sexual, religious, private, and self in society that we explore here.

References

Brucker, H. 2002. "Can International Migration Solve the Problems of European Labour Markets?" *Economic Survey of Europe*. Geneva: UN Economic Commission for Europe, Economic Analysis Division.

Chavkin, W., D. Romero, and P. Wise. 2002. "What do Sex and Reproductive Health Have to Do with Welfare?" In F. Piven, J. Acker, M. Hallock, et al. *Work, Welfare, and Politics: Confronting Poverty in the Wake of Welfare Reform*, 95–112. Eugene: University of Oregon, Wayne Morse Center for Law and Politics.

Chaya, N., and J. Dusenberry. 2004. "Where Are We Now? After Ten Years, There's Good News and Bad News in the Drive to Achieve ICPD Goals." *Countdown 2015*. (Population Action International, Washington, D.C.; Family Care International, New York; International Planned Parenthood Federation, United Kingdom.

"Chirac: Ban Headscarves in School." 2003. CNN.com, December 17.

"Facts in Brief: Sexuality Education, 2003." 2003. Alan Guttmacher Institute. http://www.agi-usa.org/pubs/fb_sex_ed02.html.

Freedman, Lynn. 1996. "The Challenge of Fundamentalisms." *Reproductive Health Matters* 8 (November): 55–69.

Freedman, L., M. Wirth, R. Waldman, et al. 2004. "Millennium Project Task Force 4, Child and Maternal Health, Interim Report." New York: Mailman School of Public Health, Bangladesh Rural Advancement Committee. February.

Ganley, Elaine. 2004. "France's Ban on Head Scarves in Schools Passes First Test." *The San Diego Union Tribune*, September 2. www.uniontrib.com.

Jacobson, J., and R. Mallik, 2002. "The Far Right, Reproductive Rights, and the U.S. International Assistance: The Untold Story Behind the Headlines." Takoma Park, Md.: Center for Health and Gender Equality. August.

Kanabus, A., and J. Fredriksson. 2004. "The History of HIV and AIDS in Thailand." *Averting HIV and AIDS (AVERT)*. http://www.avert.org/aidsthai.htm.

Krauss, C. 2004. "Letter from the Americas; When the Koran Speaks Will the Canadian Law Bend?" *New York Times*, August 4, A4.

Levin-Epstein, Jodie. 2003. "Lifting the Lid off the Family Cap: States Revisit Problematic Policy for Welfare Mothers." Washington D.C.: Center for Law and Social Policy, Childbearing and Reproductive Health Series. December. www.clasp.org.

McDonald, Peter. 2000. "Gender Equity, Social Institutions and the Future of Fertility." *Journal of Population Research* 17(1): 1–16.

Merry, Sally Engle. 2001. "Changing Rights, Changing Culture." In Jane Cowan, Marie-Benedicte Dembour, and Richard Wilson, eds., *Culture and Rights: Anthropological Perspectives*, 31–55. Cambridge: Cambridge University Press.

Millennium Development Goals. 2000. Millennium Project, United Nations. Washington, D.C.: Communication Development.

National Institute of Allergy and Infectious Disease. 2002. "Fact Sheet: The Use of Nevirapine in Preventing HIV Infection." http://www.niaid.nih.gov/factsheets/hivinf.htm.

Roosevelt, Eleanor. 1958. "Where Do Human Rights Begin?" In Allida M. Black, ed., *Courage in a Dangerous World*. New York: Columbia University Press, 1999.

Said, Edward. 1979. *Orientalism*. New York: Vintage Books.

Sunder, Madhavi. 2003. "Piercing the Veil." *Yale Law Journal* 112(6): 1,399–1,472.

Teixeira, P., M. Vitoria, and J. Barcarolo. 2003. "The Brazilian Experience in Providing Universal Access to Antiretroviral Therapy." In *Economics of AIDS and Access to HIV/AIDS Care in Developing Countries. Issues, and Challenges,* 69–88. National Association for the Research of AIDS. June. http://www.anrs.fr.

Union of Concerned Scientists. 2004. "Scientific Integrity in Policymaking: An Investigation into the Bush Administration's Misuse of Science." 1–38. http://www.ucsusa.org/global_environment/rsi/page.cfm?pageID=1641.

UNAIDS. 2004. "Executive Summary: 2004 Report on the Global AIDS Epidemic." Geneva: Joint United Nations Programme on HIV/AIDS.

United Nations. 2000. "Replacement Migration: Is It a Solution to Declining and Ageing Populations?" New York: United Nations, Department of Economic and Social Affairs.

Waxman, Henry. 2003. "Politics and Science: Investigating the State of Science under the Bush Administration." U.S. House of Representatives. August. http://democrats.reform.house.gov/features/politics_and_science/index.htm.

Women's International Coalition for Economic Justice. 2004. "Seeking Accountability on Women's Human Rights: Women Debate on the UN Millennium Development Goals." New York.

World Health Organization. 2000. "Reproductive Health Focus Trends: Reproductive and Family Health in the Western Pacific Region." Manila: WHO. http://www.wpro.who.int/themes_focuses/theme2/focus3/trends/index.htm.

———. 2001. "Global Prevalence and Incidence of Selected Curable Sexually Transmitted Infections: Overview and Estimates." Geneva: WHO.

NOTES ON CONTRIBUTORS

RADHIKA CHANDIRAMANI is a clinical psychologist working with the organization Talking About Reproductive and Sexual Health Issues (TARSUI) and is based in New Delhi, India. A recipient of the MacArthur Fellowship for Leadership Development in 1995, Ms. Chandiramani currently focuses her research on issues related to women's sexuality, pleasure, and ethics. She also writes a column for a national Indian newspaper.

WENDY CHAVKIN, M.D., M.P.H. is a physician trained in Obstetrics and Gynecology and Public Health. She has been the director of the Bureau of Maternity Services—Family Planning at the New York City Department of Health, Director of the Perinatal Epidemiology Unit at Beth Israel Medical Center, and the Chair of the Department of Population and Family Health at Columbia's Mailman School of Public Health, where she is now a professor. Dr. Chavkin edited the award-winning *Double Exposure: Women's Health Hazards on the Job and at Home*. She has written extensively in both medical and popular journals, as well as book reviews, and op-ed pieces in national newspapers, including the *New York Times* and the *Boston Globe*. She served as editor-in-chief of the *Journal of the American Medical Women's Association* for eight years and as associate editor of the *American Journal of Public Health*. She is the chair of the Board of Physicians for Reproductive Choice and Health.

ELLEN CHESLER, PH.D. is a senior fellow at The Open Society Institute, the international foundation started by George Soros. From 1997 through 2004, she directed the foundation's $35 million program in reproductive health and rights and now advises on a range of other grant making and policy development concerns. She is the author of the highly regarded *Woman of Valor: Margaret Sanger and the Birth Control Movement in America,* for which she was awarded PEN's 1993 Martha Albrand citation for the year's best first work of non-fiction. She has also written essays and articles in many anthologies and in newspapers and periodicals, including the *New York Times,* the *Washington Post,* the *New Republic,* the *Nation,* the *American Prospect* and the *Women's Review of Books.* From 1997 to 2003, she chaired the board of the International Women's Health Coalition. She now chairs the advisory committee to the Women's Rights Division of Human Rights Watch. An honors graduate of Vassar College, Chesler earned her master's and doctoral degrees in history at Columbia University.

MARTHA F. DAVIS, LL.M. is an associate professor at Northeastern School of Law in Boston, where she specializes in women's rights, immigration law, employment discrimination, and poverty law. Previously she was the vice president and legal director of the NOW Legal Defense and Education Fund in New York. She is the author of the prizewinning book *Brutal Need: Lawyers and the Welfare Rights Movement,* and has written widely on issues relating to women's rights, human rights, welfare, and violence against women. Professor Davis has participated as counsel in a number of cases before the U.S. Supreme Court.

BENNO DE KEIJZER, M.D. is a physician based in Xalapa, Mexico, who holds a master's degree in social anthropology and is completing a doctorate in community mental health. A previous recipient of Ashoka and MacArthur Foundation fellowships, Dr. de Keijzer has published two books on community participation in health and on gender and sexuality in a rural community, as well as numerous articles on men, gender, and health issues. As a cofounder of the national health network Produssep and coordinator of the nongovernmental organization Salud y Género, Dr. de Keijzer has worked for the past several years to promote health and gender equity through educational and public policy initiatives. He serves as a project-based consultant with USAID, the International Planned Parenthood Federation (IPPF/WHR), EngenderHealth, UNICEF, and the ReproSalud project in Peru.

JESSICA HORN is the program officer for women's and minority rights at the Sigrid Rausing Trust. Prior to this she worked at RAINBO as a coordinator of AMANITARE, The African Partnership for the Sexual and Reproductive Health and Rights of Women and Girls. In this capacity she led the women's rights working group for the Countdown 2015 conference on ICPD at 10. Jessica holds an MSc in gender and development from the London School of Economics and a BA in anthropology from Smith College. She has published in the journals *Feminist Africa* and *Development*. Jessica is of Ugandan and U.S. origin, has lived in Lesotho, Fiji, and the USA. She now lives and works in London.

AYESHA IMAM, PH.D. has worked extensively on research, advocacy, and education to protect and extend women's legal rights issues under customary, secular, and religious laws. She is currently the chief of Culture, Gender, and Human Rights Branch at the UNFPA. She is a core group member of the international network Women Living Under Muslim Laws (WLUML) and a founding director of BAOBAB for Women's Human Rights in Nigeria, for which she received the John Humphrey Human Rights Award in 2002. A former director of the Gender Institute in Africa, Dr. Imam has also served as the Gender Policy Advisor for the United Nations Institute for Economic Development in Senegal. Dr. Imam has published numerous journal articles, books, and program reviews, including *Engendering African Social Sciences* and two special issues of *African Development: Re-Visiting Gender I and II.*

ADRIANA ORTIZ-ORTEGA, PH.D. holds a degree in political science from Yale University. She is a professor and program coordinator of the Interdisciplinary Women's Studies Program at El Colegio de México, and a fellow of the National Research System in Mexico, a distinction awarded for research and scholarship. She is a consultant for numerous agencies, including the International Planned Parenthood Federation (IPPF), Population Council, and the Center for Women's Global Leadership. She has received research awards and fellowships from the Overseas Research Council (UK), CONACYT (Mexico), and the Ford, Rockefeller, and MacArthur Foundations. Her most recent book is *Si los hombres se embarazaran, ¿el aborto sería legal?* (*If Men Could Become Pregnant, Would Abortion Be Legal?*).

LISA ANN RICHEY, PH.D. is an assistant professor of international development studies at Roskilde University, Denmark. She holds a degree in political science from the University of North Carolina and conducted postdoctoral research in anthropological demography at the Harvard School of Public Health. She has published extensively on issues of gender and development, reproductive health, and population policy. Her current research is on the local politics of access to antiretroviral drugs in South Africa and Uganda.

MARY ROBINSON is the Executive Director of the Ethical Globalization Initiative. She served as United Nations High Commissioner for Human Rights from 1997 to 2002 and as president of Ireland from 1990 to 1997. Before her election as president in 1990, Mrs. Robinson served as senator, holding that office for twenty years. In 1969 she became the youngest Reid Professor of Constitutional Law at Trinity College, Dublin. She was called to the bar in 1967, becoming a Senior Counsel in 1980, and a member of the English Bar (Middle Temple) in 1973. Educated at Trinity College, Mrs. Robinson also holds law degrees from the King's Inns in Dublin and from Harvard University.

EDWIN WINCKLER, PH.D. is a political scientist who analyzes contemporary East Asian political development, particularly in China and Taiwan, and has taught on these subjects at Harvard University, Columbia University, and the University of California. His published works include the coedited volumes *Contending Approaches to the Political Economy of Taiwan* and *Transition from Communism in China*. Most recently, Dr. Winckler has worked closely with officials of China's population programs to assist in reorienting their programs to incorporate reproductive rights perspectives and human rights–based approaches.

INDEX

sodomy laws, 15, 250; stigma of HIV/AIDS, 134–135
Honkala, Cheri, 235, 236, 244, 248, 257, 263
honoris causa requirements for abortion, 160–161
Hoodfar, H., 44
Horn, Jessica, 28, 35–61, 274, 275, 276–277
Humanae Vitae, 166
human rights: Eleanor Roosevelt on, 1; expansion to private and local realms, 1–2, 67–68; local culture and, 66–67; origins of, 4–9; women's rights as, 3–4, 9–18, 23, 158
Human Rights Commission, 7, 8, 22
human rights movement in U.S.. *See* international law in U.S.
Human Rights Quarterly, 16, 17
Human Rights Watch, 9, 17–18, 256
Hunter, J.D., 172

Ibhawoh, B., 39
Ibrahim, J., 69
ICCPR (International Covenant on Civil and Political Rights), 8, 31, 237, 239, 240, 252, 261
ICESCR (International Covenant on Economic, Social and Cultural Rights), 8, 237–238, 242, 262
ICPD (International Conference on Population and Development), Cairo, 19–22, 35, 45, 137–138, 170, 182, 186, 239, 271
ijma, 74
ijtihad, 74
Illinois, family cap policy in, 260
Imam, Ayesha, 28, 65–92, 67, 70, 79, 80, 274, 275–277
incest, 133
India: adolescent sexuality in, 132–133; family planning in, 127–130, 138–139, 282; HIV/AIDS in, 133–137; sexual rights in, 142–144, 147–148; social norms in, 130–132, 146–147
Indiana, family cap policy in, 252, 260

India Today, 132
infanticide, 163–164
infant mortality, 104
infertility, 284
Institute of Women and Ethnic Studies, 258
Interagency Gender Working Group, 196
Interamerican Commission on Human Rights (CIDH), 156
International Association of Women Judges (IAWJ), 86
International Conference on Population and Development (ICPD), Cairo, 19–22, 35, 45, 137–138, 170, 182, 186, 239, 259, 271
International Conference on Women: in Beijing, 22–24, 137–138, 144–145, 170, 182, 186, 239, 271; in Copenhagen, 15–16; in Mexico City, 12–13; in Nairobi, 16
International Convention on the Elimination of All Forms of Racial Discrimination, 8, 15, 240–241
International Covenant on Civil and Political Rights (ICCPR), 8, 31, 237, 239, 240, 252, 261
International Covenant on Economic, Social and Cultural Rights (ICESCR), 8, 237–238, 242, 262
International Labor Organization, 7
international law in U.S., 280; approaches to domestic advocacy, 243–252; compliance with, 238; limits of, 252–256; ratification and, 237–238; reproductive rights and health and, 257–263; state courts and, 250–251, 255, 260; state and local obligations under, 239–243; Supreme Court and, 14–15, 249–250
International Monetary Fund (IMF), 7, 17, 27, 69, 88–89, 271, 272, 276, 278, 281
Iraq war, 88
Islam: female genital mutilation and, 45; French ban on headscarves, 277;

Maboreke, M., 40
Magazu, Bariya, 81, 85
Mailman School of Public Health,
    Columbia University, 3
Malik, Imam, 75–76
Maliki school of jurisprudence, 75
Mallik, R., 129, 279
Mama, A., 41
Mamdani, Mahmoud, 66–67
Mansour, A., 44, 45
March of the Americas, 237
March for Economic Human Rights, 237
March for Our Lives, 236
Marcos, Sylvia, 169
marriage: arranged, 130; gender equity
    in, 180–181; HIV/AIDS protection
    within, 107, 110, 127; of HIV-
    positive people, suspension of right
    to, 134–135; Islamic schools of law
    and, 75; promotion programs, 263;
    rape within, 44, 130; second, 181;
    sexual rights in, 140–141
Massachusetts: family cap policy in,
    252; human rights approach to
    domestic violence in, 255
Masucci, M., 236, 237
maternal mortality, 103–104, 112, 197–
    198, 273, 281, 284–285
matn, 75
Mbonye, A.K., 104, 110, 112
McCarthyism, 8
McDonald, Peter, 284
McFadden, P., 41
McGovern, Theresa, 257
media, international: HIV/AIDS and,
    105; Sharia penal code cases and,
    83–87
Mehta, Hansa, 10
Meillon, Cynthia, 23
Melara, Sonia, 247
men: childbirth, presence at, 180–181,
    190, 197; fathering skills, 190–192,
    197–198; in gender transition, 181–
    182, 282, 288; health risks of
    hegemonic masculinity, 193–195;
    participation in reproductive health

and rights initiatives, 185–193, 195–
    200, 288; socialization of, 182–185;
    unlawful sexual intercourse (*zina*),
    65–66
Menghaney, L., 136
Menon, N., 129
Merritt, D.J., 249
Merry, Sally Engle, 275
Mexico: family planning in, 166–167,
    169–170; fertility rate in, 181;
    gender transition in, 182; grassroots
    Catholic movements in, 164–166;
    male participation in repro-
    ductive health, 189–193; male
    socialization in, 184; women's
    political participation in, 170;
    women's rights in, 164, 165. *See also*
    abortion in Mexico
Mexico City, International Conference
    on Women in, 12–13
Meyer, L., 164, 165
Milani, L.R., 13, 14, 253
Mill, John Stuart, 11
Millennium Declaration, 272
Millennium Development Goals
    (MDGs), 27, 272, 286
Millennium Forum, 272
Millennium Project, 272
Miller, A.M., 140
Misra, G., 139
Missouri, juvenile death penalty in,
    250–251
Mohammed, A.S., 70
Montoya, Sandra, 154
mortality: child, 104; gender differ-
    ences in, 194; maternal, 103–104,
    112, 197–198, 273, 281, 284–
    285
Mother and Child Friendly Hospitals
    initiative, 197
Movimento Manuela Ramos, 187
Mpagi, Jane, 112
Mr. X v. Hospital Z, 134
Mubarak, Suzanne, 50
Mudanjiang family planning model,
    204–208